The Guangdong Model and Taxation in China

The Guangdong Model and Taxation in China

Formation, Development, and Characteristics of China's Modern Fiscal State-building

Jin-A Kang

Routledge
Taylor & Francis Group
LONDON AND NEW YORK

First published in 2022 by Amsterdam University Press Ltd.

Published 2025 by Routledge
4 Park Square, Milton Park, Abingdon, Oxon OX14 4RN
605 Third Avenue, New York, NY 10158

Routledge is an imprint of the Taylor & Francis Group, an informa business

ISBN: 9789463729833 (hbk)
ISBN: 9781041188100 (pbk)
ISBN: 9781003706427 (ebk)
NUR 783

Cover image: Guangzhou in the 1930s (WikiMedia Comons)

Cover design: Coördesign, Leiden

DOI: 10.5117/9789463729833

For Product Safety Concerns and Information please contact our EU representative:
GPSR@taylorandfrancis.com
Taylor & Francis Verlag GmbH, Kaufingerstraße 24, 80331 München, Germany

Table of Contents

Abbreviations 9

Acknowledgments 11

Introduction 13
The Modern Transformation of the Imperial Fiscal System: The Case of Provincial Finance in Guangdong

Part 1 New Tax Revenues in Guangdong during the Republican Era

1 Fiscal Reform in the Late Qing 23

2 Tobacco and Wine Taxes in Guangdong and Changes in the Financial Structure during Republican China 49

3 Abolition of the *Likin* and the Paradox of Tax Reform: The Special Tax 67

4 Special Taxes on Imported Rice 107

Part 2 State-led Industrialization and the State Monopoly

5 Industrial Building: Provincial Entrepreneurs 139

6 The Sugar Monopoly: From Local to National 155

Part 3 Reform of Tax Collection

7 The Building of Public Administration and Taxation 175

8 Regularization of the Tax-farming System 193

Part 4 The Transition of the Modern Chinese Tax Structure in a Global Context

9 Transition of the Modern Chinese Financial Structure 215

10 Afterword: Between Chinese Exceptionalism and Modern Fiscal State-building 245

Bibliography 259

Glossary 299

Index 307

List of Tables

Table 1.1 Total amount of revenue and expenditures in twenty-two provinces, 1908 27
Table 1.2 Comparison of historical materials in terms of the composition of Guangdong finance 30
Table 1.3 Structure of tax revenue in Guangdong, 1908–1909 33
Table 1.4 Fiscal balance in Guangdong province, including national tax income and debt income, 1912, 1924, 1926, 1930–1937 42
Table 1.5 National revenue under the control of Guangdong province, fiscal years 1930–1935 43
Table 1.6 Provincial revenue in Guangdong, excluding loans, fiscal years 1930–1936 43
Table 1.7 Breakdown of industrial and commercial taxes in Guangdong provincial revenue, 1930–1936 47
Table 2.1 Contracted amount of the *likin* for tobacco and wine in Guangzhou prefecture and Foshan district during the late Qing dynasty 53
Table 2.2 Annual revenue and expenditures in Guangdong province, 1912–1941 56
Table 2.3 Revenue from the tobacco and wine taxes and their proportion of Guangdong provincial tax revenue, 1912–1932 59

Table 2.4 Budget for tobacco and wine taxes in Guangdong province, 1930 59
Table 2.5 Revenue from the consolidated tax on cigarettes 60
Table 3.1 Special taxes in Guangdong until July 1936 69
Table 3.2 Guangdong provincial budget and collected revenue, 1933 70
Table 3.3 Guangdong provincial tax revenue, excluding national tax revenue 71
Table 3.4 Monthly tax revenue in Guangdong province, estimated as of June 1936 72
Table 3.5 Exports from Guangzhou, the Pearl River Delta, and Shanghai 88
Table 3.6 Trade balance in Guangdong province, 1928–1937 88
Table 4.1 Rice production, rice consumption, and rice shortages in Guangdong province, the 1930s 108
Table 4.2 Import volume of foreign rice and entry volume of domestic rice to Guangdong province, 1930–1937 119
Table 4.3 Average price of domestic and imported rice in the Shanghai market, 1928–1937 120
Table 5.1 Sugar imports and smuggling in China, 1928–1935 143
Table 5.2 Estimated volume of sugar smuggling in China, 1933–1936 144
Table 5.3 Newly built state-run sugar factories in Guangdong 148
Table 5.4 Value of sugar sold by the National Products Sales Department, June 1934–April 1935 154
Table 6.1 New and old sales quotas for major sugar districts in Guangdong 158
Table 6.2 Quota based on minimum consumption estimates and the highest bid sales quota for a license in seven sugar districts 158
Table 6.3 Trends in native sugar production in Guangdong 160
Table 8.1 List of files on tax contractors found among the documents of the Department of Finance, Guangdong Provincial Archives 194
Table 8.2 Monthly payments of Wanquan Company, September 1935–November 1935 199
Table 8.3 Wanquan Company's delayed payments and amount of added interest 200
Table 9.1 Tax revenue of the imperial Qing, 1766 217
Table 9.2 Tax revenue budget of the central government, 1911 222
Table 9.3 Tax revenue structure, Meiji government 224

Table 9.4 National tax revenue of the Beiyang government, 1911–1925 228
Table 9.5, Provincial tax revenue, 1915 and 1916 230
Table 9.6 National tax revenue of the Nanjing Nationalist Government, 1928–1937 232
Table 9.7 Tax structure and shares in national tax revenue, 1928–1937 233
Table 9.8 Provincial tax revenue under the Nationalist government, 1933–1936 235
Table 9.9 Tax revenue structure of the US federal government, 1880–1930 238
Table 9.10 Actual value per capita of production, expenditures, and taxes for seventy-two quarters, 1999–2016 242

Abbreviations

B&S	Butterfield & Swire Co.
BAT	British and American Tobacco
CCP	Chinese Communist Party
DFG	Department of Finance, Guangdong Province
GPG	Guangdong provincial government
KMT	Chinese Nationalist Party (Kuomintang)
NNG	Nanjing Nationalist Government

Acknowledgments

I started my research on modern China and Guangdong by writing a master's thesis at Seoul National University on building a modern sugar industry in Guangdong in the 1930s. My Ph.D. dissertation at University of Tokyo extended this theme to include a comprehensive study of how Guangdong Province attempted to rebuild its economy, finance, and trade at one province level under the adverse conditions of the World Depression. It was published in Korean by Seoul National University Press in 2005 to become the basic framework of this book project. Since then, I have published a couple of books on Cantonese merchant diaspora and their capital flow in Asian trade, but those works also reinforced my initial interest in Guangdong. This time, with the support of the Amsterdam University Press, I am very honored to be able to conduct and publish research on China's modern fiscal state-building based on Guangdong model in English.

It is highly challenging for me, a Korean scholar, to write a book in English. I could not take on this task without the encouragement of three friends: Dr. Leo M. Douw, Ms. Saskia Gieling, and Professor Parks Coble. It was Dr. Douw who requested that I publish three English articles in *Translocal Chinese East Asian Perspectives* with Brill Publishers. Fortunately, I visited the University of Amsterdam in 2015 as a presenter at his commemorative retirement conference but never thought I would be given a chance to publish with the AUP later. While staying in the United States as a visiting scholar at Harvard Yenching Institute, I presented a paper dealing with Guangdong Tobacco and Wine Taxes at the 2019 AAS Annual Conference in Denver. I was pleased but worried when I received a book publication offer from Ms. Saskia Gieling, ex-editor of the AUP, who came to Denver for a book fair. However, I hesitated in this project due to my lack of confidence in writing a whole book in English. Without Professor Coble's strong encouragement in the cafeteria at Harvard University, I could not have dared to challenge this project.

There are too many scholars, colleagues, friends and institutes that I have to thank for their guidance and help. The seven years of training I studied at the Department of Asian History, Seoul National University, molded me as a historian. I learned the basics and principles of historical research from the teaching and guidance of Professors Sungkyu Lee, Hanje Park, Keumsung Oh, Yongdeok Kim, and Hodong Kim. Above all, I would like to express my deepest gratitude and respect to two advisors, the late Professor Tuki Min, and Professor Takeshi Hamashita. Professor Toru Kubo has always supported my research since my time at University of Tokyo, and his academic achievements immensely influenced my research to the extent that this book cites his works the most. The gratitude I feel for him will never diminish. My special thanks go to Professor R. Bin Wong's constructive criticism and encouragement in peer review by revealing his real name, which gave an essential motivation for my future research.

For 22 years after receiving my Ph.D., financial support was crucial in developing my academic projects to new themes. In particular, the research funding support obtained from the Korea Research Foundation, LG Yonam Foundation, and the Harvard Yenching Institute was beneficial beyond words. Since the 1990s, the active cooperation of Sun Yat-sen University and the Guangdong Provincial Archives has been an indispensable resource for research. Especially, I would like to thank Professor Chen Chunsheng, Professor Liu Zhiwei, and Professor Zhou Xiang of Sun Yat-sen University for their consistent academic support. Also, the experience of teaching at the Institute of Chinese Modern History at the Central China Normal University (2001-2002) enhanced my understanding of Chinese society and history. I am grateful to the late Zhang Kaiyuan and Professor Ma Min for giving me such a wonderful opportunity.

The extension of my academic activities to English-speaking audience is thanks to the weekly study group for translating Chinese diplomatic documents into English starting in 2013. Dr. Cheolbae Son, the organizer of the study group, encouraged my writing in English and gave me valuable support and advice in handling English materials. Without Dr. Son's help, my academic activities would not have been able to move beyond Asia.

I would also like to thank Ms. Nancy Hearst of the Fairbank Center for Chinese Studies at Harvard University for her detailed proofreading and Ms. Victoria Blud of the AUP for her elaborate copyediting service. It is an irony that the COVID-19 pandemic contributed to the completion of this book in a logistic way. For two years, I spent most of my time in my office and at home. The AUP staff did their best to keep the book publishing schedule from being disrupted, even when working from home. I am deeply grateful. Now that the epidemic situation is showing signs of decline, I could witness the book's publication with a great pleasure.

Last but not the least, I would like to express my love and gratitude to my beloved family, the Parks: Hun, Pin Young, and Yegang.

Introduction

The Modern Transformation of the Imperial Fiscal System: The Case of Provincial Finance in Guangdong

The modern fiscal state in China was shaped in line with the creation and evolution of the modern fiscal state in the West. In the processes of state and nation-building, East Asian countries learned, imported, and transplanted the Western fiscal state system. The California School, introducing the idea of a "great divergence," argues that the advanced regions of Asia, such as the central areas of China, India, and Japan, demonstrated a level of economic development that was compatible with that of the European countries. Further, the California School argues that the economic production mode of the advanced regions of Asia, that is, a Smithian growth model,[1] was generally identical with that of Europe. However, from the perspective of a modern fiscal system, the European countries witnessed a fundamental change in their fiscal structure far earlier than the Asian advanced countries (or regions), even as there existed a considerable time lag across the European countries.[2] It was only after the late nineteenth century that the fiscal structures of the Asian countries experienced a radical change.

Throughout the twentieth century, the momentum of modern fiscal state-building expanded state power and strengthened the role of the state against autonomous management by society in the distribution of wealth. This process was fueled by the unprecedented spread and scale of wars and the ideological appeal of the socialist regimes. Today, the twenty-first century is witnessing different levels of expansion of state power in the face of the Fourth Industrial Revolution, the widening gap between the rich and poor, the growing ecological crisis, and other global crises, such as the Covid-19 pandemic. State power has begun to assume the role of protector

1 Kenneth Pomeranz, *The Great Divergence: China, Europe, and the Making of the Modern World Economy* (Princeton, NJ: Princeton University Press, 2000).

2 Bartolomé Yun-Casalilla and Patrick K. O'Brien, eds., *The Rise of Fiscal States: A Global History, 1500–1914* (New York: Cambridge University Press, 2012).

Kang, Jin-A, *The Guangdong Model and Taxation in China*. Taylor & Francis Group, 2022
DOI: 10.5117/9789463725248_INTRO

against the threats of both capitalism and communism, whereby the state obtains the authority to absorb the ever-growing ratio of national wealth for public distribution. The core of the expansion of state power is fiscal and financial power.

Current humane society faces various challenges: an unequal distrisbution of social wealth, periodic financial and economic crises, a deteriorating environment, and a public health crisis and others. In terms of endeavoring to fight against those challenges, the Chinese state model and fiscal management reveals distinctive features in contrast with the current Western states. The Chinese state-building and fiscal modernization experiences from the last century up to now were the result of several factors, including adoption of the modern Western fiscal model, socialization, and the legacy of the traditional fiscal systems. In this respect, exploring the process of financial reform in modern China helps us to understand the current Chinese state management.

This book analyzes the processes, features, and problems of Chinese fiscal modernization, primarily focusing on the case of Guangdong province, which reveals both macro and micro trends. The analysis focuses on the early Republican period, beginning from the Xinhai Revolution and ending with the Second Sino-Japanese War in 1937, in particular during the rule of the Nanjing Nationalist Government (hereafter NNG) in the 1930s. The efforts to build a modernized fiscal state, which started in the late Qing period, continued during Republican China. However, this process was suspended in 1937 due to the full-scale Sino-Japanese War and the civil war between the Chinese Nationalist Party (the Kuomintang, hereafter KMT) and the Chinese Communist Party (hereafter CCP). This research focuses on examining fiscal experiments of the Republic of China era in the sense of connecting the late Qing dynasty, a starting point for the collapse of traditional finances, with the People's Republic of China, an ongoing attempt to build a new socialist state. Therefore, if necessary, we will refer to both the early Qing period and current-day Chinese finance to situate the structural changes in the Chinese financial system during the period under discussion.

Earlier literature on modern Chinese taxation and the Chinese fiscal system mainly consists of empirical case studies of, for instance, the *likin* (the transit tax) and the consolidated tax (*tongshui*). The continuity and disconnect among traditional finance, Republican finance, and socialist finance during the People's Republic of China have been widely discussed. In Korean academic circles, however, there has been little research about modern China's fiscal history,[3] whereas there is a relatively large amount of research on this topic in Japan and China.[4] In contrast, Western academics have shown little interest in this period.[5]

As for finance during the late Qing dynasty and the early Republican period, representative works pay attention to fiscal continuities and discontinuities. In particular, there is a focus on the character and transformation of the contract and tax-farming system, which was one of the distinctive features of imperial finance. Prasenjit Duara, who traces changes in local taxation and collection in the 1920s, conceptually summarizes the transformation from a traditional local community-based tax system to tax collection through "Brockerism." He argues that this transition signaled the infiltration of state power into society.[6] According to Duara, tax reform in the Republican era was part of a violent process in which state power penetrated the private sector to acquire revenue. The profit-seeking tax collectors were not identical with the local community of taxpayers, nor did they play the protective role against state exploitation that the previous local elites administering tax collection had assumed. Susan Mann uses the term "liturgic," to describe this transition. She argues that professional tax

3 See the bibliography in this volume, especially the research by Kyung-seok Park, Jee-hwan Kim, Yeong-jin Jung, and Jin-A Kang.

4 The most active Japanese researchers are Iwai Shigeki, Kubo Tōru, Kaneko Hajime, and Tomizawa Yoshia. Iwai's ambitious articles attempt to comprehensively explain the structural consistency in the Chinese fiscal structure from the imperial to the contemporary finance, characterized by a contract system and irregular taxation. However, he focuses on criticism of the contracting system that hampered fiscal modernization while his academic interests lack of comparative historical access to the structure of fiscal-economic relations. As to the fiscal structure of Republican China, there are excellent empirical studies by Kubo, Kaneko, and Tomizawa, who are currently expanding their research to the People's Republic of China period (see the bibliography). The recently published book by Kubo Tōru, *Gendai chūgoku no genkei no shutsugen: Kokumintō tōchi ka no minshū tōgō to zaisei Keizai*) [The emergence of the modern Chinese prototype: People's integration and the financial economy under the rule of the Chinese Nationalist Party] (Tokyo: Kyūko shoten, 2020), is indicative of recent trends in Japanese literature. Finally, Chinese publications on fiscal history, although numerous, are only at an early stage in terms of theoretical access and comprehensive studies.

5 Empirical studies focusing exclusively on tax and fiscal issues in modern China remained relatively stagnant after the 1971 detailed work by Arthur N. Young, a former American adviser to the NNG. Mainstream research in modern Chinese studies focused on political and social studies until the 1980s, while taxation and finance were partially covered in the context of economic history.

6 Prasenjit Duara, *Culture, Power and the State: Rural North China, 1900–1942* (Stanford, CA: Stanford University Press, 1988).

contractors emerged with the introduction of the bidding system in the 1930s, which signaled the demise of the traditional liturgic tax systems and ideas.[7]

While Duara's and Mann's research emphasizes the disconnect in Chinese finance, Shigeki Iwai, in his study on the repartition and tax-farming system, stresses the continuity of Chinese finance. Iwai views this as a structural defect in the Chinese fiscal system, leading to extra, non-institutional taxation and corruption. Iwai's research, by examining how the Chinese financial system operated, attempts to uncover the structural flaws that have persisted from imperial finance to the present day. However, unlike Duara's and Mann's local level of analysis, his level of analysis mainly reviews the hierarchical repartition system between the central government and the local government. Even though Iwai also deals with arbitrary and additional charges in the localities, his focus is on the structural defects retaining non-budgetary finance from the perspective of central and local finance. He regards the contract system as a harmful byproduct of those structural weaknesses. In his view, the contract system might be called a remnant of tradition that has not yet been overcome.[8]

Tōru Kubo is a pioneer in the study of the NNG tariff policy and the 1935 currency reform. The division between the national tax and the local tax and the introduction of the consolidated tax are analyzed by Hajime Kaneko, who highlights the central–local struggle in terms of modern fiscal state-building. Japanese scholars tend to broaden their vision to contemporary China after the reform and opening-up policy (see n. 4).

As for overall state-building and fiscal policy during the NNG, since Young's pioneering work,[9] there have been few studies focusing exclusively on the fiscal policy of the NNG in Western languages. Until the 1980s, the finance of the NNG was only partially covered in studies on economic history. In the 1990s, the prevailing trends, focusing on social and cultural history, under the overwhelming influence of postmodernism and cultural studies, further alienated fiscal history. Therefore, the recently published book on customs in Republican China, written by Felix Boecking, was a valuable achievement to be widely welcomed. But it is a pity that the arguments are occasionally misleading due to their focus on customs statistics

7 Susan Mann, *Local Merchants and the Chinese Bureaucracy, 1750–1950* (Stanford, CA: Stanford University Press, 1987), 186–199.

8 Iwai Shigeki, "Yōeki to zaisei no aida: Chūgoku zei·eki seido no rikai teki ri kai ni mukete (1–4)" [Between corvée and finance: Towards a historical understanding of the Chinese tax and corvée system (1–4)], *Keizai keiei ronsō* 28(4), 29(1), 29(2), 29(3) (1994).

9 Arthur N. Young, *China's National-Building Effort, 1927–1937: The Financial and Economic Record* (Stanford, CA: Hoover Institution Press, Stanford University, 1971).

and their disregard of the restructuring of the tax system. For example, this book spotlights the impressive drop in tariff revenue on cigarette imports and concludes that dependence on the cigarette tax decreased.[10] But it neglects the fact that tax revenue from the cigarette industry increased considerably due to the consolidated tax.[11]

Meanwhile, Japanese studies are biased in terms of their attachment to the state–society dichotomy, in spite of their excellent empirical achievements. Most of the abundant Chinese literature on financial history during the early Republican era consists of case studies. A government-funded research project on China's financial modernization is currently underway by a joint team of three universities: Tsinghua University, Central China Normal University, and Wuhan University. Publication of the results of this research, with a long-term perspective, are forthcoming.[12]

There are inevitable difficulties incurred by clinging to historical research on Chinese finance. First, China's historical statistics have always been suspect in terms of reliability and comprehensiveness due to political instability, rampant tax avoidance, and low administrative capacity. Second, there are regional gaps in terms of financial size and structure. Even if an empirical case study of a province can successfully identify reliable long-term trends, the findings cannot necessarily be extrapolated to the country as a whole. In other words, it is difficult to draw applicable nationwide conclusions from

10 Felix Boecking, *No Great Wall: Trade, Tariffs and Nationalism in Republican China, 1927–1945* (Cambridge, MA: Harvard University Asia Center, 2017).

11 Jin A Kang, "Chunghwamin'guk shigi kwangdongsŏngŭi sul tambae kwase kaehyŏkkwa caejŏng kŭndaehwa" [The tax on wines and tobacco in Guangdong province and financial modernization during Republican China)], *Tongyang sahak yŏngu* 138 (2018): 237–286.

12 This project titled "Research on industrial and commercial taxation in modern China" is selected as one of The Major Projects of the National Social Science Fund of China Project. For the Chinese literature on fiscal and financial history of modern China, see the bibliography in this volume, especially Wang Jingyu, *Zhongguo jindai jingjishi, 1898–1927* [Modern Chinese economic history, 1898–1927] (Beijing: Renmin chubanshe, 2000); Zhou Yumin, *WanQing caizheng yu shehui bianqian* [Late Qing finance and social change] (Shanghai: Shanghai renmin chubanshe, 2000); Zhou Zhichu, *WanQing caizheng jingji yanjiu* [Research on finance and the economy in late Qing China] (Ji'nan: Qilu shushe, 2002); Zuo Zhisheng, *Zhongguo jindai caizheng shi conggao* [A collection of manuscripts about modern Chinese financial history] (Chengdu: Xi'nan caijing daxue chubanshe, 1987); Zhou Bodi, *Zhongguo caizheng shi* [Chinese financial history] (Shanghai: Shanghai renmin chubanshe, 1981). For overviews of earlier Chinese literature on the fiscal history of modern China, see Chen Feng, "20 shiji di wanQing caizhen shi yanjiu" [Research on the financial history of the late Qing dynasty in the 20th century], *Jindaishi yanjiu* 1 (2004); Shen Xuefeng and Zhang Xiaoli, "Jin shinian wanQing caizheng shi yanjiu zongshu" [A summary of research on the financial history of the late Qing dynasty in the recent ten years], *Shixue yuekan* 9 (2004); Ke Weiming, "Minguo shiqi shuishou zhidu de shanbian" [The evolution of tax system during the Republican China], *Zhongguo shehui kexue* 11 (2019).

a regional case study. To deal with these difficulties, it is necessary to focus on general trends across comparative statistics rather than to focus on the accuracy of specific statistics. Such an interpretative approach to historical studies may complement the methodology in the field of economics that focuses on numbers. It is for precisely this reason that it makes sense to focus on a specific regional case study and to combine the global, national, and regional factors, especially when examining the specific processes of financial modernization in China.

The selection of Guangdong province is therefore an appropriate focus of research for the following reasons. First, Guangdong was remarkably successful early on in the first fiscal reform of the late Qing dynasty. Its fiscal growth rate was the highest among eighteen provinces. In 1911, the year before the Qing empire collapsed, Guangdong had the lowest share of land taxes among all provinces, while its indirect taxes, such as the industrial and commercial taxes, represented the highest share. In other words, Guangdong was already breaking away from the traditional imperial financial structure even before the arrival of the Republican era.

Second, Guangdong's unique status as a revolutionary KMT base area during the early Republican period allowed the province to challenge the restoration of tariff sovereignty earlier than other provinces and to develop new tax sources. The Guangdong provincial government, set up in Guangzhou by the KMT, seized the customs by force, raised the import duty rate, and realized some "tariff autonomy," in spite of diplomatic opposition by the Western powers. In Guangzhou, the KMT also imposed various new domestic taxes on industrial and commercial goods and reformed the tax system to pay for the military spending required for the Northern Expedition. This tax and fiscal reform, centering on provincial fiscal consolidation, was directly inherited by the NNG after it succeeded in seizing power and unifying China. There is no question that Guangdong was an advanced experimental region for the creation of a financial-modernization model in China.

Taking Guangdong province as an example, this book discusses both the globalization and localization of Chinese taxation. Examining the introduction of new taxes and financial processes, along with the lessons learned from the earlier experiences of the Western powers and Japan, reveals Guangdong's pioneering efforts to transplant the model of a modern fiscal state in China. This book aims to examine the role of the Guangdong model in restructuring modern Chinese finance.

We first look at Guangdong's finance as a whole in terms of long-term trends. Part 1 is devoted to an examination of two representative new taxes in modern Guangdong: the tobacco and wine tax (*yangjiushui*) and the special tax (*zhuanshui*). Part 2 investigates the provincial-run enterprises and monopolies that were characteristic of the province. Moving on to Part 3, we examine the modernization of tax administration through the reform of tax collection. Finally, Part 4 traces the overall long-term trends of modern Chinese finance in comparison with global trends. We then extend the analysis to fiscal reform in contemporary China after the reform and opening policy in the context of the interrupted but continuing efforts toward fiscal modernization in China.

Part 1

New Tax Revenues in Guangdong during the Republican Era

1 Fiscal Reform in the Late Qing

Abstract

This chapter summarizes and characterizes the fiscal trends of Guangdong province in comparison with the rest of China from the late Qing period to the Republican era before the Second Sino-Japanese War. Beginning in the late Qing, the finance of Guangdong province differed from those of other provinces in that there was the lowest proportion of land tax revenue and the highest proportion of commercial tax revenue relative to total revenue. In terms of revenue, this second largest province tapped the industrial and commercial sectors to support the expanding provincial budget. In particular, Guangdong took the lead in tapping financial resources to build modernized government-owned industries. Such potential manifested itself during Republican China, especially in the 1930s.

Keywords: fiscal reform, China, the late Qing, the Republican China, Guangdong

The late Qing era witnessed a growing awareness of the necessity for fiscal modernization as part of the modern nation-building process. Fiscal reform efforts included the introduction of a Western budget system, enforcement of indirect taxes on the industrial and commercial sectors, and a break from the dependency on a land tax. The 1898 Hundred Days' Reform furthered discussions on financial modernization, as unfolded in the "Basic Principles of the New Policy" (*Xinzheng shiji*), written by He Qi and Hu Liyuan in 1898, on the necessity of a division between state and local taxes. After an aborted attempt, the Guangxu emperor ordered a compilation of the government budget for the first time in 1899. However, Sheng Xuanhuai's memorial about compiling an annual budget was not accepted by the imperial court amid the conservative atmosphere that dominated after the failure of the Hundred Days' Reform.[1]

1 Zhang Jiuzhou, "Lun Qingmo caizheng zhidu de gaige jiqi zuoyong" [On the reform and function of the financial system in the late Qing dynasty], *Henan daxue xuebao* (*Shehui kexue ban*)

Kang, Jin-A, *The Guangdong Model and Taxation in China*. Taylor & Francis Group, 2022
DOI: 10.5117/9789463725248_CH01

The start of the New Policy reform paved the way to full-scale modernization. Zhang Jian, a prominent reformer, in his 1901 publication "Discussion on the Reform" (*bianfa pingyi*), counted "the creation of a budget" as one of the twelve urgent tasks for the Board of Revenue (*hubu*). The Finance Office (*caizhengchu*), an institution separate from the regular bureaucracy, was finally established by the Qing court in 1903. The first government bank acting as the public treasury, Hubu Bank, was opened in 1904, with a total capital of 4 million taels.

Along with keeping constitutional reform on track, "financial reform" (*qingli caizheng*) was included as one item on the agenda of the "preliminary constitution" that the Qing court publicly declared in 1906. The Board of Revenue was renamed the Ministry of Finance (*duzhibu*) in October, and the Finance Office was incorporated into the Ministry of Finance. At the same time, the Tax Office (*shuiwuchu*), which had been established in April of the same year, took over the jurisdiction of the imperial Customs Offices and became a subordinate bureau of the Ministry of Finance. At the end of 1906, the compilation plan of the budget by the Ministry of Finance was officially confirmed.

However, the issue of how to draw up a modernized budget remained unclear. No specific measures were taken to understand each province's financial situation in real terms until 1908, which marked the beginning of the financial and administrative reforms. In 1908 the Tax Office decided to establish the Tax School (*shuiwu xuetang*) to train highly qualified tax officials. The Hubu Bank was renamed the Great Qing Bank (Ta-Ching Bank, *Daqing yinhang*), and a modern system to manage the public treasury was established with the enactment of the Banking Ordinance. In the following year, 1909, the Ministry of Finance announced the establishment of the Bureau of Financial Reform (*qingli caizhengju*), an organization tasked with investigating the local financial situation and implementing provincial financial reforms.

In 1910, Zhili province, selected as a model province for financial reform, established the Central Office of Finance (*caizheng zonghuichu*) to direct all local financial offices. Following Zhili's example, the other provinces established similar provincial offices to oversee local revenue affairs. A similar office, the Public Office of Finance in Guangdong (*Guangdong caizheng gongsuo*) was established in Guangdong province in which an

4 (2002): 52; Chi-ho Chŏng, "Ch'ŏngmal yanggyech'oŭi chaejŏnggaehyŏgan'gwa kungmin'gukka" [Liang Qichao's financial-reform plan and the idea of a nation-state I in the late Qing dynasty], *Myŏngch'ŏngsa yŏn'gu* 39 (2013): 147.

Administrative Commissioner (*buzhengshi*) took over the position of the Chief Manager (*zongban*). At the same time, the Bureau of Military Revenue (*shanhouju*) and the Central Bureau of *Likin* (*liwu zongju*) were abolished.[2]

Based on these institutional rearrangements, the Ministry of Finance in Beijing ordered that the twenty-two Bureaus of Financial Reform in the provinces sort out and clarify all revenue and expenditures by item and telegraph the results to Beijing by the end of the 35th year of the Guangxu emperor (1909). These reports were summarized and compiled into one table, titled "The Total Amount of Revenue and Expenditures of Twenty-two Provinces in the 34th Year of Guangxu."[3] The primary goal of this compilation was to clarify the amount of "unreported local spending" (*waixiao*) among the provincial revenue, which had previously been exempt from reporting to the Board of Revenue in Beijing. Earlier statistics, compiled in Beijing, had been based solely on the amount of "reported local spending" (*zouxiao*). This groundbreaking move in 1910 allowed the imperial court to understand the full extent of local finance.

A further step was taken to clarify local revenue. A series of compilations, the "Financial Statement" (*caizheng shuomingshu*) projected the finance in each province. These compilations, produced by the Bureaus of Financial Reform in the twenty-two provinces, were detailed and voluminous reports on revenue and expenditures in the 34th year of Guangxu (1908) and the first year of Xuantong (1909). Because administrative ability and official expectations of financial reform varied by province, the publication dates of these compilations also varied. Among the twenty-two provinces, the Guangdong compilation is noted for its detail and accuracy.[4] The *Guangdong Financial Statement* (*Guangdong*

2 Chen Feng, "WanQing caizheng yusuan de yunniang yu shishi" [Preparation and implementation of the financial budget in the late Qing dynasty], *Jianghan luntan* 1 (2009): 78–90; Satō Junpei, *Kindai chūgoku zaiseishi: 'Gaishō' kara 'chihō' e* [A fiscal history of modern China: Changing central-provincial relations in the late Qing and the early] (Tokyo: Tōkyō daigaku shuppankai, 2020), chaps. 1 and 2.

3 Beijing tushuguan chubanshe yingyinshi, ed., *Qingmo Minguo caizheng shiliao jikan* [Financial historical materials of the late Qing dynasty and Republican China, Vol. 1] (Beijing: Beijing tushuguan chubanshe, 2007), 165–171.

4 This compilation was edited in the second half of 1910 and first published in 1911 by the Bureau of Finance Reform of Guangdong (*Guangdong qingli caizhengju*) before being published twice during the Republican era by the Economic Association (*Jingji xuehui*) in 1915 and by the National Tax Service's Office (*Guoshui guanli weiyuanhui gongshu*) in 1928. In 1997 Guangdong Economic Publishing House published a fully edited new version; see Guangdongsheng caizheng kexue yanjiusuo (Fiscal Science Research Center, Department of Finance, Guangdong), ed., *Guangdong caizheng shuomingshu* [Guangdong financial statement] (Guangzhou: Guangdong jingji chubanshe, 1997).

caizheng shuomingshu) is thus a valuable record for historians to use in exploring the transformation of imperial finance and taxation during the late Qing period. The experience of Guangdong demonstrates the rise and expansion of the *likin* tax revenue, the structural changes in the traditional finance reliance on a land tax, and provincial endeavors to build a modern fiscal state.

Fiscal scale of Guangdong province in late Qing China

Before examining Guangdong's provincial revenue, it is helpful to compare Guangdong province with the other provinces to understand the distinct features of Guangdong finance. Other than the aforementioned "Total Amount of Revenue and Expenditures of the Twenty-two Provinces in the 34th Year of Guangxu," there are no data comparing the financial size of each province during the late Qing. However, due to the different local currencies and the overlapping calculations of remittances to the other provinces (*xiekuan, xiexiang*), remittances to the Ministry of Finance in Beijing (*jiexiang, jingxiang*), and the financial subsidies from the Board of Revenue in Beijing (*bubokuan*), it is almost impossible to calculate the exact amount of central and provincial revenue.

However, Han Xiang of the People's University has made valuable progress in this respect by scrutinizing the previous calculations.[5] In particular, he finds that the earlier research uncritically copies the errors regarding Guangdong silver tael revenue in the *Supplementary Documents in the Qing Dynasty* (*Qingchao xu wenxian tongkao*) written by Liu Jinzao, which overestimated the total amount of Guangdong provincial revenue by more than 30 million taels by falsely adding 10 million taels to the silver tael revenue item.[6] Nevertheless, Han Xiang fails to produce reliable alternative statistics and the *Guangdong Financial Statement* remains a reliable basis for research. He roughly estimates the combined total amount of central and local revenue in the 34th year of Guangxu at about 240 million taels. Keeping these limitations in mind, we will now take a look at "The Total Amount of Revenue and Expenditures of the Twenty-two Provinces in the 34th year of Guangxu."

5 Han Xiang, "WanQing caizheng guimo gusuan wenti chutan" [Research on the problem of estimating the scale of public finance in the late Qing], *Zhongguo jingjishi yanjiu* 3 (2014): 25–41.
6 Han Xiang, "WanQing caizheng guimo gusuan wenti chutan," 27.

Table 1.1 Total amount of revenue and expenditures in twenty-two provinces, 1908

Province	Revenue	Expenditures
Fengtian	15,807,272 taels	15,587,889 taels
Jilin	4,858,702 taels	5,355,657 taels
Heilongjiang	933,256 taels Heilongjiang cash 4,855,040 strings Russian rubles 102,803 yuan Gold 306 liang	2,290,906 taels Heilongjiang cash 2,596,495 strings Russian rubles 16,385 yuan Silver dollar 5 million yuan
Zhili	21,658,597 taels	23,574,139 taels
(Rehe)	806,385 taels	841,264 taels
Jiangsu Ningshu	25,496,890 taels	25,745,182 taels
Jiangsu Sushu	20,403,020 taels	24,890,000 taels
(Jiangbei)	132,525 taels Xiangping silver coin 1,506,987 taels standard cash 28,739,667 pieces	116,244 taels Xiangping silver dollar 1,126,814 taels standard cash 28,331,479 pieces
Anhui	6,006,729 taels	6,741,779 taels
Shandong	11,311,699 taels	10,529,028 taels
Shanxi	5,871,806 taels	6,140,252 taels

Province	Revenue	Expenditures
Gansu	3,121,780 taels standard cash 2,518,798 pieces	3,290,757 taels standard cash 3,900,539 pieces
Xinjiang	3,172,300 taels	3,346,564 taels
Fujian	6,721,105 taels	6,941,107 taels
Zhejiang	8,148,581 taels Silver dollar 4,633,444 yuan Silver 10-cent, 20-cent coin 657 *jiao* (1 *jiao* = 10 cents) Standard cash 24,914,477 pieces	8,473,207 taels Silver dollar 4,489,848 yuan Silver 10-cent, 20-cent coin 288 *jiao* (1 *jiao* = 10 cents) Standard cash 30,178,722 pieces
Jiangxi	7,569,863 taels	7,895,177 taels
Hubei	16,545,200 taels	18,521,400 taels
Hunan	6,028,100 taels Silver dollar 476 yuan Standard cash 662,200 strings	6,424,200 taels Silver dollar 160 yuan Standard cash 582,500 strings
Sichuan	15,320,657 taels	14,964,926 taels
Guangdong	Minyin silver 7,259,463 taels Foreign silver dollar 20,018,317 taels	Minyin silver 6,568,526 taels Foreign silver dollar 21,041,711 taels

Province	Revenue	Expenditures	Province	Revenue	Expenditures
Henan	6,885,117 taels	6,600,094 taels	Guangxi	4,890,643 taels	4,992,157 taels
Shaanxi	3,963,702 taels	4,127,565 taels	Yunnan	6,011,502 taels	6,983,166 taels
			Guizhou	1,533,270 taels	1,791,056 taels

Source: "Guangxu sanshisinian ershier zhisheng suiru suichu zongshu biao" [The total amount of revenue and expenditures of the twenty-two provinces in the 34th year of the Guangxu emperor], in Han Xiang "WanQing caizheng guimo gusuan wenti chutan," 26, Table 2.
Note for translation of currencies and units:
tael: *liang,* standard silver bullion currency unit scaled by the Board of Revenue, 37.5 g
liang: weight unit
silver dollar: *yinyuan*
yuan: *yuan,* silver dollar unit, 0.72–0.73 tael
standard cash: *zhiqian,* official copper cash
piece: *wen,* standard cash unit
string: *chuan,* a bundle of 1,000 pieces of copper cash tied with a string in principle Heilongjiang
cash: *zhongqian*
Russian ruble: *qiangqian*
foreign silver dollar: *yangyin*
Minyin silver: *minyin,* pure silver bullion, namely, de facto standard silver bullion
Xiangping silver coin: *xiangping,* silver coin minted in Kashgar, Xinjiang
silver 10-cent, 20-cent coin: *xiaoyinyuan,* subsidiary silver coin
jiao: *jiao,* 10-cent silver unit
gold: *jinsha*

As can be seen, the reports on provincial revenue used varying currency units, including the silver tael unit of the Board of Revenue (*Kuping* tael), pure silver bullion, the silver dollar, gold, and numerous different copper coins. While most provinces used the Kuping tael as the primary currency unit in their revenue reports, Guangdong's report adopted two currency units—silver bullion and foreign silver dollars. However, the revenue in foreign silver dollars was converted to the Kuping tael. The amount of revenue in foreign silver dollars was 20.01 million Kuping taels, 2.7 times more than the 7.25 million Kuping taels of silver bullion revenue. This means that in practice, Guangdong province widely used silver dollars, unlike the other provinces. As to the volume of provincial revenue, Guangdong's provincial revenue was 27.27 million Kuping taels, which is the highest among the twenty-two provinces, nearly 18 times more than the 1.53 million taels in Guizhou province, which had the smallest amount of provincial revenue. However, since Jiangsu province was divided into two districts, Ning (*Ningshu*) and Su (*Sushu*), in terms of its reported revenue, the real revenue of Jiangsu province should equal the sum of the two districts.[7] Accordingly, the total amount of revenue in Jiangsu province totaled about 46 million taels, which is the largest sum in real terms, and Guangdong province had the second highest amount of provincial revenue.

Detailed information about Guangdong's tax revenue, tax structure, and fiscal balance can be found in the *Guangdong Financial Statement*. This book presents detailed figures and tables for each revenue and expenditure item for two years, the 34th year of Guangxu and the first year of Xuantong. Overall, there are ten major categories of revenue and fourteen major categories of expenditures. At a more detailed level, there are 812 revenue items and 1,094 expenditure items. However, the actual amounts of taxes and expenses are estimated to be far higher than those that appear in the statement. For example, looking at the revenue item under the "Miscellaneous Taxes of Each Prefecture" (*gexian xiaoshui*), we find that some of the miscellaneous taxes across the different prefectures are only partially listed. The same situation applies to expenditures at the prefecture level, thus complicating the finance situation in Guangdong

The national taxes and the local taxes are not recorded separately in the *Guangdong Financial Statement*, while the "draft government budget in the 4th year of Xuantong (1912)" drawn up in 1911 finally compiled the tax revenues, divided between the two categories of national taxes and local taxes. Besides these two sources, the *Gazetteer of Guangdong Province: Finance*, published in 1999, offeres useful categorization which attempts to reorganize the revenue categories in the *Guangdong Financial Statement* in line with the categories used during the Republican era. Table 1.2 compares the categories adopted by these three sources.

The tax on domestic opium (*tuyaoshui*), which was on the tax list in the *Guangdong Financial Statement*, disappeared from the budget in the 4th year of Xuantong because the constitutional movement had prohibited the use of opium and abolished the tax on opium. In addition, because the revenue from the sale of official positions (*juanshu*) was assigned to the national tax category in the budget in the 4th year of Xuantong, this revenue disappeared from the provincial revenue items. Along with the principle of making a division between the national budget and the local budget,

7 During the Qing dynasty, Jiangsu province was uniquely divided into two Financial Commissioner's Offices: The Financial Commissioner's Office of Right Jiangnan (*Jiannan you buzhengshi si*) and the Financial Commissioner's Office of Left Jiangnan (*Jiangnan zuo buzhengshi si*). Ji Haopeng, "Ningshu haishi sushu: Xinren zhiji Jiangsu shenghui zhi zheng" [Belonging to Ningshu or Suzhou: The Debate during the Jiangsu Province Conference in 1911–12], *Jiangsu shehui kexue* 2 (2017): 239.

Table 1.2 Comparison of historical materials in terms of the composition of Guangdong provincial finance

Revenue			**Expenditures**		
Statement	**Budget of 1912**	***Gazetteer of Guangdong Province***	***Statement***	**Budget of 1912**	***Gazetteer of Guangdong Province***
Land tax	Land tax	Land tax	Remittances to the capital		Remittances to the capital and other provinces and forced assignment of payments
Salt tax	Salt tax	Industrial and commercial tax	Remittances to other provinces		
Tariff	Tariff		Total administrative expenses	Foreign affairs expenses	Administrative expenditures (administrative, ceremonial, diplomatic, and judicial costs)
Regular and miscellaneous taxes	Regular and miscellaneous taxes	Deed taxes, fees, public property, forfeitures, and donation income	Negotiation expenses	Interior expenses	
Opium tax	-		Civil service expenses	Financial expenses	
likin	*likin*		Financial expenses	Education expenses	Military and security expenditures
Regular and miscellaneous levies	Regular and miscellaneous levies		Ceremony expenses	Army expenses	
Sales of official positions	-		Education expenses	Navy expenses	
Income of government enterprises	Income of government enterprises	Government-run enterprises incomes		Judicial expenses	Economic and construction expenditures
Miscellaneous income	Miscellaneous income			Agricultural and commercial expenses	
		Subsidies from the central government and other provinces		Transportation expenses	Education and health expenditures
		Debt income			Social relief expenditures

Source: Guangdongsheng caizheng kexue yanjiusuo [Fiscal Science Research Center, Department of Finance, Guangdong], ed., *Guangdong caizheng shuomingshu* [Guangdong financial statement] (Guangzhou: Guangdong jingji chubanshe, 1997), 12, 375; Han Xiang, "WanQing caizheng guimo gusuan wenti chutan," 31; Guangdongsheng difang shizhi bianzuan weiyuanhui [Compilation Committee for The Gazetteer of Guangdong Province], *Guangdongsheng zhi: Caizheng zhi* [Gazetteer of Guangdong Province: Finance], compiled by Guangdongsheng defang shizhi bianzuan weiyuanhui [Gazetteer compilation ommittee of Guangdong province] (Guangzhou: Guangdong renmin chubanshe, 1999), 49–124.
Note: "Statement" refers to the *Guangdong Financial Statement* (191)1; "Budget of 1912" refers to the "draft government budget in the 4th year of Xuantong (1912)";
Gazetteer of Guangdong Province refers to *Gazetteer of Guangdong Province: Finance* (1999).

remittances to Beijing (*jiekuan, jingxiang*) and subsidies to neighboring financially poor provinces (*xiekuan, xiexiang*) were assigned to the category of national expenses.

There have been considerable changes in the naming of the items for revenue and expenditures. Along with incorporating the poll tax into the land tax during the reign of Kangxi, the land and poll tax (*didingyin*) was substituted by the land tax (*tianfu*) during the earlier stage of the *Guangdong Fiscal Statement*. Changes in expenditures are more prominent. Before the Opium War, official expenditures were divided into twelve major categories (*jisi, yixian, weishi, kechang, xianggan, yizhan, chashan, shangxu, xiushan, zhizao* [Guangdong did not have this item], *caiban*, and *gonglian*). These were all substituted by fourteen more modern categories in the *Guangdong Financial Statement*, out of which only three categories, such as remittances to the Beijing, remittances to other provinces, and ceremonial expenses (*dianlifei*) can be considered to be traditional expenditure items.[8]

Because the *Guangdong Financial Statement* only records tax revenue for some essential items, it is difficult to determine its exact amount. The financial scale in Guangdong province is estimated to be approximately 23.4 million taels in 1908 and 37.4 million taels in 1909.[9] This indicates an explosive increase of more than 10 million taels in a single year, while the steep rise in Guangdong provincial revenue was not seen until after the First Sino-Japanese War. In 1849, the total amount of provincial revenue was only 3.2 million taels, and actual local spending was only 1.5 million taels (not including remittances to Beijing and neighboring provinces). Meanwhile, in 1893, the amount of provincial revenue and expenditures increased to 11.09 million taels and 11.28 million taels, respectively, of which 6.78 million taels was spent within the province. Provincial revenue and expenditures in 1909 increased to 37,396,473 taels and 38,326,867 taels, respectively, an increase of more than 300 percent.[10] As pointed out by many studies, due to the forced payment of the Boxer Indemnity (*tanpai*) and the financial burden of having to pay for the New Policy, the populations in all provinces faced the imposition of exploitative tax collections and the provinces witnessed their highest rise in revenue. The extent of fiscal expansion in Guangdong surpassed that of the other twenty-two provinces.

8 Wang Tingkui, "Minguo yiqian weiyi de Guangdong caizheng jupian: Xijian Qingmo 'Guangdong caizheng shuomingshu' zhengli ben wenshi" [The sole financial comprehensive record of Guangdong provincial finance prior to Republican China: Thinking about the publication of the "Guangdong Financial Statement" in the late Qing], *Guangdong shizhi* 2 (1998): 71.

9 Han Xiang, "WanQing caizheng guimo gusuan wenti chutan," 41.

10 Wang Tingkui, "Minguo yiqian weiyi de Guangdong caizheng jupian," 72.

Fiscal features of Guangdong province in the late Qing

How was such a feat of fiscal expansion possible? A comparison with the fiscal composition in the early Qing can provide some clues. In 1685, Guangdong's provincial revenue amounted to 1.598 million taels in Kuping silver taels, out of which the land tax accounted for 71.7 percent, the salt tax 11.69 percent, and the toll and commercial taxes 16.61 percent. This was a typical tax structure in traditional China, which was characterized by heavy reliance on land and salt taxes. However, by the end of the nineteenth century, military expenses and war indemnities led to the imposition of numerous new taxes, such as the *likin*, the gambling tax, the opium tax, and miscellaneous other taxes, whereby the irregular and additional taxes surpassed the regular taxes. In 1893, the *likin* tax accounted for 38.91 percent (1.676 million taels) of the composition of provincial revenue (4.309 million taels) and it replaced the land tax as the largest source of revenue. In contrast, out of the 19.83 million taels of Guangdong's provincial revenue in 1909, excluding customs and debt income, the gambling tax accounted for 17.85 percent (3.539 million taels), the salt tax accounted for 17.16 percent (3.402 million taels), and the *likin* tax accounted for 13.8 percent (2.737 million taels). These commercial taxes all overtook the 5.57 share of the land tax (1.104 million taels).[11] Table 1.3 below shows the itemized distribution of the actual amount of tax collected in the silver dollar standard.

The largest amount of revenue came from the regular and miscellaneous levies (*zhengza gejuan*), in which the gambling tax was included. The *likin* tax ranked second in the tax-revenue rankings. Therefore, as indicated above, the revenue structure of Guangdong relied less on the land tax and more on the *likin* and the gambling taxes. An examination of 1908 and 1909 reveals that revenue increased considerably, by 2.7 million taels. While most of the revenue items showed an increase, only the levies and miscellaneous income (*za shouru*) were drastically reduced. The reason was due to the decline in the gambling tax revenue, which was reduced by more than 0.8 million taels, from 4.35 million taels to 3.54 million taels. Originally, the gambling tax was spent on military spending, but in 1909 the house of provincial representatives (*ziyiju*), which was born out of the constitution movement, launched a campaign to ban gambling. This campaign caused a

11 *Guangdongsheng zhi: Caizheng zhi* [Gazetteer of Guangdong Province: Finance], compiled by Guangdongsheng defang shizhi bianzuan weiyuanhui [Gazetteer compilation ommittee of Guangdong province] (Guangzhou: Guangdong renmin chubanshe, 1999), 49; *Guangdong caizheng shuomingshu*, 49.

Table 1.3 Structure of tax revenue in Guangdong, 1908–1909 (unit: taels)

Source	1908		1909		+/-
	Collected amount	Share	Collected amount	share	
Land tax	2,934,386.717	10.55	3,141,562.061	10.30	207,175.344
Salt tax	2,808,142.851	10.09	3,470,574.486	11.38	662,431.635
Tariff	6,995,224.208	25.15	7,309,794.122	23.97	314,569.914
Regular and miscellaneous taxes	1,466,664.180	5.27	1,920,084.019	6.29	453,419.839
Opium tax	338,396.277	1.21	343,047.507	1.13	4,651.230
Likin	3,151,832.108	11.33	3,394,259.219	11.13	242,427.111
Regular and miscellaneous levies	6,222,690.250	22.37	5,801,906.437	19.02	-420,783.813
Sales of official positions	217,573.092	0.78	921,464.097	3.02	703,891.005
Income from government industry	381,078.560	1.37	1,188,274.456	3.89	807,195.896
Miscellaneous income	3,295,698.712	11.85	2,998,919.789	9.83	-296,778.923
	27,811,686.955		30,489,886.193		2,678,199.238

Source: collected data from *Guangdong caizheng shuomingshu*.
Notes: This table records the amount to the 3rd digit, disregarding the 4th digit in the sources. The Guangdong opium tax was managed collectively under the name of the Guangdong Guangxi Consolidated Opium Tax (*liangguang tuyao tongshui*). In addition, because the standard year of the opium tax ranged from the 11th month to the next 10th month, the amount of the opium tax in the 34th year of Guangxu was the amount of tax collected in Guangdong from the 11th month of the 33rd year of Guangxu to the 10th month of the 34th year of Guangxu. The amount of the land tax revenue in the above is close to 3 million taels in both years, which is much larger than the 1.104 million taels presented in the *Guangdongsheng zhi*. This is because the *Guangdongsheng zhi* only calculates the regular and the additional "land and poll tax" (*didingyin*) as the land tax revenue, whereas the "Guangdong Financial Statement" includes the land and poll tax as well as all other taxes on land, such as the "mass rice" (*minmi*) tax, the "grain donation" (*liang juan*) tax, and other additional taxes.[12]

steep drop in revenue from the gambling tax. A complete ban on gambling was implemented in 1911. Second, less miscellaneous income was collected due to the centralization of local finance. The major tax revenue item in this category came from the interest income generated by grain loans administered by the provincial government to peasants from the disaster relief fund and the warehouse reserves. However, the central government thereafter began to directly control these financial institutions.

12 *Guangdong caizheng shuomingshu*, 54, 77.

On the other hand, the item with the largest rise in revenue was enterprise income, that is, the income from the management of various state-run enterprises. The amount accounted for by this item increased by more than 0.8 million taels, enough to make up for the decrease in the gambling taxes. The profits of the two state-run financial institutions, the Canton Mint (*zaobi Yuechuang*) and the Official Silver Copper Money Bureau (*guan yinqianju*) increased from 330,000 to 770,000 silver taels and from 20,000 to 400,000 silver taels, respectively. The second most significant increase in revenue was the income from the sale of official positions, recording an increase of 700,000 taels within one year. As a result, the combined share of government enterprise income and income from sales of official positions in provincial income jumped from 2.15 percent in 1908 to 6.91 percent in 1909.

In conclusion, both continuities and discontinuities can be found in an analysis of provincial revenue in these two years. First of all, the earlier trend continued in terms of an increase in total revenue and a high reliance on the *likin* and the gambling tax. Nevertheless, the extent of the dependence on the gambling tax declined in terms of both in quantity and share, whereas new fiscal resources, such as the income from state-run enterprises, increased impressively. Furthermore, the various currencies seen in earlier official reports disappeared, and revenue was estimated and reported exclusively by conversion to silver taels.

Disorder in terms of measures and currencies had been a long-standing problem in Chinese finance. The attempt to unify fiscal money represented a giant step forward in the direction of fiscal modernization. The pioneering effort to adopt silver dollars as the monetary standard unfolded in the *Guangdong Financial Statement* of 1909.[13]

The building of government enterprises in Guangdong in the decade prior to the end of the Qing dynasty

The item "income from government enterprises" was classified as the ninth revenue category in the *Guangdong Financial Statement*. The state-run companies belonging to this category were the Canton Mint, the Provincial Bank, Xicun Cement Plant, the Official Printing Office, Ruyuan Coal Mine, and Qujiang Antimony Mine. Government and merchant joint ventures (*guangshang heban*) were also assigned to this category, including Zengyuan Paper Company, the water supply company, and the electric power company.

13 *Guangdong caizheng shuomingshu*, 5–11.

Finally, a so-called "government supervised, privately-run company" (*guandu shangban*), the antimony mine at Mt. Maan in Qujiang, was also assigned to this category.[14]

The most important revenue sources were the Canton Mint and the Provincial Bank, with profits from the other companies remaining minimal until the demise of the Qing empire. The Canton Mint (later the Guangdong Provincial Mint) originated from the Official Copper Coin Bureau (*guanqianju*), founded in 1887, which started to mint legal copper cash (*zhiqian*) for the first time in China in 1889, through the use of imported machines. The bureau was renamed the Canton Mint in 1890, the first official modern mint to cast silver dollars in China. The Canton Mint recorded total profits of 2.855 million taels from 1889 to 1899, with average yearly profits amounting to about 0.28 million taels. The launch of minting copper ten cash (*dangshi tongyuan*) in large quantities produced additional massive profits for the Canton Mint, leading to high profit of as much as 0.76 million (759,100) taels in 1909. The total profits of the Canton Mint from 1889–1909 amounted to 8,974,000 taels. In 1906 the Canton Mint was transferred to the jurisdiction of the Ministry of Finance by the Qing court and it was no longer a provincial enterprise. However, while 40 percent of the total profits was assigned to the Ministry of Finance, 60 percent continued to belong to the provincial treasury at this time.

The Provincial Bank was initially called the Official Silver Copper Money Bureau when it was established in 1904. It was later renamed the Guangdong Provincial Bank. Its main business was to issue convertible banknotes for the silver currency minted by the Canton Mint. This banknote was called an official silver banknote (*guanyinpiao*). In addition, the Provincial Bank was responsible for issuing the silver money minted by the Canton Mint. Total issuance of banknotes in the late Qing amounted to 10 million taels. The Provincial Bank already had modern banking functions, such as lending issued banknotes to the private sector, receiving interest, and opening accounts to pay interest on private savings. The Provincial Bank's net profits were modest, as little as 21,300 taels in 1908, but they jumped to 396,100 taels in the following year.[15]

There were multiple currencies circulating for daily transactions in the mid-nineteenth century in Qing China: silver ingots, silver dollar coins, and copper cash. By the end of the nineteenth century, the Qing court and several provincial governments attempted machine-based modern

14 *Guangdong caizheng shuomingshu*, 24–25.
15 *Guangdong caizheng shuomingshu*, 297–301.

coin-casting. The first successful mint was the Canton Mint, followed by other provincial mints.

The pioneering development and high profits of the Canton Mint and the Provincial Bank in the late Qing resulted in the formation of a distinct monetary zone in Guangdong, which, in the long run, was separate from the rest of China. Guangdong province remained a distinct market based on the so-called "Small Money" standard, in contrast to the so-called "Big Money" zone centered in Shanghai until the 1930s.

So-called "Small Money" (*xiaoyang, haoyang, xiaoyuan, haozi, xiaoyinyuan, jiaoyang, haoyin*, etc.) originally referred to 0.2 silver dollar (20 cents, *shuanghao*) and 0.1 silver dollar (10 cents, *danhao*) as subsidiary currencies, while "Big Money" (*dayang*) referred to 1 silver dollar. When the Canton Mint (later the Guangdong Provincial Mint) started to mint silver coins for the first time in 1890, one silver dollar consisted of 90 percent silver content, whereas the 20-cent silver coin had 86 percent silver content and the 10-cent silver coin had 82 percent. This means that there were greater profits in producing 20-cent and 10-cent coins than in producing one silver dollar.[16]

Based on the decimal system, ten *danhao* or five *shuanghao* were supposed to be equivalent to one silver dollar. However, the traditional market practice was to reassess the value of currency according to weight and purity, regardless of the face value. The Chinese government tried to introduce a modern currency system based on face value and counting. Initially, despite the lower silver content, the 20-cent and 10-cent silver coins in Guangdong were accepted in the market according to their legal face value. Five 20-cent silver coins and ten 10-cent silver coins could be converted to one silver dollar because the steep rise in the value of copper cash had led to its meltdown in large scale around 1890, and the resultant cash shortage had led to an urgent need for 20-cent and 10-cent silver coins in the market. In other words, because of high demand the Chinese temporarily began to

16 Xiong Li, "Yuebi shiyao" [A brief history of currency in Guangdong], *Guangdongsheng Yin hang yuekan* 1(1) (1937): 58; Miyashita Tadao, *Chūgoku heisei no tokushu kenkyū: kindai chūgoku ginryō seido no kenkyū* [Special study of the Chinese monetary system: A study of the modern Chinese silver system] (Tokyo: Maruzen kabushiki kaisha, 1952), 47; Tōa dōbunkai, ed., *Shina shōbetsu zenshi daiikken kantonshō fu honkon makao* [Complete gazetteer of each Chinese province, Vol. 1 Guangdong Province, Appendix: Hong Kong and Macau] (Tokyo: Tōa dōbunkai, 1917), 1037–1039, 1041–1042. Meanwhile, other records note that the *dayang* silver, and the *shuanghao* and *danhao* silver coins had 90.27 percent, 80 percent, and 85 percent silver content, respectively; see Gu Yu, "Guangdongsheng sannian shizheng jihua zhong bizhi gaige fang'an zhi niyi" [The draft currency reform in the three-year plan of Guangdong province], *Xin Guangdong* 3 (1933): 13.

accept the modern concept of currency valued by counting, instead of the traditional concept of currency valued by weight and purity. In contrast, there was limited market need and popularity for one silver dollar, firstly because it was too valuable for daily transactions, and secondly because forging one silver dollar was easier relative to small silver money due to its bigger size. Guangdong province not only limited minting quantity but also market circulation of "Small Money," and merchants in the province and the general population came to make business settlements exclusively in "Small Money."[17]

Because of the larger seigniorage and the Cantonese preference for "Small Money" for settlement of daily transactions, the Canton Mint almost exclusively cast "Small Money," accounting for 98 percent of the total amount of silver dollars cast by the Canton Mint from 1890 until 1900. Due to the growing financial burdens, the provincial government in the 1900s further dropped the purity of silver coins to pursue seigniorage. Gresham's Law worked as well, causing an outflow of "Big Money" from the province. Hence, the Guangdong market was filled almost exclusively with "Small Money." Finally, the legal decimal system collapsed. One silver dollar *yuan* in Guangdong under the "Small Money" system corresponded in value to five *shuanghao* or ten *danhao*, whose value was less than the one silver dollar *yuan* in Shanghai under the "Big Money" system. The Chinese market started to discount "Small Money" against "Big Money" in actual transactions. Accordingly, the legal decimal regulation was taken over by market custom, leading to systematic separation of '"Small Money" from "Big Money" and daily fluctuations in exchange rates between the two. From the late Qing, Guangdong province used 10-cent and 20-cent silver coins for actual payments, while the accounting and price standard was one silver dollar *yuan*, [which indicated] the value of five 20-cent silver coins,[18] or one "Small Money *yuan*" (*xiaoyang yuan*, *haoyuang yuan*).

If a visitor from another province carried one silver dollar ("Big Money"), he had to exchange it for 20-cent or 10-cent coins in Guangdong to make payments. For trans-provincial transactions, a daily exchange rate between 1 *yuan* in Guangdong ("Small Money") and 1 *yuan* in other provinces ("Big Money") was set by the market.[19]

17 Zhongguo renmin yinhang zonghang canshishi [Counselor's office of the People's Bank of China], ed., *Zhonghua Minguo huobishi ziliao dierji* [Monetary history of the Republic of China, Part 2] (Shanghai: Shanghai renmin chubanshe, 1991), 7.

18 Gu Yu, "Guangdongsheng sannian shizheng jihua," 13.

19 Xiong Li, "Yuebi shiyao," 54.

The minting of copper ten cash (*tongyuan*) was another example whereby the Canton Mint pursued seigniorage. The copper ten cash had the face value of ten pieces of cash, while its minting cost was at most two to three pieces of cash. Therefore, the Canton Mint could enjoy enormous profits.[20] The value of copper ten cash was very useful for daily payments in China. The problem was that Cantonese people preferred small silver money for payments over copper ten cash. The circulation of copper ten cash remained modest in Guangdong, with most used as small change, and market needs for copper ten cash were meager. Taken together, it seems strange that the amount of copper ten cash castings was so significant, making up about 61 percent of the total issued coins cast by the Canton Mint before the demise of the Qing dynasty. But the Canton Mint could find a market outside of the province. Most of its castings were transported to Shanghai for export and sold to other provinces.

The profits from the casting of copper ten cash paid for Guangdong's provincial spending for subsidies to suppress a rebellion in Guangxi. The initial purpose of issuing copper ten cash was to link copper cash with the silver dollar in the decimal system, with 100 copper ten cash to be equal to 1 silver dollar *yuan*. That is why copper ten cash was called copper *yuan* in Chinese. However, because of the separation between "Small Money" and "Big Money," the market continued to discern copper money from silver money according to their actual value and market needs, failing to link copper ten cash to the silver dollar. Therefore, the Qing court relinked copper ten cash to copper cash and changed the English inscription on the copper ten cash from *one cent* to *ten cash*. Despite the legal exchange rate whereby 1 silver dollar was equal to 100 pieces of copper ten cash, the market exchange rate between 1 silver dollar and copper ten cash fluctuated sharply from 80–95 (in 1900 to 1904) to 150 (in 1906) to 170–180 (in 1909).[21]

20 *Guangdong caizheng shuomingshu*, 298.

21 Xu Sidao, "Guangdong tongyuan de zhuzao he liutong" [Casting and circulation of cash], in *Jindai Guangdong jinrong Guangdong wenshi ziliao diliushi jiu ji: Yinhai zong heng* [Literary and historical materials on modern finance in Guangdong, Vol. 69: The vast sea of silver], ed. Zhongguo renmin zhengzhi xieshang huiyi Guangdongsheng weiyuanhui wenshi ziliao yanjiu weiyuanhui [Committee on the Study of Historical Materials the Guangzhou Municipal Branch of the Chinese People's Political Consultative Conference] and Zhongguo Renmin Yinhang Guangdongsheng fenhang jinrong yanjiusuo [Financial Research Institute of the Guangdong Branch of the People's Bank of China] (Guangzhou: Guangdong renmin chubanshe, 1992), 4–15. By the beginning of the Republican era, copper ten cash was again similar to the "Small Money" silver coins. The exchange rate for a 10-cent silver coin tended to decrease in value from twelve pieces of copper ten cash between 1918 and 1922, to twenty pieces in 1923, and twenty-five to pieces in 1934. Xu Sidao, "Guangdong tongyuan," 13.

There were two attempts to reform the "Small Money" world of Guangdong before the end of the Qing. One was an order by Zhou Fu, viceroy of Liang-guang in 1907, and the other was an order issued by the Ministry of Finance in 1908, the purpose of which was to decrease the casting volume of "Small Money" and to increase the casting volume of "Big Money." But a reluctance to accept "Big Money" in the Guangdong market and the outflow of "Big Money" thwarted both attempts.[22]

Apart from the Canton Mint and the Provincial Bank, the other provincial enterprises could not demonstrate impressive success in terms of profits. However, these pioneering provincial ventures were unique in Guangdong and they had fully developed by the beginning of the Republican era. Chinese people were becoming familiar with cement through the treaty ports. The Xicun Cement Plant was set up in 1906 in Guangzhou. Because cement produced in British cement factories in Macau and Hong Kong enjoyed high popularity in the Guangdong market, the Guangdong provincial government invested as much as 0.5 million taels from the salt tax revenue to build this factory. However, the plant was not producing cement and bricks until May 1909. Although it is difficult to make a judgment about the contribution of this factory to financial revenue due to its short lifespan, this factory developed into one of the largest provincial industries in Guangdong during the Republican era.

The Zengyuan Paper Company was originally a private plant. It was restructured into a "government–merchant joint venture" in 1905, with the government holding some 90 percent of the stock. Between 1905 and 1909, the total amount of paper sales amounted to about 400,000 taels. However, net profits were modest, with only 3,016 taels recorded in 1908 and 4,300 taels recorded in 1909. Another important provincial industry was the water supply company, in which as much as 1.2 million taels was invested, split 50–50 between the government and overseas Cantonese merchants. This company was established in the winter of 1905 and by 1908 it began supplying water. In its initial years, few households applied for water, and real profits remained modest. An electric power company was established in 1909, and it was reopened as a "government–merchant joint venture" after the provincial government purchased the Canton Electricity Company from Russell & Co. (*Qichang yanghang*). The provincial government raised private capital as merchant stock. Although the water supply company and the electric company were both government–merchant joint ventures, in practice all operations

22 Xiong Li, "Yuebi shiyao," 60.

as well as management were left to the merchant stockholders, with the Guangdong provincial government only receiving dividends for its investment.

These provincial companies and government–merchant joint ventures did not contribute significantly to provincial finance due to the collapse of the Qing only a few years after their opening. However, the early presence of provincial enterprises in Guangdong province, which were extremely rare in the rest of the country until the end of the Qing, is indicative of the advanced nature of fiscal policy in Guangdong. Another reason for this was the existence of an overseas Cantonese community, which backed commerce and industry in the province. Cantonese had been among the first overseas Chinese migrant laborers in the nineteenth century, and in 1949 the Cantonese population still constituted over 70 percent of the total overseas Chinese population. Overseas Cantonese actively responded to the motherland's calling to construct modern infrastructure facilities in their hometowns. In combination with the official endeavor to attract overseas Chinese capital to build modern industries, a rudimentary but pioneering building of provincial industries began in Guangdong province ahead of any other region of China.[23]

The fiscal structure of Guangdong province during the Republican era

During the Republican period, the Guangdong provincial government was composed of four departments: civil affairs, finance, construction, and education. Each department managed poorly reported special financial resources, including illegal revenue such as the opium tax, additional fees, and smuggling.[24] In spite of such unrecorded hidden revenue, it is still useful to look at the official revenue records to understand overall trends in provincial finance. Guangdong province was the headquarters of Sun Wen and the Kuomintang's (hereafter KMT) independent regime during the late

23 Xiang Jun, "WanQing Huaqiao yu Zhongguo jingji xiandaihua yanjiu" [Overseas Chinese in the late Qing and China's economic modernization] (PhD diss., University of Ji'nan, 2007), 135–137.

24 "Nankin seifu no kantonshō kinyu zaisei seiri no genkyō" [The current situation of financial and fiscal consolidation in Guangdong led by the Nanjing Government], *Tōa* 9 (11) (1936): 81. For the opium policy of the Chen Jitang regime, see Xavier Paulès "Unacceptable but Indispensable: Opium Law and Regulations in Guangdong, 1912–1936," *Cross-Currents: East Asian History and Culture Review* 1(7) (2013).

1910s and the 1920s. Therefore, provincial finance faced an urgent need to fund the KMT's political campaign against its rival, the Beiyang government in Beijing (also known as the Peking government, 1912–1928). After 1937, the Second Sino-Japanese War and the Civil War hampered normal operations of provincial finance. It is most useful to compare provincial finance of the late Qing with that of the Republican era in Guangdong during the period of rule by warlord Chen Jitang (1926–1936) when the financial situation was relatively stable.

The most representative record about revenue in Guangdong province in the 1930s is *The Record of Guangdong Provincial Finance* published in 1933 by the Department of Finance, Guangdong province (hereafter, the DFG). Chapter 4 of Volume 4 provides information on the "settlement of accounts" from 1912 to 1932. In addition, the *Gazetteer of Guangdong Province: Finance,* which was published in 1999 by the DFG, presents complete data about provincial revenue during the Republican era. The data for 1912 to 1932 is copied from the *Record of Guangdong Provincial Finance*. In addition to these published data, it is also helpful to check the scattered data in contemporaneous official reports. For example, the Guangdong Provincial Bank launched a monthly journal in 1937, with the founding issue including tax revenue and debt income for the province until 1935.[25]

However, the problem is that the numbers in these materials, in terms of total revenue and the respective revenue amount for each item, are contradictory. Additionally, the tax revenue figures for the 1930s in the *Gazetteer of Guangdong Province: Finance* exclude national tax income that was illegally held and used in Guangdong without remittances to Nanjing. So, to analyze total revenue, including national tax income, Tables 1.4 and 1.5 below use the data in the *Record of Guangdong Provincial Finance* until 1932 but use the data in the *Guangdong Provincial Bank Monthly* for 1933 to 1935. Other data are used to supplement the above. The data in the *Gazetteer of Guangdong Province: Finance* are used to analyze revenue by item in Table 1.6.

25 Guangdongsheng Caizhengting [Department of Finance, Guangdong], *Guangdongsheng caizheng jishi* [Record of finance in Guangdong province] (Guangzhou: Guangdongsheng caizhengting, 1933); Guangdongsheng defang shizhi bianzuan weiyuanhui [Compilation Committee for the Gazetteer of Guangdong Province], *Guangdongsheng zhi: Caizheng zhi* [Gazetteer of Guangdong Province: Finance] (Guangzhou: Guangdong renmin chubanshe, 1999); Guangdongsheng yinhang [Guangdong Provincial Bank], "Appendix: Provincial revenue of Guangdong," *Guangdongsheng yinhang yuekan* [Monthly Journal of Guangdong Provincial Bank], inaugural issue (1937).

Table 1.4 Fiscal balance in Guangdong province, including national tax income and debt income, 1912, 1924, 1926, 1930–1937 (unit: in *haoyang* 10,000 *yuan* for 1912–1936, in *Fabi* 10,000 *yuan* for 1937)

Year	Revenue			Expenditures		
year	National tax	Provincial tax	Total	National tax	Provincial tax	Total
1912	*	*	3813.9	*	*	3813.9
1924	*	*	1208.1	*	*	1219.6
1926	*	*	12655.0	*	*	12543.0
1930	5262.9	6846.5	12109.4	5664.8	6566.6	12231.4
1931	6568.0	5743.8	12311.8	6547.1	5726.0	12273.1
1932	5556.4	6743.9	12300.3	5594.8	6396.9	11991.7
1933	4963.6	5666.3	10629.9	4951.7	5291.8	10243.5
1934	7152.8	7422.7	14575.5	7224.4	7293.3	14517.7
1935	6996.7	7963.1	14959.8	7006.2	8033.3	15039.5
1936	–	3119.4	–	–	3111.0	–
1937	–	3291.1	–	–	3002.8	–

Source: The figures for between 1912 and 1932 come from "Appendix: Final Accounting of Revenue and Expenditures," *Guangdongsheng caizheng jishi*, Vol. 4, Part 4 and the data for 1933 and 1935 come from "Appendix: Provincial Revenue of Guangdong," *Guangdongsheng yinhang yuekan* [Monthly journal of The Guangdong Provincial Bank], inaugural issue (1937).

Note: Each year indicates the fiscal year, starting in July of that year and ending in June of the following year.

* From 1912 to 1929, there was no division between the national tax and the local tax. But beginning in 1930 the two taxes, the national treasury and the provincial treasury, were divided accordingly.

** National tax revenue for 1936 and 1937 are unknown.

In 1919 fiscal income in Guangdong was recorded at 38.13 million *yuan*. Thereafter it fluctuated at around 30 million *yuan*, hitting a historical low of 12.08 million *yuan* in 1924 when the province was under KMT rule led by Sun Wen. However, the establishment of the Guangdong National Government, combined with the fiscal reconstruction directed by Song Ziwen (T. V. Soong), successfully promoted effective financial institutionalization to fund the military spending for the Northern Expedition in 1926–1927, leading to a tenfold increase in revenue compared to the two previous years. In 1926, total revenue in Guangdong exceeded the 100-million-*yuan* threshold for the first time. By law, the national tax was to be separated from the local tax in 1930, but in practice, under Chen Jitang's rule, most national taxes, except tariffs, were withheld for provincial use. The combined revenue of the national tax and the local tax gradually fell in fiscal year 1933, but the tide was soon reversed to reach a peak in fiscal year 1934 and fiscal year 1935, when Chen Jitang's regime undertook military expansion against the Nanjing Nationalist Government (hereafter NNG). Table 1.5 shows that loan income was the largest source of the national tax under the Guangdong provincial government, and the consolidation tax was the second-largest source of the national tax, followed by the opium tax and the salt tax. In terms of expenditures, military spending constituted 70–80 percent of total national expenditures. Provincial fiscal revenue, excluding national treasury income and loans is presented in Table 1.6.

Table 1.5 National revenue under the control of Guangdong province, fiscal years 1930–1935 (unit: *haoyang* 10,000 yuan, the fiscal weight in terms of % is in parentheses)

Fiscal year	Salt tax	Tobacco and wine tax	Consolidated tax	Income from the ban on opium	Debt	Total
1930	832.5(15.8)	410.3(7.8)	127.6(2.4)	599.5(11.4)	2319.4(44.0)	5262.9
1931	692.9(10.6)	552.9(8.4)	905.7(13.8)	836.2(12.7)	2775.8(42.3)	6568.1
1932	705.4(12.7)	463.6(8.4)	1017.7(18.3)	869.9(15.7)	1810.7(32.6)	5556.4
1933	396.9(7.9)	506.4(10.2)	1004.3(20.2)	935.8(18.9)	1803.6(36.3)	4963.6
1934	384.9(5.4)	386.9(5.4)	1173.7(16.4)	867.0(12.1)	3843.0(53.7)	7152.8
1935	490.0(7.0)	424.0(6.0)	1048.4(14.9)	735.9(10.5)	3823.1(54.6)	6996.7

Source: See Table 1.4
Note: The two sources, *Guangdongsheng caizheng jishi* and *Guangdongsheng yinhang yuebao*, have the same data for each tax revenue item in 1933 except for the debt figures.

Table 1.6 Provincial revenue in Guangdong, excluding loans, fiscal years 1930–1936

Fiscal year	Provincial revenue	Land tax	Industrial and commercial tax	Enterprise income
1930	4506.3	415.0(9.2%)	2470.9(54.8%)	*
1931	4328.1	448.3(10.3%)	2545.8(58.8%)	*
1932	4897.1	430.5(8.7%)	2820.0(57.5%)	*
1933	4940.9	419.1(8.4%)	4287.1(86.7%)	*
1934	6029.4	472.2(7.8%)	5091.7(84.4%)	133.3(2.2%)
1935	6181.9	301.9(4.8%)	4035.2(65.2%)	1241.5(20.0%)
1936	3119.4	462.0(14.8%)	2035.9(65.2%)	49.5(0.1%)

Source: Guangdongsheng difang shizhi bianzuan weiyuanhui [Compilation Committee for The Gazetteer of Guangdong Province], *Guangdongsheng zhi: Caizheng zhi* [Gazetteer of Guangdong Province: Finance] (Guangzhou: Guangdong renmin chubanshe, 1999), 51.

First, total revenue in Guangdong fluctuated in alignment with changes in central versus local politics. According to Table 1.6, Guangdong provincial revenue for 1930–1936 ranged from 50 million *yuan* to 60 million *yuan*, almost double the 20 million taels (about 30 million *yuan*, excluding tariffs and debts) at the end of the Qing dynasty. In 1935, it reached a record high of 61.81 million *yuan* as the conflict between Chen Jitang and Jiang Jieshi (Chiang Kai-shek) intensified. Nevertheless, when Chen Jitang stepped down and Guangdong province was taken over by the NNG in 1936, provincial revenue plunged by nearly half within a year. Second, Guangdong's revenue structure moved along the trajectory of fiscal modernization that had been established in the late Qing. The weight of the land tax in total revenue fell to a single digit, and the share of the commercial tax was growing, indicating that the fiscal shift that appeared in the late Qing was further strengthened during the Republican era.

One of the features of the commercial taxes in Guangdong in the 1930s was the substitution of the *likin* by a newly introduced special tax and an excise tax following the announcement of the abolition of the *likin* in 1929. From 1912 to 1929, the total amount of *likin* in Guangdong came to 153.22 million *yuan* (*haoyang*), which accounted for 34.6 percent of total tax revenue in the province.[26] As compensation for the loss to provincial revenue that came with the abolition of the *likin*, the NNG allotted the land tax to the local tax. However, unlike other major provinces, such as Hunan, Jiangxi, Zhejiang, and Jiangsu that relied on the land tax for over half of their provincial tax revenue, the share of the land tax in provincial tax revenue in Guangdong was only about 10 percent. Instead, the gambling tax and the opium tax accounted for 34 percent of the total provincial tax revenue.[27] In other words, the structure of tax revenue during the late Qing, which was heavily dependent on gambling taxes and opium taxes, did not change during the Republican period. Guangdong province responded to the abolition of the *likin* by creating new taxes levied on imports and commerce at the provincial level.[28] We will return to this issue in Chapters 3 and 4.

In the 1930s, there were new attempts to make progress in terms of fiscal modernization. One such attempt was the first appearance of "enterprise income" in the provincial revenue items in 1934. So-called "enterprise

26 "Rikin teppai mondai" [The issue of the abolition of the *likin* tax], *Tōa* 4(4) (1933): 102–3; *Guangdongsheng zhi: Caizheng zhi*, 72–79, 131.

27 *Guangdongsheng caizheng jishi*, Vol. 1. Part 1, 67–68.

28 For pioneering research on the special tax in Guangdong, see John Fitzgerald, "Increased Disunity: The Politics and Finance of Guangdong Separatism, 1926–1936," *Modern Asian Studies* 24(4) (1990): 745–775.

income" (*shiye shouru*) refers to income from industries run by the Guangdong provincial government, which was identical to the "government enterprise income" (*guanye shouru*) that one finds in the budget for 1912. Government-run industries were introduced as a new potential source of financial revenue, but the revenue from these industries still remained modest in the late Qing. The Guangdong provincial government, under the rule by Chen Jitang, began to expand the government-run industries in 1933. As a result, the amount of "enterprise income" increased rapidly in 1935, accounting for about 20 percent of Guangdong province's fiscal revenue. Unlike other provinces that focused on expanding commercial taxes to increase revenue, the Guangdong provincial government looked for a way to fund its increasing spending by building full-scale, state-run industries, leading to provincial economic development.

Chen Jitang's regime drafted and promoted the Three-Year Administrative Plan of Guangdong (*Guangdong shizheng sannian jihua*) from 1932 to 1935 and invested a large sum—35 million *yuan*—to establish about twenty modern manufacturing plants within a short period. Among such plants, the scale of the Xicun Cement Plant, which had been established in the late Qing, was expanded, bringing in a profit of 17 million *yuan* in the 1930s. But sugar refineries were by far the biggest and most lucrative ventures. The plan to build sugar refineries began in 1933, with a collaboration with American sugar capital and Czech machinery companies, and thereafter generated an annual profit of more than 30 million *yuan*. Initially, the profits from plants run by the Guangdong provincial government were not included in the provincial treasury and instead they fell into the hands of the military commanders. However, in 1935, part of this income, amounting to 12.41 million *yuan*, of which 3.549 million *yuan* came from the sugar refineries, was diverted to provincial revenue to make up for the sharp drop in financial income due to the abolition of the *likin*. That is the amount seen in Table 1.4, and it means that the financial contribution of state-run industries to the provincial government must have been much greater than that indicated in Table 1.4.[29]

However, to maximize profits by removing potential rivals to the state-run plants, the Guangdong provincial government created special local taxes corresponding to the protective tariffs that were levied on imports and Chinese products, as long as these goods entered Guangdong from outside the province. Merchants in the rest of China, especially Shanghai merchants who controlled distribution of the domestic market, criticized

29 *Guangdongsheng zhi: Caizheng zhi*, 84–85.

the Guangdong provincial government for being a warlord autarky. So-called "official smuggling," without paying the tariffs levied by the NNG, became an important means through which to extort money for Chen Jitang's regime, in combination with the monopolies and high protective taxes. This smuggling refers to the act of importing finished goods, such as sugar and cement, without paying the tariffs for the raw materials to the state-run plants, in defiance of the NNG's high tariff policy. This was an act that openly ignored the high tariff policy of the NNG and intercepted the tariff revenue of the NNG. Therefore, the NNG abolished all tax preferences for the state-run plants once it took over Guangdong after repressing the coup by Chen Jitang. The share of "enterprise income" relative to the total provincial revenue dropped dramatically to 0.1 percent in 1936. Despite this short setback, Guangdong's fiscal model for procuring revenue through state-run industries and monopolies deeply affected fiscal management by the NNG. Combined with the high wartime demand for revenue due to the Sino-Japanese War and thereafter the Civil War with the Chinese Communist Party (hereafter CCP), the NNG established a kind of state-monopoly capitalism under which the government sector overwhelmingly outstripped the private sector in terms of production, distribution, and sales. Along with this trend, the share of "enterprise income" in total provincial revenue surged to 50 percent up to 80 percent in the 1940s.[30] Table 1.7 below provides more detailed information about the industrial and commercial taxes in Guangdong before the outbreak of the Sino-Japanese War.

The most significant change was the introduction of the newly established special tax (*zhuanshui*) and other similar taxes including the tax on imported agricultural products, 20 percent additional charge on the special tax, and the sales tax on petroleum. Revenue from the three taxes totaled 14 million *yuan* in 1933 and 26 million *yuan* in 1934.

Again, the share of the total three taxes relative to total industrial and commercial tax revenue rose from 32.6 percent in 1933 to 51.3 percent in 1934. Even after the NNG took control of Guangdong in 1936, these taxes were maintained to fund the war, with only slight name changes. While the industrial and commercial tax revenue dropped steeply to 16.46 million *yuan* in 1937, to 6.26 million *yuan* in 1938, and then rising to 12.22 million *yuan* in 1939 due to the war, reliance on the special taxes rose to more than 50 percent. Once it took over, the NNG inherited the fiscal strategy that had been introduced by Chen Jitang's regime.

30 *Guangdongsheng zhi: Caizheng zhi*, 85.

Table 1.7 Breakdown of industrial and commercial taxes in Guangdong provincial revenue, 1930–1936

	1930	1931	1932	1933	1934	1935	1936	Total
Business tax	–	–	–	76.2 (1.7%)	101.2 (1.9%)	83.1 (2.0%)	177.1 (0.6%)	437.6 (1.8%)
Slaughter tax	–	–	–	183.0 (4.2%)	300.9 (5.9%)	116.5 (2.8%)	224.1 (11%)	824.5 (3.5%)
Sales tax on petroleum	–	–	–	230.1 (5.3%)	396.7 (7.7%)	340.8 (8.4%)	184.7 (9.0%)	1152.3 (4.9%)
Special tax on agricultural products	–	–	–	1086.3 (25.3%)	1798.5 (35.3%)	1526.8 (37.8%)	881.3 (43.2%)	5292.9 (22.7%)
20% additional charge on the special tax	–	–	–	88.5 (2.0%)	426.0 (8.3%)	191.3 (4.7%)	11.3 (0.5%)	717.1 (3.0%)
Military payment fund	1452.9 (58.8%)	1358.4 (53.3%)	1737.1 (61.5%)	1800.0 (41.9%)	1464.9 (28.7%)	1196.8 (29.6%)	126.2 (6.1%)	9136.3 (39.2%)
Likin and levies	98.7 (3.9%)	228.2 (8.9%)	177.1 (6.2%)	112.1 (2.6%)	51.6 (1.0%)	29.6 (0.7%)	–	697.3 (2.9%)
Other	919.3	959.2	905.8	710.9	551.9	550.3	431.2	5028.6
Total	2470.9	2545.8	2820.0	4287.1	5091.7	4035.2	2035.9	23286.6
Index	100	103	114.1	173.5	206.1	163.3	82.4	

Source: *Guangdongsheng zhi: Caizheng zhi,* 83, Tables 1-1-2-8. The percentages are added.

As analyzed above, looking at the overall trends in official fiscal statistics allows us to understand the complicated dynamics of fiscal rivalry between the central and provincial governments as well as Guangdong province's fiscal state-building efforts at the local levels. We will now track the experiences of Guangdong province and examine in depth its course of trial and error.

2 Tobacco and Wine Taxes in Guangdong and Changes in the Financial Structure during Republican China

Abstract

This chapter explores the history of the tobacco and wine taxes in Guangdong in the context of China's fiscal transformation. This case highlights the experience of Guangdong as a pioneering model for the Chinese fiscal state. The tobacco and wine taxes in China began as a type of likin in the late Qing in response to the needs of the military budget, but it gradually developed into an independent tax. The taxation on cigarettes was distinctive in that it was a tax on a modern enterprise. The revolutionary Nationalist regime in Guangzhou reorganized and effectively enforced tobacco and wine taxes in Guangdong. Other new taxes, such as the consolidated tax, first introduced in Guangdong, were expanded nationwide by the Nanjing Nationalist Government.

Keywords: tobacco tax, wine tax, consolidated tax, China, Guangdong

This chapter explores the history of the tobacco and wine taxes in Guangdong in the context of China's financial transformation. This case highlights the experience of Guangdong as a pioneering model for the Chinese fiscal state. The financial system of the central government in the Qing dynasty mainly relied on land taxes from the provinces, with few tax sources exclusively controlled by the central government. This financial structure did not change until the end of the late Qing dynasty. With the beginning of the Republican era, the central government sought to ensure its continued access to independent financial resources through a division between national and local taxes. The most prominent feature of China's financial transformation in the twentieth century was the growing importance of

Kang, Jin-A, *The Guangdong Model and Taxation in China*. Taylor & Francis Group, 2022
DOI: 10.5117/9789463725248_CH02

industrial and commercial taxes as a form of indirect taxes. Even in the twenty-first century, almost half of Chinese tax revenue is derived from indirect taxes, while the proportion of direct taxes, such as the income tax or the inheritance tax, remains low.

Of the several new taxes introduced in modern China, the tobacco and wine taxes were the only successful taxes that survived and developed into a main source of tax revenue during the Republican era. Under Nationalist rule, business taxes, income taxes, and other modern taxes were modestly and only partially introduced. With the founding of the PRC, these taxes were abolished due to the socialization of production and they were not restored until the reform and opening-up policy.

The development and transformation of the tobacco and wine taxes are closely related to industrialization. With the advent of machine-produced cigarettes, the tobacco trade underwent tremendous changes in the twentieth century. Cigarettes soon occupied an overwhelming proportion of the tobacco products market, and the cigarette industry became one of the most important and lucrative modern industries. The taxation on cigarettes was distinctive in that it was a tax on a modern enterprise. This was not exceptional in China. Consolidated taxes (*tongshui*) introduced by the NNG were levied on the manufacturing of items, first on cigarettes and then on cotton yarn, flour, matches, and cement, but cigarettes quickly became a core source of tax revenue. The modern industrialization of cigarette production facilitated the collection process and reduced collection expenses for the taxation administration.[1] Modernization of the tobacco industry in the form of cigarettes was an important backdrop to the increasing proportion

1 "Previous research on the tobacco and wine taxes mostly focused on sales by the Beiyang government. Li Qingyu, "Minguo Beijing zhengfu yanjiu gongmai shulun" [Research on the tobacco and liquor monopoly by the Beiyang government], *Lishi jiaoxue* 10 (2017); Guo Xu, "Qingmo Minchu jiushui zhidu yingelun" [History of the liquor tax system in the late Qing and early Republic], *Guizhou wenshi congkan* 4 (2011); Liu Qi and Huang Tianhua, "Minguo shiqi zhuanmai zhidu yanjiu" [Research on the monopoly system during the Republican period], *Caizhengshi yanjiu* 4 (2012). There are several comprehensive and grounded analyses about the introduction of these taxes and well-documented case studies. He's and Xiao's studies on the tobacco and wine taxes in the *likin* tax during the late Qing are worthy of note. He Hanwei, "Qingmo fushui jizhun de kuoda jiqi juxian: Yi zashui zhong de yajiushui he qishui weili" [Expansion and the tax basis and its limitations in the late Qing: The case of the tobacco and wine tax and the deed tax in the miscellaneous taxes], *Taiwan zhongyang yanjiuyuan jindaishi yanjiusuo jikan* 17(2) (1988). Xiao Junsheng, "WanQing jiushui zhengce de yanbian lunxi" [Analysis of change in the liquor tax policy during the late Qing], *Shehui kexue jikan* 3 (2008). Fang's paper summarizes the general history of the tobacco tax, dating from the introduction of cigarettes through Joseon Korea to the Inner Mongolian region to the early Republican period. Fang Jianchang, "Neimenggu yancao xiaoshi: Jianlun Minguo qianqi Neimeng de yanshui ji youguan jigou" [The history of tobacco

of tobacco and wine taxes in modern finance. Ultimately, the justifications for the taxation on tobacco and wine were the same worldwide in terms of being sumptuary taxes against luxurious trends and for guarding public health, which tended to reduce popular resistance to the high rate of taxation. It is important to note that the incubation of the idea of a consolidated tax first occurred in Guangdong, which was the revolutionary base of the Kuomintang (hereafter KMT). The perspective of the local context, through the case of Guangdong's tobacco and wine taxes, served as a model for Nationalist policy.

The introduction of tobacco and wine taxes in the late Qing dynasty: From the *likin* to the tobacco and wine taxes

The beginning of tobacco and wine taxes in the late Qing dynasty

The *likin* in the late Qing dynasty was the first form of tax on tobacco and wine, and the tax rate on tobacco and wine originally was the same as that on other commodities: 1 percent of the price. Later, however, it rose to 4 percent or more of the price. This rate was higher than the average *likin* tax rate, which was 2.26 percent. With the outbreak of and then defeat in the First Sino-Japanese War (1894–1895), the enormous indemnities and the resultant financial pressures forced the Qing government to pay more attention to taxation on tobacco and wine. But even then, the tax rate was still not very high. Along with the Boxer Rebellion and the launch of Guangxu's New Policy, the Qing dynasty enforced tax apportionment to local governments in 1903. This practice, called *tanpai*, led to a rapid increase in the financial burden on local governments. Some provincial governments gradually separated the tax on tobacco and wine from the *likin* while significantly increasing the tax rate.

Zhili province was the top revenue-generator in tobacco and wine taxes. Governor-General Li Hongzhang and Yuan Shikai paid particular attention to the tax revenue from tobacco and wine and developed various tax collection methods. As a result, the tax on tobacco and wine in Zhili recorded revenue of 717,900 taels in 1905, 722,000 taels in 1906, and 773,500 taels in 1907, making it the highest revenue-generator in the country. Sichuan province was a latecomer, as its tax on tobacco and wine was not enacted until 1904, but

in Inner Mongolia: The Cigarette tax in Inner Mongolia and its related organizations in early Republican China], *Yinshan xuekan* 1 (1998).

it quickly caught up with Zhili province in terms of the amount of revenue generated. In spite of its late start, the revenue from the tax on tobacco and wine in Sichuan rose sharply, reaching 1 million taels by the eve of the Xinhai Revolution and the demise of the Qing dynasty in 1911. This amount was much higher than 0.7 million taels from the *likin* and it accounted for nearly 6 percent of the 17.3 million taels of Sichuan's fiscal revenue and one-ninth of the 9.14 million *yuan* of China's total tobacco and wine tax revenue.[2]

The expansion of taxation on tobacco and wine in the late Qing was closely related to the war and the demand for military funding. The first tax on tobacco and wine was enacted during the Taiping rebellion. In 1884, the Qing court again levied a license tax on retailers of tobacco and wine due to the military demands of the Sino-French War. Ten years later, in order to cope with the military budget of the First Sino-Japanese War, the Qing court imposed additional taxes on tobacco and wine. Later, in order to raise funds to cover the training expenses for the Beiyang New Army, Zhili province implemented a measure to separate the tobacco and wine tax from the *likin*, making it into an independent tax. In 1904, Sichuan province levied its first wine tax to fund the training expenses for the New Army and the military budget for the Tibet campaign.[3]

In 1910, the Qing court experimented with introducing a fiscal budget system and it planned to make a division between national taxes and local taxes, which signaled an effort to systematically modernize its fiscal and tax systems. It was planned that the tobacco and wine taxes in various forms would be consolidated into one national tax. The collection agency would be established as a special bureau under the direct control of the central government, with subordinate agencies from the provincial branches down to the county and prefectural levels. However, these plans were not implemented due to the 1911 Revolution and the demise of the Qing dynasty; the task of financial reform was hence handed over to the Republic of China.

Tobacco and wine taxes in Guangdong province

Compared to Zhili and Sichuan provinces, Guangdong province did not witness significant development of the tobacco and wine taxes in the late Qing dynasty. Tobacco and wine taxes in Guangdong constituted only a small proportion of the provincial tax revenue. Moreover, in contrast to Zhili and Sichuan, the tobacco and wine taxes in Guangdong did not

2 Xiao Junsheng, "WanQing jiushui zhengce de yanbian lunxi," 150153.

3 Xiao Junsheng, "WanQing jiushui zhengce de yanbian lunxi," 154.

develop into an independent tax. In a previous analysis of the *Guangdong Financial Statement*, I pointed out that Guangdong's finance had already been transformed into a modern system in two key ways: the dominant proportion of revenue stemming from indirect taxes compared to the land tax, and the emergence of government industry incomes. These two features of Guangdong finance were clearly distinct from those of the other provinces. However, with respect to the development of the tobacco and wine taxes, Guangdong lagged behind the other provinces.

The *Guangdong Financial Statement* records the first tobacco and wine taxes in the category of a "*likin* on all kind of goods" (*baihuo lijin*)." The *likin* was introduced in Guangdong province in 1862 and was levied on tobacco and wine in 1869.[4]

The first expansion of the tobacco and wine tax occurred in 1895 and 1896, just after the First Sino-Japanese War. During this period, the tax rate rose by 330 percent. However, the tax increase was not fully implemented. It was collected by local merchant guilds on the basis of the traditional contract system, but these merchant guilds effectively resisted the tax increase through petitions and bargaining tactics.[5]

Table 2.1 Contracted amount of the *likin* for tobacco and wine in Guangzhou prefecture and Foshan district in the late Qing dynasty (unit: tael)

Region	Type of business	Name of guild contractor	Contracted amount		
			1869	Since 1901	
Guangzhou	Cut tobacco	Chongantang	2,592	10,368	+300%
Guangzhou	Tobacco leaf in Heshan	Gonghetang	1,200	6,240	+420%
Guangzhou	Wine	Fuzhitang	2,940	5,880	+100%
Guangzhou	Strip tobacco	Chongdetang	280	-	-100%
Foshan	Cut tobacco	Unknown	240	348	+45%
Foshan	Wine	Unknown	1,440	240	-83%
Foshan	Wine in Shiwan	Unknown	480	960	+100%
			9,172	24,036	+162%

Source: *Guangdong caizheng shuomingshu*, 230–231; *Guangdong yanjiushui yange*, 20.

4 Yu Qizhong, *Guangdong yanjiushui yange* [The evolution of the tobacco and wine tax in Guangdong] (Guangzhou: Guoli Zhongshan daxue chubanbu, 1933).

5 Guangdongsheng caizheng kexue yanjiusuo [Fiscal Science Research Center, Department of Finance, Guangdong], ed., *Guangdong caizheng shuomingshu* [Guangdong financial statement] (Guangzhou: Guangdong jingji chubanshe, 1997), 49.

Table 2.1 shows that the contracted amount did not actually increase by 330 percent as the regulation had proposed, with the exception of Heshan, and in two cases it even decreased.

Following the *likin*, different types of taxes on tobacco and wine appeared. First, the "fortress and cannon fee" (*taipao jingfei*) was a unique tax in Guangdong, which was temporarily levied on dealers of tobacco and wine in Guangzhou in 1890 to raise funds to procure guns for coastal security. But the original purpose of this temporary tax was soon transformed and it was established as a regular tax. Second, two other taxes on tobacco and wine are found in the "miscellaneous tax" category of the *Guangdong Financial Statement*: the "steaming bucket fee" (*jiuzeng paifei*, 1902) and the "county tax on wine for levies and donations" (*shengwai geshu shou jiujuan baoxiao gekuan*). These miscellaneous taxes were all invented to procure funds for the New Policy, which included funds for the establishment of schools, police stations, and workhouses.[6]

The author of the *Guangdong Financial Statement*, emphasizing Japanese success in raising as much as 63 million *yen* in revenue from the wine tax, repeatedly cites Meiji Japan's policy as an example of the successful collection of a wine tax. The author advocates a government monopoly on wine, as in the case of the Meiji government, and insists that taxpayers would not feel burdened by the heavy tax rate because of the characteristics of an indirect tax. Additionally, the high tax rate on wine would prevent people from indulging in excessive drinking and luxurious spending. However, the author warns of the side-effects of too high tax rate on wine, suggesting that a sharp increase in the price of Chinese wine would encourage domestic sales of imported wine while subsequently decreasing the tax revenue due to the declining sales of Chinese wines. The late Qing government's idea of a modern state tax policy was based on reference to the experience of foreign countries.[7]

How much tax did Guangdong collect on tobacco and wine in the late Qing dynasty? Even though it is difficult to calculate the exact value due to incomplete data, a simple sum of the tobacco and wine taxes in the *Guangdong Financial Statement*, calculated by exempting the transit tax, amounts to no more than 220,000 taels.[8] This value is far less than that in Zhili (700,000 taels) and Sichuan (about 1 million taels).[9] Moreover, in Guangdong province, the tobacco and wine tax did not develop into an

6 *Guangdong caizheng shuomingshu*, 230–231, 235–240.
7 *Guangdong caizheng shuomingshu*, 259–260.
8 Guo Xu, "Qingmo Minchu jiushui zhidu yingelun," 26.
9 Xiao Junsheng, "WanQing jiushui zhengce de yanbian lunxi," 155.

independent tax category, unlike in Zhili and Sichuan, until the demise of the Qing dynasty. One factor that may account for the underdevelopment of the tobacco and wine tax in Guangdong province, despite the highly advanced structure of Guangdong finance, is its geographical remoteness from the central government and the traditional powers of local merchant guilds for tax collection. However, with the dawn of the Republican era, Guangdong province surpassed the other provinces in terms of the amount of revenue generated and the varieties of tobacco and wine taxes.

Tobacco and wine taxes during the Republican era

The general trend of Guangdong provincial finance during the Republican era (except for debt) is seen below in Table 2.2. According to Table 2.2, the revenue of Guangdong province dropped sharply to less than 10 million *yuan* in 1923 and 1924, but starting in 1925, there was a rapid increase, reaching a record of almost 70 million *yuan* in 1929. After 1930, the tax revenue returned to the level of 30 million yuan, but in 1934 and 1935, it rose to about 50 million *yuan* and then decreased in 1936 to about 20 million *yuan*, which is equivalent to the value during the period of the early Beiyang government.

This trend is unique to Guangdong, which is clearly different from other provinces. Guangdong province had been a revolutionary base for the Chinese Nationalist Party (the Kuomintang, hereafter KMT), led by Sun Wen. In 1923 and 1924, Sun Wen established a military government in Guangzhou, which ruled until the confrontation between the Northern and Southern governments. At that time, the military government of Guangdong actually occupied only the one city of Guangzhou, while the rest of Guangdong was not under its control. Since the actual collection of taxes was only implemented in Guangzhou, the total value of Guangdong provincial revenue was drastically reduced during these two years. After Sun's death in 1925, under the collective leadership of Jiang Jieshi and Wang Jingwei, the Guangdong Nationalist Government was formally established and it launched an expedition into the interior of Guangdong province. The successful expedition expanded the KMT's control into the whole province, leading to a sharp rise in tax revenue. The start of the Northern Expedition by the KMT in 1926 led to an explosive increase in the military budget. The Northern Expedition marked the beginning of the peak period of fiscal expansion in Guangdong province because the revenue from this single province inevitably had to pay for the nationwide military campaign under the flag of the legitimate central government.

Table 2.2 Annual revenue and expenditures in Guangdong province, 1912–1941 (unit: 10,000 *yuan*, *Guobi*, National Currency)

Year	Revenue	Expenditures	Year	Revenue	Expenditures
1912	2,669.7	2,228.3	1927	5,539.7	7,787.2
1913	1,377.5	2,643.4	1928	5,888.6	8,674.4
1914	1,429.9	1,608.2	1929	7,034.7	9,601.8
1915	1,395.6	1,698.2	1930	3,457.7	4,596.6
1916	1,753.9	2,679.1	1931	3,029.6	4,008.2
1917	1,961.1	2,812.1	1932	4,048.9	3,876.0
1918	2,020.5	2,807.9	1933	3,966.4	3,704.2
1919	2,252.4	3,293.9	1934	5,195.9	4,905.2
1920	1,566.7	2,568.5	1935	5,574.1	5,623.0
1921	2,132.6	2,875.3	1936	2,609.7	3,394.0
1922	1,678.5	2,359.2	1937	3,291.1	3,002.7
1923	967.2	1,170.6	1938	1,320.3	1,302.5
1924	682.2	853.7	1939	2,754.6	2,775.5
1925	2,525.9	4,919.8	1940	6,509.3	5,407.7
1926	5,937.7	8,780.1	1941	16,117.11	15,124.0

Source: Zhang Xiaohui, *Minguo shiqi Guangdong shehui jingjishi* [A socioeconomic history of Guangdong during the Republican period] (Guangzhou: Guangdong renmin chubanshe, 2005), 300.
Note: The figures for 1912–1929 are the combination of the national treasury and provincial treasury; the figures for 1930–1941 are the figures for the provincial treasury alone.

The Nationalist regime in Guangdong denied the legitimacy of the Beiyang government and asserted itself as the legitimate central government, while the Ministry of Finance of the Nationalist government was actually in Guangzhou. Its administration could only exercise power first in Guangzhou, then in Guangdong province as a whole. Therefore, at that time there was no distinction between a national tax and a local tax in Guangdong. Guangzhou became the temporary capital of the Nationalist regime, and Guangdong province took on a status similar to that of the traditional Zhili province during the Qing dynasty, which had been under strong administrative control. The record-breaking revenue in Guangdong was the result of this geopolitical shift as well as the surge in military and financial demands.

Following the success of the Northern Expedition, the Nationalist government left Guangzhou, moving northward through Wuhan to Nanjing. The NNG reunified China to declare the completion of the Northern Expedition in 1928. In the same year, the Ministry of Finance in Nanjing announced the division of national taxes and local taxes. As a result, provincial tax revenue in Guangdong dropped dramatically after 1930. On the one hand, the financial burden of Guangdong province eased as the central government moved to Nanjing, but, on the other hand, many of its taxes and fees were allotted to the category of a national tax for use by the national treasury in Nanjing.[10]

Table 2.3 lists the formal amounts in the provincial treasury. In fact, the national taxes from Guangdong were not fully remitted to the central government in Nanjing but, rather, were retained for provincial use. This was the so-called *jieliu,* a pervasive phenomenon during the Republican period when the warlords in each province withheld tax revenue.[11] After the departure of the Nationalist regime from Guangdong and a number of military coups, provincial power in Guangdong fell into the hands of Chen Jitang, a local military leader. Even though he was first credited by the NNG for holding provincial power, Chen Jitang joined the anti-Jiang group in alliance with Hu Hanmin and the Southwest Government Committee of the KMT in 1932. His purpose was to establish a semi-independent separatist regime in Guangdong province. Due to the potential military confrontation with the NNG, Chen Jitang increased the military budget. Regardless of whether it was due to national tax or provincial taxes, Guangdong's tax revenue had increased substantially, and the provincial tax broke through the 50-million-*yuan* barrier. It was not until the Liangguang Incident, an abortive military coup by Chen Jitang in 1936, that the NNG recovered control of Guangdong province, and the Guangdong provincial treasury returned to its normal level in 1936.

10 A draft for the division between national and local taxes was compiled in 1913, but it was never implemented (*huofen guojiashui difangshui fa*). The Guangdong Nationalist Government began to discuss this issue in 1924. The Minister of Finance, Gu Yingfen, submitted a "Proposal for Permission for the Division of National and Local Taxes" in 1927 (*huofen guojia shouru difang shouru xuke an*). In the next year, 1928, the newly appointed minister of Finance, Song Ziwen, held a national finance conference that drafted a new plan (*huofen guojia shouru difang shouru* [*zhichu*] *biaozhun*). In 1929, Song Ziwen visited Guangdong province to divide the main taxes of Guangdong into two categories. He assigned fourteen types of taxes to the national tax and twelve types of taxes to local taxes (Zhang Xiaohui, *Minguo shiqi Guangdong shehui jingjishi,* 280). For the detailed process behind the division between national taxes and local taxes, see Kaneko Hajime, "Chūgoku no tōitsuka to zaisei mondai: 'Kokuchi zaisei kakubun' mondai o chūshin ni" [China's unification and financial problems: A focus on the "division between national and local taxes], *Shigaku kenkyū* 179 (1988); Satō Junpei, *Kindai chūgoku zaiseishi: 'Gaishō' kara 'chihō' e* [A fiscal history of modern China: Changing central-provincial relations in the late Qing and the early] (Tokyo: Tōkyō daigaku shuppankai, 2020): 94–101.

11 Qin Qingjun, "Minguo shiqi Guangdong caizheng shiliao 1911–1949" [Historical materials on finance in Guangdong province during the Republican period 1911–1949], *Guangdong wenshi ziliao xuanji* 29 (1983): 87, 150–153.

Zhang Xiaohui's research (in the report which appears in *Bank of China Monthly Journal*, Vol. 5, Issue 3, September 1932) observes that the average annual revenue from Guangdong's tobacco and wine taxes was about 4 million *yuan*, which is equivalent approximately to 14.5 percent of the average provincial tax revenue (27.65 million *yuan*), during the twenty years (1912–1931) before the Sino-Japanese War.[12] This proportion of total tax revenue in Guangdong province was much higher than the 6 percent in Sichuan province, which had been the largest tobacco and wine tax revenue source during the late Qing dynasty. It is clear that the tobacco and wine taxes in the total tax revenue of Guangdong province expanded substantially during the Republican era from their modest beginning during the late Qing period.

Both *The Evolution of the Tobacco and Wine Taxes in Guangdong* (*Guangdong yanjiushui yange*), written by Yu Qizhong in 1933, and *The Record of Guangdong Provincial Finance* contain detailed records of the taxes on tobacco and wine during the Republican periods. These two sources complement each other in terms of filling in missing information, as can be seen in Table 2.3.

The general trend in revenue from the tobacco and wine taxes in Guangdong as seen in Table 2.4 does not differ substantially from that in Table 2.3. The taxes on tobacco and wine increased rapidly during the period of the Northern Expedition that began in 1926, reaching nearly 5 million *yuan*. But there are also some significant differences. In comparison to the revenue of the late Qing period, the revenue from the tobacco and wine taxes recorded a substantial increase to about 3 million *yuan* in the late 1910s and early 1920s as provincial revenue shrank considerably. That is to say, the tobacco and wine taxes in Guangdong attracted substantial attention as new tax sources as early as the period of the Beiyang government. Actually, the tobacco and wine taxes accounted for about 10 percent of the provincial tax in the early 1920s. This significant share of provincial tax revenue increased further in the 1930s.

After national and local taxes were divided in 1929, the Guangdong Tobacco and Wine Bureau (*Guangdong yanjiu shiwuju*) compiled a budget table for the Guangdong tobacco and wine taxes in 1930, as shown in Table 2.4. These statistics offer insights into the potential amount of revenue from the tobacco and wine taxes in Guangdong.

12 Zhang Xiaohui, *Minguo shiqi Guangdong shehui jingjishi*, 315.

Table 2.3 Revenue from the tobacco and wine taxes and their proportion of Guangdong provincial tax revenue, 1912–1932 (unit: *yuan*)

Year	Source No. 1	Source No. 2	%
1912	649,000		2.4
1913	1,778,000	1,778,233	12.9
1914	2,355,000	2,357,798	16.5
1915	1,274,000	1,273,393	9,1
1916	1,595,000	1,594,799	9.1
1917	2,008,000	2,009,265	10.2
1918	2,318,000	2,318,851	11.4
1919	3,146,000	3,145,816	13.9
1920	2,324,000	2,324,016	21.1
1921	3,167,000	3,033,892	13.8
1922	1,867,000	1,865,998	11.1
1923	263,000	262,713	2.7
1924	544,000	548,204	8.0
1925	1,784,000	1,781,872	7.0
1926	3,221,000	4,805,000	5.4–8.0
1927	5,657,000	5,227,000	9.4–10.2
1928	5,843,000	6,119,558	9.9–10,4
1929	5,011,000	5,307,241	7.1–7.5
1930		4,991,974	14.4
1931		5,276,124	17.4
1932		5,249,041	12.9

Sources: *Guangdong yanjiushui yange*, 288; Guangdongsheng Caizhengting [Department of Finance, Guangdong], *Guangdongsheng caizheng jishi* [Record of finance in Guangdong province] (Guangzhou: Guangdongshengcaizhengting, 1933), Vol. 2, 161, 167.

Table 2.4 Budget for tobacco and wine taxes in Guangdong province, 1930

Taxes	Tobacco tax	Tobacco leaf tax	Tobacco license tax	Additional charge for tobacco license			Subtotal
Revenue	1,654,428	490,578	181,580	36,262			2,362,848
Taxes	**Wine tax**	**Wine cake tax**	**Imported wine tax**	**Industrial ethanol stamp tax**	**Wine license tax**	**Wine license tax additional charge**	**Subtotal**
Revenue	2,336,193	360,000	89,580	208,596	525,230	105,070	3,624,669
Adjustments							300,000
Total Budgeted Amount							**6,287,517**

Source: *Guangdong yanjiushui yange*, Appendix, Table 2.

The tax target from the tobacco and wine taxes was relatively high, amounting to more than 6.2 million *yuan*. This figure is comparable to the entire provincial tax revenue of a poor province such as Guizhou. According to this budget, the tobacco tax revenue and the wine tax revenue amounted to 2.3 million *yuan* and 3.62 million *yuan*, respectively. But the former figure can be misleading because the tax on cigarettes is not included here, owing to the fact that the NNG implemented a new type of "consolidated tax" on cigarettes as a national tax. Statistics about actual revenue from the consolidated tax on cigarettes can be found in the *Record of Guangdong Provincial Finance*, as shown in Table 2.5.

Table 2.5 Revenue from the consolidated tax on cigarettes

Fiscal year	Total revenue from the consolidated tax	Revenue from the tax on cigarettes in the consolidated tax
1929	-	3,093,616.56
1930 (first half)	-	4,041,978.51
1930 (second half)	3,019,984.68	
1931	8,703,709.79	-
1932	10,494,178.36	-

Source: *Guangdong yanjiushui yange*, 289–290; *Guangdongsheng caizheng jishi*, Vol. 2, 220.
Note: The NNG's fiscal year began in July and ended the following June.

The total revenue from the consolidated tax in 1931 and 1932 amounted to about 8.7 million *yuan* and more than 10 million *yuan*, respectively. The amount of revenue from the tax on cigarettes within the consolidated tax reached more than 3 million *yuan* in 1929 and more than 4 million *yuan* in 1930, representing the highest share of the total consolidated tax. The Ministry of Finance in Nanjing levied this tax on cigarettes for the first time in 1929 and then in 1932 extended the tax to four other modern commodities: cement, matches, flour, and cotton yarn. The sudden increase in the consolidated tax in 1932 may be due to the increase in taxable items. Factoring the revenue from the tax on cigarettes within the consolidated tax, we find that tobacco tax revenue surpassed wine tax revenue in Guangdong province. Despite the large expected budget of 6.8 million *yuan*, actual revenue from the tobacco and wine taxes in 1930 amounted to 4,991,974 *yuan*, not a small amount. When the 4,041,978 *yuan* from the consolidated tax revenue from cigarettes is taken into account, the total revenue from the tobacco tax becomes almost 10 million *yuan*. In comparison with the 1 million *yuan* tax revenue from tobacco and wine taxes during the period of the Beiyang government, the tax revenue from tobacco and wine taxes in Guangdong can be considered enormous.[13] This is indicative of the importance of the wine and cigarette taxes to provincial finance in Guangdong.

The expansion of tobacco and wine taxes and Guangdong province

This section will examine the concrete process of how Guangdong province expanded the scope of taxation on tobacco and wine during the Republican era. Yu Qizhong, author *of The History of the Guangdong Tobacco and Wine Taxes*, identifies more than twenty kinds of taxes on tobacco and wine in Guangdong and classifies them into five categories according to the subject of taxation and the mode of production: the native tobacco and wine tax, the license tax on tobacco and wine, the wine cake tax, the imported wine tax, and the cigarette tax.[14]

The first category consists of the original taxes on tobacco and wine that began in the late Qing dynasty as a type of *likin* in 1869. A substantive change took place in 1912, after the collapse of the Qing. The *likin* on tobacco and wine became independent taxes, that is, the tobacco and wine taxes. With the experience of Zhili and Sichuan as precedents, this marked the official beginning of tobacco and wine taxes in Guangdong. In April 1915, the Ministry of Finance in Beijing announced implementation of the tobacco and wine public sale system (*yanjiu gongmaizhi*), which aimed to centralize taxation on tobacco and wine. Although this reform only resulted in an increase in the tax rate without any institutional reform, one meaningful change was that the currency standard for the collection of the tobacco and wine taxes in Guangdong was changed from the "Small Money" of the local currency to the "Big Money" of the national currency. This was a step forward in the direction of national monetary integration.[15]

In spite of the gradual increase in the tax rate, the tobacco and wine taxes in Guangdong were singular independent taxes on these two items during the early Republican period. But under Nationalist control, various

13 The Beiyang government stipulated that the tobacco and wine taxes, the charge for the public sale of tobacco and wine, and the tobacco and wine license tax belonged to the national tax category. However, between 1917 and 1923 an average of less than 10 percent of the total tax revenue from these three taxes was remitted to Beijing (Guo Xu, "Qingmo minchu jiushui zhidu yingelun," 3–31; Li Qingyu, "Minguo Beijing zhengfu yanjiu gongmai shulun," 55).

14 Yu Qizhong, *Guangdong yanjiushui yange*, 2–3.

15 Yu Qizhong, *Guangdong yanjiushui yange*, 19–34.

new taxes on tobacco and wine were imposed. For example, 1926 saw the establishment of a tobacco leaf production tax, a tobacco entry tax, and a license tax on medicated wine, imported wine, and bottled wine sales. In 1927, the Guangdong provincial government began to levy a toll tax on native wine and doubled the tax rate on tobacco and wine as a whole.[16]

The second of the five categories was the license tax on tobacco and wine dealers. The license tax appeared in Guangdong for the first time in 1912. It was originally called a license fee (*paizhao fei*), but it was renamed a license tax (*paizhao shui*) in October 1914. The third category was the wine cake tax, which started in 1926 and continued during the period of Northern Expedition. The fourth category included various taxes on imported wines that were broadly divided into a license tax and a stamp tax. In 1926, the Guangdong provincial government began to levy the taxes on imported wines at different rates from those levied on native wines, thereby canceling the previous flat rate. To protect domestic products, the tax rate on imported wines was as high as 50 percent of the price. By 1928, the NNG had reduced the tax rate from 50 percent to 30 percent. However, the Guangdong provincial government insisted on a 50 percent tax rate and stipulated that 30 percent of it would be allotted to national revenue and 20 percent to provincial revenue, starting on 1 March 1929. In August, the Ministry of Finance in Nanjing canceled the 20 percent provincial tax. However, after 1932 when Chen Jitang joined the anti-Jiang camp, the taxes on imported wines were no longer remitted to the national treasury.[17]

The last and most important tax category was the consolidated tax on cigarettes. Cigarettes were widely sold in China after the founding of British American Tobacco (BAT) in 1902. BAT had dominating strength in both the imported and the domestic cigarette markets. In 1937, its sales volume in China reached 1.12 million boxes, accounting for 67.2 percent of total cigarette sales in the country. BAT enjoyed a low tax rate and rapid development in the Chinese market. In the early twentieth century, governments all over the world designated cigarettes as luxury goods and imposed heavy taxes to collect additional revenue. The international cigarette tax rate generally ranged from 75 percent to 200 percent of the price, but the Qing court levied taxes on BAT cigarettes only at a rate of from 0.3 percent to 0.7 percent of the price. During the Republican era, based on a compromise with BAT in October 1921, the Beiyang government increased the tax rate to 2.5–5 percent and then again to 5 percent in March 1925. In general, however, this rate

16 Yu Qizhong, *Guangdong yanjiushui yange*, 36–37.

17 Yu Qizhong, *Guangdong yanjiushui yange*, 87–100, 117, 125–138.

was modest in comparison with international levels. It was the NNG that succeeded in increasing the tax rate considerably. The NNG announced a 50 percent tax rate on cigarettes, including BAT cigarettes in June 1927. After several rounds of negotiations, the NNG and BAT reached agreement on a tax rate of 27.5 percent for imported products and 22.5 percent for domestic products.[18]

However, Guangdong province experienced a different trajectory. The first attempt to levy a tax on cigarettes in Guangdong province occurred in 1921. At that time, Sun Wen was elected the Grand Marshal of his self-proclaimed military government in Guangzhou. After the separation of the Northern and Southern governments, the military government in Guangzhou levied 20 percent of the stamp duty on cigarettes in order to raise military funds, regardless of whether the products were imported or domestic. Only goods with an attached stamp were allowed to be sold in the market. This relatively high tax rate on cigarettes was successfully enforced due to Sun Wen's head-on confrontation with the West, unlike the Beiyang government, which had relied heavily on the Western powers both politically and financially. The same applied to the action to increase the cigarette tax in 1925 taken by the Guangdong Nationalist Government and the KMT after Sun Wen's death. This Nationalist regime in Guangzhou announced that it would raise the tax on imported cigarettes by 40 percent and the tax on domestic cigarettes by 20 percent. Even though this tax rate was lower than international levels, it was still higher than the 5 percent of the Beiyang government. When the military budget in the middle of the Northern Expedition sharply increased in May 1927, the tax rate on both domestic and imported cigarettes in Guangdong jumped to 50 percent of the wholesale price.

By the following month, the newly established NNG announced a special 50 percent tax on cigarettes. In fact, this was an extension of Guangdong province's cigarette tax that the Nationalist regime was implementing at the national level. When the consolidated tax on cigarettes was finally implemented at the rate of 32.5 percent, after negotiations between the NNG and BAT at the end of 1928, Guangdong province insisted on collecting a 50 percent tax on cigarettes, out of which 32.5 percent was allotted to the

18 Wang Zhijun, "Lun Ying Mei yan gongsi yu jiu Zhongguo de 'xieding yanshui'" [Research on the British American Tobacco Company and the 'Agreement on the Cigarette Tax' of old China], *Xuchang xueyuan xuebao* 3 (2006): 99–105; Kyung-seok Park, "Namkyŏngkukminchŏngpuŭi sesuchŏngch'aekkwa chaechŏngkipanŭi sulip: ikŭm·t'ongsechŏngch'aekŭl chungsimŭlo" [Fiscal policy and revenue stablization of the Nanjing Nationalist Government: The case of the lijin and the consolidated tax policy], *Tongyang sahak yŏn'gu* 61 (1998): 127–130.

national treasury and 17.5 percent to the provincial treasury. As mentioned earlier, this exceptional situation did not end until November 1929 when a special order by the NNG cancelled this provincial quota. With the anti-Jiang movement of 1932, Chen Jitang's regime in Guangdong regained control over cigarette tax revenue. After the short period between the Liangguang Incident in 1936 and the outbreak of the Sino-Japanese War in 1937, national integration and reform of the tax system in Guangdong province were once again delayed due to the urgent demands of wartime finance.[19]

Legacy of the tobacco and wine taxes

The tobacco and wine taxes in China began as a type of *likin* in the second half of the nineteenth century in response to the needs of the military budget, but it gradually developed into an independent tax. When modernizing its taxation system, the Qing government referenced the Meiji Japanese model. In addition to discussing taxation on wine and cigarettes, the government reviewed the monopoly policy and the heavy tax rates in Meiji Japan. The Meiji government in Japan also experienced two wars—the Sino-Japanese War (1894–1895) and the Russo-Japanese War (1904–1905)—that transformed its fiscal structure into a modern financial system. First, the main source of taxes changed from land taxes to indirect consumption taxes. Among the different types of indirect consumption taxes, the taxes on tobacco and wine were particularly important in Japan. As early as 1899, revenue from the wine tax exceeded that from the land tax, becoming the largest source of tax revenue. In 1901, a consumption tax was implemented, targeting wine, soy sauce, and sugar. Textiles were added to this list in 1904. At the same time, the tobacco industry was included in the monopoly system, with tobacco leaves being included in 1898, and finished products such as cigarettes being included in the monopoly in 1904. Revenue from the Japanese wine tax revenue reached 13.9 million *yen* (about 13 percent of tax revenue) in 1890, 50.29 million *yen* (about 17 percent) in 1900, and 86.7 million *yen* (about 13 percent) in 1910. Revenue from the tobacco monopoly was 7.24 million *yen* in 1900 and 62.09 million *yen* in 1910. By 1910, total revenue from the wine tax and the tobacco monopoly exceeded 100 million *yen*. Total fiscal revenue in Japan, including revenue from monopolies, state-run firms, and bonds, amounted to 678.87 million *yen* in 1910, of which 14.7 percent came from the tobacco monopoly and the wine tax.

19 Yu Qizhong, *Guangdong yanjiushui yange*, 165–171.

The introduction of the Japanese model in China was not as successful as it had been in Japan. Under the unequal treaty system, China had difficulty imposing both custom duties and domestic taxes. The public sales of the Beiyang government and the consolidated tax of the NNG could only be effective after very tough negotiations with the Western powers, the local merchant guilds, and the provincial warlords.

During the Republican era, Guangdong became a new model, or experimental area, in terms of the reform of China's tax system. Guangdong's experience in reforming its taxes was then expanded by the NNG throughout the country. The tobacco and wine taxes in Guangdong were reorganized and enforced effectively by the Nationalist government in the course of its rivalry with the Beiyang government. Other new taxes, such as the consolidated tax, which was first introduced in Guangdong, were expanded nationwide by the NNG.

Moving forward, what is the experience of the taxation on wine and cigarettes in China today? After the reform and opening-up period, China implemented a tobacco monopoly system in 1983. Between 1994 and 2007, revenue from the tobacco tax ranged from 11.9 percent (at its highest, in 1995) to 7.6 percent (at its lowest, in 2001) of the total tax revenue of the central government. The tax rate began at 38 percent but then fluctuated between 20 percent and 40 percent. In 2016, the total annual revenue of the Chinese government was 15.96 trillion *yuan*, with 7.24 trillion *yuan* in the national treasury and 8.76 trillion *yuan* with the local governments. According to a 2016 report by the State Tobacco Monopoly Administration, total industrial and commercial tax revenue generated by the tobacco monopoly was 1.8 trillion *yuan*, of which 1.06 trillion *yuan* belonged to the national treasury. The taxes on wine are scattered among various other taxes, but the total tax revenue from the wine industry is reported to be around 1 trillion *yuan*. The fiscal revenue from both the tobacco and wine taxes constituted almost 15 percent of the total fiscal revenue in China. Coincidently, the taxes on tobacco and wine in Guangdong under Nationalist rule represented more than 14 percent of total provincial revenue, and were thus almost equal to its present share of total revenue. The legacy of the reform of the tobacco and wine taxes launched in Guangdong province seems to have been inherited by the NNG and has survived to present-day China.

3 Abolition of the *Likin* and the Paradox of Tax Reform: The Special Tax

Abstract

From the late Qing to the 1920s, abolition of the likin was always a priority on the Chinese tax reform agenda. The newly established Nationalist Government in Nanjing finally announced the policy of "abolishing the likin and creating a new tax" in conjunction with restoring tariff sovereignty. This chapter examines how the Guangdong provincial government responded to the central government's policy by focusing on creating the Special Tax. The Chen Jitang separatist regime in Guangzhou responded to preemptively abolishing the likin and miscellaneous taxes and reinventing the special tax as a kind of local tariff instead. The special tax became the largest source of financial revenue in Guangdong province through the 1930s.

Keywords: Special Tax, Guangdong, local tariff, China

From the late Qing to the 1920s, abolition of the *likin* was always a priority on the Chinese tax reform agenda. But it was not until the establishment of the Nanjing Nationalist Government (hereafter NNG) that the policy of "abolishing the *likin* and creating a new tax" (*caili jiashui*) was implemented in conjunction with the restoration of tariff sovereignty. The NNG secured high-revenue income by raising the tariff rate instead of promising abolition of the *likin* from the Western powers. To compensate for the loss of expected revenue loss due to the abolition of the *likin*, the NNG allocated land taxes to the local governments. However, Guangdong province, which was already highly commercialized, could not match the loss of the *likin* with gains from the land tax. This chapter examines how the Guangdong provincial government (hereafter, the GPG) responded to the central government's policy to abolish the *likin* in the 1930s by focusing on the creation of the "special tax."

Kang, Jin-A, *The Guangdong Model and Taxation in China*. Taylor & Francis Group, 2022
DOI: 10.5117/9789463725248_CH03

The origins of the special tax: Between the *likin* and tariffs

The special tax was a local tariff on foreign goods transferred to Guangdong province. However, in reality it was more complicated. First, it had the nature of a tariff in that it targeted imported goods. Second, it had the nature of the *likin* in that domestic cargo from other provinces could also be subject to this taxation. Third, it had the nature of a consolidated tax or a special consumption tax in that the Department of Finance of Guangdong Province (hereafter DFG) established a special bureau to impose direct and unified collection throughout the province. Some researchers have suggested that the special tax was a unique tax found only in Guangdong province, but others claim it was nothing more than a variant of the *likin*. It is difficult to attach numbers to the special tax because some local tariffs on foreign goods fell under the category of an extra tax (*teshui*) rather than a special tax (*zhuanshui*). Despite those ambiguities, it is possible to categorize the special tax based on several shared features. First, it was a provincial tariff on imported or transferred goods from outside of Guangdong to the provincial territory. Second, imported goods were taxed by a separate bureau following customs clearance procedures. Third, the GPG promoted the legitimacy of the taxation by claiming that it served to protect local products from import substitution. Nevertheless, the NNG criticized this local tariff for interfering with unified administration of national tariffs and the national policy to abolish the *likin*. The special tax is first found in historical records from April 1930. This was a "Special Tax on Artificial Fiber," which was nothing other than a renaming of the earlier *likin*, without any change in the tax rate or the subjects of taxation. A series of other special taxes followed this first appearance. Table 3.1 below provides details about the special taxes that existed at the time of Chen Jitang's abortive military coup in July 1936 (the Liangguang Incident).[1]

1 Kawai Tatsuo, Consul General of Guangdong→Hirota Kōki, Minister of Foreign Affairs of Japan,"Goma abura ni gaikoku nōsanpin senzei tekiyō kata ni kansuru ken" [Application of the Special Tax on Sesame Oil Agricultural Products], 10 September 1935, E.1.3.2.1-004 Chūgoku ni okeru sozei oyobi futankin kankei zakken [Miscellaneous matters related to taxes and contributions in China, Vol. 4], Gaimushō, Gaikō Shiryōkan [Diplomatic Archives of the Ministry of Foreign Affairs of Japan], Tokyo; Kawai Tatsuo→Hirota Kōki, "Gaikoku hikaku zei no zeiritsu hikiage ni kansuru ken" [On the increase in the tax rate on foreign leather], 6 July 1935, E.1.3.2.1-004.

Table 3.1 Special taxes in Guangdong until July 1936 (unit: haoyang yuan)

Name	Starting time	Collection agency	Proto-type	Estimated yearly income
Imported Cement Tax	1924	STB*		0.6 million
Special Tax on Artificial Fiber	April 1930	Commis-sioner	*Likin*	0.2 million
Imported Leather Tax	July 1931	STB		0.5 million
Special Tax on Imported Paper	Nov. 1931	STB		0.4 million
Special Tax on Imported Wax	Feb. 1932	Tax contractor**	*Likin*	0.3 million
Special Tax on Imported Pigment	Feb. 1932	STB	*Likin*	0.3 million
Special Tax on Imported Fertilizer	June 1932	STB		0.2 million
Special Tax on Imported Clothing	June 1932	STB	*Likin*	0.4 million
Special Tax on Agricultural Products	August 1933	STB		7–9 million
Special Tax on Imported Dried Fruits and Seafood	1934			
Special Tax on Imported Machinery	1935			
Special Tax on Used Rubber Tires	1935			
Special Tax on Imported Timber	June 1936			
Special Tax on Imported Rubber Products	June 1936			
Special Tax on Imported Porcelain and Glass Metal Products	1936			
Special Tax on Imported Cosmetics and Toys	1936 (est.)			
Special Tax on Imported Sugar	1924	STB		0.5–1.1 million
Sales Tax on Petroleum	Oct. 1934	Commis-sioner		0.85 million

Source: Guangdongsheng difang shizhi bianzuan weiyuanhui [Compilation Committee for The Gazetteer of Guangdong Province], *Guangdongsheng zhi: Caizheng zhi* [Gazetteer of Guangdong Province: Finance] (Guangzhou: Guangdong renmin chubanshe, 1999), 80; Liu Han [Fiscal Science Research Center, Department of Finance, Guangdong], "Bolai wuchan zhuanshui, kai ting zheng ji: Xiezai 'Guangdongsheng zhi: Caizheng zhi' chuban zhi qian" [The beginning and end of the special tax collection on imported products: Written before publication of the *Gazetteer of Guangdong Province: Finance*]. Unpublished draft. Presented by the author during a visit to the Fiscal Science Research Center, 4 July 1999: Harada Chūichirō, Consul of Shantou→Arita Hachirō, Minister of Foreign Affairs of Japan, Harada. 17 April 1936, E.1.3.2.1-2-1 Santō mondai kome senzei [The Shantou issue: the Special Tax on Rice], Gaimushō, Gaikō Shiryōkan [Diplomatic Archives of the Ministry of Foreign Affairs of Japan], Tokyo.

Note:

* STB refers to the Special Tax Bureau of Agricultural Products.

** The contractor was the Heyi Company.

Table 3.1. lists the special taxes as extensively as possible. The Imported Cement Tax, the Sales Tax on Petroleum, and the Tax on Imported Sugar Products were not called special taxes, but they were identical to the special tax in nature, leading to wide criticism from the Western powers that they were illegal taxes. The GPG began to levy the tax on imported cement in 1924 to raise the construction costs for Sun Yat-sen University, but the category of a special tax did not start until about 1930. In particular, creation of the Special Tax on Agricultural Products in 1933 played a decisive role in creating the special tax as a unique type of revenue-raising taxation, which attracted criticism both in and out of Guangdong province. Along with the expansion of the tax subjects, tax collection services for all kinds of special taxes were gradually integrated into the Special Tax Bureau for Agricultural Products. It is no wonder that the Special Tax on Agricultural Products came to represent all kinds of special tax revenue in the accounting of the provincial government.

Table 3.2 shows the proportion of special tax income in the total revenue of Guangdong province. In the first year of the GPG's Three-Year Plan, 1933, the two major taxes in the special tax category, the Sales Tax on Petroleum and the Special Tax on the Agricultural Products, were created.

Table 3.2 Guangdong provincial budget and collected revenue, 1933 (unit: 10,000 *haoyang yuan*)

Name	Land tax	Deed tax	Pawn tax	Slaughter tax	House levies	Likin	Ship levies	Business tax
Budget	623	259	12	210	4	158	47	150
Revenue	438	215	17	167	2	183	12	89
Over budget			5				35	
Under budget	185	44		43	2	25		61

Various levies	Local property income	Local administrative income	Local business income	Military Pay Fund	Prefectural and county commercial taxes	Others	Special Tax on Agricultural Products	Sales Tax on Petroleum
560	13	88	9	1472	171	10	-	-
390	33	48	10	1927	144	186	177	17
	20		1	455		176	177	17
170		40			27			

Source: Qin Qingjun, "Guangdong sannian shizheng jihua xia yi nianlai caizheng zhi huigu" [Review of finance during the past one year under the Three-Year Administrative Plan of Guangdong province], *Xin Guangdong* 15 (1934): 12.

As shown in the table, despite various attempts to raise income during the period of the Three-Year Plan, actual revenue from most tax items was much less than that which was budgeted, except for the Military Pay Fund (*chouxiang*), the Sales Tax on Petroleum, and the Special Tax on Agricultural Products. Excluding these three items, settlement of the accounts resulted in a deficit of 3.6 million *yuan*. The surplus of 6.49 million *yuan* from these three eventually contributed to a surplus of 2.89 million *yuan*. The Military Pay Fund included various gambling taxes. The sharp increase in gambling tax revenue was due to the introduction of the public bidding system (to be discussed in Part 3).

The amount of revenue raised in the two months after introduction of the Special Tax on Agricultural Products and the Sales Tax on Petroleum was shockingly large, coming in at 1.77 million *yuan* (from October to December) and 170,000 *yuan* (from November to December), respectively. The special tax was undoubtedly the main financial source for the GPG to fund the growing provincial expenditures during the Three-Year Plan period. The financial weight of these two taxes in Guangdong province is confirmed in Tables 3.3 and 3.4 below.

Table 3.3 Guangdong provincial tax revenue, excluding national tax revenue (unit: 10,000 *haoyang yuan* / (%))

Fiscal year	Revenue	Land tax	Special Tax on Agricultural Products	Sales Tax on Petroleum
1933	4940.9	419.1 (8.5%)	1086.3 (22%)	230.1 (4.7%)
1934	6029.4	472.2 (7.8%)	1798.5 (29.8%)	396.7 (6.6%)
1935	6181.9	301.9 (4.9%)	1526.8 (24.7%)	340.8 (5.5%)
1936	3119.4	462.0 (14.8%)	881.3 (28.3%)	184.7 (5.9%)
Total	2,0271.6	1655.2 (8.1%)	5292.9 (26.1%)	1152.3 (5.7%)

Source: *Guangdongsheng zhi: Caizheng zhi*, 50–51, 83.

According to Table 3.3, the Special Tax on Agricultural Products always maintained a share of nearly 30 percent of provincial tax revenue. Revenue from the Sales Tax on Petroleum outplayed land tax revenue in 1935. Table 3.4 is the report sent in July 1936 to Kong Xiangxi, Ministry of Finance, Nanjing, from Tang Haian, director of the Maritime Services of Shanghai,

Table 3.4 Monthly tax revenue in Guangdong province, estimated as of June 1936) (unit: *haoyang yuan*)

Tax	Monthly income	Tax	Monthly income	Tax	Monthly income
Land tax	253,486	House levies	1,548	Sales Tax on Petroleum	150,627
Deed tax	69,673	Business tax	53,496	Special Tax on Agricultural Products	1083,727
Pawn tax	46,410	Military Pay Fund	861,244	20% additional charges	134,637
Slaughter tax	112,810	Various levies	374,338	Local administrative income	156,202
Shop tax	5,198	Local property income	249	Government industry income	16,000
Ship tax	766	Other	25,503	Retained *likin*	5,632

Source: "Tang Haian baogao youguan Guangdong caizheng shouzhi qingxing zhi Kong Xiangxi midian" [Confidential telegram sent by Tang Haian to Kong Xiangxi, reporting on financial revenue in Guangdong], July 1936, in *Zhonghua Minguo shi dang'an ziliao huibian diwuji diyibian caizheng* [Compilation of archives on the history of the Republic of China, Collection 5, Part 1 finance and economy, Vols. 1–9] (Nanjing: Jiangsu guji chubanshe, 1994), 684–688.

who had been dispatched to Guangzhou. It reveals the financial situation in Guangdong province on the eve of Chen Jitang's coup. According to Table 3.4, the ratio of the Special Tax on Agricultural Products to total provincial revenue was at its height, at 32 percent, even higher than the 28.3 percent in 1933 (Table 3.2). However, apart from this ratio, the value of each year's tax revenue tended to shrink due to the steep drop in the absolute value of imports caused by the repeated increase in the tariff rate. In Guangzhou, income from the Special Taxes on Sugar, Beans, Rice, and Flour dropped to 27.5, 75.1, 25.3, and 28.8, respectively, from an index of 100 in 1933. The GPG, which succeeded in reducing imports but was hit financially, responded by expanding the tax objects subject to the special tax. In particular, as military tensions between the NNG and the Chen Jitang's regime in Guangdong increased in 1936, successive new special taxes were announced.

As shown above, the special tax was the largest source of financial revenue in Guangdong province through the 1930s. Nevertheless, it is important to examine how the special tax could play such a role, and only in Guangdong province. We turn to a more detailed discussion of the special tax in the context of tax reform and political change in Guangdong province.

Creation of the special tax in the 1930s

"Abolition of the *likin* and creation of new taxes" and the special tax

Abolition of the likin

The special tax in Guangdong was motivated by a series of central government tax-reform actions, in particular "abolition of the *likin* and the creation of new taxes" and the "division of national and local taxes" (*guodi huafen*). The NNG declared the nationwide abolition of the *likin* beginning on 1 January 1931. Because the *likin* was a major source of local finance, it was originally expected that this measure would lead to local financial deficits and resistance at the local levels.

The *likin* had been first introduced in Yangzhou in 1853 as a temporary way to fund the military campaigns to suppress the rebels. But it soon came to be expanded across the country as it was sanctioned by the Qing court to finance local military expenditures during the Taiping and Nian rebellions. It was in 1858 that the *likin* was first introduced in Guangdong. It was levied on goods in transit or as a sales tax in shops, originally, applied on an ad valorem basis, with rates varying from an original 1 percent to over 10 percent. The *likin* became a permanent tax and an important source of revenue for the local government until the end of the Qing. Since the *likin* was levied on imports in transit, foreign merchants criticized it as identical to a tariff, and hence called for its prompt abolition. Abolition of the *likin* was first promised in the British–Qing treaty of 1902. During the Republican era, the Treaty of Washington in 1922 and the Special Conference on the Chinese Customs Tariff in 1925 discussed Chinese tariff autonomy instead of abolition of the *likin* by the Chinese government. The eventual abolition of the *likin* had to wait until 1 January 1931, when the NNG implemented a revised tariff rate (*diyici xiuzheng jinkou xin shui*).[2]

Among all the provinces, Guangdong had collected the *likin* most vigorously. From 1919 to 1929, revenue from the *likin* totaled 153.22 million *yuan* (*haoyang*), constituting 34.6 percent of the total commercial and industrial tax revenue. When the NNG resumed talks with the Western powers in 1928

2 "Rikin teppai mondai" [The issue of the abolition of the *likin* tax], *Tōa* 4(4) (1931): 101. For details on the process of restoring China's customs autonomy, see Kubo Tōru, *Senkanki chūgoku "jiritsueno mosaku" kanzei tsūka seisaku to keizai hatten* [Seeking for "self-reliance" in China during the interwar period: Tariff and monetary policy and economic development] (Tokyo: Tokyo daigaku shuppankai, 1999), chaps. 1, 2.

regarding abolition of the *likin*, *likin* revenue amounted to 16.5 million *yuan*, 14.5 percent of the total provincial tax revenue.[3]

However, the expected loss of the *likin* revenue was not the only factor that jeopardized Guangdong's finances. The NNG announced a tax reform package at the same time as the abolition of the *likin*. In general, the target of the reform was to clean up the overlapping miscellaneous taxes and to replace them with a new tax. The new tax, designed by the NNG as a resource to replace the *likin* or the miscellaneous taxes, included special consumption taxes (*tezhong xiaofei shui*), factory taxes (*chuchuang shui*), and the business taxes (*yingye shui*). The former two were assigned as a national tax, and the latter was a provincial tax. The three principles of tax unification fixed before the abolition of the *likin* had already made it clear that the salt tax and the special consumption tax should be subject to national administration. A report from Fan Qiwu, then director of the Guangdong Finance Department, referred to the expected outcome for provincial revenue from the tax reform implemented under central guidelines.

Guangdong province's 1930 budget consisted of 25.77 million *yuan* in revenue and 36.88 million *yuan* in expenditures, with a revenue shortfall of 11.11 million *yuan* (all units in *haoyang*). Combined with the loss of 1.89 million *yuan* (7 percent of the total revenue) caused by abolition of the various prefectural taxes, there was an annual loss of 0.41 million *yuan* (1.6 percent) caused by the central action that allowed the provincial cement plant to be administrated by the Consolidated Tax Bureau, a loss of 1.27 million *yuan* (5 percent) caused by the abolition of the *likin*, and a loss of 14.17 million *yuan* (55 percent) caused by the gambling prohibition. As a

3 "Rikin teppai mondai," 102–105. These numbers are far higher than other numbers because of Japan's wide interpretation of the category of the *likin* tax. Guangdongsheng difang shizhi bianzuan weiyuanhui [Compilation Committee for The Gazetteer of Guangdong Province], *Guangdongsheng zhi: Caizheng zhi* [Gazetteer of Guangdong Province: Finance] (Guangzhou: Guangdong renmin chubanshe, 1999), 31, 72–79. The tax revenue and the fiscal weight of the *likin* in the 1930 fiscal year increased largely because the national tax and the savings tax were added to calculate the income. But because the fiscal year of 1931 ran from July 1931 to June 1932, the income for the 1931 fiscal year was reduced to half that of the 1930 fiscal year. In the annual statistics, there are records of 6.98 million *yuan* in 1928, 7.71 million *yuan* in 1929, and 6.39 million *yuan* in 1930 (not the fiscal year). See Guangdongsheng Caizhengting [Department of Finance, Guangdong], *Guangdongsheng caizheng jishi* [Record of finance in Guangdong province] (Guangzhou: Guangdongshengcaizhengting, 1933), Vol. 2: 2. For a detailed table of the abolished *likin* checkpoints and the previous monthly tax quotas, see *Guangdongsheng caizheng jishi*, Vol. 1, 82–84.

result, provincial tax revenue dropped to just 8.02 million *yuan*. Later, the revenue shortfall would rise to 28.87 million *yuan*.[4]

Of course, new income was expected, which the NNG allotted to the GPG as compensation—for instance, tax revenue from the business tax and the land tax. But the GPG had to forgo 4.52 million *yuan* due to the advance abolition of numerous *likin* taxes. Moreover, it was difficult to expect that a new operating tax would guarantee an immediate solid income. The land tax revenue was no more than half of the gambling tax revenue in Guangdong, but a land survey had to be carried out across the province in order to properly overhaul the land tax. Still, it was simultaneously impossible to carry out the survey in all ninety-four prefectures. It took time and money, so an increase in the land-tax revenue could not be expected immediately. In other words, the central guidelines implied virtual bankruptcy for Guangdong province.[5]

Provincial initiatives for the abolition of the miscellaneous taxes after 1931

Joining the anti-Jiang campaign in 1931 offered the GPG a chance to promote its own tax-reform program. The GPG had reorganized its tax sources with its own programs, in keeping to some extent with the NNG's guidelines. In content, the direction of the GPG reform program was not much different from that of the NNG in terms of unification of taxes and expansion of taxation on commercial activities.

As a follow-up to the 1931 abolition of the *likin*, the NNG in 1934 promulgated a new policy to abolish the miscellaneous taxes. But in this action, the GPG was one step ahead as it had abolished considerable miscellaneous taxes in the previous year. The Three-Year Plan, starting in January 1933, had included tax reform, targeting the creation of a new tax and a readjustment of the miscellaneous taxes.

First, action was taken to assess the local situation. In July 1933, the GFD organized a special team that was dispatched throughout the province to investigate taxes, levies, and charges in all counties and towns. The investigation team's mission was to screen the local archives about taxation, determine the actual conditions of the local tax system, and hear local opinions about future reforms. To prevent fraud, bribery was strictly

4 Prior to 1937, Guangdong province used the "Small Money" (*haoyang, xiaoyang*) standard as the monetary unit for official statistics, including government accounting. Unless otherwise specified, Guangdong statistics in this book are in units of *haoyang*. *Guangdongsheng caizheng jishi*, Vol. 4. 22.

5 *Guangdongsheng caizheng jishi*, Vol. 1, 67–68.

prohibited. The investigation team left Guangzhou on 16 August 1933, starting with Nanhai and Foshan, and then gradually expanding its investigation.[6]

Second, there was an attempt to enhance supervision and monitoring of local taxation. On 14 March 1933, the DFG established a committee to monitor unified taxation at local levels (*Guangdong guosheng shuijuan tongyi jiancha weiyuanhui*) and in early April it set up inspection offices in various regions to begin their work. However, after failing to produce significant results, the GPG established a new inspection bureau to crack down on smuggling (*jisi zongchu*) under the DFG, which began work in late October. It served as an important organization supporting the policy of the DFG until 1936.[7]

Based on the above work, the GPG phased out the miscellaneous taxes. Fifty-four provincial taxes with revenue of 3,081,981 *yuan* (*haoyang*) and 153 sub-local taxes were abolished between January 1933 and late July 1934, when the NNG announced a national order to abolish the miscellaneous taxes.[8]

6 Yoshida Tanichirō, Acting Consul General of Guangdong→Uchida Kōsai, Minister of Foreign Affairs of Japan, "Kanton zaiseichō no kenshi zeien oyobi Tesūryō nado chōsadan soshiki ni kansuru ken" [Department of Finance, Guangdong's organization of the special investigation team on taxes, levies, and charges in counties and towns], 20 July 1933, E.1.3.2.1-004; Yoshida Tanichirō, Acting Consul General of Guangdong→Uchida Kōsai, Minister of Foreign Affairs of Japan, "Kanton zaiseichō shusai no kenshi zeien chōsadan so no go" [The situation after the Department of Finance, Guangdong, organized a special investigation team on taxes, levies, and charges in counties and towns], 15 August 1933, E.1.3.2.1-004.

7 Yoshida Tanichirō→Uchida Kōsai, "Kanton koku shō zeien tōitsu kensa iinkai no seiritsu ni kansuru ken" [Establishment of the Guangdong Unified Inspection Committee on National and Provincial Taxes and Levies], 18 March 1933, E.1.3.2.1-004; Yoshida Tanichirō→Uchida Kōsai, "Kōshū santō sansui kōmon kaku kensajo shokuin ninmei no ken" [Staff Appointments for the Guangzhou, Shantou, Sansui, and Jiangmen Inspection Offices], 8 March 1933, E.1.3.2.1-004; Yoshida Tanichirō→Uchida Kōsai, "Kanton zaiseichō shushi sōsho ni kansuru ken" [Department of Finance, Guangdong, Anti-smuggling General Office], 29 September 1933, E.1.3.2.1-004.

8 Chen Baozhi, "Ershisannian shengzheng sheshi zhi huigu" [Review of the performance of provincial administration in the twenty-third year of the Republic of China (1934)], *Xin Guangdong* 26 (1935): 8, 21; Chen Baozhi, "Minguo ershisinian shengzheng sheshi gaikuang" [Performance of the provincial administration in the 24[t]h year of the Republic of China (1935)], *Xin Guangdong* 36 (1935): 12; Qin Qingjun, "Guangdong sannian shizheng jihua xia yi nianlai caizheng zhi huigu" [Review of finance during the past one year under the Three-Year Administrative Plan of Guangdong province], *Xin Guangdong* 15 (1934): 14–29; Hattori Tsuneo, Acting Consul General of Guangdong→Hirota Kōki, Minister of Foreign Affairs of Japan, "Kantonshō no zatsuzei seiri jijō ni kansuru ken, Kantonshō zaisei tōkyoku no haishi zatsuzei ichibetsu hyō, January 1933–August 1934" [Guangdong province's miscellaneous consolidated tax situation, table of the miscellaneous taxes abolished by the finance authorities of Guangdong province], 18 August 1934, E.1.3.2.1-004; Yoshida Tanichirō→Uchida Kōsai, "Zaiseichō no zatsuen haishi kata ni kansuru ken" [The way to abolish the miscellaneous levies of the Department of Finance], 4 January 1933, E.1.3.2.1-004.

This proactive action was a measure independently implemented by the GPG, and it had the effect of preventing interference from the NNG and a propaganda effect for Chen Jitang's regime. For example, in April 1934 the NNG held the National Finance Conference (*quanguo caizheng huiyi*) in Nanjing to discuss fiscal reform. However, the director of the DFG, Qu Fangpu, did not participate, claiming he was too busy. When the order to abolish the current miscellaneous taxes, which had been approved at the conference, arrived in Guangdong, the GPG responded that it had already activated its own program to abolish the miscellaneous taxes. How was the GPG able to secure its own financial revenue despite the abolition of so many miscellaneous taxes?

Central versus provincial rivalry over the new taxes

In 1933, new taxes were introduced in succession by the GPG. For example, the Special Tax on Agricultural Products was introduced on 16 September 1933, and the Sales Tax on Petroleum was introduced on 16 October 1933. The NNG conceded to each province the License Tax on Tobacco and Wine (established on 1 July 1934) to cover the losses caused by the abolition of the miscellaneous tax. The GPG widely promoted that the Special Tax on Agricultural Products and the Sales Tax on Petroleum would protect the rural economy and local industries by guarding against imported goods in Guangdong.[9] These taxes, however, were mostly variants of the previous *likin*, with only a small change in terms of form and name. Nevertheless, there were some changes as well.

First, the Sales Tax on Petroleum was a sales tax on gasoline stores. The attempt to raise revenue from sales of imported oil in Guangdong had begun in 1925, when a state monopoly on the retail sales of gasoline was introduced. In the next year, the Nationalist government in Guangdong canceled the monopoly and instead imposed a new extra tax on gasoline (*meiyou teshui*), with a tax rate fixed at 2 *yuan* (*haoyang*) per container (=10 gallons). In 1929, the NNG integrated this extra tax on gasoline with a tariff by entrusting the Maritime Customs Service with the task of tax collection. However, the GPG introduced the Sales Tax on Petroleum and set up another special office of the Specialized Tax Bureau in October 1933. The tax rate was set at 3 *yuan* (*dayang*) per container and was converted to 3.9 *yuan* (*haoyang*) by applying a 30 percent premium on *dayang*. The rate then rose to 5 *yuan*

9 See the report by Guangdong governor, Lin Yungai, on administration of the Provincial Council in Guangdong dang'anguan, *Chen Jitang yanjiu shiliao, 1928–1936* [Historical materials for research on Chen Jitang] (Guangzhou: Guangdongsheng dang'anguan, 1985), 289.

(*dayang*) per container. In June 1934, the GPG extended taxation to diesel oil. Stores dealing with oil, whether imported or domestic, had to pay a new provincial tax as a sales tax in addition to the tariffs.

The three major oil conglomerates—American Mobil, Texaco, and the British Asiatic Petroleum Company—publicly opposed this tax. But the GPG enforced tax collection against the opposition, claiming that the sales tax was levied on business owners and had nothing to do with foreign companies. However, foreign oil companies fabricated the price and quantity when selling oil to brokers to help the oil brokers, and retail shops evaded this sales tax.[10] In 1935, this practice forced the GPG to change the procedure for tax collection to prevent tax evasion. The tax was no longer collected by retailers and it was collected instead on the amount of imports of diesel oil and gasoline.[11] Tracing the trajectory of the GPG's taxation on gasoline and its adjustment against tax evasion, some emerging trends in terms of financial resources become apparent. First, the central government tried to integrate the distribution of the miscellaneous taxes with the tariffs, whereas the GPG tried to combine the miscellaneous taxes into a single provincial tax. Second, to prevent a backlash against double tariffs, the new provincial tax took the form of taxation on local shops and Chinese merchants. Third, to prevent tax evasion by merchants and foreign companies, this tax eventually came close to being a tariff belonging to the treasury of the central government. In the end, the NNG and the GPG could not help but become rivals over financial resources. This rivalry is well illustrated in the case of the special tax.

The GPG created the Special Tax on Artificial Fiber in April 1930, which was the first tax on a specific commodity in an attempt to support a local industry. The GPG announced that they had decided to levy this tax because the silk industry in Guangdong had been hit hard by the import of artificial fibers. Whether imported from abroad or domestic goods in transit, all artificial fibers transported to Guangdong should be subject to the new tax.[12] This special tax was integrated into the category of the Special Tax on Imported Cloth in September 1933.

10 Deng Yanbin, "Chen Jitang kaizheng meiyan fanmai ying shui" [Chen Jitang's launch of the Sales Tax on Petroleum], *Guangzhou wenshi ziliao* 16 (1965): 43–48; Chen Boren, "Chen Jitang tongzhi jituan de hengzheng baolian" [Tyrannical rule and excessive exploitation by the ruling group in the Chen Jitang regime], *Guangzhou wenshi ziliao* 16 (1965): 108; Qin Qingjun, "Guangdong sannian shizheng jihua," 31.

11 Chen Baozhi, "Ershisannian shengzheng," 20.

12 *Guangdongsheng caizheng jishi*, Vol. 2, Part 3, 837. Apart from taxation on Imported goods such as the Special Tax on Artificial Fiber, a unified provincial tax on local Silk products (*silei*

In fact, the Special Tax on Imported Cloth had originated from the *likin* tax. Apart from the previous *likin* on cotton cloth, the GPG started to levy a "domestic *likin* tax on cotton cloth" (*neidi pilei lijin*) beginning in 1925, stating that this tax was to be levied only on Western cotton cloth produced in Chinese factories. The tax rate varied from 5 percent to 12.5 percent of the price and it was the Chinese merchants exclusively who were forced to pay this tax. If the importer was Chinese, the goods were taxed as soon as the customs clearance process was completed. If the importer was a foreign merchant, the taxation occurred when the foreign merchant handed over the goods to Chinese merchants. Combined with the tariff, Chinese importers were to pay about 12 percent of the price of cotton cloth.[13] The domestic *likin* tax on cotton cloth was similar to the special tax in the 1930s. Although this *likin* was abolished in 1931, it was later revived as Special Tax on Machine-Made Cotton Cloth (*yangbu pitou zhuanshui*).[14]

The Special Tax on Imported Sugar (*bolai tangleijuan*), was also similar to the *likin* on sugar, which had been abolished in May 1934. This de facto special tax had been part of a grand project to expand sugar plantations in the agricultural sector, to build modernized state-run sugar refineries in the industrial sector, and to construct a tariff wall in the financial sector[15] (to be further discussed in Part 3).

As the above examples show, most special taxes originated from the *likin* tax. In effect, the disappearance of the *likin* in Guangdong province was not due to the abolition order by the central government but rather to its substitution by a new special tax with a higher tax rate.[16]

teshui, the exclusive tax on silk thread) was created in 1929 to promote exports. *Guangdongsheng caizheng jishi*, Vol. 1, Part 1(62), 79–80.

13 Gaimushō tsūshōkyoku [Trade Bureau, Ministry of Foreign Affairs, Japan], *Saikin No kanton keizai jijō* [The recent economic situation in Guangdong] (Tokyo: Gaimushōtsūshōkyoku, 1927), 35.

14 *Guangdongsheng caizheng jishi*, Vol. 2, Part 3, 826.

15 Katō Hiyoshi, Acting Deputy Consul of Shanghai→Taiwan seitō kabushiki Kaisha kōbe seitōjo (Taiwan Sugar Co., Ltd Kobe Sugar Refinery), 19 June 1928, E.1.3.2.1-004; Chen Boren, "Chen Jitang tongzhi jituan de hengzheng baolian," 112.

16 The gambling tax also increased the tax rate. At the same time as the official prohibition of gambling in August 1934, the GPG decided to raise the contracted amount of the gambling tax as well as that of the opium tax to support the opium and gambling ban in Guangdong province. The case of substituting a special tax for the *likin* included abolition of the Fortress and Cannon Fee. Although this *likin* had been abolished by the NNG, the GPG revived it on 16 July 1931. However, as many of the products belonging to this *likin* taxation base were subject to the special tax collection, the GPG announced the complete abolition of the Fortress and Cannon Fee from 1 January 1932. Instead, the Guangzhou Chamber of Commerce Collected and paid 80,000 *yuan* to the GPG in a lump sum. Suma Yakichirō, Acting Consul General

From the stance of the NNG, the existence of the special tax in Guangdong was unacceptable because it interfered with the NNG's policy of dividing the *likin*, the tariffs, and the taxes between the central and local governments. The NNG ordered the GPG to abolish the additional import tax of an "inland 2.5 percent tax" (*neidi erwu shui*) in 1928 (with the exception of Shantou where it was abolished in 1929), to abolish the *likin* tax in 1931, and to abolish the miscellaneous taxes in 1934, gradually pressuring the sources of local taxes. Although these three abolition orders seem to refer to different tax categories, in effect they were actually the same kind of action. When the "inland 2.5 percent tax" should have been abolished, the local governments expanded the *likin* tax. Facing the abolition of the *likin*, local governments instead began to increase the various miscellaneous taxes. In other words, the vigorous push by the Guangdong government to abolish the miscellaneous taxes prior to the NNG's 1934 order was tantamount to the GPG taking the initiative to clean up those tax sources that were favorable to Guangdong provincial finance. The idea of tax reform was shared by the NNG and the two only differed in terms of whether the new tax would be a national tax or a provincial tax. Underpinning the separatist regime in Guangdong province and the NNG's decision to temporarily avoid a frontal confrontation, the DFG pushed for an independent tax-reform program to generate a considerable rise in provincial revenue. Qu Fangpu, director of Finance in Guangdong, made four major readjustments to the miscellaneous taxes between 6 May 1932, and July 1934, leading to a total increase of 0.47 million *yuan*. As a result of the reform of the gambling tax, annual revenue rose from 14.63 million *yuan* in the previous years to 16.40 million *yuan* in 1934.[17]

of Guangdong→Shidehara Kijūrō, Minister of Foreign Affairs of Japan, "Kōshū shi ni okeru zari hōdai hi fukki kata ni kansuru ken" [How to revive the Fortress and Cannon Fee in Guangzhou City], 16 July 1931, E.1.3.2.1-003 Miscellaneous matters related to taxes and contributions in China, Vol. 3; Suma Yakichirō→Shidehara Kijūrō,"Sekitan fuka zei chūshi setsu ni kansuru ken" [Rumor about cancellation of the coal tax], 20 August 1931, E.1.3.2.1-003; Suma Yakichirō→Shidehara Kijūrō, "Sekitan fuka zei chūshi ni kansuru ken" [Cancellation of the coal surcharge tax], 7 September 1931, 1.3.2.1-003; Suma Yakichirō→Inukai Tsuyoshi, Minister of Foreign Affairs of Japan, "Zari hōdai hi teppai ni kansuru ken" [Cancellation of the Fortress and Cannon Fee], 26 December 1931, E.1.3.2.1-003; Chen Boren, "Chen Jitang tongzhi jituan de hengzheng baolian," 111; Chen Boren, "Caizheng he shuijuan" [Finance and taxes and levies], in *Nantian suiyue: Chen Jitang zhu Yue shiqi jianwen shilu* [Days of the southern sky: Records of personal experiences about Guangdong under the rule of Chen Jitang], ed. Guangdongsheng zhengxie wenshi ziliao yanjiu weiyuanhui (Guangzhou: Guangdong renmin chubanshe, 1987), 296.

17 Chen Baozhi, "Ershisannian shengzheng," 21.

How was the idea of a special tax as a quasi-tariff realized?

Guangdong's unique history can explain why the special tax was only enacted in Guangdong province and why it was different from the other provinces' similar *likin* tax. Guangdong province had been the cradle of the revolutionary regime and by the 1920s it had the political legitimacy and legacy required to collect quasi-tariffs in the name of the revolution.

Except for a few disruptions, Guangdong province had been home to the Nationalist party and its revolutionary government from 1917 to 1926. This regime always claimed that it was the legitimate central government, even though in reality it was limited geographically to Guangzhou. As the capital of Guangdong province, Guangzhou was a major trade port where the maritime services were installed. Thus, a tug-of-war over tariff revenue, which had important diplomatic and financial implications, was ongoing. Instead of recognizing the commissioner for Guangzhou appointed by the inspector-general, Sun Wen and the military government in Guangzhou was allotted about 2.77 million Haikwan taels (*haiguan liang*) in tariff revenue from the Guangzhou Chinese Maritime Customs Service from July 1919 to March 1920. After rebuilding the government in February 1923 in the wake of expelling his rival, Chen Jiongming, from Guangzhou, Sun Wen claimed rights to 13.5 percent of the tariff revenue from the diplomatic representatives of the foreign powers. In spite of facing initial rejection, the Nationalist government in Guangzhou finally was granted the rights to 13.5 percent of the tariff revenue on the condition that this fund should be exclusively used for public works such as irrigation.

Shortly thereafter, the Nationalist government in Guangzhou announced enforcement of a provisional 2.5 percent tariff (*erwu zanding fujia guanshui*) on the foreign powers, which was met with strong opposition. On 11 October 1926, Song Ziwen, director of Finance, established the Bureau on the Inland Tax on Goods in Transit (*zhengshou chuchan yunxiao wupin neidi shuiju*), right next to the Maritime Customs Service, to collect a 2.5 percent ad valorem tax on exports. This tax was widely called the "inland 2.5 percent tax." In the face of strong opposition from the foreign powers, Song Ziwen declared that this tax was not a tariff but a domestic consumption tax. Collection of this tax continued until February 1929.[18]

18 Na Hyŏn-su, "Pukpŏl ch'ogi kungminjŏngbu ŭi taeoe gwan'gye ŭi chŏn'gae: Chamjŏng bugagwanse ŭi chingsu rŭl chungshim ŭro" [The Nationalist government's foreign relations during the early Northern Expedition period: Focusing on the collection of the 2.5 percent provisional tariffs], *Yŏksa hakpo* 99/100 (1983): 275–300.

There was also interference with the Maritime Customs Service in May 1931. A new Nationalist government was set up in Guangzhou by anti-Jiang factions in the Kuomintang (hereafter KMT), and Chen Jitang reappointed Sir Frederick Maze as inspector-general in the name of the central government and allowed him to go to Guangzhou. This maneuver was actually an effort to take over the Maritime Customs Service in Guangzhou. The NNG conceded Guangzhou's tariff revenue to the group in Guangdong in order to continue the tariff service uninterrupted. After an agreement was reached between the NNG and the anti-Jiang group in Guangdong to cancel the rivaling government in Guangzhou, the tariff revenue was returned to the control of the central government in Nanjing. However, even after that there was an abortive attempt to use the tariff revenue for provincial expenditures. Feng Zhuman, director of Finance in Guangdong, sought to use the tariff revenue to fund the monetary reform and the military campaign against the Communists in Jiangsu.[19] In retrospect, the history of the dispute over tariff revenue in Guangdong was completely unique, as a result of the conflict between China and the foreign countries, the confrontation between central and local politics, and its revolutionary legacy.

Nevertheless, the special tax in the 1930s was not a repetition of a disguised domestic tax or quasi-tariff of the 1920s. Provincial endeavor in developing agricultural and industrial production on the supply side was an essential factor to make the special tax a sustainable tax source. The success of import substitution, to some extent, supported its duration. Otherwise, the reckless raising of taxes would have resulted in a decrease in imports and a shortage of goods in the provincial market. In this respect, the special tax, designed to fight the Great Depression, could base its legitimacy on its protection of provincial industries and the planned economy.

19 The specific process is detailed in the following file. E.3.4.0.3-4-2 Chūgoku Zeikan kankei zakken: Kaigan kanshō mondai/ Kanton kaigan [Miscellaneous affairs relating to the Chinese Maritime Customs Service: Interference with the Maritime Customs Service / Guangdong Customs Service] (May 1931). However, the Salt Tax was successfully retained, and the director of Guangdong's Salt Tax Office received an appointment from the anti-Jiang Guangdong Nationalist Government, and the Salt Tax was credited to the Guangdong Central Bank. Later, the Guangdong Central Bank was reorganized as the Guangdong Provincial Bank. In 1932, the NNG implemented a "Salt Tax reform" to strengthen central control, but it was not especially applied to Guangdong until 1936. The Salt Tax revenue in Guangdong under Chen Jitang's rule was seized by Chen Youzhou, Chen Jitang's brother, assumed the position of the Salt Commissioner for Guangdong and Guangxi. Arthur N. Young, *China's National-Building Effort, 1927–1937: The Financial and Economic Record* (Stanford, CA: Hoover Institution Press, Stanford University, 1971): 59.

What positive impact did the special tax have on the economy in Guangdong province? Echoing the slogan of import substitution, the trade deficit in 1936 decreased sharply to one-quarter of the 220 million *yuan* recorded in 1932. Furthermore, Guangdong province witnessed outstanding development of the industrial sector. By 1936, over twenty provincial-government factories were in operation. They were generally the largest and most modernized plants, which had adopted advanced technologies in China as of the 1930s. The total capital of state-run plants rose from about 50,000 *yuan* in the early 1930s to over 70 million *yuan* in 1936. The number of private companies increased to about 2,000 during the Three-Year Plan period, of which 347 were said to be modern companies. It is remarkable that the total capital of private companies more than doubled, rising from 6.54 million *yuan* in 1930 to 15 million *yuan* in 1936. According to calculations by the DFG, the Xicun Cement Plant and six sugar refineries could substitute 24.3 million *yuan* and 30 million *yuan* of the value of imports, respectively. Because income from state-owned enterprises went to the GPG, the government could provide subsidies to the rural areas and eliminate the miscellaneous taxes, costing some 3 million *yuan*. In this respect, the "state-building" efforts by the GPG should not be ignored.[20]

Meanwhile, the limits of the special tax were self-evident. First, there were two aspects to this tax, one of which was its protective function for local industry. The other was its financial function, that is, to fund military expenditures for the Guangdong separatist regime. Whenever political tensions between Nanjing and Guangzhou escalated, the money-raising aspect of the special tax would take priority over its protective aspect. As a result, the special tax was subject to a loss of public support among the local people and its legitimacy was subject to erosion.

20 Yu Yanguang and Chen Fulin, *Nanyue geju: Cong Long Jiguang dao Chen Jitang* [The separatist regime of southern Guangdong: From Long Jiguang to Chen Jitang] (Guangzhou: Guangdong renmin chubanshe, 1989), 329–335. Efforts to build a Guangdong sugar industry in the 1930s are discussed in detail in the following studies. Kang Jin-A, "1930 nendai kanton Chinsaitō seiken no seitōgyō kensetsu" [Building of the sugar industry under the Chen Ji-ang regime in Guangdong province in the 1930s], *Chikakini Arite* 30 (1996); Jin-A Kang, "1930 nyŏndae chunggugŭi sŏlt'ang chŏnmaewa hongk'ong t'aegodangbang: Taegonghwangesŏ saranamgi" [The politics of the Taikoo Sugar Refinery Co. in Hong Kong against the Chinese sugar monopoly during the 1930s: Survival during the Great Depression], *Chungguk kŭnhyŏndaesa yŏngu* 85 (2020); Emily M. Hill, "The Life and Death of Feng Rui (1899–1936): Sugar Mills, Warlord Rule in Guangdong, and China's Agrarian Economy" (PhD diss., Cornell University, 1996), later published as *Smokeless Sugar: The Death of a Provincial Bureaucrat and the Construction of China's National Economy* (Vancouver: University of British Columbia Press, 2001).

Second, the self-protectionist slogan of the special tax was a double-edged sword for Guangdong. The idea of taxing goods not only in foreign countries but also in other parts of China to protect Guangdong's industry should have been called local tariffs. They represented nothing less than a head-on challenge to unified customs administration by the NNG and they provoked strong opposition from merchants in other parts of China. In February 1936, the DFG declared an increase in the special tax rate, using the protection of Guangdong's state-run industries as an excuse. Shanghai's business associations wired the GPG requesting its cancellation but with no success. However, two months later, Lin Yungai, governor of the GPG, demanded that the NNG provide a preferential tax rate for products from state-run plants to be exported to other provinces, citing the protection of national goods against foreign goods in the domestic market. This demand was not accepted and it further exacerbated criticism from merchants in Shanghai and elsewhere.[21]

Finally, there was a negative socioeconomic impact on the local economy when the excessive collection of the special tax caused a shortage of supplies in the provincial market due to the failure to replace the decline in imports by local production. In particular, taxation on daily necessities resulted in panic. The severe food crisis that hit Guangdong province in 1937 was the result (see Section 3 of this chapter).

The special tax born from Guangdong's financial and economic structure

The reason why the special tax took up such a high proportion of Guangdong's finances in the 1930s and caused a nationwide controversy can be found in Guangdong's economic and financial structure.

It is helpful to describe the features of Guangdong's economy and to compare them with those of Shanxi province, which was another prominent warlord-led economy. And both provincial governments were harshly criticized as military autarkies by Shanghai media in the 1930s. Shanxi was not a wealthy province. Total tax revenue in Guangdong was almost three times larger than that in Shanxi. Meanwhile, the total amount and share of the land tax in Guangdong provincial tax revenue in the total was 4.19 million *yuan* (8.4 percent) in 1933, 4.72 million *yuan* (7.8 percent) in 1934, 3.01 million *yuan* (4.9 percent) in 1935, and 4.62 million *yuan* (14.8 percent) in 1936 (units all *haoyang*). In the case of Shanxi province, the amounts and shares were

21 *Shenbao* (Shen Bao Daily), 6 February, 11 April 1936.

6.52 million *yuan* (48.4 percent) 1933, 6.52 million *yuan* (51.1 percent) in 1934, and 6.6 million *yuan* (53.1 percent) in 1935 (units all *dayang*). If there was a 20 percent discount for *haoyang* silver *yuan*, the absolute amount of the land tax in Shanxi was about twice as large as that in Guangdong. The share was more than five times that in Guangdong. On the other hand, the amount and share of the industrial and commercial tax in total Guangdong provincial tax revenue was 42.87 million *yuan* (86.8 percent) in 1933, 50.91 million *yuan* in 1934 (84.4 percent), 40.35 million *yuan* (65.2 percent) in 1935, and 20.35 million *yuan* (65.2 percent) in 1936.[22]

In sum, Guangdong relied more heavily on indirect taxes, with the nature of the tariffs and the sales tax related to commercial activities rather than to traditional tax sources, such as the land tax.[23] Unfortunately, this financial

22 Myŏng-hŭi Kang, "Mobŏmsŏng ŭi hŏ wa shil: Min'guk shigi sansŏsŏng chŏngbu ŭi chŏngch'i gaehyŏk kwa kyŏngje kŏnsŏl" [The rhetoric and reality of the model province: Political reform and economic construction of the Shanxi provincial government during the Republic of China] (PhD diss., Seoul National University, 1995), 148, Table 2. For a comparative table of each province's tax structure in the 1930s, see Uchida Tomoyuki, 1930 nendai ni okeru En Sekizan seiken no zaisei seisaku" [Fiscal policy of the Yan Xishan regime in the 1930s], *Ajia Keizai* 25(7) (1984): 21, 27, Tables 4, 15. According to a nationwide survey conducted by the Ministry of Industry, the proportion of the agricultural population relative to the total provincial population in Guangdong was 63.7 percent, the lowest in China. That of Shanxi was 82.8 percent, and the national average was 74.5 percent (*Shenbao*, 3 October 1933). This survey does not include the three provinces of Qinghai, Xikang, and Guangxi.

23 Uchida argues that Shanxi province in the 1930s had a more robust financial base than the rest of the provinces due to the higher fiscal weight of the land tax, resulting in the relative stability of the Yan Xishan regime (Uchida, "1930 nendai ni okeru En Sekizan seiken," 28). However, there was not always a correlation between a higher fiscal ratio of the land tax and the strength of a political entity. Instead, the deciding factor was the provincial capacity of fiscal policymaking to fit the wide range of different economic and tax environments in each province. The absolute amount of land tax revenue in Guangdong province also rose steadily after the GPG reformed the traditional land-poll tax (*tianfu*) to a provisional land tax (*Guangdongsheng zhi: Caizheng zhi*, 63). Nonetheless, the decisive success in financing the military expenses relied on the surge in indirect tax revenue. In this respect, the financial scale was essential, and the larger the financial scale, the more critical was the industrial and commercial tax revenue than the rigid land tax revenue. Even in the case of Shanxi, the Yan Xishan regime experienced success in the consolidation of the industrial and commercial taxes but not in the land-poll tax reform. See Uchida Tomoyuki, "En Sekizan seiken no zaisei seiri jigyō: 1930 nendai chūgoku ni okeru gunbatsu chihō kakkyo ni tsuite no ichikōsatsu" [The fiscal consolidation project of the Yan Xishan regime: A study of regional separatism of the warlord in China in the 1930s], *Hitotsubashi ronsō* 91(6) (1984): 844. Many studies have pointed out that in the 1930s, the focus of public finance gradually shifted from a land tax to an industrial and commercial tax. See Kubo Tōru, "Kokumin seifu no zaisei to kanzei shūnyū, 1928–1937 nen" [The finance of the Nationalist government and customs revenue, 1928–1937], in *Chūgokushi ni okeru shakai to minshū* [Society and people in Chinese history], ed. Masubuchi tatsuo sensei taikan kinen ronshū kankōkai [Publication committee for Tatsuo Masubuchi's retirement memorial collection] (Tokyo: Kyūko shoin, 1983); Kaneko

structure of Guangdong resembled the financial structure of the central government (NNG), resulting in competition between the two over financial resources.[24] However, the merchants' reactions to the fiscal and economic policy was quite different in Guangdong and in Shanghai. The NNG's high tariff policy combined with its import substitution industrialization policy was welcomed and promoted by Shanghai business circles. Unlike the Shanghai merchants, however, the Guangdong merchants were less responsive to the GPG's policy and political propaganda.

On 3 July 1934, at a meeting held by the Department of Construction, representatives of merchants agreed to collect the special taxes on imported goods but they stood united in opposition to the imposition of the special taxes on domestic goods in transit.[25] The Guangzhou Chamber of Commerce (in the *Chamber of Commerce Weekly*) expressed concern that imposition of a tax on domestic goods in transit could endanger domestic industry, and the Shanghai Chamber of Commerce dispatched a representative to Guangzhou to cancel the special tax.[26] In addition, the Chinese General Chamber of Commerce in Hong Kong issued an appeal in its monthly journal that Hong Kong products should be viewed as national goods and hence be exempt from the special tax.[27]

It was natural for merchants in Shanghai and Hong Kong to voice their opposition to the attempt to levy a tax on their products, but why did the merchants in Guangdong strongly oppose such an attempt? The fundamental reason can be found in Guangdong's economic structure, as opposed to that of Shanghai, and the ramifications of the economic policy decisions in the two cities were most important for the NNG and the GPG, respectively.

Guangzhou lost its status to Shanghai as the leading trade port in the middle of the nineteenth century. Guangzhou's export volume was 73 percent of that of Shanghai in 1883, but it had dropped to 31 percent by 1924. In addition, compared with the diversity of exports from Shanghai, in Guangzhou there was a higher export dependency on a single item—silk. Silk exports

Hajime, "Chūgoku no tōitsuka to zaisei mondai: 'Kokuchi zaisei kakubun' mondai o chūshin ni" [China's unification and financial problems: A focus on the "division between national and local taxes"], *Shigaku kenkyū* 179 (1988).

24 For the detailed tax structure of the NNG, see Kubo Tōru, "Kokumin seifu no zaisei to kanzei shūnyū."

25 Guangzhoushi shanghui [Guangzhou Chamber of Commerce], "Zhaoji ge hangshang taolun zhengshou waihuo teshui qingxing" [Calling on all merchants to discuss the situation of the Special Tax on Foreign Goods], *Shishanghui zhoukan* 9 (6 July 1934): 2.

26 Untitled article, *Shishanghui zhoukan* (6 October 1934): 4.

27 Chen Xingyuan, "Zenyang fazhan huanan zhi shangye" [How to develop commerce in South China], *Xianggang huashang zonghui yuekan* 1(5) (1935).

constituted more than half of the total export volume in Guangzhou. This explains the highly risky and fragile character of Guangzhou's export business in the ever-changing international market. As the silk industry was the first to be affected by the worldwide depression in the 1930s, repercussions in Guangzhou were more severe than those in Shanghai.[28]

David Faure states that Guangzhou could not effectively reinvest the benefits of the economic boom in various crops and other economic sectors due to its need to import a large volume of foreign rice, and also because of the decline in disposable income. This contrasted with the virtuous circle in Shanghai, combined with its development of foreign trade and commercial crop cultivation, increase in income and consumption, and economic stimulus to develop various crops, including rice farming.[29] However, these results can be interpreted from another point of view. Shanghai could expand its production partly because it had a vast hinterland along the Yangtze River, while Guangzhou lacked comparable land resources. In addition, the price of domestic rice in the Shanghai market had been competitive with that from Southeast Asia until the 1920s. In contrast, from the end of the nineteenth century domestic rice in the Guangzhou market had been more expensive than Southeast Asian rice, and the long-term consumption of indica rice imported from South Asia had gradually changed the palate of local people. By the 1930s, Guangdong people were paying more for high-grade imported rice than for domestic rice. Therefore, survival strategies in the two regions took different paths. Guangdong province found its own hinterland in Southeast Asia. Migrant laborers and merchants who entered Southeast Asia to cultivate and trade various commercial crops, including rice. While Guangdong surely imported rice from Southeast Asia, it also sent a mass migration of laborers to Southeast Asia, making direct inroads into Southeast Asia's agriculture, commerce, and industry.

Table 3.6 shows that Guangdong province suffered from an overwhelming trade deficit. In particular, the surge in the trade deficit from 1931 to 1933 was caused by a sharp drop in exports, mostly silk, rather than an increase in imports. Guangdong's economic structure was gradually shifting to a typical import-dependent economy.

28 For a comparison of the silk industry in Guangdong and Shanghai, see Robert Y. Eng, "Chinese Entrepreneurs, the Government, and the Foreign Sector: The Canton and Shanghai Silk-Reeling Enterprises, 1861–1932," *Modern Asian Studies* 18(3) (1984): 353–370.

29 David Faure, "The Plight of the Farmers: A Study of the Rural Economy of Jiangnan and the Pearl River Delta, 1870–1937," *Modern China* 11(1) (1985): 3–37.

However, this explanation is only based on customs data drawn by national borders. In the 1920s, about 100 million *yuan* of Chinese remittances flowed into Guangdong every year, offsetting the excess imports and maintaining a high level of consumption in Guangdong. In terms of imports and exports, which are distinguished by the border, Guangdong's economy may have been unbalanced with a huge deficit. However, including Southeast Asia's economy as its hinterland, Guangdong's economy can be considered internally balanced in terms of production and consumption. In other words, commercial and financial activities that moved large amounts of income and remittances were another economic engine of Guangdong province.

Table 3.5 Exports from Guangzhou, the Pearl River Delta, and Shanghai (unit: million Haikwan taels)

Year	Guangzhou and Pearl River Delta		Shanghai		
	Total value of exports	Silk	Total value of exports	Silk	Cotton
1883	17.1	10.1(59%)	23.3	14.5(62.2%)	3.9(16.7%)
1904	67.3	31.6(47%)	80.2	33.4(41.6%)	26.3(32.7%)
1924	120.6	62.6(52%)	384.4	48.6(12.6%)	124.1(32.2%)

Source: Based on data in David Faure, "The Plight of the Farmers: A Study of the Rural Economy of Jiangnan and the Pearl River Delta, 1870–1937," *Modern China* 11(1) (1985): 13–14, Table 4 and Table 5.

Table 3.6 Trade balance in Guangdong province, 1928–1937 (unit: 1,000 *yuan*)

Year	Imports	Exports	Deficit	Year	Imports	Exports	Deficit
1928	249,345	175,947	73,398	1933	269,169	94,456	174,713
1929	229,488	182,343	46,145	1934	156,553	82,026	74,527
1930	243,916	164,654	79,264	1935	150,269	75,268	75,001
1931	276,243	152,035	124,208	1936	130,171	84,547	45,624
1932	314,259	92,538	221,721	1937	180,024	130,065	49,959

Source: Hirano Ken, *Kanton no genjō* [The current situation in Guangdong] (Guangzhou: Kanton nihon shōgyō kaigisho, 1943), 108.

By the 1930s Guangdong province, with Guangzhou as its capital, was characterized by a decline in its status as a port of trade, sluggish exports and instability, dependence on food imports, a huge trade deficit, and close links with the Southeast Asian economies. When considering its heavy dependence on the commercial and external economies, it was difficult for Guangzhou's merchants to fully support the special tax, which can be said to have interfered with commercial activities. A future vision of fostering provincial industry was just a plan.

Moreover, the special tax that was unfavorable to Chinese interests in Southeast Asia was not welcomed by commoners who subsisted on remittances from family members working abroad. In this respect, national interests did not coincide with local interests. The same applied to merchants who had import businesses with Southeast Asia. Trade barriers to Southeast Asia, such as the special tax, were not necessarily favorable to the provincial economy. Underdevelopment of the production factor lowered merchant expectations for an alternative industrialization vision offered by the GPG. Furthermore, the idea that the fruit of industrialization based on state-run plants could be shared with the private sector was also questionable.

The economic structure defined the trade and fiscal structure of Guangdong. Guangdong's main tax targets overlapped with those of the central government, such as the indirect tax on commercial activities, resulting in Guangdong's vulnerability to political tensions with the NNG. Due to the lack of a production sector, it was difficult for such an autarkic model based on self-sufficiency, like that of Shanxi, to succeed. Interference with trade activities could weaken political legitimacy by losing the support of merchants. This was in stark contrast to the NNG's protectionist policies, which won strong support from Shanghai's business circles who wanted to curb imports. The Guangdong economic structure was the fundamental reason why the GPG's self-protectionist appeal was not echoed by most of the Guangdong population.

The special tax and merchants in Shantou

The special tax faced criticism not only from the NNG but also from the merchant groups and foreign consulates in Guangdong. In Guangzhou, where the administrative power of the GPG was based, collection of the special tax was carried out as planned, while various frictions over the special tax continued in Shantou and the Chaozhou area, in the northern part of Guangdong. Shantou, known as Swatow, was the center of the Chaozhou area. This city was a treaty port opened by the Tianjin Treaty of 1858, and it was the second-largest trading port in Guangdong. Geographically, this port city was located far from Guangzhou; rather, it was closely linked culturally and economically with Fujian province and Shanghai. The position of the merchant groups with respect to the special tax helps to understand the presence of the special tax in Shantou.

Prelude: The 1929 general strike against the inland 2.5 percent tax in Shantou

In early 1929, the strong merchant-led campaign against taxation that swept Shantou provided the background to the later struggle with the GPG in the 1930s. On 11 October 1926, Guangdong's Nationalist Government started to impose a new tax on local goods and imported goods in transit to the inland area of Shantou.[30] This tax was a 2.5 percent additional tariff, acknowledged by the Treaty of Washington in 1922. However, the Guangdong government was a revolutionary regime controlling only small localities in the south, and its legitimacy was not recognized by the foreign powers that supported the Beiyang government. Therefore, the Nationalists had to collect this tax, even in the treaty ports in Guangdong, in their own way, thus creating the so-called "inland 2.5 percent tax." The tax target was expanded to the local goods in transit in the treaty ports. The income was substantial, with revenue of some 7.7 million *yuan* in 1928. In 1928 when the inland tax on the treaty ports in Guangdong was abolished, the GPG decided to temporarily maintain the inland tax in Shantou because of its source of revenue. On 24 February 1929, the DFG officially confirmed the abolition of the inland tax in Shantou, dating back to 1 February. Behind this abolition order there was, in fact, a persistent opposition movement led by the Shantou merchants.[31]

The tax had earlier been highly praised as an important source to fund the Northern Expedition and leading to tariff autonomy.[32] However, not only foreign but also Chinese merchants had to endure the burden of the tax payments, causing considerable controversy throughout Guangdong. In particular, the merchant association in Shantou organized a tenacious movement to oppose the inland tax.

To eradicate tax evasion, the GPG twice, in February and March 1928, announced a new regulation regarding payment of the inland tax. The Shantou Chamber of Commerce responded to this action by sending a petition to DFG calling for abolition of the inland tax. The petition asked that

30 For the detailed process of the diplomatic controversy over the Inland tax, see Na Hyŏn-su "Pukpŏl ch'ogi kungminjŏngbu ŭi taeoe gwan'gye ŭi chŏn'gae," 261–312.

31 *Guangdongsheng caizheng jishi*, Vol. 2, 2–3.

32 *Guangdongsheng caizheng jishi*, Vol. 2, 2; Na Hyŏn-su, "Pukpŏl ch'ogi kungminjŏngbu ŭi taeoe gwan'gye ŭi chŏn'gae," 288–291.

the Inland Tax Bureau and the 2.5 percent inland tax be incorporated with the Customs Service, as in the case of other provinces. However, in contrast to the demands of the petition, the Inland Tax Bureau issued additional regulations to further strengthen the documentary requirements and the exemption qualifications for payment of the inland tax. Furthermore, a new regulation was announced in May that allowed merchants to export goods only after clearing cargo inspection in the Inland Tax Bureau. The bureau argued that the purpose of this action was to eradicate smuggling.[33]

Shantou merchant groups criticized the new regulations because they interfered with normal commercial transactions, citing the requirement that cargo be searched one by one and the high risk of delayed urgent cargo.[34] After numerous attempts to cancel the new regulations failed, on 10 September forty-eight trade associations in Shantou organized a "Committee Supporting Domestic Exports" (*guochan chukou weichi weiyuanhui*) and wired information about the illegality of the new regulation throughout the country and in Hong Kong. The campaign against the inland tax escalated to a general strike against shipments, leading to the shutdown of the port of Shantou. On 11 September, a steamer to Hong Kong (the "Chaozhou"), a steamer to Vietnam (the "Yuanli"), and two steamers to Shanghai (the "Hanzhou" and the "Yisheng") could not depart from Shantou because their shipments had been rejected. At the port of Shantou, access to ships was cut off.[35] On 9 October, the Ministry of Finance of the NNG ordered that the new regulation be deferred. The Shantou merchants rejoiced and lifted the strike by resuming export shipments. However, the GPG sent a telegram to the Inland Tax Bureau demanding that the regulation be implemented and warning of the imposition of penalties on non-registered shipments. Because of the so-called "divergence in orders from the central government and the provincial government," the GPG was inundated with protests from all over the country, including the National Merchants' Association. Meanwhile, despite the NNG's mediation, the GPG and the Shantou merchants failed

33 Beppu Kumakichi, Consul of Shantou→Tanaka Giichi, Minister of Foreign Affairs of Japan, "Kaku shōgyō kōkai no naichi zeikyoku saitetsu undō ni kansuru ken" [The Commercial Associations' Movement for the abolition of the Inland Tax Bureau], 18 April 1928, E.1.3.2.1-02, Miscellaneous matters related to taxes and contributions in China, Vol. 2.

34 Zhang Ouru, "Shantou neidi shuiju houlun lingdan fengchao zhi jingguo jiqi ganxiang" [The experience and thoughts about the unrest over ticket regulation prior to shipment by the Shantou Inland Tax Bureau], *Chaomei shanghui lianhehui banyuekan* 1(1) (1929): 16–18.

35 Beppu Kumakichi→Tanaka Giichi, "Shūsei naichisanka shukkō hōzei Benhō hantai undō ni kansuru ken" [The movement against the report on the revised regulations on local products], 14 September 1928, E.1.3.2.1-004.

to reach a compromise. The merchants in Shantou decided to resume their strike, leading to an unprecedented financial and economic crisis for Shantou society, including a series of bankruptcies of large-scale native banks.[36]

The reason why the GPG took the risk to disobey an order of the central government was due to the importance of the revenue from the inland tax in Shantou. The amount of revenue raised by the January 1929 tax that was sent from the Inland Tax Bureau to the Shantou sub-treasury was 387,488 *yuan*. Therefore, even if there were monthly gaps, the Inland Tax Bureau submitted between 3 million *yuan* and 5 million *yuan* per year.[37] In February 1929, Feng Zhuwan, director of the DFG, declared the abolition of the inland tax.[38] However, the emergence of similar domestic taxes was inevitable unless the central government were to compensate for the loss. One year later, on 19 February 1930, the GPG started to impose a 10 percent temporary levy on national taxes. On 1 August, it canceled the temporary levy and instead began collecting a 20 percent additional tax. However, all of these attempts failed due to strong opposition from foreign and Chinese merchants.[39] This eventually set the stage for the second round of confrontation between the GPG and the merchants in Shantou over the Special Tax.

Structure of the special tax issue in Shantou

Merchants' campaign against the Special Tax

Shantou was known for its trade with northeastern China, Shanghai and the Yangzi River basin, and Southeast Asia. Its merchants exported sugar and palm oil and they imported beans, bean cake, peanuts, and so forth through trade with northeastern China. In addition, they imported rice and dried fish from Southeast Asia while exporting native goods. This trade had a long history that had been undertaken by the so-called South and North Guilds (*nanbeigang huowu yunshu gongshui, nanbeihang* for short). The two other major merchant associations affiliated with this trade were

36 Zhang Ouru, "Shantou neidi shuiju houlun," 18–20.

37 "Shantou fenjinku yi yue fen shouru zhi diaocha" [Survey of the revenue of the Shantou sub-treasury in January], *Chaomei shanghui lianhehui banyuekan* 1(3/4) (1929): 12.

38 Zhang Gonglue, "Xin shangren" [The new merchant], *Chaomei shanghui lianhehui Banyuekan* 11(1929): 13.

39 Yano Makoto, Consul General of Guangdong→Tanaka Giichi, Minister of Foreign Affairs of Japan, 30 January 1929, E.1.3.2.1-002; Beppu Kumakichi→Shidehara Kijūrō, "Kokuzei ni taishi niwari huka ni kansuru ken" [20 percent additional charge on the national tax], August 1930, E.1.3.2.1-002.

the Food Grain Trade Guild (*zaliang gonghui*) of grain importers and a brokerage union of wholesalers.[40]

The two most significant imported goods were rice from Southeast Asia and soybean cakes from northeastern China, which were subject to the Special Tax on Agricultural Products and the Special Tax on Imported Fertilizers, respectively. Therefore, Shantou's trade was deeply affected by the introduction of the Special Tax, and the three aforementioned guilds launched a relentless campaign against the Special Tax.

It is necessary to look at the trade structure in Shantou in the 1930s. Bean cake, imported from Dalian, Andong, Niuzhuang, Shanghai, and Hankou, was used as fertilizer on sugar cane farms and rice farms in the Chaozhou area. The volume of yearly imports amounted to 800,000 piculs in the 1930s. Interestingly, the import business of soybean cakes showed signs of booming due to the revival of traditional sugar manufacturing in Chaozhou in the 1930s. Sugar cane cultivation returned to the limelight due to the GPG's plan to build state-run sugar refineries. As sugar cane cultivation increased, the demand for soybean cakes for fertilizer flourished. The GPG's encouragement of sugar cane cultivation to provide the raw material for sugar refineries also increased demand for imported rice because rice had been competing with sugar cane in decision-making regarding farm crops. Rice was the top imported good in Shantou throughout the twentieth century. Next to Jiulong (the entry port of Guangzhou), Shantou was the second-largest rice import port, occupying 20–30 percent of all Guangdong rice imports between 1932 and 1936. Peanuts and oil were also among the main imports. Even though oil extracted from peanuts was largely replaced by kerosene, there was still a high demand for oil for home lighting and food.[41]

All of the above major imports were daily necessities or products required for agricultural production. In addition, Shantou's economy mainly depended on agriculture and commerce, and industry was less developed. There were

40 *Shenbao*, 17 September 1935. For the South and North Guild and its trade during the late Qing, see Miyata Michiaki, "Shinmatsu chōshū chihō ni okeru satō bōeki no tenkai to chiiki shakai: Santō kō no ryūtsū jōkyō o chūshin toshite" [Development of the sugar trade and local communities in the Chaozhou region during the late Qing: Focusing on the status of distribution in the Shantou port], in *Kanda nobuo sensei koki kinenronshū: Shinchō to higashi ajia* [Memorial collection celebrating the 70th birthday of of Nobuo Kanda: The Qing dynasty and East Asia], ed. Kanda Nobuo sensei kok kinen ronshū henshū iinkai [Compilation committee for the memorial collection celebrating the 70th birthday of Prof. Nobuo Kanda] (Tokyo: Yamagawa shuppansha, 1992), 489–512.

41 "Shantou lai chunmi ji doubing shijia zhi yuce" [Prediction of the market price of spring rice and soybean cake entering Shantou], *Chaomei shanghui lianhehui banyuekan* 1(2) (1929): 19–20; *Shenbao*, 1 December 1932.

few industrialists welcoming the high-tariff policies. Moreover, the GPG's Three-Year Plan focused on Guangzhou, alienating Shantou and Chaozhou. Among the newly built state-run sugar refineries, five were located in the Guangzhou area, whereas only one was built in Jieyang in Chaozhou prefecture.[42] On the whole, the cause of promoting local industry hardly resonated with Shantou merchants who viewed the Special Tax as another rent-seeking activity.

It was in November 1932 that there was an attempt to impose a tax on soybean cakes. Before this, there had been no taxes on soybean cakes. However, after the 1931 Mukden Incident, the NNG applied high tariffs on the entry of Manchurian goods in the name of an economic blockade. Seeing their chance, the GPG announced a special tax on all soybean cakes imported to Guangdong. Simultaneously, the Soybean Cake Trader Associations throughout the country immediately launched a campaign against the GPG's action. Shanghai's association (*Shanghaishi zaliang youbingye tongye gonghui*) was at the forefront.[43] This was because after the Mukden Incident, Shanghai and cities in the Yangtze River Delta rapidly increased their soybean cake production to substitute for Manchurian products in the domestic market. The largest markets were in Guangzhou and Shantou. In other words, this Special Tax would block not only Manchurian soybeans but also soybeans from central China. Facing a nationwide opposition movement, the GPG declared on 7 December 1932 that this special tax would be levied exclusively on Manchurian soybeans.

However, in March 1933, Taili Company, which was a tax-farming company for the Special Tax on Imported Fertilizers, in effect the soybean tax, and Shantou police detained more than ten ships carrying "domestic soybean cakes" on charges of tax evasion. The police argued that these soybean cakes were all Manchurian products shipped to Shanghai as a transit port. The Shantou merchants, the owners of the detained ships, insisted that they all were domestic products. There was no way to confirm who was correct. Finally, the GPG surrendered to public pressure and released the detained ships.[44]

42 The local community primarily accepted a modernized sugar factory (the Jieyang sugar factory) as a threat to the traditional sugar manufacturers in the Chaozhou area. This was quite different from Guangzhou's situation, where modern sugar factories, newly built by the government, substituted for the imported sugar without rivalry with the local private manufacturers (Kang Jin-A, "1930 nendai kanton Chinsaitō seiken no seitōgyō kensetsu," 89).

43 *Shenbao*, 1 December 1932.

44 *Shenbao*, 31 March 1933.

In May 1934, yet another detention related to soybean cakes took place. A new tax-farming company, Huifeng Company, detained the steamer "Zhongxing," which was carrying 18,200 pieces of soybean cake from Shanghai to Shantou. Due to the active lobbying by the Shanghai merchant associations and advertisements attesting to the fact that they were domestic products, the "Zhongxing" was rereleased.[45]

However, the situation deteriorated even further. On 1 September 1935, the newly appointed tax-farming company, Lianan, announced an expansion of taxation on all domestic products, at the rate of 0.25 *yuan* per 1 picul. Soybean cake manufacturers and traders throughout the country responded to this announcement by staging a general strike. Representatives from Shanghai, Wuxi, Changzhou, and Kunshan delivered a petition to the NNG. Soybean merchants in Guangzhou, Hankou, and Shantou joined the strike.[46]

With the start of taxation, Shantou merchants had already become passive players in the strikes. This was because, firstly, the Shantou merchants were too weak to bear the burdens of a strike. During the previous years, repeated campaigns against taxation had led to heavy losses, amounting to 1 to 2 million *yuan,* for Shantou dealers. They were on the verge of bankruptcy owing to the collapse of agriculture due to the worldwide depression and the massive prevalence of smuggling. Within a year, half of Shantou's shops had closed. The capital of thirty-four closed companies ranged from 100,000 *yuan* to 1 million *yuan*, showing that recurrent strikes had seriously weakened even large companies in Shantou. Secondly, it was the producers, not the merchants, whose survival was at stake. For Shantou merchants, it would be far better to import high-quality Manchurian products without exemptions over low-quality domestic products. This taxation continued until the end of Chen Jitang's regime.[47]

Interestingly, in this process Shanghai merchants and Shantou merchants all accused "one foreign country" from profiting from this dispute. This was a reference to Japan, a euphemism due to the censorship of anti-Japanese media. The NNG strictly censored news and reports against Japan in order to avoid any additional conflicts. However, the Shanghai newspaper, *Shenbao,* reported on the smuggling from Manchuria to Shantou by Japanese companies.

In reality, Japanese nationals in Shantou operated organized smuggling of soybean cakes from Manchuria via Shanghai, relying on the diplomatic

45 *Shenbao*, 16 May 1934, 31 August 1935.

46 *Shenbao*, 31 August 1935.

47 *Shenbao*, 1, 3, 6, 10, 12, 15, 17, 19, and 20 September 1935, 11 June 1936.

protection of the Japanese consul in Shantou. This situation forced the GPG to enact controversial taxation on all domestic soybean cakes. Why was the influence of Japan so strong in Shantou? The rise of a Japanese presence in Shantou dated back to the Guangzhou–Hong Kong strike of 1925–1926, caused by British oppression of the 30 May 1925 movement. Taking advantage of the British capital's retreat from Guangdong for more than a year, Japanese companies, including steamship companies such as Osaka, Nisshin, and Yamashita, made their way to Shantou. Trading companies such as Mitsui and Mitsubishi, which had been forced to downsize their branches or to withdraw from Guangdong, reopened and enlarged their branches. In 1927, the number of Japanese residents in Guangdong jumped from about 200 to 450.[48]

Shantou in particular witnessed a growth in Japanese activities because of historical and cultural ties with Fujian province. The Chaozhou area was not only geographically closer to Fujian province than to Guangzhou and Hong Kong, but also closer in terms of language and culture, as the majority of Chaozhou people stemmed from Fujian. Chaozhou merchants and laborers had formed an independent transnational diaspora while demonstrating a close kinship with the Fujian diaspora. Shantou, the exit port for the Chaozhou area, had a long history of trade with Shanghai and Southeast Asia as the hometown of the Chaozhou network.[49] Once Taiwan, whose population largely originated from Fujian, was colonized by Japan, more Taiwanese people entered Shantou business through the Fujian network. As a result, the number of Japanese traders in Shantou jumped to more than 500, most of whom were Taiwanese.[50]

The other factor that strengthened the economic ties between Shantou and Japan was the Japanese invasion of Manchuria. Heavy reliance on Manchurian products, such as soybean cakes and grains, boosted activities by Japanese merchants in Shantou. They started to import soybean cakes from the Northeast (Manchuria) to trade with Taiwan, and to become involved in intermediary rice trade via Hong Kong.[51] More than anything, the high tariffs and the subsequent smuggling inspired Japanese commercial

48 Gaimushō tsūshōkyoku, *Saikin no kanton keizai jijō*, 39-44.

49 Hamashita Takeshi, "Imin to shōgyō nettowāku: chōshū gurūpu notaiimin to hongoku sōkin" [Immigration and commercial network: Chaozhou immigrants in Thailand and their remittances to China], *Tōbunken kiyō* 116 (1992): 65.

50 *Shenbao*, 1 October 1935.

51 Harada Chūichirō, Consul of Shantou→Hirota Kōki, Minister of Foreign Affairs of Japan, "Kantonshō kome zenzei ni kansuru ken" [The Special Tax on rice in Guangdong province], 8 October 1935, E.1.3.2.1-004.

activities. In the 1930s, Japan systematically carried out massive smuggling operations from north to south across China, neutralizing the high tariff policy of the NNG. In Guangdong, Shantou became another major smuggling point to incapacitate the Special Tax policy of the GPG. The Shantou market was soon flooded with smuggled products.

Lack of legitimacy as a local tariff and foreign pressures

The high tariffs imposed by NNG were a government-led legitimizing act based on tariff autonomy, which was recognized by the foreign powers. However, the Special Tax in Guangdong did not have international legal binding force. Therefore, Japanese merchants refused to pay the Special tax, claiming that it violated the trade treaty. Apart from this logic, however, there was a precedent whereby local tariffs were imposed on foreign countries based on justification by force, such as the 1926 inland tax. In practice, the financially troubled governments in Guangdong had always attempted to impose taxes on the goods of foreign merchants. As a case in point, let us take a look at the history of interactions with the Japanese.

The Japanese government enumerated the illegal taxes levied by Guangdong on imports in 1927 as the following: tobacco and wine stamp duties (May 1921), cement tax (January 1924), petroleum and alcohol tax (February 1925), the inland tax (2.5 percent provisional surcharge), luxury goods tax (11 October 1926, 6 June 1927), and *likin* taxes. Beginning in June 1925, the Guangdong Nationalist Government ordered that the *likin* be collected from foreigners in the wake of the anti-British movement. In March 1927, the *likin* was levied on the goods of Japanese merchants as well.

The GPG's efforts to impose local tariffs continued in 1928. The GPG enforced a 10 percent local surcharge on tariffs on foreign merchants to fund financial maintenance, disaster relief, and recovery projects. This attempt was frustrated due to united objections by the foreign powers. The GPG again tried in May 1928 to levy a 20 percent surcharge on tariffs for six months, but this effort was similarly aborted.[52]

52 Beppu Kumakichi→Yoshizawa Kenkichi, Minister Extraordinary and Plenipotentiary of Japan to China, "Kanton zengo kinyū iji oyobi shinsai fukazei ni kansuru ken" [Tax surcharge for Financial maintenance and disaster relief in Guangdong], 13 March 1928, E.1.3.2.1-001, Miscellaneous matters related to taxes and contributions in China, Vol. 1; Beppu Kumakichi,Yoshizawa Kenkichi, "Shinsai fukazei wo naichi zeigyoku ni chōshū seshimuru no ken" [Collection of disaster relief tax surcharges by the Inland Tax Bureau], 27 April, 8 June 1928, E.1.3.2.1-001; Morita Kanzō, Consul General of Guangdong→Tanaka Giichi, "Shinsai fukazei chōshū ni kansuru ken" [The collection of disaster relief tax surcharge], 29 May 1928, E.1.3.2.1-001.

Since the 1930s, the conflict with Japan had been intensifying. Many large-scale Japanese cotton textile mills were built in Shanghai and Tianjin (called *Zaikabo* in Japanese) with direct capital investments. In early 1930, the GPG announced it would levy a special tax on the *Zaikabo*'s cotton cloth entering Guangdong. In June the taxation was interrupted due to strong opposition from the Japanese side but it began again in July.[53] However, this time collection at entry in the customs office was adjusted to collection by the Chinese merchants when the Japanese merchants handed over the imports at the warehouses. The GPG was thus able to successfully implement the taxation.[54]

This episode shows the nature of the special tax well. The 1928 attempt to collect the tariff surcharge can be considered a revival of the 1925 inland tax at the local level. The nature of the two taxes is identical. Nonetheless, while the Guangdong Nationalist Government in 1925 succeeded in suppressing the opposition by foreign powers to levy the inland tax, the GPG in 1928 failed to do so. This was because the GPG was a provincial government lack of legitimacy to debate this issue. Therefore, the local tariff was transformed into a domestic tax, and the burden fell on the Chinese merchants.

Nationalism, localism, and profiteering: The 1935 Shantou Incident

The fiscal readjustment after 1933 produced some results. But the escalating conflict between Chen Jitang and Jiang Jieshi forced the GPG to repeatedly raise the rate of the Special Tax to fund the growing military spending. The high tax rate resulted in discouraging imports and encouraging smuggling. As the crackdown on smuggling intensified, the distribution cycle of goods was obstructed, causing a backlash from the merchants. However, foreign merchants (who had been exempt from taxation at the port of entry to Guangdong) and certain Guangdong merchants collaborated to take advantage of loopholes to evade the special tax.

Japanese nationals looked to the import companies in Shantou to organize an "import business without paying the Special Tax," that is,

53 In the late 1930, more than 50 percent of the imported cotton cloth in Guangdong consisted of Japanese products, and the rest were from Great Britain and Shanghai.

54 Suma Yakichirō→Shidehara Kijūrō, 6 July, 22 July 1931, E.1.3.2.1-003.

to engage in smuggling. The GPG had to extend the taxation to foreign merchants, including the Japanese, and decide whether to crack down on the smuggling or to protect the local merchants who were paying taxes. The 1935 Shantou Incident dramatically reveals the tensions growing across the country.

On 10 and 11 September 1935, an anti-smuggling crackdown squad in Jieyang county confiscated 16.2 tons of rice and 140 bags of soybeans that had been brought into the country by Japanese merchants, on charges of tax evasion.[55] Nevertheless, on 12 September, seven Japanese navy vessels entered the Shantou port without prior notification to the Chinese side. The GPG and the Shantou city government issued a strong protest to the Japanese consuls in Guangzhou and Shantou. The Japanese side responded by saying that the warships' entry was a legitimate measure taken to protect the Japanese residents in Guangdong. It argued that it was illegal to detain Japanese goods in Jieyang and it asked for immediate return of the seized goods to the original owners. In order to press the GPG further, three more vessels entered the port of Shantou on 25 September. The so-called Shantou Incident was reported by the nationwide media.[56]

Why did the situation worsen until the military was brought in? Furthermore, how could the Japanese side react so quickly in only one day? In reality, the conflict between the GPG and the Japanese in Guangdong had already become serious even before the confiscation in Jieyang. Earlier, on 3 September, the Japanese consulate in Shantou had obtained secret telegram exchanges between the commanders of the garrison corps in Guangdong. They were consulting to coordinate a crackdown on Japanese smuggling organizations (*honghui*) in the Shantou and Chaozhou areas. The Japanese side drew up countermeasures with the Japanese consul-general in Guangzhou and the Japanese navy's torpedo squadron commander before dispatching Japanese naval vessels to Shantou. The case of confiscation in Jieyang served as an excuse for a prepared show of force.[57]

55 Harada Chūichirō→Hirota Kōki, 15 September 1935, E.1.3.2.1-2-1 Santō mondai kome senzei [The Shantou issue: the Special Tax on Rice].

56 According to reports in *Shenbao Daily*, the US also dispatched a ship to Shantou following the entry of the Japanese navy. But there were no US-related reports on this issue. *Shenbao*, 1 and 6 October 1935.

57 Nakahara Saburō, Japanese Navy Officer and Military attaché in Guangdong→Vice Chief of the Army General Staff, Chief of Staff of the Three Fleets, Commander of the Five Water Wars, Satō Okota Military attaché with the Chinese legation, 6 September 1935, E.1.3.2.1-2-1; Kawai Tatsuo, Consul General of Guangdong and Harada Chūichirō→Hirota Kōki, "Nihonjin mitsuyusha shikei no ken" [Japanese smugglers executed], 6 September 1935, E.1.3.2.1-2-1.

The two diplomatic reports about negotiations between the GPG and Japan addressed the vast gaps between their respective views. In a meeting with the Japanese consul-general in Guangdong, Chen Jitang complained about Japanese smuggling activities, whereas Counsel-General Kawai said that the imposition of a tax on Japanese citizens was a treaty violation.

Another negotiating table was set up between the Japanese consul in Shantou, Harada Chūichirō, and the Shantou city government. The representative of the Shantou city government criticized the fact that Japanese merchants had organized a large-scale rice import trade union exclusively to import tax-exempt foreign rice to Shantou. As a result, the business of the innocent taxpayers, the South and North Trade Union (*nanbeihang*), would be seriously damaged. Meanwhile, Consul Harada argued that Chinese merchants were losing out in the competition because of the heavy Special Taxes, saying, "The real intention (of the Chinese merchants' petition to the GPG) is to ease the heavy tax burden."

However, the Shantou side replied that the revenue from the Special Tax belonged to the provincial budget, and thus it could not reduce it on their own. In reality, the monthly revenue from the Special Tax in Shantou that formerly had amounted to 1.2–1.3 million *yuan* had dropped to 0.2 million *yuan* by 1935. The sharp drop in tax revenue had forced the government to take countermeasures to protect the volume of transactions by Chinese merchants on whom they could levy the tax.[58]

In fact, subsequent actions by Shantou merchants favored Consul Harada's argument. On 14 September, the South and North Trade Union submitted a petition to the GPG asking for cancellation of the Special Tax Bureau and integration of the taxation service into the Customs Services. This request coincided exactly with the request by the Shantou merchants in the 1928 inland tax conflict. However, cancellation of the separate taxation meant a loss of tax control on the part of the GPG and thus it was unacceptable.[59]

It should be noted that the Japanese merchants, called "national merchants (*hōshō*)" or "Japanese nationals (*sekimin*)" in Japanese consul reports, were technically Taiwanese who received Japanese nationality after the 1895 Japanese colonization. In the wake of the Shantou Incident, the Ministry of Foreign Affairs in Tokyo was divided into hard-liners and soft-liners. The soft-liners interpreted the current situation as being caused

58 Kawai Tatsuo→Hirota Kōki, 11 September 1935, E.1.3.2.1-2-1; Harada Chūichirō→Hirota Kōki, "Dōgyōkumiai ni kansuru kō sanji mōshide hōkoku no ken" [Report on Huang's proposal about the industrial union], 13 September 1935, E.1.3.2.1-2-1.

59 Harada Chūichirō→Hirota Kōki, 20 September 1935, E.1.3.2.1-2-1.

by Taiwanese merchants with Japanese nationality who had abused the consular jurisdiction against the Chinese crackdown in collaboration with the Japanese consulate in Shantou. Moreover, the import tariff rate on rice in the rest of China was higher than the Special Tax rate on imported rice in Guangdong. It would have been better for the Japanese importers to pay the Special Tax in the name of the Chinese buyers. This was based on a report by the Japanese Army in China, which prioritized Manchuria, as opposed to the Japanese Navy's aggressive strategy in southern China toward Southeast Asia. At first, Foreign Minister Hirota seems to have accepted the soft-liners' argument.[60]

However, there was an immediate and intense backlash from the hard-liners, especially the Japanese consuls and the navy officials in Guangdong. According to their counterargument, after repeated rate rises, the Special Tax rate on rice was already higher than the import tariff on rice levied in the rest of China by the NNG. Moreover, as this Special Tax was a newly enforced illegal local tax, there was no need to negotiate it any longer. A strong show of force would assure invalidation of the tax.[61] These debates implied that Japanese traders had imported foreign rice in Guangdong without paying the import tariff on rice to the Customs Services after the NNG began to levy the tariff on imported rice.

In reality, Guangdong became a tax-free zone for foreign rice importers as long as the GPG continued to collect the Special Tax on Imported Rice not from foreign importers but from Chinese traders who bought the imported rice after customs clearance. Once the GPG raised the special tax rate higher than the tariff and extended the taxation to foreign importers, it came to oppose the Special Tax.

The NNG and the merchant groups out of Guangdong criticized that Guangdong's Special Tax was illegal and merely a variant of the *likin* tax. However, Japanese involvement in this issue through the Shantou Incident subtly changed their attitudes about the Special Tax. Japan was the last country to recognize Chinese tariff autonomy among the foreign powers. After reluctant acceptance of Chinese tariff sovereignty, Japan staged the Mukden Incident

60 Usuda Hirozo, Janapese Army Officer, Lieutenant Colonel, Military attaché in Guangdong→Vice Chief of the Army General Staff, 3 October 1935, E.1.3.2.1-2-1; Hirota Kōki→Kawai Tatsuo, 3 October 1935, E.1.3.2.1-2-1.

61 Nakahara Saburō, Japanese Navy Officer and Military attaché in Guangdong→Vice Chief of the Army General Staff, Chief of Staff of the Three Fleets, Commander of the Five Water Wars, Satō Okota Military attaché with the Chinese legation, 24, 27 September 1935, E.1.3.2.1-2-1; Commander of the Five Water Wars→Vice Chief of the Army General Staff, Chief of Staff Of the Three Fleets, 3, 4 October 1935, E.1.3.2.1-2-1; Harada Chūichiro→Hirota Kōki, 8 October 1935, E.1.3.2.1-2-1.

in 1931 to seize China's Northeast territory (Manchuria) and its market by force. Furthermore, Japan neutralized the NNG's protective tariff policy by bringing Japanese goods into the Central China market through demilitarized North China without paying tariffs.[62] Consequently, as soon as a similar case of Japanese smuggling and menacing military power appeared in the south, a wave of strong nationalism arose throughout the country. Nationalistic sentiment toward Japan further complicated the nature of the Shantou Incident.

The media in Guangdong and Hong Kong strongly criticized the Japanese acts of smuggling. Doubts about the legitimacy of the Special Tax in Guangdong were buried in the surge of nationalism.[63] However, the Shanghai merchants heaped criticism on both the GPG and the Japanese merchants. The GPG was condemned for imposing heavy taxes on food to harm the people's livelihood under the guise of domestic protection. They complained that other provincial merchants—like those in Shanghai, who had to pay high taxes—were disadvantaged. Nonetheless, the Chinese media in Shanghai concluded that the Japanese should still pay the Special Tax since the Special Tax was part of the tariff.[64]

The attitude of the NNG was identical to that of the Shanghai media. On the Japanese Navy's entry to Shantou, Chen Jitang requested aid from the NNG. The NNG viewed this as an excellent chance to negotiate with the GPG a reintegration of the Customs Service. Director of Shanghai Maritime Customs Service, Tang Haian, was dispatched to Guangzhou. The NNG asked the GPG to cancel the Special Tax on Imported Rice by integrating it into the rice import tariff on the condition of promising all revenue from the rice import tariff in Guangdong to the GPG. In addition, the Finance Minister, Kong Xiangxi, visited Guangzhou to suggest integrating the Special Tax on Sugar into the consolidation tax. This was an expression of the NNG's willingness to lose the tax revenue for the cause of reunifying fiscal administration. The GPG still refused to accept the NNG's proposal while it insisted that the NNG recognize the Special Tax as an independent provincial tax.[65]

One month after the Shantou Incident, agreement was reached on 14 October 1935, and Jieyang county returned the confiscated goods to the Japanese owners on the condition of confirming that all Chinese buyers

62 For the detailed reaction of Japan against Chinese tariff autonomy, see Kubo Tōru, *Senkanki chūgoku "jiritsueno mosaku"*, chap.14; Na Hyŏn-su, "Pukpŏl ch'ogi kungminjŏngbu ŭi taeoe gwan'gye ŭi chŏn'gae," 303.

63 Mizuzawa Kōsaku, Consul General of Hong Kong→Hirota Kōki, 16 September 1935, E.1.3.2.1-2-1.

64 *Shenbao*, 4 October 1935.

65 Harada Chūichirō→Hirota Kōki, 20 September 1935, E.1.3.2.1-2-1; Harada Chūichirō→Arita Hachirō, 17 April 1936, E.1.3.2.1-2-1.

would first pay the Special Tax before taking imports from foreign importers. Nevertheless, this was only a temporary concession. From then on, anti-Japanese sentiment in Shantou was growing. Tensions escalated with the detention of Japanese merchants and clerks, assaults on Chinese employees working for Japanese companies, and bloody clashes between Taiwanese and crackdown squads. These did not end until the collapse of Chen Jitang's regime in July 1936.[66]

The NNG's adjustment of the Special Tax after retaking Guangdong in 1936

After Chen Jitang went into exile on 18 July 1936, following the coup's failure, the NNG reorganized the GPG to carry out the task of centralization. One of the priorities on its agenda was fiscal reform, especially a redefinition of national and local taxes from the existing taxes in Guangdong.[67] The Special Tax on Imported Rice was absorbed into the tariff. Furthermore, the Central Bank of China decided to unify customs administration by establishing a branch in Guangdong province and assuming responsibility for overall business related to tariffs, for which the Bank of China was responsible in the rest of China.[68]

Song Ziliang, the younger brother of Song Ziwen, was appointed the new director of the DFG. The new DFG abolished 561 miscellaneous taxes, amounting to 26.1 million *yuan* between August 1936 and March 1937, and wrote off the overdue land taxes, which amounted to 12 million *yuan*. Beginning on 1 September, gambling and opium sales were banned, at the cost of 15.6 million *yuan* and 10.8 million *yuan* in revenue, respectively. These acts of benevolent and good governance resulted in a significant drop in

66 Lian Bingyi, "Chen Jitang Yu Hanmou shiqi Chaoshan ji zong duiri shijian" [Several anti-Japan incidents in the Chaozhou-Shantou district during the period of rule of Chen Jitang and Yu Hanmou], *Guangzhou wenshi ziliao* 4 (1961), 171–179; Chen Boren, "Caizheng he shuijuan," 299.
67 Kong Xiangxi, minister of Finance, repeatedly ordered Song Ziliang to carry out a clear- cut division between national and local taxes. "Kong Xiangxi zhi Song Ziliang midian gao" [Secret telegram from Kong Xiangfu to Song Ziliang] (25 July 1936), in Zhongguo dier lishi dang'anguan [Second historical archives of China], *Zhonghua Minguo shi dang'an zilia huibian diwuji diyibian caizheng jingji* [Compilation of archives on the history of the Republic of China, Collection 5, Part 1: Finance and economy, Vols. 1–9] (Nanjing: Jiangsu guji chubanshe, 1994), 682–683.
68 All the tariff revenue was under the control of the Central Bank of China from March 1932 (Kaneko Hajime, "Chūgoku no tōitsuka to zaisei mondai," 22). However, Guangdong's tariff revenue was deposited in the Bank of China until 1936 because the Guangzhou branch of the Central Bank of China was reorganized into the Guangdong Provincial Bank in 1932.

provincial revenue, which recorded a deficit of 24 million *yuan* in the first year after Song's inauguration. Without these two major revenue sources, the gambling tax and the opium tax, the centralized Guangdong province had no option but to appeal to the NNG. Zeng Yangfu, who succeeded Song and became director of the DFG on 10 April 1937, then asked for central subsidies to rescue the province from its finance deficit. One month later, 18 million *yuan* in subsidies was transferred to Guangzhou.[69] The Nanjing government's appeasement policy and aid to Guangdong saved Guangdong's finances, but provincial finance was transformed from self-reliance to dependence.

Nonetheless, unlike in the case of the opium tax and gambling tax, the NNG took a flexible and cautious attitude toward arrangements for the Special Tax. Although the merchants' groups requested the immediate abolition of all kinds of Special Taxes, the NNG's final decision on the Special Tax was unsatisfactory.

On 28 August, the DFG announced the decision to rearrange the Special Tax. First, the name of the Special Tax was changed from the "Special Tax on Agricultural Products" (*bolai nongchanpin zaxiang zhuanshui*) to "Guangdong Province's Tax on Imported Products" (*Guangdongsheng bolai wupinshui*). Second, the tax was to be imposed on imports and not on domestic goods in transit. However, there were exceptions. The DFG declared that all oils and beans transported to Guangdong would continue to be taxed due to so-called "special circumstances." Third, full abolition of the Special Tax was abandoned; instead, a gradual step was taken. Tax items that hurt domestic industry, hindered the people's livelihood, or interfered with central tax revenue were to be eliminated first. According to this standard, the GPG decided to abolish the Special Taxes on Imported Rice, Waste Rubber Tire, and Machinery, and the additional tax on imported cement. The Sales Tax on Petroleum was also abolished because it was considered double taxation. The previous 20 percent surtax was canceled. Meanwhile, abolition of the fourteen other special taxes was delayed. The Special Tax survived legally by enacting "the Regulation on the collection of all kinds of Special Taxes."[70]

69 "Ben shengshi ge xianshi caizheng jinxun" [Recent news about finance at all levels of cities in our province], *Guangdongsheng yinhang rikan* 1(1) (1937): 131; "Nankin seifu no kantonshō kinyu zaisei seiri no genkyō" [The current situation of financial and fiscal consolidation in Guangdong led by the Nanjing Government], *Tōa* 9(11) (1936): 92–93; Nakamura Toyoichi, Consul General of Guangdong→Hirota Kōki, 1 September 1936, E.1.3.2.1-005, Miscellaneous matters related to taxes and contributions in China, Vol. 5.

70 Guangdong caizhengting bishushi [Secretary's Office, Department of Finance, Guangdong], *Guangdong caizheng jiyao* [Financial summary of Guangdong] (Guangzhou: Guangdong caizhengting,

Merchants in Guangdong and Shanghai responded to this undetermined decision by calling for complete abolition. The Shanghai Chamber of Commerce in May 1937 and the Guangzhou Grain Association in July 1937 repeatedly appealed to the NNG for abolition of the Special Tax on Agricultural Products. Despite initial confirmation of full abolition, the NNG and the new GPG decided to partly preserve the Special Tax, firstly because of financial constraints and secondly to block grain imports by the Japanese occupying the Northeast. Shanghai merchants complained that the NNG gave preferential treatment to Guangdong to appease the local people.[71]

Moreover, on 1 April 1938, nine months after full-scale war between China and Japan broke out, the GPG declared a special tax on domestic goods shipped from Japanese-occupied areas, including Beijing and Tianjin, Nanjing, and Shanghai. In addition, the name of the special tax was changed to an "entry tax on cargo from lost territory" (*shidi huowu rukoushui*). Director of the DFG, Zeng Yangfu, stressed the inevitability of taxation to prevent "smuggling" of Japanese products repackaged as domestic products by Japanese merchants. Taxation on domestic goods entering Guangdong was perfectly legal at this time.

Interestingly, the name of the special tax itself soon reappeared. The GPG finally revived the Special Tax in 1939. From 1 June 1939, "Wartime Tax Regulations for the Guangdong Special Tax on Imported Products" (*Guangdongsheng bolai wuchan zhuanshui zhanshi shuize*) were enacted. The object of this taxation as stipulated in Article 1 included not only imported foreign products but also products entering from the rest of China and products entering from Communist territory in Guangdong. Twelve items were subject to the Special Tax: imported agricultural products, imported timber, cosmetics and decorations, toys, imported glass and metal products, rubber-made goods, pigments, foreign paper, imported clothes, imported sugar, imported leather, confectionery, seafood, and wax. There were no differences between the Special Tax items during the Chen Jitang period in terms of the name of the tax, the nature of taxation, and the taxed items.[72]

1937), 57; *Shenbao*, 31 July 1936. The order to abolish the Sales Tax on Petroleum was not implemented. The share of the Sales Tax on Petroleum to the total industrial and commercial tax revenue increased from 7.46 percent (1933–1936) to 7.72 percent (1937–1941). *Guangdongsheng zhi: Caizheng zhi*, 81.

71 "Yuesheng nongchanshui yijiu cunzai" [Guangdong agricultural tax still exists], *Yinhang zhoubao* 21(21) (1937): 7–8.

72 Guangdongsheng caizhengting, ed., *Guangdongsheng bolai wuchan zhuanshui zhanshi shuize* [Wartime Tax Regulations for the Guangdong Special Tax on Imported Products], printed on 1 January 1940 (collection of Sun Yat-sen Library, Guangzhou).

The term Special Tax could still be found in the "Regulations on Guangdong Local Taxes" (*Guangdongsheng difang shuize*) published in 1943. There were seven Special Taxes, including on sugar (16 January 1940), on paper (10 February 1941), on wax (1 January 1941), on cassia and cassia-made products (1 June 1942), on beans (*youdou*, 17 June 1941), on pigment (19 November 1941), and on rubber and rubber-made products (19 November 1941).[73]

In sum, after the NNG retook Guangdong the Special Tax was gradually reinstated in the Guangdong tax system. The reason that the Special Tax reappeared was down to nothing more than the onset of serious financial difficulties and the Sino-Japanese War. In terms of fiscal unification, as in other areas, the Sino-Japanese War seriously interrupted the NNG's state-building and state integration efforts. Central government subsidies were the only alternative to compensate for the projected losses after overall abolition of the Special Tax. These did not end until the conclusion of the war.

From the perspective of Cantonese traditional concept, however, there may be another explanation for the continued survival of the special tax in Guangdong. Okamoto Takashi points out that trade with Southeast Asia had long been categorized as domestic trade under the Canton system of the Qing. He contrasts this with the Shanghai system that was built up with the modern Maritime Customs Service, which clearly divided trade between domestic and international on the basis of borders.[74] The ambiguity between "in" and "out" in terms of tariffs might have persisted in Guangdong society, which was deeply connected with Southeast Asia both in terms of labor and trade. It may be the case that the rest of China was more "out" of Guangdong than Southeast Asia was.

This explanation may appear to go too far. However, the Special Tax on Rice highlights the complicated and conflicting rivalry in taxation between the GPG, Guangdong merchants, and Shanghai merchants as representatives of merchants in the rest of China. In addition, taxation on rice was also closely related to the food supply and livelihood of local society, leading to the nationwide controversies on it. By focusing on the Special Tax on Rice, the next chapter will discuss the special taxes from another perspective.

73 Zai kanton nihon taishikan jimusho [Office of the Embassy of Japan in Guangdong], ed., *Kantonshō chihōzei zeisoku* [Local tax regulations in Guangdong province], Guangzhou: printed in November 1943 (collection of Sun Yat-sen Library, Guangzhou), 79–84.

74 Okamoto Takashi, *Kindai chūgoku to kaikan* [Modern China and the Maritime Customs] (Nagoya: Nagoya daigaku shuppankai, 1999), 148.

4 Special Taxes on Imported Rice

Abstract

The controversial success in raising revenue in the 1930s Guangdong was the Special Tax on Imported Rice. This issue highlights the central-local rivalry in taxation and inter-regional conflicting interests between Guangdong and the rest of China. People in Guangdong have struggled to resist any tax on imported rice since the 1920s. But, when the central government in Nanjing began to levy a tariff on imported rice to raise the slogan of "food self-sufficiency." Chen Jitang regime in Guangzhou announced instead to charge the Special Tax on it. However, Guangdong merchants appealed that imported rice from Southeast Asia was not a "foreign rice" but a "national rice." Finally, the food crisis in 1936 resulted in the tariff exemption to Guangdong province.

Keywords: Special Tax, Guangdong, imported rice, food, self-sufficiency

Food supply in Guangdong province

Since the middle of the Ming dynasty, Guangdong province had been known for running short of provisions. According to Lou Tongmao's calculation, which was used in 1936 for the Guangdong provincial government (hereafter, the GPG)'s policy-making, the average yearly non-glutinous and glutinous rice production in Guangdong province was about 131 million piculs. In comparison, the amount of polished rice circulating in the market was only 78.69 million piculs due to the 40 percent loss in rice processing. However, applying the average annual consumption of rice per capita as 3.5 piculs and multiplying it by the population of 33,461,320 (1936), total rice consumption in Guangdong province was 117,114,651.5 piculs, hence a shortfall of 28,424,651.5 piculs. Other contemporaneous data, from the Agriculture and Forestry Bureau in 1935, reported that the total arable land area of Guangdong province was 23,897,804 *mu* and yearly rice production

Kang, Jin-A, *The Guangdong Model and Taxation in China*. Taylor & Francis Group, 2022
DOI: 10.5117/9789463725248_CH04

was 113,046,249 piculs. Both data reveal a shortfall in the food supply within the province.[1]

Table 4.1 below shows that the shortfall totaled 16,958,758 piculs, slightly less than the above calculation. In particular, the Chaozhou and Shantou areas were the most rice-deficient localities in the province.

Table 4.1 Rice production, rice consumption, and the rice shortage in Guangdong province, the 1930s (unit: picul)

District	Average annual production	Average annual consumption	Surplus (+)/shortage (-)
Central Guangdong	34,379,945	38,430,363	(-)4,050,418
Eastern Guangdong	31,554,382	39,398,666	(-)7,844,284
Northern Guangdong	13,136,620	9,561,734	(+)3,574,886
Western Guangdong	9,887,500	11,432,396	(-)1,544,896
Nanlu	15,275,000	22,982,086	(-)7,707,086
Qiongya	8,512,900	7,899,860	(+)613,040
Total	112,746,347	129,705,105	(-)16,958,758

Source: Lian Haowu (Alfred H. Y. Lin), "Ershi shiji sanshi niandai Guangdong mihuang wenti de yanjiu" [Research on the rice famine in Guangdong in the 1930s], *Zhongguo jingjishi yanjiu* 4 (1996): 11, Table 1

The main strategy for filling this shortage was importing rice and grains from Southeast Asia (*yangmi* and *yanggu*). According to statistics of the Chinese Maritime Service, the total amount of rice imported to China from abroad during the twenty-seven years from 1910 to 1936 was 321,873,456 piculs, with an average of 11,921,242 piculs per year. However, Guangdong province imported 212,077,106 piculs during the same period, with a yearly average of 7,854,710 piculs, accounting for 65.88 percent of China's total rice imports. During these twenty-seven years (1910–1936), there were six years when Guangdong province imported more than 10 million piculs of rice, eight years when Guangdong's rice imports exceeded 80 percent of China's total rice imports, and fifteen years when Guangdong imports exceeded 70 percent of China's total rice imports. In short, Guangdong was the biggest rice import market in China.[2]

1 Min Shu, "Guangdong shiliang wenti zhi jiantao" [Examination of the food problem in Guangdong], *Xin Guangdong* 38 (1936): 23–24. *Xin Guangdong*, 38.

2 Guangdong nonglinju [Bureau of Agriculture and Forestry of Guangdong Province], "Yuesheng migu zengchan wunian jihua" [The Five-Year Plan to increase rice and grain production in Guangdong province], *Yinhang zhoubao* 22(15) (1938): 7–9.

The first rice imports to Guangdong province took place in 1722 when 300,000 *shi* of rice was imported into Fujian, Guangdong, and Ningbo as a form of tributary trade to solve the food shortages. Because food provision was related to the people's livelihood, the rice imports were tax-free from 1722 until 1933.[3]

The rice import business from Thailand was initially dominated by Amoy merchants in Fujian province. However, by the mid-eighteenth century, the merchants of Chaozhou in Guangdong province had the upper hand. The success of the Chaozhou merchants' business was stimulated firstly by the surge of Chaozhou immigrants to Thailand from the seventeenth century onwards, and secondly by the Qing policy of allowing rice imports to solve the chronic food shortages in southern China.[4] Out of Thailand's population of 20 million in the 1930s, about 3 million were Chinese, most of whom had come from Chaozhou. The Thai Chinese were not only rice farmers but also rice millers, and they dominated the rice-processing industry. In other words, the so-called foreign rice was produced and transported to China by other Chinese. About 70 percent of the imported foreign rice until 1920 was sold in Guangdong.[5]

However, initially the amount of imported rice did not surpass the amount domestic rice in the Guangdong market. The middle and upper reaches of the Yangtze River were the largest rice-producing areas in Qing China. For example, in 1881, merchants from Guangzhou and Zhaoqing prefectures were the biggest buyers of rice in Wuhu, the largest rice market along the Yangtze River.

Over time, Guangdong's rice market gradually came to be dominated by overseas products.[6] First, imported rice was good quality, cheap in price, and convenient for transportation, even though the freight rate varied according to the distance. Furthermore, in the case of domestic rice, the many *likin* tax checkpoints before entering Guangdong province

3 Some research argues that the tax exemption began on exported rice began with the Exemption in 1728 by the Yongzheng emperor. Lian Haowu (Alfred H. Y. Lin), "Ershi shiji sanshi niandai Guangdong mihuang wenti de yanjiu" [Research on the rice famine in Guangdong in the 1930s], *Zhongguo jingjishi yanjiu* 4 (1996):17.

4 Hamashita Takeshi, "Imin to shōgyō nettowāku: chōshū gurūpu no taiimin to hongoku sōkin" [Immigration and commercial network: Chaozhou immigrants in Thailand and their remittances to China], *Tōbunken kiyō* 116 (1992): 63–69.

5 Thereafter, foreign rice made rapid inroads in the Shanghai market. The rice industry in the three largest rice exporting countries, Thailand, Vietnam, and Burma, was controlled by overseas Chinese, especially Chaozhou immigrants. *Shenbao*, 9 October 1933, 26 February 1934.

6 Sheng Huanming, "Yuesheng yang gumi mianshui wenti" [The controversy over tax exemptions on foreign rice and grain in Guangdong province], *Yinhang zhoubao* 21(16) (1937): 13–19.

levied miscellaneous taxes to raise market prices. Second, the domestic transportation routes were underdeveloped. Prior to 1936, the Yuehan (Guangzhou to Hankou) railway had not been completed. Merchants had to transport rice purchased in Wuhu, Hubei, and Anhui via Shanghai by sea. At that time, the seacoast between Shanghai and Guangzhou was dominated by three foreign steamship companies: the China Coast Steam Navigation Company (founded by Jardine, Matherson & Co.), the China Navigation Company (founded by Butterfield & Swire Co.), and the Nisshin Kisen Kaisha (of Nissin Steamship Co.). Shipping rates were expensive, and contracts favored these companies. In contrast, through Hong Kong dealers, merchants in Guangdong could buy as much Southeast Asian rice as they needed. The distance between Hong Kong and Guangzhou was short enough to complete the trip within a day, which helped merchants to respond in a timely manner to market changes. The rice trade was highly competitive, so timeliness and a stable supply were most important. Third, the existence of non-economic obstacles in the domestic rice market was also a factor driving Guangdong merchants toward foreign rice. Provincial governments often banned rice exports if food shortages were expected. Hence, unilateral reliance on domestic rice could negatively affect people's livelihoods in Guangdong.[7]

As a result, the import of foreign rice in Guangdong increased to an average of 10.3 million piculs per year between 1922 and 1934, while the average amount of domestic rice transported to Guangdong dropped to 1.6 million piculs, accounting for only 10 to 20 percent of the total rice imports. Big companies in Guangdong opened branches in Vietnam and Thailand to buy rice, and small merchants bought rice from rice shops in Hong Kong. The two major cities to import rice were Guangzhou and Shantou. Rice import companies in Guangzhou were concentrated across the foreign settlement of Shamian. In Shantou, rice shops (*mihang*) gathered on Yongan Street, nicknamed "rice shop street" (*mihang jie*). The rice import business was closely related to the shipping and banking businesses. Capital for these businesses varied from thousands to tens of thousands of *yuan*, relying solely on native banks (*yinzhuang*) for their liquidity. More than a few native banks operated rice shops as subsidiary businesses.

7 Chen Boren, "Caizheng he shuijuan" [Finance and taxes and levies], in *Nantian suiyue: Chen Jitang zhu Yue shiqi jianwen shilu* [Days of the southern sky: Records of personal experiences about Guangdong under the rule of Chen Jitang], ed. Guangdongsheng zhengxie wenshi ziliao yanjiu weiyuanhui (Guangzhou: Guangdong renmin chubanshe, 1987), 294–305; Sheng Huanming, "Yuesheng yang gumi mianshui wenti," 13–19.

Therefore, a failure of the rice import business could lead to bankruptcy and financial ruin.[8]

As reviewed above, even though Guangdong's rice trade was mostly related to the people's livelihoods, due to its low food self-sufficiency, the rice business in Guangdong was characterized by instability because it was vulnerable to fluctuations in market prices. Consequently, imposition of the Special Tax on Imported Rice could have implications for Guangdong society beyond its fiscal meaning.

The campaign of the merchant class against the Special Tax on Imported Rice

Early attempts to impose a tax on imported rice

The governing authorities in Guangdong were well aware of the enormous expected revenue that taxing rice imports could generate. However, public opinion was strongly against the taxation on rice, the rationale being that it could harm the people's livelihood. An earlier controversy over taxation on imported rice can be found in *The Gazetteer of Guangdong Maritime Customs* (*Yuehai guanzhi*) published in 1839 and written by Liang Tingnan. Although there had been several discussions about rice import tariffs, the Chinese emphasis on moral principles kept imported rice exempt until the 1930s. The regime of Chen Jitang was the first authority to levy a tax on rice imports. In 1929, the Department of Finance of Guangdong had tried to levy a tax on imported rice by giving the tax-contractor Lǚ Jingxi the right to tax so-called "rice crumbs."[9] But this attempt was blocked by a strong anti-taxation movement by rice shops in Guangdong and repeated appeals to the Nanjing Nationalist Government (hereafter NNG). Soon thereafter, however the Department of Finance, Guangdong province (hereafter, the DFG) drafted new tax regulations requiring a certificate for every imported rice transaction and collection of a stamp tax. But this move was also frustrated after a petition campaign to the NNG staged by rice merchants.

8 "Shantou mishi zhi diaocha" [Survey of the market price of rice in Shantou], *Chaomei shanghui lianhehui banyuekan* 1(1) (1929): 12–15; "Shantou lai chunmi Ji doubing shijia zhi yuce" [Prediction of the market price of spring rice and Soybean cake entering Shantou], *Chaomei shanghui lianhehui banyuekan* 1(2) (1929): 19–20.

9 The so-called "tax on rice crumbs" had already been established in 1928. *Shenbao*, 18 November 1928.

In 1931, the DFG started to collect an additional tax on rice piculs (*dantou fujiashui*) for the sale of imported brown rice and glutinous rice. Domestic rice merchants saw this tax as a de facto rice import tax and immediately launched a campaign against it. After negotiations between the Association of Rice Traders and the DFG, the rice traders collected funds to make a one-time payment to the DFG. Instead, the regulation's enactment was suspended.[10] However, it was later revealed that the brief suspension was only a preparatory step before the Special Tax on Imported Rice would be implemented. The GPG's repeated attempts to tax imported rice had failed because both merchants and the NNG shared a sense that they should not tax staple foods that supported the people's livelihoods. Nevertheless, the 1930s saw another strong moral appeal from a different angle, which would subdue this common-sense approach.

At the time of the dispute over rice taxation in Guangzhou, simultaneously there was a sharp debate in newspapers throughout the country over whether an import tax should be levied on rice. Confronting the traditional opinion of refraining from taxing rice, those in favor sought to find a broader market for domestic rice and to become self-sufficient in food. In 1929 the Shanghai Municipal Commission proposed an import tax on foreign rice to the Shanghai Municipal Government. In response, in 1930 the central government in Nanjing ordered that related ministries engage in joint research.

What set the stage for taxing imported rice was the steep drop in rice prices in 1930. Due to the severe drought, large quantities of rice and grains had to be imported in 1929. However, in 1930 a bumper crop, 40 percent more than that in the previous year, resulted in an oversupply and a resultant heavy drop in rice prices. The price of rice in 1931 was almost half what it had been in 1930. In 1931, in addition to the fall in price, economic conditions for the peasants worsened due to flooding.[11]

To help the peasants, five main rice-producing provinces in the Yangtze River Basin (Hunan, Anhui, Jiangxi, Henan, and Hubei), in conjunction with the Shanghai merchant groups, submitted a joint petition to the NNG that called on them to tap the domestic market for their rice by levying a tax on imported rice. They argued that the dumping of foreign rice had caused a

10 Liang Yong, "Chen Jitang tongzhi jituan de hengzheng baolian" [Tyrannical rule and excessive exploitation of the ruling group in the Chen Jitang regime], *Guangzhou wenshi ziliao* 16 (1965): 123–125; Chen Boren, "Caizheng he shuijuan," 303–304.

11 "Miye qingjin yangmi maifen jinkou" [The rice business circle requests a ban on the import of foreign rice and wheat flour], *Yinhang zhoubao* 15(14) (1931): 6–7.

plunge in domestic prices which had exacerbated the rural economic crisis. Moreover, if imported rice were to be taxed, they argued, domestic rice could help to regain the lost Guangdong and Guangxi markets.[12]

Ma Yinchu, the prestigious contemporary economist, pointed out that the crisis in the rural economy was due to institutional obstacles, such as the ban on rice exports and the reckless *likin* taxation that blocked market flows and led to the erosion of the domestic market by imported rice. Therefore, he argued that the government should not only collect a tax on imported rice and grain but also cancel the local bans on domestic rice exports and liberalize trans-provincial rice trade. Nevertheless, the immediate attention of the public was focused on whether or not imported rice would be taxed.[13]

Finally, in September 1932 when the Ministry of Finance held a conference on food for the people (*minshi huiyi*), Song Ziwen and Chen Guofu proposed their respective schemes to maintain rice prices. Song's proposal was biased on guaranteeing free trade: reducing taxes on rice and grains, collecting import taxes on rice and grains, encouraging banking loans for the peasants, and improving the farmers' purchasing power. Meanwhile, Chen's proposal was a more state-controlled and traditional solution, emphasizing maintaining a storage system to control food demand and supply. The final decision by the NNG in October generally followed Song's proposal to impose a tax on imported rice. Importantly, the import tax rate was to be calculated in accordance with the fluctuation in rice prices. If the price of rice was less than 9 *yuan* per picul, 30 percent of the import price would be taxed; 5 percent would be collected if the price ranged between 13.5 *yuan* and 15 *yuan*; and if the price was over 15 *yuan*, it would be exempt from the import tax.[14]

However, the GPG expressed its total opposition to the NNG's initiative, turning sharply away from its previous stance on taxing rice imports. The Southwest Political Council of the Nationalist Party opposed the collection of a rice import tax following the stance of the GPG. This autonomous party institution, independent from the NNG, was installed by senior party

12 "Zhengshou yangmi jinkoushui wenti" [On the issue of import duties on Foreign rice], *Yinhang zhoubao* 17(35) (1933): 1–2.

13 Ma Yinchu, "Cong weichi mijia wenti shuodao qianbi geming" [Talking about issues from maintaining rice prices to the currency revolution], *Yinhang zhoubao* 17(7) (1933), 5.

14 Taxation on imported flour, but not rice, was already attempted in 1928. Beppu Kumakichi, Consul of Shantou→Tanaka Giichi, Minister of Foreign Affairs of Japan, "Yunyū mugiko ni taishi unshōzei kafu kata ni kansuru ken" [How to levy the transit and sales tax on imported wheat flour], 18 August 1928, E.1.3.2.1-001. Chūgoku ni okeru sozei oyobi futankin kankei zakken [Miscellaneous matters related to taxes and contributions in China, Vol. 1], Gaimushō, Gaikō Shiryōkan [Diplomatic Archives of the Ministry of Foreign Affairs of Japan], Tokyo.

leaders of the anti-Jiang movement, who then backed Guangdong separatism until 1936. The issue reached a deadlock. On 12 September 1933, the NNG passed the regulation of rice import tax in the Administrative Yuan and submitted it to the Legislative Yuan for enactment. However, four days later, on 16 September, the GPG suddenly declared the provincial Special Tax on Agricultural Imports. On 19 September, the Southwest Political Council ratified the decision of the GPG.[15]

As a result, there was a split between the national and provincial governments in terms of taxation on imported rice. Beginning in September 1933, the Chinese Maritime Customs in the territory of the NNG collected import tariffs on rice nationwide, but with the exception of Guangdong province. The Ministry of Finance in Nanjing dispatched Chen Qilai, a director of the Consolidated Tax Bureau, to Guangzhou in early December to unify collection of the rice import tax, but the negotiations ended in failure. The NNG was forced to tolerate Guangdong's Special Tax on Imported Rice.[16]

After imposition of a tax on imported rice was aborted between 1929 and 1932, the GPG finally succeeded in taxing imported rice to increase its source of revenue. It was only possible by taking advantage of national public opinion in demanding taxation on rice imports and because of the policy decision by the NNG. In this sense, the Special Tax was possible because the GPG borrowed the authority of the NNG to suppress potential opposition by Guangdong merchants. It can also be attributed to the NNG's import-substitution policy, protective tariff policy, and the ever-growing nationalist sentiment of the National Goods Movement. The GPG used the issue of food self-sufficiency to promote the legitimacy of the Special Tax on Imported Rice among Guangdong's population and put forward the issue of food self-sufficiency in its Three-Year Plan. Integral parts of this plan included an expansion of rice paddies and improved varieties. To promote rice farming, 30 million *mu* of land (out of the 40 million *mu* of arable land) was allotted to rice cultivation. High-producing rice varieties were developed at Son Yat-sen University under the guidance of Ding Ying, the prestigious agricultural scientist and dean of its Agricultural College.[17]

15 *Shenbao*, 19 September, 1 October 1933.

16 Tsukamoto Tsuyoshi, Consul of Amoy→Hirota Kōki, Minister of Foreign Affairs of Japan, 18 December 1933, E.1.3.2.1-004, Miscellaneous matters related to taxes and contributions in China, Vol. 4; "Yangmi zhengshui wenti" [On the issue of levying an import duty On foreign rice], *Yinhang zhoubao* 17 (38) (1933): 2.

17 Yu Yanguang and Chen Fulin, *Nanyue geju: Cong Long Jiguang dao Chen Jitang* [The separatist regime of southern Guangdong: From Long Jiguang to Chen Jitang] (Guangzhou: Guangdong renmin chubanshe, 1989), 336.

Merchants' resistance to the Special Tax on Imported Rice

Once the GPG announced it would collect the Special Tax on Imported Rice, Guangzhou merchants dealing in the rice trade united to demand immediate cancellation of the tax. The anti-taxation movement was led by the chairman of the Rice Wholesalers' Association, Huang Yongyu. The Rice Wholesalers' Association had been established in 1928, but with origins dating back to the Hall of Nurturing (*yanghetang*), a rice merchants' guild in Qing China. In the days of the Guangxu emperor, Huang's father had operated a wholesale rice shop called the Rice Market of Harmony (*heji mishi*), which dealt with both domestic and imported rice. Huang Yongyu, one of the largest rice wholesalers in Guangzhou and owner of seven rice shops, was elected the first chairman of the association. He was a man of significant influence in Guangzhou business circles, being the chairman of the Automobile Trade Association, a standing member of the Guangzhou Chamber of Commerce, and chairman of the Guangdong Provincial Federation of Commerce. Above all, he had earned his reputation in Guangzhou business circles by leading the successful petition to the NNG to frustrate the DFG's two attempts to tax imported rice in 1929 and 1930.[18]

On this occasion, Guangdong's merchants cooperated with overseas business partners to defeat the GPG's taxation movement. Rice shops in Hong Kong stopped delivering rice to Guangdong province in protest after receiving a telegram about the taxation from the GPG on 19 September. Vietnamese and Thai rice exporters declared that they would not transport rice to Guangdong unless the Special Tax on Imported Rice was canceled. However, registration and taxation had already been imposed on cargo that entered Guangzhou from Hong Kong on 16 September. Thus, the Guangzhou merchants could not avoid a head-to-head confrontation with the GPG.[19]

On 16 September, the first day of implementation of the Special Tax on Imported Rice, Guangzhou's rice shops refused to pay the tax, and tens of thousands of piculs of rice were detained at a checkpoint. Huang Yongyu succeeded in reclaiming the detained rice through negotiations with the authorities and promising that he would persuade the merchants to accept the tax. Despite official concessions and issuance of an ultimatum to pay the

18 Liang Yong, "Chen Jitang tongzhi jituan de hengzheng baolian," 123–125.

19 "Yangmi jinkoushui jiang shixing zhengshou" [Foreign rice import duty to be issued], *Yinhang zhoubao* 17 (37) (1933): 8.

tax, the merchants continued to refuse to pay the Special Tax on Imported Rice until December. The GPG arrested Huang on charges of "tax evasion" on 20 December.[20] During his detention, the GPG succeeded in defeating the resistance and collecting the Special Tax on Imported Rice.[21] The reluctant acceptance by the merchants was, to some extent, because the rice import tax (tariff) was already being collected in the rest of China, and partly because it was difficult to resist a slogan to substitute import rice with "national" rice.

According to Article 3 of the regulation on Special Tax on Imported Rice (announced on 26 September 1933), the tax payment was a "buyer's" burden. It was a preliminary action against criticism from foreign countries who must argue that it was a variant of the *likin* or unfair tariffs. Accordingly, the GPG emphasized that this tax was to be levied only on Chinese merchants in the city. The taxation was based on the "Big Money" standard, and the surcharge on the conversion to "Small Money" was 30 percent.[22]

The tax rates for this tax were frequently revised.[23] Initially, the tax rates were 1 *yuan* ("Big Money") for one picul of imported rice and 0.6 *yuan* for one picul of imported grain. Meanwhile, the NNG set the tariff rates on imported rice and grain at 1 *yuan* (customs gold unit) per 1 picul, higher than the rate of the Special Tax on Imported Rice. However, on 20 March 1934, the rate of the Special Tax on Imported Rice was raised to 1.2 *yuan*. Less than one month later, on 15 April the GPG increased the rate by 20 percent to reduce the circulation of banknotes after financial panic in Guangdong had caused a bank run. On 16 June an official countermeasure to quell the financial panic was announced, in which the rate of the Special Tax on Imported Rice was increased again by 20 percent. As a result, the rate of the Special Tax on Imported Rice climbed from 1 *yuan* ("Big Money") to 1.2 *yuan* (20 March 1934), to 1.44 *yuan* (15 April), and again to 1.728 *yuan*

20 "Yuesheng juban bolai nongchanshui" [Tax on imported agricultural products in Guangdong province], *Yinhang zhoubao* 17(39) (1933): 6; *Shenbao*, 20 September, 3 October, 7 October 1933; Chen Boren, "Caizheng he shuijuan," 303–304.

21 *Shenbao*, 21 December 1933; Chen Boren, "Caizheng he shuijuan," 303–304.

22 Qin Qingjun, "Guangdong sannian shizheng jihua xia yi nianlai caizheng zhi huigu" [Review of finance during the past one year under the Three-Year Administrative Plan of Guangdong province], *Xin Guangdong* 15 (1934): 32–35; Chen Baozhi, "Ershisannian shengzheng sheshi zhi huigu" [Review of the performance of provincial administration in the twenty-third year of the Republic of China (1934)], *Xin Guangdong* 26 (1935): 18–19.

23 More than 100 kinds of agricultural products were subject to the Special Tax on Imported Agricultural Products. "Yuesheng juban bolai nongchanshui" [Tax on imported agricultural products of Guangdong province], *Yinhang zhoubao* 17(39) (1933): 6–7.

(16 June). The tax rate for imported grain also increased from 0.6 *yuan* to 0.864 *yuan* per picul.[24]

Consequently, the rate of the Special Tax on Imported Rice finally surpassed the customs tariff rate. During the first year of the launch of the Special Tax on Imported Rice from 16 September 1933 to October 1934, the GPG secured revenue amounting to 14,660,586.13 *yuan* (*haoyang* unit, "Small Money").[25] Even after 1934, the tax rate continued to rise. In October 1935, the NNG rate on imported rice was 3 *yuan* per picul, while the rate of the Special Tax rate on Imported Rice in Guangdong was 3.5 *yuan* per picul by the "Big Money" standard.

In April 1936, the GPG asked the central government in Nanjing to recognize the Special Tax on Imported Rice. According to a report sent by Japanese Consul in Shantou, the NNG replied, "this tax is a national tax, and recognizing this tax as a provincial tax will disrupt the financial system and the maritime administration." Instead, the NNG suggested that the central government willingly compensate the GPG for the loss of revenue from the Special Tax on Imported Rice if tax services in Guangdong could be unified with the customs administration.[26] However, this tax issue was not settled until the central government took over Guangdong province in 1936.

Changes in the structure of the Guangdong provincial food market

The tax debate was related to the issue of food self-sufficiency at the national level. When the GPG issued an announcement about the new tax regulation, Vietnamese and Thai rice merchants, the biggest foreign suppliers of rice, boycotted exports to Guangdong. As a result, rice imports decreased significantly beginning in September 1933. Initially, the GPG planned actively to purchase domestic rice in consideration of national public opinion, which required Guangdong society to exclusively use domestic products for the procurement of food. The product discussed at the initial stage was Hunan rice, and the negotiations started at the level of the provincial governments. On 29 September, He Jian, governor of Hunan province, sent a telegram to Chen Jitang, expressing his strong support for the Special Tax on Imported Rice policy and his gratitude for the large-scale buying of Hunan rice,

24 Tsukamoto Tsuyoshi→Hirota Kōki, 18 December 1933, E.1.3.2.1-004; Harada Chūichirō→Hirota Kōki, 8 October 1935. E.1.3.2.1-004.

25 Chen Baozhi, "Ershisannian shengzheng," 18–19; *Shenbao*, 16 March 1934.

26 Harada Chūichirō, Consul of Shantou→Arita Hachirō, Minister of Foreign Affairs of Japan, 17 April 1936, E.1.3.2.1-2-1. Santō mondai kome senzei [The Shantou issue: the Special Tax on Rice].

which was heavily stocked after a bumper harvest. On the same day, rice merchants in Guangdong contracted with the Hunan provincial government to purchase 1 million piculs of rice from Hunan through official-merchant joint management. But the next day, 30 September, Guangdong rice shops held a meeting of business associations to ask for a reduction in the tax rates and a change to ad valorem taxation.[27] This means that the merchants' final intention was to lower the tax burden, even though they could not resist the cause supporting the use of domestic products. From the standpoint of the rice-producing provinces, it did not matter at all if there was a Special Tax on Imported Rice or an import tariff. What was most important to them was that there be a market for their rice.[28] On 20 October 1933, the National Food Conference (*gesheng liangshi huiyi*), held in Nanchang and to which the GPG had dispatched Wen Zhongqi as Guangdong provincial representative, pledged to solve the food shortage in Guangdong by using domestic rice.[29]

The cooperation between Guangdong province and other rice-producing provinces seems to have worked well. However, changes in circumstances divided the two sides. The governments of the rice-exporting countries in Southeast Asia came up with various export incentives to offset China's tariff barriers so as to support the devastated rural areas due to the world depression. The Dutch government in Java exempted the export tax to maintain its competitiveness.[30] At first, in September 1933, Thailand, the largest exporter, drastically reduced its exports to Guangzhou and Shantou in protest against the Special Tax. Hundreds of thousands of piculs of domestic rice were transferred from Wuhu to Shantou via Shanghai to compensate for the decrease in imported rice. However, the rice crop in Thailand had flourished due to an abundant harvest, and the price of rice plummeted in 1933. Therefore, Thai rice was still cheaper than domestic rice in the Shantou rice market, even after adding payment of the Special Tax. Moreover, Thai rice exporters decided to cancel their shipping strike and to resume exports

27 In 1931, when the Anhui government collected a new tax on local rice exported to Guangdong, the rice merchants in Guangdong boycotted the transportation and purchase of rice from Wuhu. Further, the two merchant associations for rice and grains in Guangzhou held a meeting that decided to buy rice from Thailand and Vietnam (*Shenbao*, 27 February, 2 April 1931). This experience further strengthened Guangdong merchants' distrust of domestic rice and preference for imported rice.

28 *Shenbao*, 30 September 1933.

29 *Shenbao*, 18 October 1933.

30 Hu Shi, "Xinnian mengxiang" [Dream of a new year], *Dagongbao*, 30 December 1934, E.1.3.2.1-004.

to Guangdong after seeing the massive input of domestic rice in the market. As a result, imports from Thailand surged again beginning from November, with more than 66,600 piculs of Thai rice being imported every day.[31]

To understand the GPG's intention and the nature of the Special Tax, it is worth examining the ban on imported Thai rice in 1935, which ended in controversy. In protest against the Thai authorities' policy against Chinese immigrant laborers, Guangdong society organized an economic campaign against Thailand. As a result, the Food and Grain Control Commission (*liangshi tongzhi weiyuanhui*) in Guangdong passed a bill banning Thai rice imports on 30 March. In May, however, the Guangdong provincial government changed its ban on imports of Thai rice to a general rise in the Special Tax on Imported Rice.[32] In short, despite the Special Tax, rice imports continued, and the GPG's policy was more of a financial priority that emphasized the tax revenue from the Special Tax on Imported Rice, rather than an attempt to eliminate rice imports and replace them with domestic rice. Table 4.2 shows the ratio of domestic rice transferred to Guangdong province to foreign rice imported in Guangdong province.

Table 4.2 Import volume of foreign rice and entry volume of domestic rice to Guangdong province, 1930–1937 (unit: picul)

Year	Volume of foreign rice imports		Volume of domestic rice transferred to Guangdong		Total volume of rice shipped to Guangdong
	piculs	percent	piculs	percent	
1930	5,117,801	87.92	702,945	12.08	5,820,746
1931	5,448,802	75.19	1,797,650	24.81	7,246,452
1932	13,576,542	94.56	780,590	5.44	14,357,132
1933	16,974,581	84.16	3,193,781	15.84	20,168,362
1934	8,320,219	82.46	1,770,363	17.54	10,090,583
1935	8,169,390	89.97	910,798	10.03	9,080,188
1936	4,545,324	55.03	3,714,720	44.97	8,260,044
1937	5,068,974	47.44	5,616,868	52.56	10,685,842

Source: Lian Haowu, "Ershi shiji sanshi niandai Guangdong mihuang wenti de yanjiu," 17, Table 3.

31 *Shenbao*, 10 November 1933.

32 *Shenbao*, 31 March, 20 May 1935.

Table 4.3 Average price of domestic and imported rice in the Shanghai market, 1928–1937 (unit: picul, *yuan*)

Year	Price of silver (US cents/ oz.)	Price of foreign rice in Guang zhou	Price of foreign rice in Shanghai	Silver movement (1 million *yuan*)		Foreign rice import (1 million picul)	
				From Shanghai into the country	Im- ported into China	Into Pearl River Delta	Into Shanghai
1928	60.10	9.20	7.50	*	160	7.8	0.1
1929	52.0	10.50	9.10	58	159	6.0	0.5
1930	38.80	12.50	11.50	32	101	3.7	7.1
1931	31.50	10.60	8.70	53	68	4.1	0.8
1932	27.60	9.80	9.30	-143	*	9.5	3.8
1933	34.80	10.90+	6.30	-83	-14	11.9	0.9
1934	48.70	8.00	7.10	*	-280	6.1	1.0
1935	65.40	7.60	8.30	*	-289	5.7	9.7
1936	47.30	10.90	7.40	*	-290	2.9	0.2
1937	45.80	*	8.40	*	-398	3.2	0.5

Source: David Faure, "The Plight of the Farmers: A Study of the Rural Economy of Jiangnan and the Pearl River Delta, 1870–1937," *Modern China* 11(1) (1985): 28, Table 9: Import of foreign rice and related factors.
Note: + possible error. See the source.

Table 4.2 shows that the total amount of income/entry peaked in 1932 and 1933 and decreased after 1933, the year that collection of the Special Tax on Imported Rice began. However, considering the exceptionally high numbers in 1932 and 1933, the total amount of imports/entry from 1934 to 1935 was still about 40 to 50 percent higher than that in 1930 and 1931. Additionally, there was no significant change in 1936 when the NNG recovered control of Guangdong province. Consequently, the high dependency on food from outside of Guangdong province did not improve throughout the 1930s. The food self-sufficiency policy promoted by the Guangdong provincial government was insignificant.

The change in the composition of imported rice and domestic rice fluctuated along with the political changes. During the Chen Jitang regime, cheap imported rice continued to constitute around 80 percent of total imports and entries before and after collection of the Special Tax. But because there was a significant amount of smuggling between 1934 and 1935, the actual amount of imported rice was probably higher than that shown by the statistics.

The entry amount of domestic rice jumped to about 3.2 million piculs in 1933, a fourfold increase from that in the previous year. This reveals the attempt by the GPG to meet national demand and to use more "national goods." However, the entry volume soon dropped rapidly and returned its pre-1933 level. It was after the centralization of Guangdong province in 1936 that a significant shift occurred in the composition of the rice supply. The amount of imported rice plunged to half the level in the previous year, and domestic rice accounted for about 50 percent of total imports and entries in both 1936 and 1937. However, the amount of imported rice in 1936 and 1937 was similar to that in 1930 and 1931 in terms of absolute volume. In other words, the most significant change since 1936 was the surge in the entry of domestic rice into Guangdong.

Therefore, first of all, despite collection of the Special Tax on Imported Rice, the proportion of rice imports remained high and there was with no significant decrease. Second, Guangdong province's low self-sufficiency rate did not improve, but what did change was that, beginning in 1936, it relied on domestic rice rather than imported rice. Third, the food supply and demand structure in Guangdong province changed significantly from 1936 due to the great leap in the amount of domestic rice transported to the Guangdong market rather than due to a decline in rice imports.

Table 4.3 demonstrates price trends in the rice market of Guangzhou and Shanghai. The price of rice in Guangzhou was generally higher than that in Shanghai. It was only in 1935 that the price of rice in Guangzhou was lower than that in Shanghai. This might be attributed to the rampant smuggling in Guangdong, but it requires further investigation. In addition, rice prices in both Guangzhou and Shanghai declined in 1934 and 1935, despite the tax hikes on imported rice beginning in 1933. Because of the world depression, rice from Southeast Asia was dumped in China, further exacerbating the price drop. However, the circumstances of the rice trade changed along with the resilience of the Southeast Asian economies from the depression. This was a factor that forced the rice price in Guangzhou to soar, leading to a severe food crisis in 1936. The political crisis deepened the food crisis in Guangdong, which caused conflicts over finding a solution.

The food crisis and the conflicts over exemptions from the rice import tax in Guangdong

After the aborted coup by Chen Jitang in 1936, the NNG canceled the Southwest Political Council and integrated the Special Tax on Imported Rice into the rice import tax to unify the customs administration. Nonetheless, a new barrier loomed over the unification process. The new obstacle was not warlordism, an easy target morally, but stabilization of the people's livelihoods by securing food, a much trickier target morally.

The food crisis in Guangdong province and the "Sale of Hunan Rice to Guangdong" movement

Guangdong province, especially Guangzhou, had been suffering from severe food shortages since the spring of 1936. There were several reasons for the food crisis. First, the GPG's separate currency reform as opposed to the NNG's *fabi* (legal tender) currency unification in November led to the collapse of the foreign exchange market, where Guangdong legal currencies plunged. In consequence, import prices soared due to the heavy discount on Guangdong currency. Second, Southeast Asian authorities canceled their low-price policies because the dumping had almost depleted their rice stocks in 1934 and 1935. Third, there was widespread panic buying due to anxiety about food shortages and speculative hoarding in expectation of a further surge in prices. Those purchases drowned the rice stock quickly to hamper circulation in Guangzhou's rice market, further aggravating the food situation in Guangzhou. Fourth, as rice merchants in other localities in Guangdong or near Guangdong hoarded rice for speculative purposes, rice-producing prefectures in Guangdong issued a ban on rice transfers to maintain their local food supplies.

In March 1936, Zhongshan, Qingyuan, Dongguan, and Huiyang counties declared a ban on rice exports because of excessive purchases of local rice by outside merchants. On 22 March, the Wuzhou Chamber of Commerce of Guangxi province filed a petition with the Changwu county government to impose a ban on rice exports, arguing that Guangdong merchants' excessive buying had raised the price of rice in Wuzhou. Guangdong's rice shortage thus affected the rice market of the neighboring province of Guangxi. Ironically, the local governments' issuance of a ban on rice exports compelled the rice merchants throughout the province to rush to Guangzhou to buy rice. Most of them were merchants from Shantou and Jiangmen.

The Association of Rice Shops in Guangzhou, conscious of the risks of a rice shortage, requested a ban on rice exports from Guangzhou and a temporary exemption from the Special Tax on Imported Rice. The GPG rejected the demand for a full tax exemption but temporarily lowered the special tax rate by 25 percent from April to 21 May 1936.[33] However, the food

33 *Shenbao*, 29 March 1936.

crisis showed no signs of abating, and it deteriorated even further with the repeated occurrence of rice riots. The GPG was compelled to implement a tax exemption beginning from the end of May.[34]

In June and July, Chen Jitang's coup was quelled. After integrating the special tax's services with the Customs, the Customs office in Guangzhou started to collect the Special Tax on Imported Rice. This led to a strong protest by rice merchants in Guangzhou, who had enjoyed the tax exemption in June under Chen Jitang's regime. The new DFG announced that the exemption by the old GPG had been illegal and it asked merchants to pay the import tax, in order to "maintain the agriculture of our country and to maintain the entirety of the tariffs."[35]

However, the food shortage was worsening, and the protests by Guangdong merchants persisted. The NNG adopted a policy of appeasing Guangdong public opinion. The central government in Nanjing acknowledged a temporary tax exemption on imported rice from 20 July to 10 August, saying it was related to the "people's food problems" (*minshi wenti*). It was announced that the tax rate would be lowered by 50 percent until the end of August, to be followed again by full collection. Instead of making these concessions, the new DFG required that the Commercial Federation of Guangdong Province (*Guangdongsheng shanglianhui*) purchase domestic rice to solve the food shortage.[36] Thereafter, there was a confrontation over the solution to the food crisis in Guangdong province, that is, whether to rely on duty-free imported rice or to increase the transfer of domestic rice.

The governments and rice traders in the rice-producing provinces in the Yangtze River Basin and the rice merchant groups in Shanghai insisted on solving the shortages in Guangdong by relying on domestic rice. This group, which supported the exclusive use of "national rice," can be called the National Rice Group. Their specific solution or slogan was "Sell Hunan Rice to Guangdong" (*Xiangmi xiaoYue*).[37]

34 *Shenbao*, 5, 16 April, 9 June 1936.

35 *Shenbao*, 24 July, 3 and 10 August 1936.

36 *Shenbao*, 25 August 1936.

37 For the agricultural structure and food shortages in Guangdong in the 1930s, see studies by A. H. Y. Lin and D. Faure. Lin argues that there was a "virtual disappearance of an arable land frontier" in Guangdong and the lack of social and political power to promote agricultural production had led to the food shortage. According to Lin, the increase in rice imports resulted from rice shortages caused by the shift of cultivation to commercial crops to profit from foreign trade. On the other hand, David Faure argues that rice imports were not due to food shortages. Rather, farmers chose a reasonable strategy to improve living standards by consuming imported rice and cultivating commercial crops. Regarding the food crisis of the 1930s, Lin states that the food crisis was an agricultural crisis and had nothing to do with changes in rice prices.

In the spring of 1936, the rice yield in Hunan province had already reached three-quarters of its yearly average and was expected to exceed the record-breaking 1933 crop of 2 million *shi*. The year 1939 witnessed the centralization of Guangdong in July and the full opening of the Yuehan railway (*yuehan tielu*), the railway between Guangzhou and Hankou in September.[38] In particular, expectations from the opening of the Yuehan railway were high, drawing keen attention to the exchange of goods between Hunan and Guangdong provinces. The railway connection was expected to allow mass transportation and the sale of domestic rice to Guangdong. The line was 1,100 kilometers long, from Wuchang station in Hubei to Huangsha Station, a terminal station in Guangzhou, connecting the three provinces of Hubei, Hunan, and Guangdong. Completion of the entire railway route shortened the transport time between Hunan and Guangdong from six to seven days to about forty hours. Railway transport was also expected to

Therefore, the action to exempt the rice import tax failed to increase rice imports and to stabilize the surging rice prices. Faure attributes the food crisis to the Great Depression, the outflow of silver, and the decline in peasants' purchasing power, which was rooted in the downfall of the Guangdong silk industry. When Miyata discusses agriculture in the Chaozhou area during the Qing dynasty, he argues that the conversion of cultivated land from rice to sugar cane in the Chaozhou area was a rational choice by the peasants based on regional specialization to secure high incomes. However, it is necessary to review the food shortage with respect to the policy of the provincial government. In the 1930s, the Guangdong provincial government promoted a food self-sufficiency policy while it encouraged cultivation of sugar cane as a commercial crop for the Sugar Industry Rejuvenation Plan. As a result, this inconsistency between policies recreated the rivalry between rice and sugar cane in the Chaozhou area. Lian Haowu, "Sanshi niandai Guangdong nanlu de tudi liyong yu nongye gaikuang yanjiu" [A study on land use and agriculture in Nanlu district of Guangdong in the 1930s], in *Shisi shiji yilai Guangdong shehui jingji de fazhan* [Development of the social economy in Guangdong since the fourteenth century] (Guangzhou: Guangdong gaodeng jiaoyu chubanshe, 1992), 78–94; "Ershi shiji sanshi niandai Guangdong mihuang wenti de yanjiu," 10–20; "WanQing shiqi Guangdongsheng de duiwai maoyi jiqi dui nongcun shehui jingji de yingxiang" [Foreign trade in Guangdong and its impact on the rural social economy in the late Qing period], *Qingdai quyu shehui jingji yanjiu (xia)* [Research on the regional social economy in the Qing dynasty. Vol. 2], ed. Ye Xianen (Beijing: Zhonghua shuju,1992), 1165–1192; David Faure, "The Flight of Farmers: A Study of the Rural Economy of Jiangnan and the Pearl River Delta, 1870–1937," *Modern China* 11(1) (1985); Miyata Michiaki, "Shinmatsu chōshū chihō ni okeru satō bōeki no tenkai to chiiki shakai: Santō kō no ryūtsū jōkyō o chūshin toshite" [Development of the sugar trade and local communities in the Chaozhou region during the late Qing: Focusing on the status of distribution in the Shantou port], in *Kanda nobuo sensei koki kinenronshū: Shinchō to higashi ajia* [Memorial collection celebrating the 70th birthday of Nobuo Kanda: The Qing dynasty and East Asia], ed. Kanda Nobuo sensei kok kinen ronshū henshū iinkai [Compilation committee for the memorial collection celebrating the 70th birthday of Prof. Nobuo Kanda] (Tokyo: Yamagawa shuppansha, 1992).

38 Tang Qijun, "Xiangmi xiao Yue wenti" [On the issue of selling Hunan rice to Guangdong], *Yinhang zhoubao* 20(36) (1936): 27–28.

reduce freight rates. Yu Jifu, director of the Department of Construction, Hunan Province, visited Guangzhou to consult on the sale of Hunan rice to Guangdong with the new GPG officials. The NNG helped this project by allowing the Bank of Communications to provide financial support. In August 1936, Hunan and Guangdong provinces succeeded in agreeing on mutual economic cooperation, announcing a "regulation on the sale of Hunan rice" (*tuixiao xiangmi banfa*) and the "principles for economic cooperation" (*jingji hezuo yuanze*). These regulations gave preferential tax and transportation treatment to Hunan rice, the establishment of a joint government–merchant company exclusively for this project, and the organization of a banking trust to offer cheap credit.[39]

Under the above agreement, two joint companies between the government and the merchants were established in Guangzhou (*xiangyue yunmi gongsi*) and in Shantou (*liangshang guochang gongsi*). Zou Dianbang, chairman of the Guangzhou Chamber of Commerce, and Zou Minchu, ex-director of the DFG and a founder of Guohua Bank, signed an agreement for a joint venture for Hunan rice transportation and marketing in Guangdong province (*heban xiangmi yunxiao Yuesheng tiaoyue*) on 8 September. The two sides agreed to fund the venture with 50,000 *yuan* respectively, to pool 0.1 million *yuan*, with which each company would transport and sell 100,000 *shi* (sacks) of Hunan rice in Guangzhou and Shantou. For working capital, the Bank of Communications would lend as much as 70 percent of the purchase price of 0.2 million *yuan* at a loan interest of 7 percent.[40]

However, once the first order for Hunan rice arrived in Guangdong via the Yuehan railway in November 1936, complaints poured in from all sides. First, the railway's actual transportation capacity was lower than expected because the railway service only ran one way, once a day. Daily transportation of about 100,000 bags could not meet the sharp decline in imports after the resumption in the collection of the rice import tax and could not stabilize the skyrocketing rice prices in Guangdong. Second, the quality of Hunan rice was inferior to that of imported rice. Despite the initial set of high standards for the quality of Hunan rice, the standards later continued to be lowered to collect rice in time to meet urgent demand. Consequently, the upper limit of impurities or moisture content in white rice rose significantly,

39 Tang Qijun, "Xiangmi xiao Yue wenti," 27–28; "YueHan lu yanxian wuchan diaocha" [Investigation about the products in the regions along the YueHan railway], *Yinhang zhoubao* 20(38) (1936): 5–8.

40 "Xiangmi xiao Yue yu Xiang Yue jingji hezuo" [Sales of Hunan rice to Guangdong and economic cooperation between Hunan and Guangdong], *Yinhang zhoubao* 20(38) (1936): 1–2.

which led to a worsening of the quality of Hunan rice. A third factor was the inexperience of the Hunan merchants. From 1921 to 1931, there were eight years when Hunan provincial authorities had banned rice from moving to other regions. Competitive trading organizations, such as rice sales organizations in Southeast Asia, had found it challenging to develop their business in the area of Hunan province, which fluctuated between being open and closed to trade. Although Changsha was the central rice market in Hunan, its trading volume was small and its sources of rice were complex. It was not easy to order and purchase certain kinds of rice in large quantities in the Changsha rice market. The underdeveloped and immature market system caused anxiety about the stability of the supply in Guangdong. Furthermore, as demand surged, the Hunan side raised prices and began to hoard. A lack of commercial morality created distrust among the merchants in Guangdong. This kind of unpleasant experience ironically revealed the advantages of the imported rice. In comparison with Hunan rice, there was a competitive and more market-driven system for Southeast Asian rice, which guaranteed quick delivery, a stable supply, and different varieties of rice. It took only two weeks from order to delivery. Quick delivery and intense competition in Southeast Asian rice market suppressed spectacular price hikes.[41]

The sale of Hunan rice in Guangdong resulted in the completely paradoxical effect on the Guangdong population of confirming the merits of imported rice. As rice merchants in Guangdong accused the Hunan side of being insincere, the Guangdong Provincial Government finally moved against this project. On 30 November, Huang Musong, governor of Guangdong province, and Yu Hanmou, the top military officer in Guangdong, sent a joint telegram to the NNG petitioning an exemption of the rice import tax. When this news appeared in the media, the rice merchants in Guangdong stopped selling Hunan rice, resulting in a dramatic drop in sales of Hunan rice in the Guangdong market.[42]

In the meantime, an incident occurred that disrupted the project. In December, Hunan rice waiting for delivery to the Guangdong market was seized in Changsha by the Bureau of Commodity Inspection (*Changsha shangpin jianyanju*) on charges of failing to be tested.[43] In fact, the bureau detained the rice because the merchants had refused to pay a so-called inspection fee. Therefore, transport of rice to Guangdong province was

41 Sheng Huanming, "Yuesheng yang gumi mianshui wenti," 13–19.

42 *Shenbao*, 1 December 1936.

43 "Xiangmi xiao Yue cheng wenti" [The problem of selling Hunan rice to Guangdong], *Yinhang zhoubao* 20(49) (1936): 5–6; *Shenbao*, 26 December 1938.

suspended. Rice merchants in Guangzhou and Shantou immediately announced the suspension of the purchase of rice from Hunan. Further, they openly demanded that the authorities abandon the project and cancel the rice import tax.[44]

This demand was rejected by the Ministry of Finance in Nanjing. In December 1936, the Ministry of Finance confirmed once again that the food shortage in Guangdong province should be resolved with domestic rice.[45] Because of widespread complaints about Hunan rice, the GPG sought imports of Guangxi rice, but the Guangxi provincial government rejected its proposal, saying that it would affect its ability to be self-supporting. At the time, the Hunan rice was still being detained in Changsha. Transport from both the domestic market and the international market was blocked, and the price of rice in Guangdong continued to soar.

However, just in time, a new movement emerged. Song Ziliang, director of Finance in Guangdong, decided to establish a new institution called the "Guangdong Food Regulation Committee" (*Guangdong minshi tiaojie weiyuanhui*), which was expected to be fully responsible for procuring rice from other provinces to solve the Guangdong food shortages. On 22 December, the regulation on the Food Regulation Committee was passed at a provincial administrative conference. The Guangdong Food Regulation Committee was to be managed by the standing committee consisting of fifteen members, including two government representatives and three bank representatives. The two government representatives were Song Ziliang and Zeng Yangfu. Unlike the project for sales of Hunan rice that was promoted by the Department of Construction, this new initiative was designed and executed by the Department of Finance.[46] Liu Weichi, director of the Department of Construction in Guangdong, also submitted a similar proposal to set up a new institution to control the purchase of rice from outside the province. In Liu's proposal, the capital for the new committee was increased fivefold to 5 million *yuan,* and the committee was a larger and more powerful organization than the Guangdong Food Regulation Committee. After that, the Guangdong food market began to show signs of a controlled economy.[47]

44 Sheng Huanming, "Yuesheng yang gumi mianshui wenti," 13–19.

45 Uuknown editor and publisher, *Yue sheng yang mi mianshui wenti hui ji* [A collection of discussions on the foreign rice tax exemption in Guangdong province], Collection in the Sun Yat-sen library, Guangzhou (1937), 1–3.

46 "Yueshe minshi tiaojiehui" [Guangdong province's establishment of the Food Regulation Association], *Yinhang zhoubao* 21(1) (1937): 6–8.

47 Xiong Li, an officer of the Department of Finance during Chen Jitang's rule, was a member of the Economic Design Committee, participated as a government representative in the control

Meanwhile, the Hunan provincial government took action to reverse the negative opinions of Guangdong society regarding Hunan rice. Taking advantage of the opportunity for Song Ziwen, chairman of the National Economic Commission (*Quanguo jingji weiyuanhui*), to go to Guangzhou, the Hunan provincial government, on 26 December, dispatched He Haoruo, director of Finance in Hunan, to Guangzhou. He Haoruo tried to talk with the Guangdong authorities through Song Ziwen. However, he did not have a chance to meet with Song, and his suggestion to the GPG about barter trade between the two provinces ended in failure.[48]

The rise of Song Ziwen during this process is noteworthy. Considering Song's complete control over the sale of rice in Guangdong province thereafter, the Guangdong Food Regulation Committee's establishment in December 1936 might have been a preliminary step for Song's grand plan for food control and management of Guangdong. Moreover, Song Ziliang, director of the DFG and a planner on the Guangdong Food Regulation Committee, was Song's younger brother. The food issue in Guangdong, initially led by the Ministry of Industry, was left to Song Ziwen and the Ministry of Finance in Nanjing. Kubo's study on the tariff policy of the NNG points out that the Ministry of Industry led by Chen Gongbo eagerly advocated the protection of domestic industry, while the Ministry of Finance, led by Song Ziwen, made securing revenue a priority.[49] In some way, this classification matches that of food issue in Guangdong.

of commerce debate (14 September 1934) held by the Guangzhou Chamber of Commerce, and supported the government's control of commercial activities. *Shishanghui zhoukan* 18(21) (September 1934): 1–5.

48 "Xiangmi xiao Yue cheng wenti," 5–6; "Yuesheng zushe liangshi zong gongsi" [Guangdong province sets up a Food company], *Yinhang zhoubao* 20(48) (1936): 2–3. When the sale of Hunan rice was put on hold, representatives from Jiangxi, Hubei, and Fujian provinces rushed to Guangzhou to promote their rice.

49 Kubo Tōru, "Chūgoku kokumin seifu ni yoru kanzei seisaku kettei katei no bunseki: 1932. 1934 nen" [Analysis of the tariff process: Policy-making of the Nationalist government of China, 1932–1934], *Tōyō bunka kenkyūjo* 92 (1983), 184–185; Kubo Tōru, "Kokumin seifu no yushutsu sokushin seisaku to chūka kōgyō kokugai bōeki kyōkai: 1930 nendai chūgoku ni okeru yushutsu shikō kōgyōka no mosaku" [The export promotion policy of the Nationalist government and the Chinese Industrial Foreign Trade Association: The Search for export-oriented industrialization in China in the 1930s], *Tōyō bunka kenkyūjo* 100 (1987): 81–113. There has been a long-standing academic debate over the extent to which the policy of the NNG reflected the interests of the capitalists. Kaneko Hajime, "Sanhai shihonka kaikyū to kokumintō tōchi" [The Shanghai capitalist class and Kuomintang governance (1927–29)], *Shigaku kenkyū* 176 (1987); Kubo Tōru, "1930 nendai chūgoku no kanzei seisaku toshihonka kaikyū" [China's tariff policy and the capitalist class in the 1930s], 42–64. *Shakakeizai shigaku* 47(1) (1981); Parks Coble, Jr., *The Shanghai Capitalists and the Nationalist Government, 1927–1937* (Cambridge: Harvard University Press, 1986). It was not

The project for the sale of Hunan rice in Guangdong was forced to retreat significantly from its original goal, and the complete substitution of imported rice in the Guangdong market was abandoned.[50] Which side was responsible for the failure of the project? Despite the transfer of responsibility between the two sides, Guangdong and Hunan provinces made no concessions, each putting their local interests first. The differences lie in the logic of rationalizing their self-interest. The GPG's argument was based on the market advantages between imported rice and domestic rice to stabilize the people's livelihood, while Hunan province's argument was based on the issue of self-sufficiency and nationalistic sentiments about supporting domestic rice.

The food problem in Guangdong province entered a new stage in 1937 when the GPG petitioned the NNG for exemption of the rice import tax, thus reviving the increasingly fierce controversy over the tax exemption.

The petition movement for exemptions from the rice import tax and the backlash

The first united petition was submitted by Yu Hanmou and Huang Musong on 30 November 1936. In January 1937, four repeated petitions were reported in the media. Entering 1937, the rice price in Guangzhou rose out of control. The rice price per picul in a normal year was 7 *yuan*, but in August 1936, it had already jumped to 10 *yuan*. On 19 January 1937, rice prices soared again, and Hunan rice prices in Guangzhou jumped more than 16 *yuan* per picul. Rice riots occurred frequently. The three rice and grain merchants' associations dispatched representatives to petition for a temporary tax exemption for imported rice to stabilize the rice market, arguing that the supply of Hunan rice could not meet demand.[51] On 21 January, the NNG announced a temporary action for Guangdong (*zanshi Yuesheng mihuang banfa santiao, banshui jizhang jinkou banfa*) that allowed 300,000 kilograms

easy to unify the interests of the capitalist class and the interests of the Nationalist government to produce a concept of "national benefit." There were various contending interpretations of the content of "national interests" within the NNG. Once China moved toward a wartime system in the wake of the outbreak of the Second Sino-Japanese War, the command economy—prioritising defense—was identified with national interests, which did not coincide with the interests of the capitalists.

50 *Shenbao*, 6 February, 15, 27, and 28 March 1937.

51 *Shenbao*, 1 December 1936 and 9, 17, and 20 January 1937; Quanshi (penname), "Yuesheng qingqiu yangmi mianshui wenti" [Guangdong province's request for a tax exemption on foreign rice], *Yinhang zhoubao* 21(3) (1937), 1–2.

of imported rice to be imported after paying only half of the import tax, while the second half would be recorded for future payment. Later, the upper limit of the preferential rice imports increased to 1.3 million piculs (78,000 tons).

By the end of February, rumors had spread that Guangdong would be allowed a complete exemption. Despite am initial denial in February, on 1 April the Ministry of Finance in Nanjing announced that it would grant a full exemption of the import tax on as much as 2 million piculs (120,000 tons) of rice and grain imported to Guangdong between 1 April and 31 August. The abrupt decision to allow the tax exemption and the enormous volume beyond expectations shocked the national rice group. As soon as the tax exemption was announced, domestic rice prices fell and sales dropped in the Guangzhou market. The national rice group, including the Shanghai Rice Merchants Associations and the governments and merchant associations in the five rice-producing provinces, organized a special mission to protest and lobby.[52]

In the process of the half-exemption measure in January to the full duty-free permit in April, there was a paper war between the national rice group in the Yangtze River Basin and the tax exemption group in Guangdong. The policy of the NNG was affected by political factors as it became more entangled in this debate.

The argument for duty-free rice imports

The group that demanded duty-free rice imports consisted of the GPG as the authority responsible for the solving food shortages, the people of Guangdong (who favored imported rice in terms of price and taste), the Guangdong merchants (who preferred the imported rice business), and the Southeast Asian Chinese who operated the international rice trade from production to distribution.

Rice and grain prices per picul in Guangdong, which were recorded at 7.7 *yuan* and 4 *yuan* respectively in 1935, soared to 16.6 *yuan* and 9 *yuan* in 1937. Qiongya region (present-day Hainan province) was in the worst situation because the price of rice per picul exceeded 20 *yuan*.[53]

52 *Yue sheng yang mi mianshui wenti hui ji*, 1–3.

53 Bogong (pen name), "Yangmi mianshui jinkou wenti" [Duty free imports of foreign rice], *Banyue pinglun* 1(5) (1937): 6–9; "Yang gumi yun yue an gao yi duanluo" [The case of transporting foreign rice to Guangdong has come to an end], *Yinhang zhoubao* 21 (17) (1937): 5. However, there were negative opinions against rice import tax exemptions within the GPG, expressing doubt that the rice price surge in 1937 and the food crisis was due to speculation by the rice merchants. Xiong Li seems to have held this opinion. He was released from his official position

Unlike most Shanghai commentators, Sheng Huanming, of Fudan University, contributed an article to Shanghai's influential journal *Bank Weekly* (*Yinhang zhoubao*) openly advocating an exemption from rice import tax for Guangdong.[54] He attributed the food shortages in Guangdong to internal problems of the domestic market, which failed to balance supply and demand. Furthermore, the Southeast Asian rice that had been imported to Guangdong for over fifty years had built up good credit in Guangdong, and many Guangdong immigrants were making a living by rice farming. In other words, in the eyes of the Guangdong population, the imported rice was being cultivated and sold by their relatives living in Southeast Asia. Therefore, both economically and emotionally, the imported rice was not a so-called "outside" product.

In fact, Guangdong rice merchants and Southeast Asian Chinese merchants appealed that Southeast Asian rice was not a "foreign rice (*yangmi*)" but a "national rice (*guomi*)."[55] The concept of nation was still in limbo as transnational connections clearly dominated the local economy and human networks. At that time, the NNG recognized the dual citizenship of the overseas Chinese, and Chinese societies in Southeast Asia supported the Nationalist Party and Sun Wen. The national revolution led by Sun Wen and the process of building the NNG can be said to have awakened Southeast Asian Chinese to the idea of a Chinese national consciousness. Against this backdrop, Southeast Asian rice came to be seen as "national rice."

This process of instilling nationalism and linking the merchants to self-organization was also applied to organizing the Thai Chinese, especially the Chaozhou natives. Chen Shouming, a Chaozhou native, assumed the role of president of the Chinese General Chamber of Commerce in Thailand from 1932 to 1936. Once the Sino-Japanese War broke out in July 1937, the Chinese in Thailand, led by Chaozhou native organizations, supported the

on the Guangdong Food Regulation Committee due to the merchants' strong protest against suspension of duty-free permits for 700,000 bags of imported Vietnamese and Thai rice. Rice merchant organizations claimed that Xiong Li intentionally delayed the tax exemption in collusion with the speculative traders. But others protected him and argued that he was falsely accused of being tough on rice speculation. It has also been observed that this was a fabricated case, reflecting the struggle over interests within the provincial government. In an interview with Wang Zemin, a retired researcher who participated in the financial takeover in the 1950 Guangdong operation, he testified that Xiong Li's corruption case was not genuine. The interview was held in July 1999 at the Fiscal Science Research Center, Department of Finance, Guangdong.

54 Sheng Huanming, "Yuesheng yang gumi mianshui wenti," 13–19.

55 Chen Xingyuan, "Zenyang fazhan huanan zhi shangye" [How to develop commerce in South China], *Xianggang huashang zonghui yuekan* 1(5) (1935): 5.

NNG by issuing national salvation bonds and transporting rice to Shantou at reduced prices.[56] Chen's argument fit the reality of the time.

Furthermore, Chen rebutted the national rice group's claim that a decrease in rice imports could revive the rural economy and improve the peasants' lives, and that China could achieve food self-sufficiency. Chen said that the current low price of rice in the rice-producing provinces was not caused by the oversupply of rice in the market and could not suggest the readiness of self-sufficiency. Instead, according to him, underdeveloped transportation and disintegrated domestic markets led to a wide price gap within China. He cited the example that the price of rice exceeded 13 *yuan* per picul in Guangzhou, whereas in Hunan, rice was used to feed pigs due to the collapse of prices. Actually, in Guangzhou, the price of rice exceeded 16 *yuan* per picul in 1937, while the price of rice in Shanghai varied from 7 *yuan* to 9 *yuan*.

Pointing out the low quality and high price of Hunan rice in Guangdong, Sheng Huanming concluded that the NNG's high tariff policy to block rice imports caused a shortfall in supply and led to soaring prices and the suffering of the people. He further added, "I cannot agree with raising the price of rice to exploit the people of Guangdong and to use it as capital to revive rural China."[57]

The National Rice Group

The National Rice Group argued that the rice price gap between Shanghai and Guangdong was due to a depreciation in the value of Guangdong currency and the soaring exchange rate between Shanghai and Guangdong. Therefore, once monetary unification was completed, the price of rice in Guangdong would be stabilized. Through April 1937, the Rice and Grain Dealers Association and the Shanghai Chamber of Commerce repeated their petitions to cancel the tax exemption for Guangdong. Li Quanshi, an influential writer, published an article in *Bank Weekly* supporting the National Rice Group's argument. His main argument against the tax exemption was that the exemption action would destroy the unification of the customs administration. He argued that Guangdong province's duty-free claim was due to nothing but local selfishness, adding, "If the taste of national rice

56 Hamashita Takeshi, "Imin to shōgyō nettowāku," 70–71. For the financial contributions of the overseas Chinese during the war against Japan, see Kikuchi Kazutaka, "Kōnichi sensō jiki no kakyō to chūgoku kōgyō gassaku undo" [Overseas Chinese and the Chinese Industrial Collaboration Movement during the Anti-Japanese War], *Rekishi hyōron* 549 (1996): 28–29.

57 Sheng Huanming, "Yuesheng yang gumi mianshui wenti," 13–19.

is not agreeable to their palate, they will suit themselves whether or not they eat it for a long time. " He claimed, "If saying that the interests of the Chinese rice business in Thailand and Vietnam should be protected, the rural interests of the four provinces, Hunan, Hubei, Jiangxi, and Anhui, should be far more protected."[58]

The joint protest letter submitted to the NNG on 9 April named 163 organizations across five provinces and Shanghai. In particular, the opposition movement in Shanghai was extremely enthusiastic. In a petition sent to the NNG, the Shanghai Chamber of Commerce criticized the tax exemption action, saying, "Even if we accept that food is scarce in Guangdong, we should seek relief within the scope of maintaining policies to protect domestic agricultural products."[59] At first glance, their arguments exuded an intense nationalism, but it would be misleading to interpret this enthusiasm as mere nationalistic sentiment. Shanghai merchants had a large interest in purchasing and transporting domestic rice to Guangdong. The National Rice Group was a conglomerate interwoven with business interests. It took up the cause of nationalism only to promote the purchase of domestic rice.

Both the National Rice Group and the Tax Exemption Group were trying to mobilize and reinterpret "nationalism" for their own interests. While the National Rice Group excluded the overseas Chinese communities due to the territorial border, the Tax Exemption Group interpreted nationalism only on the basis of ethnicity, thus including overseas Chinese.

Change in the Nanjing Nationalist Government's food policy in Guangdong

The NNG rejected the joint petition by the National Rice Group to cancel the tax exemptions. Political considerations to appease local opinion worked behind the tax exemption decision. Concerned about provoking Guangdong regionalism in the process of his takeover, Jiang Jieshi himself sent a secret telegram to Kong Xiangxi, in which he stated that it was crucial to prevent the Guangdong people from feeling that the central government had taken away their rights and status.[60] This policy decision undoubtedly had a

58 Quanshi, "Yuesheng qingqiu yangmi mianshui wenti," 1–2.

59 "Yue sheng yang mi mianshui wenti" [The issue of the foreign rice tax exemption in Guangdong province], *Yinhang zhoubao* 21(13) (1937): 3–6.

60 "Tang Haian baogao youguan Guangdong caizheng shouzhi qingxing zhi Kong Xiangxi midian" [Confidential telegram sent by Tang Haian to Kong Xiangxi, reporting on financial revenue in Guangdong], July 1936, in *Zhonghua Minguo shi dang'an ziliao huibian diwuji diyibian*

conciliatory overtone. However, there must have been another intention. In line with the tax exemption measures, the state's food control policy was placed on the national agenda by the NNG.

On 1 January 1937, the Ministry of Finance announced the official establishment of the Food Transport and Sales Bureau (*liangshi yunxiaoju*) as a government office specializing in coordinating and managing food production and sales across the country. A few days earlier, on 21 December 1936, the Guangdong Food Regulation Committee had been established. These two movements, one at the local level and the other at the national level, were interrelated. Moreover, in the following month of February, the establishment of the Food Transport and Sales Company (*liangshi yunxiao gongsi*) was announced as an executive organization.[61] This company, belonging to a private agency that would pool capital by attracting investments from banks, overseas Chinese, and domestic investors, aimed to balance food supplies and prices across the country. The backer behind this company was Song Ziwen, who said that when he had visited Guangdong, he had been inspired to establish the company. The founding members of the company, which was later renamed the Southern China Rice Business Limited Company (*Huanan miye gufen youxian gongsi*),[62] also included many high-ranking Guangdong natives in the NNG, such as Sun Zhesheng and Wu Tiecheng.

The Ministry of Finance chose a multifaceted relief system to mobilize all sources, both domestic and imported rice, to relieve the food crisis in Guangdong.[63] This policy shift sought to strengthen the state's food control, to ease the import barriers by recognizing the tax exemptions, and to shift the priority from self-sufficiency to food security. The impending war against Japan certainly worked as one of the factors behind this policy shift.[64] The priority during the wartime economy was to reserve as much food as possible in the case of an emergency. There are three reasons for

caizheng [Compilation of archives on the history of the Republic of China, Collection 5, Part 1 finance and economy, Vols. 1–9] (Nanjing: Jiangsu guji chubanshe, 1994), 681.

61 "Caizhengbu liangshi yunxiaoju chengli" [The establishment of the Food Transportation Bureau of the Ministry of Finance], *Yinhang zhoubao* 21(1) (1937) 6.

62 "Song Ziwen deng chouzu liangshi yunxiao gongsi" [Song Ziwenand others are preparing to set up the Food Transportation Company], *Yinhang zhoubao* 21(8) (1937): 1–2.

63 "Yue sheng yang mi mianshui wenti," 3–6.

64 It should be noted that the GPG did not abandon its original policy of prioritizing domestic rice. The higher risk of a full-scale war against Japan forced Guangdong to rely on food self-sufficiency. For example, as of August 1937, right after the outbreak of the war, a survey of rice stocks in Guangzhou showed 36,000 piculs of rice from duty-free imported grains and 1.26 million piculs of rice from domestic rice sources in other provinces. "Guangdong yuchou minshi wenti" [Guangdong planned to solve the peoples' food problem], *Yinhang zhoubao* 21(30)(1937): 4–6.

this interpretation. First, the policy shift to state control overlapped exactly with the emergency period from 12 to 25 December, during which the Xian Incident occurred and Jiang Jieshi was released after promising an active response to the Japanese invasion. Second, Song Ziwen was the leader of the pro-US and anti-Japanese clique in the NNG, supporting a war against Japan. Third, it was confirmed by the policy of NNG after the outbreak of the Sino-Japanese War.

Multiple actions to solve the food crisis of Guangdong finally succeeded, with the rice prices in Guangdong heading toward stabilization. However, the outbreak of the Sino-Japanese War on 7 July suddenly reversed the rice prices in Guangdong and drove them up once again. War caused the rice-buying rush nationwide. Rice merchants from the rest of China rushed to Guangzhou to buy tax-exempt imported rice. Rice brokers from Shandong province entered Guangdong territory to embark on rampant rice-buying, draining the rice market. Prefectural and county governments within Guangdong scrambled to issue a ban on rice exports, and people stockpiled food.[65] Unlike one year earlier, Guangdong could not expect a supply of rice from the other provinces, even if it wanted it. Under these circumstances, the state's food control system worked efficiently to secure a food supply, and the Southern China Rice Business Limited Company assumed the role of a control tower for provincial food supply and distribution. Rice merchants in prefectures and counties begged for their allotment of rice from the company's local storehouses. In October 1934, merchant associations in Shantou petitioned for a local allotment of rice and duty-free rice imports. In November, the Southern China Rice Business Limited Company actually released 10,000 bags of rice to merchants in Shantou to meet local demand.[66] Jiang Jieshi finally granted an exemption from the rice import tax in March 1938.[67]

However, it was just a matter of time before rice imports by sea would be blocked due to the Japanese occupation of the coastal region. Therefore, the

65 "Guangdong yuchou minshi wenti," 3–6.

66 Shantou shi Chaoyang gonghui changwu dongshi, Ma Zonghan, Deng Jieqing, Wu Huisheng, Hong Zijian, Lin Weimin (The senior members of the laborers union of Chaoyang district, Shantou)→Caizhengting (Department of Finance, Guangdong), 6 October 1937, 4(2)130(1) Guangdong Provincial Archives in Guangzhou; Lufeng xian xianzhang Ou Rujun (The Lufeng county magistrate Caizhengting tingzhang Zeng Yangfu: Director of the Department of Finance, Guangdong province; hereafter, the DFG), 27 October 1937, 4(2)130(1); Shantou shi Chaoyang gonghui changwu dongshi Ma Zonghan deng→Caizhengting, 3 November 1937, 4(2)130(1).

67 "Jiang weizhang hezhun yangmi mianshui ru Yue" [Chairman Jiang approves foreign rice to enter Guangdong duty-free], *Yinhang zhoubao* 22(10) (1938): 4–5.

GPG concluded that it should further strengthen control over food by shifting the focus of its policy from outside procurement to food self-sufficiency within the province. This transition appeared in the form of the drafting of the Five-Year Plan to increase rice and grain production in Guangdong (*Yuesheng migu zengchan wunian jihua*) in April 1938. According to reports in *Bank Weekly*, in February 1938 the GPG still focused on food procurement from outside sources.[68] However, at the start of April, the Five-Year Plan was published and the GPG established a Production Committee, suggesting bank loans to increase rice production.[69] This Five-Year plan aimed to achieve complete self-sufficiency in order to feed the 33 million people in Guangdong by increasing food production to 250 million piculs within five years.[70]

This transition can be said to have come about due to the wartime situation, when supplies from the outside were unavailable. Nonetheless, it should be pointed out that this policy was consistent with the food policy under Chen Jitang. To achieve future food self-sufficiency, the policy emphasized cheap bank loans to farmers, improvement of rice varieties at the research centers, and extension of improved technologies. The Agriculture and Forestry Bureau was the most active executor and planner in promoting improvements in crop variety during the period of Chen Jitang's rule. The focus of the Five-Year Plan in 1938 was on the improvement of varieties of rice. Although the food self-sufficiency efforts under Chen Jitang ended without positive results before Chen's resignation, the policy orientation and the previous achievements in improving varieties were handed down through the continuity of the bureaucracy.

In fact, the self-sufficiency policy of Guangdong did not materialize, and only the state's strong grip on food remained. However, this is not the end of the story. During the Civil War, Song Ziwen, who took over as governor of the Guangdong province on 1 October 1947, established a food monopoly organization, the Guangdong Food Economic Committee (*Guangdong liangshi jingji weiyuanhui*).[71] At the time, there was no greater leap between the state-controlled economy of the Nationalist Party and the socialization of the agricultural economy until the early People's Republic of China.

68 "Yue sheng she liangshi teweihui" [Guangdong province sets up special food committee], *Yinhang zhoubao* 22(5) (1938): 1.

69 "Yue kuoda zengjia nongye shengchan" [Guangdong province to increase agricultural production], *Yinhang zhoubao* 22 (14) (1938): 2.

70 Guangdong nonglinju, "Yuesheng migu zengchan wunian jihua," 7–9; "Yue tongzhi churukou maoyi" [Guangdong controls import and export trade], *Yinhang zhoubao* 22(20) (1938): 4–5.

71 Wang Song, Jiang Shimin, and Rao Fanghu, *Song Ziwen zhuan* [Biography of Song Ziwen] (Wuhan: Wuhan chubanshe, 1996), 274–277.

Part 2

State-led Industrialization and the State Monopoly

5 Industrial Building: Provincial Entrepreneurs

Abstract
The construction of state-owned enterprises is one of the outstanding characteristics of Guangdong finance in the 1930s. Chapter 5 focuses on the Three-year Plan for the Rejuvenation of the Sugar Industry in Guangdong. With the most significant amount of invested capital among government factories, building modern sugar refineries was most successful. To protect the government sugar mills, the Guangdong provincial government followed an import substitution policy to impose the Special Tax on Sugar Imports, which became a significant revenue source. However, the largest profits came from the sugar monopoly that began in 1934. Like the traditional salt monopoly, the government took control of local sugar products and control over the distribution of imports for sales by licensed merchants.

Keywords: Sugar, Guangdong, the Great Depression, monopoly

The construction of state-owned enterprises is one of the outstanding characteristics of Guangdong finance in the 1930s. Although there was some building of provincial government industries in the late Qing, the building of government industries during the Three-Year Administrative Plan (1933–1936) represented a significant success. In terms of the scale of investment and profits, Guangdong's building of twenty-four government factories was the biggest project in China in the 1930s. This chapter focuses on the construction of sugar refineries to analyze China's financial and fiscal strategy during this period. With the greatest amount of invested capital among government factories, the project to build modern sugar refineries was most successful. To protect the government sugar mills, the Guangdong provincial government (hereafter, the GPG) followed an import substitution policy to impose the Special Tax on Sugar Imports, which also

Kang, Jin-A, *The Guangdong Model and Taxation in China*. Taylor & Francis Group, 2022
DOI: 10.5117/9789463725248_CH05

became a significant source of revenue. The largest profits, however, came from the sugar monopoly that began in 1934. Like the salt monopoly, a major tax source in traditional China, the GPG took control not only of provincial sugar products but also control over the distribution of imports for sales by licensed merchants. The strategy of the GPG, which combined government factories and a sales monopoly to maximize government income, had a significant impact on the Nanjing Nationalist Government (hereafter NNG).

The declining sugar industry in Guangdong in the early 1930s

China had been a major sugar-producing country, with Fujian, Taiwan, Sichuan, and Guangdong as centers of sugar cane cultivation and sugar manufacturing that became important sites for trade with northern and central China. After the opening of the treaty ports, Chinese sugar was exported overseas until the 1880s. But with the development of the machine-processed sugar industry in Hong Kong and the increase in refined sugar imports, China became a net sugar importer in 1893, competing with Hong Kong sugar, Japanese sugar, Java sugar, and other imported sugars. In 1929, sugar imports amounted to 100 million taels, ranking as China's second-largest import item after cotton products.[1]

In 1933–34, China produced 5.28 million piculs of sugar, of which 4.73 million piculs were produced in Sichuan and Guangdong. These native sugars were all produced with manual labor by boiling and using stone rollers. Sichuan's sugar was mostly used to achieve provincial self-sufficiency, whereas Guangdong's sugar was primarily sold beyond the provincial borders. With 46.2 percent of the total sugar production in Guangdong exported for sales outside of the province, Guangdong sugar accounted for 85.8 percent of China's total out-of-province exports. Nonetheless, due to the decades-long decline in sugar manufacturing in China since the 1890s, by the 1930s the number of traditional sugar manufacturers and merchants had declined. The share of sugar exports relative to total exports in Shantou dropped from 60–90 percent in 1866–1891 to about 10 percent in 1926.

The experience of Shanghai sugar market, the largest sugar market in China, was indicative of the decline of Guangdong sugar in the domestic market. The share of domestic sugar products in the total sugar imports to

1 Shiyebu Zhongguo jingji nianjian bianzuan weiyuanhui [China Economic Yearbook Compilation Committee of the Ministry of Industry and Commerce], *Zhongguo jingji nianjian* [China Economic Yearbook], Vol. 2 (Shanghai: Shangwuyin shuguan, 1934), 139.

Shanghai plunged from 93 percent in 1867 to 0.96 percent in 1930. The rest of the sugar products consisted of imported sugar. In the 1930s, the Chinese market was mainly contested by Hong Kong sugar, Japanese sugar, and Java sugar. Hong Kong sugar had pioneered and monopolized the refined sugar market in China since the 1880s. Still, Japanese sugar made its way to China after the Russo-Japanese War and grew thereafter to become the most formidable rival to Hong Kong. In addition, the anti-British movement, ignited by the May Thirtieth Incident in 1925, ruined British business in China.[2]

Hong Kong had two representative sugar refineries: one was the China Sugar Refining Co., Ltd, which had been established by Jardine, Matheson & Co., Ltd in 1878, having taken over from Wahee & Co. The second refinery was Taikoo Sugar Refinery Co., Ltd, which had been founded by Butterfield & Swire Co. in 1881 and had entered into full operation in 1884. These two refineries dominated the East Asian market in the 1880s and 1890s. However, the China Sugar Refining Co. failed to recover from the losses caused by the anti-British boycott and was closed down in 1928, leaving Taikoo Sugar as the sole survivor.[3]

Hong Kong sugar lost the Manchurian and the North China markets to Japanese sugar because of the sharp drop in the exchange rate of the Japanese *yen*, slumping sales, and the Japanese military invasion. Moreover, the Java sugar business, which had supplied raw sugar to the sugar refineries in Japan and Hong Kong, began to export Java white sugar directly to China in the mid-1920s. By the early 1930s Java sugar outperformed Hong Kong sugar and Japanese sugar in the Chinese market. Java White was cheaper and similar in color to refined sugar, meeting market demand in China during the economic depression of the 1930s.

Growth of the sugar industry is a typical case of import-substituting industrialization in the economic history of the West. Due to not only its large population but also its loss of tariff autonomy, the Chinese sugar

2 For the long-term trends in sugar production and markets in Asia, see Jin-A Kang, "Kŭntae tongasia sŏlt'ang sichangkwa hongk'ong chetangŏp: sangin tiasŭp'olanŭn chisok kanŭnghanka?" [Sugar markets in modern East Asia and the Hong Kong sugar industry: Is the Merchant diaspora sustainable?], *Yŏksa pip'yŏng* 130 (2020). For statistical trends in Chinese sugar imports during the 1920s and 1930s, see Yŏng-gu Chŏng, "1902–1930 Chungguk paeksŏlt'angshijangŭi sŏnggyŏk" [Features of the Chinese white sugar market, 1902–1930], *Chungguksa yŏn'gu* 121 (2019); Hirai Kensuke, *Satō no teikoku nihon shokuminchi to ajia shijō* [Empire of sugar: External forces of change in the economies of the Japanese colonies] (Tokyo: Tōkyō daigaku shuppankai, 2017).

3 Sugiyama Shinya, *Nichiei Keizai kankeishi kenkyū 1860–1940* [Historical study of Anglo-Japan Economic Relations] (Tokyo: Keiō gijuku daigaku shuppankai, 2017), 208–209.

market became the most extensive free market in the world. However, the NNG in December 1928 regained tariff sovereignty and in February 1929 it raised custom duties steeply. The Chinese sugar market was transformed from a free and open market into a regulated and closed market.

The Wall Street Crash in the United States in 1929, which triggered the Great Depression, had different effects in terms of time and intensity in various parts of Asia. Japan and Southeast Asia, which had adopted the gold standard for currency, experienced an immediate economic downturn in their industrial sectors beginning in 1930. Meanwhile, in China, which had adopted the silver standard for its currency, the recession spread from the collapse of the rural economy to urban commerce and industry in 1932.

The sugar cane industry was hit especially hard worldwide. Unfortunately, when the abrupt global economic depression occurred, Cuba and Java, which ranked first and second among world raw sugar makers, were setting new records by producing 5 million tons of sugar in 1929 and 3 million tons in 1930. However, the global demand for sugar fell sharply in the 1930s due to the economic downturn. In the worldwide dog-eat-dog competition for sugar, there was a vicious cycle of overstocking, slumping sales, and low profits in the global sugar business. Against this backdrop, China, the largest sugar market in Asia, attempted to close the doors on its "open market."[4]

Conversely, this represented a golden opportunity to build the Chinese sugar industry. In 1931, the NNG announced a plan to build twelve major industries selected by the Ministry of Industry, one of which was the sugar industry. In cooperation with capital from Cuban sugar, the government planned to set up a sugar refinery in Shanghai with a daily output of 1,000 tons. However, the contract was canceled after Japan bombed Shanghai in the wake of the Manchurian Incident. In 1934, the Ministry of Industry, together with Cuba, announced a four-stage renewed plan to build modern sugar refineries throughout the country, including in Shanghai, Guangdong, Hainan, Sichuan, Hankou, and Chongqing. To protect the incipient domestic sugar industry, the tariff rate on imported sugar was raised to 27.5 percent of the import price in 1929, but it jumped to 150 percent after gradual increases in December 1930, May 1933, and June 1934.[5] Under this protective umbrella

4 G. Roger Knight, "Exogenous Colonialism: Java Sugar between Nippon and Taikoo Before And During the Interwar Depression, c. 1920–1940," *Modern Asian Studies* 44(3) (2010): 480.

5 Jin-A Kang,"1930 nyŏn chungkukŭi kyŏngchekaepalesŏ nat'ananŭn sŏngkwa chungang —'kwangtongtang'ŭi sanghaechinch'ulkwa namkyŏngchŏngpu" [Center and local in Chinese economic development in the 1930s: Launch of Guangdong sugar in the governments of Shanghai and Nanjing], in *Chungkuk kŭnhyŏntaesaŭi chaechomyŏng* [Reconsideration of the history of modern China], ed. Sŏultaehakkyo tongyangsahakkwa yŏn'gushil (Seoul: Jisiksanupsa, 1999),

of tariffs, which effectively blocked imports, the NNG attempted to build state-run sugar refineries to monopolize the domestic market, expecting that they would reap huge financial profits.

Despite high protective tariffs, this was very different from the sugar policy in Meiji Japan. In the production sector, the Japanese government, through government subsidies and domestic tax incentives, had induced private companies to invest in sugar refineries. Japan chose institutional control instead of operating state-run industries. The Federation of Sugar Industry deliberately regulated the production, distribution, and sale price of Taiwan raw sugar through the Agreement on Sugar Production Disposal and the Agreement on Raw Sugar Purchases.[6] This system had the effect of de facto market control. Rather than encouraging private companies, the Chinese government put state-led industrialization on the agenda as soon as it restored customs sovereignty. This shows that the priority of the NNG was to secure revenue. The high tariffs were not much of a benefit to the private merchant class. Furthermore, they were not welcomed by ordinary consumers, who as a result had to buy more expensive sugar. The result was a rise in smuggling.

Table 5.1 Sugar imports and smuggling in China, 1928–1935 (unit: 1,000 tons)

	Index (1929 =100)	Imports	Regular imports					Smuggling				
				Java	HK	Japan	Taiwan		Java	HK	Japan	Taiwan
1928	40	766	748	503	32	213	0	18	18	0	0	0
1929	100	777	759	546	38	175	0	18	18	0	0	0
1930	100	707	676	436	49	191	0	30	24	0	6	0
1931	175	684	610	399	42	156	13	75	48	0	24	3
1932	350	519	340	188	66	67	18	180	137	0	60	12
1933	350	420	252	153	36	60	3	168	130	0	36	2
1934	350	419	243	137	38	68	1	176	156	0	19	0
1935	350	413	245	93	26	106	20	167	128	0	18	2

Source: Hirai Kensuke, *Satō no teikoku nihon shokuminchi to ajia shijō,* 122.

285; "A proposal for the development of the sugar industry on Hainan Island," H. C. Lin→Messrs. Dodwell & Co., Ltd, 24 May 1934, JSS 5-1-9 (Messrs. Butterfield & Swires. Hong Kong (hereafter Hong Kong)→Messrs. John Swire & Sons, Ltd London (hereafter London), 3 August 1934, JSS 5-1-9. Attachment [3]) John Swire & Sons Ltd Archive, London University SOAS Library Special Collections.

6 Hirai Kensuke, *Satō no teikoku nihon shokuminchi to ajia shijō*, 38.

According to Table 5.1, after the first tariff rise in 1929 (27.5 percent of the price), the tariff rate on sugar had increased to 3.5 times its previous level by 1932. Official sugar imports, excluding smuggling, plunged from about 760,000 tons to 250,000 tons during the same period. In contrast, the volume of smuggling increased from 18,000 tons to 170,000–180,000 tons. Actual imports combining both official imports and smuggling were significantly reduced from a total of about 800,000 tons to 580,000 tons. Table 5.2 below presents alternative smuggling statistics.

Table 5.2 Estimated volume of sugar smuggling in China, 1933–1936 (unit: 1,000 tons)

Year	Smuggling estimates via Manchuria	Smuggling estimates via Hong Kong	Total
1933	25.9	23.1	49.0
1934	18.8	53.3	72.1
1935	14.9	22.4	37.1
1936	115.0	33.0	148.0

Source: Based on Nihon tōgyō rengōkai, *Manshūkoku chūkaminkoku no satō bōeki narabini juyōryō ni kansuru tōkeiteki ichikōsatsu* [A statistical consideration of sugar demand as well as sugar trade in Manchuria and the Republic of China] (Tokyo: Nihon tōgyō rengōkai, 1938), 35. Table 32.

The volume of smuggling in Table 5.1 is steady, without fluctuations, in the range of 170,000 to 180,000 tons, whereas Table 5.2 shows the volume of smuggling to be 50,000 to 70,000 tons, decreasing in 1935 and increasing significantly in 1936. Although the difficulties in compiling smuggling statistics should be taken into account, the overall trend might well be reflected in Table 5.2, where the scale of smuggling doubled in 1934, then declined sharply in 1935, but then increased again in 1936. These data coincide with the rise and fall of the state-run sugar refineries in Guangdong that fundamentally changed China's sugar market. Beginning in 1934, Guangdong province promoted provincial government sugar refineries via operation of its sugar monopoly. The GPG strictly prohibited smuggling and all private sugar trade that was outside of the monopoly system. But Chen Jitang's military officials brought in large amounts of Java and Hong Kong sugar, bypassing the customs in Guangzhou. They reaped enormous profits from the smuggled sugar that they then sold in Guangdong at the monopoly price. However, when the new sugar refineries began full-scale operation in 1935, the GPG strengthened its crackdown on private smuggling and reduced the entry of Hong Kong and Java sugar.

After centralization of Guangdong in 1936, sugar refineries in Guangdong were no longer favored.

Although the NNG regained tariff autonomy in 1929, import-substituting industrialization via the sugar industry remained unrealized in China by 1933. Protective tariff walls were put up, but smuggling was rampant, and the domestic sugar industry showed no signs of revival. The task of economic revival or rebuilding was handed over from the NNG to the warlord separatist government in Guangdong.

The push for the construction of modern sugar refineries by the Guangdong provincial government: Three-Year Plan for Rejuvenation of the Sugar Industry

Guangdong province, a former sugar exporter, had become a sugar importer by the 1930s. Its total sugar consumption was estimated to be 300,000 tons (5 million piculs) per year, which in the 1920s was met by 216,000 tons (3.6 million piculs) of native sugar (brown sugar made by traditional sugar-processing mills) and 144,000 tons (2.4 million piculs) of imported sugar. However, because Guangdong province collected the Special Tax on Sugar Imports to raise revenue, the official amount of imported sugar continued to drop. Imports were reported to be 112,860 tons (1,881,000 piculs) in 1930, 66,480 tons (1,108,000 piculs) in 1931, and 35,880 tons (598,000 piculs) in 1932. Combined with the smuggling, the actual volume of imported sugar is estimated to be more than 140,000 tons annually. According to a report by the Japanese Consulate in Guangzhou, 11,100 tons (185,000 piculs) of sugar were imported into Guangzhou from April 1932 to March 1933. Most of it, some 164,000 piculs, was from Java.[7]

After the anti-Jiang movement in 1931, Chen Jitang's regime struggled to strengthen military power by training soldiers and purchasing arms. In 1931, expenditures to maintain the military increased from 1.8 million *yuan* to 4.2 million *yuan* per month. By the end of June 1932, troops had already been in arrears for five months. The printing of notes was the easiest way to finance the military. In April 1932, the GPG issued Guangdong Defense Fortress Debt in as much as 30 million *yuan*, which was the largest

7 Kawagoe Shigeru, Consul General of Guangdong→Hirota Kōki, Minister of Foreign Affairs Of Japan, 19 June 1934, S5160-25, Kantonshō no bu [Guangdong Province File], Nihon Gaimushō monjo kantonshō no bu [Diplomatic Archives of the Ministry of Foreign Affairs of Japan], Microfilm Collection, National Assembly Library of Korea.

public debt issued by the provincial government between 1912 and 1940. In 1933, the GPG issued Guangdong Provincial Banknotes in an amount of 27 million *yuan* with a reserve of only 5 million *yuan*. However, the market soon discounted the banknotes, whereupon financial fluctuations and inflation followed.[8]

In 1932 discussions began about securing financial stability through industrialization. On 27 September, the Three-Year Plan, to begin on 1 January 1933, was passed by the Southwest Political Council. The key point of the plan was to find and invest in industries with low capital, high profits, and a fast pay-off. It was Feng Rui, chief of the Bureau of Agriculture and Forestry of the Guangdong Provincial Department of Reconstruction, who strongly recommended to Chen Jitang that they focus on the sugar industry.[9]

Feng Rui was a native of Panyu county, Guangdong, who had studied the Chinese agricultural economy at Jinling University and had obtained his PhD from Cornell University. He participated in the Rural Reconstruction Movement in Ding county of Hebei (the Ding Xian Experiment) before Hu Jixian, director of the Department of Reconstruction, asked him to head the Bureau of Agriculture and Forestry in 1931. Feng Rui believed that the collapse of China's rural economy had resulted from the invasion of imported agricultural products, so he strongly supported the government project to revive and modernize Guangdong's sugar industry. His goal was to achieve self-sufficiency, first in Guangdong and then in China. After Chen Jitang sanctioned this proposal, Feng Rui visited the Philippines in 1933 to sign a contract with the Honolulu Ironworks Co., an American machinery manufacturer, to build and equip a sugar factory in the Guangzhou district (later called the Xinzao Sugar Plant). In December 1933, Feng also contacted Škoda Works, a Czech machinery company that had just entered China, and in March 1933 he signed a formal contract for another sugar factory (later called the Shitou Sugar Plant). By offering favorable payment terms, these two rival companies continued to sell machinery and equipment for

8 Li Jiezhi, "Chen Jitang tongzhi Guangdong de shimo" [The whole story of Chen Jitang's rule of Guangdong], in *Chen Jitang yanjiu shiliao, 1928–1936* (Historical materials for research on Chen Jitang, 1928–1936), ed. Guangdong dang'anguan (Guangzhou: Guangdongsheng dang'anguan, 1985), 406; Qin Qingjun, "Minguo shiqi Guangdong caizheng shiliao, 1911–1949" [Historical materials on finance in Guangdong during the Republic of China, 1911–1949], *Guangdong wenshi ziliao xuanji* 29 (1983): 111, Table 13:
List of bonds issue by Guangdong province, 1912–1940.

9 Chen Shaoyu, *Guangdong tangye yu Feng Rui* [The Guangdong sugar industry and Feng Rui] (Hong Kong: n.p., 1937), 1–3, 8.

sugar plants and distilleries during the next three years.[10] Feng Rui could enjoy unconventionally favorable contract terms because sugar processing machinery was not sold during the global depression. This was the beginning of the myth of China "building industry without capital" (*wuben ban gongye*). In May 1934, the Guangdong provincial government officially announced the Three-Year Plan for Rejuvenation of the Sugar Industry (*tangye sannian fuxing jihua*) and declared construction of new state-run sugar factories and a sugar monopoly within the province. As of 1933, only small-scale private sugar mills that used stone rollers and boilers to produce brown native sugar operated in Guangdong. Six mechanized sugar factories were built between 1934 and 1936. To ensure a stable and uninterrupted supply of raw material and to encourage farmers to cultivate more sugar cane, the government distributed better seeds for free and provided credit loans of 25 *yuan* per mu. The total amount of loans to the sugar farms increased from 398,000 *yuan* in 1934 to 700,000 *yuan* in 1935 and 108,000 *yuan* by September 1936.[11]

According to the account books, before 1936 Feng Rui and the GPG financed this project by investing 9 million US dollars (about 40 million *yuan*) in the sugar factories (other sources claim that 50 million *yuan* was spent on actual construction of the factories). This amount is equivalent to the total annual income of the GPG, which ranged from 40 million to 60 million *yuan* in the 1930s. Initially, Feng Rui and the GPG requested that Song Ziwen, minister of Finance of the NNG, lend the money on behalf of industrial reconstruction, but this request was rejected. In the end, funds had to be procured from within the province. The main source was the newly

10 According to the Škoda documents in Czech, the order to establish the Shitou Sugar Factory (C. Antonio, Sze-Tow) was decided in January 1934, and the official contract was signed in March 1934. Construction of the Shunde Sugar Factory (San Pedro, Shuntak) was completed in 1935. In March 1935, construction of a third factory, the Dongguan Sugar Plant (Santa Anna, Tung Koon), was signed between Škoda and the GPG. In March 1936, the most important contract was signed, a project to double the size of the Shitou Sugar Factory. The contract price amounted to 25 million crowns, accounting for half the total sales of Škoda in China in 1936. The Honolulu Ironworks Co. built the Huiyang Sugar Factory (Waichow, Ping Tam), but Škoda won the contract for parts procurement. Aleš Skřivan, "Škodovy závody a výstavba cukrovarů v Číně před druhou světovou válkou" (Skoda Works and the construction of sugar refineries in China before World War II), *ICaŘ* 127(11) (2011): 363. The Škoda Works, the leading Czech military and machinery company, had exported weapons and machinery to China since the 1920s. For its activities and profits, see Ales Skrivan Jr., "Czechoslovak Export of Arms to China in the Interwar Period," *ÖT KONTINENS 1*, (2010).

11 Chen Shaoyu, *Guangdong tangye yu Feng Rui*, 48; "Kuangtung Government Sugar-factory," *Chinese Economic Journal and Bulletin* 18(2) (1936): 168. For details about the sugar industry reconstruction in Guangdong, see Kang Jin-A, "1930 nendai kanton Chinsaitō seiken no seitōgyō kensetsu" (1996).

Table 5.3 Newly built state-run sugar factories in Guangdong (unit: ton)

Factory name***	Location	Builder *	Payment plan(installment)	Daily squeeze ability	Operation start date
Xinzao	Near Guangzhou	H	18 months	500	December 1934
Shitou**	Near Guangzhou	S	20 months	1,000	December 1934
Shunde	Near Guangzhou	S	34 months	1,000	December 1935
Jieyang	Near Chaozhou	H	20 months	750	December 1935
Dongguan	Near Guangzhou	S	40 months	1,000	January 1936
Huiyang	Huizhou	H	–	1,000	November 1934

Source: "Kuangtung Government Sugar-factory," *Chinese Economic Journal and Bulletin* 18(2) (1936): 160–162, 248.

Notes:

* H refers to Honolulu Ironworks Co.; S refers to Škoda Works.

** The daily squeeze ability of the Shitou sugar factory increased to 2,750 tons by December 1936.

*** The former four sugar factories constituted the business of the provincial government. Dongguan and Huiyang belonged to the First Force of Guangdong Army.

launched Special Tax on imports of rice, grains, tobacco, oil, and chemical fertilizer. In January 1935, Feng Rui encouraged the Guangdong Provincial Bank to negotiate a loan with Shanghai banks, using the sugar factories as collateral. Another way to collect money was simply to issue more money. It is said that 37.2 million *yuan* of secretly issued Guangdong Provincial Banknotes was spent on the construction of state-run industries, of which a considerable part went to the sugar factories. In addition, the GPG raised 30 million *yuan* in loans from foreign banks in the United States and Sweden.[12]

There were also many favorable conditions for capital savings in the building of the sugar industry. Two global sugar plant importers allowed payment in installments for several years and guaranteed complete installation and operation by dispatching their own engineers. Java sugar exporters allowed for deferred payments for raw sugar. Finally, the global depression provided good opportunities for latecomers.

12 Li Jiezhi, "Chen Jitang tongzhi Guangdong de shimo," 406; Nihon tōgyō rengōkai, *Shina no tōgyō: Kotoni nanshi saikin no tōgyō jijō ni tsuite* [China's sugar industry: Especially on the recent situation of the sugar industry in South China] (Tokyo: Nihon tōgyō rengōkai, 1939), 19–21.

Official smuggling

One of the major means of raising funds was officially organized smuggling. Due to the unstable supply of raw materials from the sugar cane growers, sugar factories only operated for three months per year, far below the initial goal of the 120-day operations, and not enough sugar was produced to meet provincial demand. To make up for the supply shortage, the GPG and Feng Rui decided to import Hong Kong and Java sugar. However, this sugar was imported without going through customs inspections and it was then repackaged, at a sugar factory that was still under construction, as a product labeled "Five Rams Brand," the brand of the state-run companies built by the GPG. This sugar sold as a provincial product was mockingly called "smokeless sugar" (*wuyantang*), meaning that the factory was not running, so there was no smoke from the chimney, but the sugar was still produced.

The GPG dispatched three ships to Hong Kong to purchase refined sugar from the Taikoo Sugar Refinery. It was escorted to Guangdong tariff-free by two armed anti-smuggling patrol boats, the "Haiwei" and the "Haizhou." This was an act of "smuggling" that sought to take advantage of the huge price gap when the price of sugar in Guangdong was more than double that in Hong Kong because of the heavy tax and monopoly price.

It is difficult to determine the scale of the illegal profits brought in by this so-called official smuggling. Reportedly, between June and December 1934 there were profits of about 4 million *yuan* from repackaging and selling nearly 30,000 tons. Feng Rui himself admitted that during the initial stage the profits from the repackaging amounted to 3.45 million *yuan*. Other reports claimed that the profits from smokeless sugar were equivalent to the total amount of the assets of Xinzao and Shitou, the first two state-run sugar factories (about 9 million *yuan*).

The Swire Archive, held in the special collection of the SOAS Library, London, provides detailed reports about the building of the sugar factories, Feng Rui's activities, and the sugar transactions with the GPG. Butterfield & Swire in Hong Kong (hereafter B&S) was a subsidiary of John Swire & Sons Ltd, London. On 26 September 1933, B&S first reported to London about the Guangdong provincial project to build sugar refineries. Three days later, a report dated 29 September contained detailed information about the first factory to be built in Xinzao (Suntso [sic]), near Huangpu in the Guangzhou district. This information was provided by Y. K. Mok (Mok Ying Kwai), manager of the sugar department. He reported that the GPG banned the establishment of a private sugar mill with more than 50,000 *yuan* in capital to protect the state-run sugar factories. This fact is consistent with later information.[13] Y. K. Mok was a member of the Mok family, the famous Taikoo comprador family that had monopolized the Chinese comprador position in B&S for over sixty years. As a comprador but an independent sugar dealer, Y. K. Mok was responsible for general sales of Taikoo sugar. He eventually left his position at B&S and became involved in the business of a licensed sugar sale agency of the GPG.[14]

At that time, the GPG was seeking to buy Java sugar through Pentreath & Co., one of Hong Kong's leading sugar importers. For the Guangdong market, refined sugar was to be supplied from Taikoo (B&S) and Java sugar from Pentreath & Co.[15] At the beginning of the sugar monopoly in May 1934, a warship dispatched by the GPG shipped 500 tons of Java sugar from Hong Kong to Huangpu in Guangzhou.[16] On 21 June, Feng Rui, the B&S, and the Taikoo Sugar Refinery met to sign a first contract of 240 tons (4,000 piculs).[17]

On two occasions, the B&S sent C. P. Wong, who had replaced Y. K. Mok as new sugar comprador, in Guangzhou (9–11 and 15–19 August 1934) to observe the new sugar factory in Xinzao.[18] His report is more detailed than that found in other archival material on the sugar factory and sugar sales. In the two months after the beginning of the sugar monopoly, the GPG purchased a large amount of Java white sugar from various suppliers: 6,000 tons from Pentreath & Co., 750 tons from the influential Chinese sugar capital in Java, Messrs. Kian Gwan (sic),[19] 500 tons from the German Erdmann & Sielcken,[20] and 200 tons from other dealers in Hong Kong. All purchased

13 Hong Kong→London, 26, 29 September 1933, JSS 5-1-8; London→Hong Kong, 27 October 1933, JSS 5-1-8.

14 Mo Yinggui (Mok Ying Kui), "Yingshang Taigu yanghang jin bainian zai Huanan de yewu huodong yu moshi jiazu de guanxi" [The business activities of the British company, Butterfield & Swire Co., during the last 100 years and its relationship with the Mok family], *Guangdong wenshi ziliao* 44 (1985): 77–82.

15 Hong Kong→London, 27 April 1934, JSS 5-1-9.

16 Hong Kong→London, 18 May 1934, JSS 5-1-9.

17 Hong Kong→London, 21, 29 June 1934, JSS 5-1-9.

18 Hong Kong→London, 24 August 1934, JSS 5-1-9; C. P. Wong→Hong Kong, 23 August 1934, JSS 5-1-9.

19 For Oei Tiong Ham (Huang Zhonghan in Mandarin) and the Kian Gwan (Jianyuan in Mandarin) Company, see Yoshihara Kunio, ed., *Huang Zhonghan caituan: Dongnanya diyi qiye diguo*, tr. Zhou Nanjing [The Oei Tiong Ham concern: The first business empire of Southeast Asia] (Beijing: Zhongguo huaqiao chubanshe, 1993); Cai Renlong, "Huang Zhonghan jiazu yu Jianyuan gongsi" [The Oei Tiong Ham family and the Kian Gwan company], *Nanyang wenti* 1 (1983): 15, 18–19, 22.

20 "Messrs. Erkman's representative" in Wong's report might be misspelled as "Erdmann." Messrs. Erdmann & Sielcken was one of the large sugar exporters in Java.

sugar was repackaged into bags weighing 1.5 piculs and stamped with the logo of the Five Rams brand. In addition, 7,000 and 2,500 piculs of candy, which was in high demand, was purchased from Messrs. Nam Cheong and Messrs. Chun Wah, in Mongkok, Jiulong (Kowloon) Peninsula, respectively. The Guangdong Navy transported the Taikoo refined sugar from Hong Kong to the dock opposite Whampoa Military Academy, where local junk ships carried it to the Xinzao Sugar Factory.

Wong estimated that the GPG sold 54,000 piculs in July. At the same time, the authorities cracked down on the smuggling and seized sugar of 16,000 piculs, while 20,000 piculs were successfully smuggled in and released to the market. Feng Rui purchased Java White from Pantres at 5.75–6 *yuan* per picul and distributed it within Guangdong province at a controlled price of 20 *yuan* per picul. The monopoly-controlled price of refined sugar purchased from Taikoo was originally set to be 26 *yuan* per picul, but it was soon lowered to 23 *yuan* due to sluggish sales. Additionally, 3,000 piculs of brown candy had been purchased from Messrs. Nam Chen, Hong Kong's local candy dealer, at 7.10 *yuan* per picul. After being repackaged as Five Rams brand, it was sold in Shantou for 23 *yuan* per picul. In early July, when this repackaged Five Rams brand candy was shipped to Shanghai for trial sales, the Shanghai customs doubted whether it was really a domestic product. Furthermore, Wong reported that the GPG had signed a contract to exclusively supply sugar to the Guangxi province market under the Five Rams brand. The GPG sold the Java brown sugar at 20 *yuan* per picul to Guangxi on the condition that the GPG would allow free delivery to Wuzhou, Guangxi. The Guangxi provincial government earned 25 percent of the sales price, that is, 5 *yuan* per picul.

Wong accompanied Feng Rui on a tour of two factories, the Xinzao and the Shitou factories built in Panyu county, the hometown of Feng Rui. The two factories were scheduled to enter into operation in December 1934. Wong visited the sugar cane plantation, which was breeding new seeds from the Philippines. The Xinzao factory built by the Honolulu Iron Works had a crushing capacity of 500 tons per day to produce brown sugar within seven hours, and the Shidou factory, built by Škoda Works, doubled this capacity by crushing 1,000 tons of cane per day. Both factories had an alcohol distillery unit, which used crushed sugar cane as fuel and distilled alcohol from molasses separated from centrifuges in the sugar factories. The Baist Co. equipped the two alcohol distilleries for 20,000 Hong Kong dollars. Wong said Feng Rui signed a contract with the Honolulu Iron Co. to build another sugar plant in Shantou, later called the Jieyang Sugar Factory. The three plants were provincial government industries directly under the administration of

Feng Rui. In addition, Wong reported that there was another sugar factory controlled by the First Force of Chen Jitang, the Waichow Mill (sic), with a cane-crushing capacity of 1,000 tons per day. It is possible that this was the Huiyang Sugar Factory, which entered into operations in November 1934.[21]

How much was Taikoo sugar sold to the GPG for the Guangdong sugar monopoly? According to annual reports from 1934, 1935, and 1936, B&S sold about 56,000 piculs (3,360 tons) in 1934, 30,780 piculs (1,846 tons) in 1935, and 29,700 piculs (1,782 tons) in 1936.[22]

Profitability of the sugar factories and their financial contribution

Political protection and control over the market and prices guaranteed considerable profits to the state-run sugar factories. The GPG allowed duty-free imports of machinery and raw materials for the sugar factories, while levying a heavy tax on sugar imports. At that time, white sugar was priced 10.02 *yuan* per picul in Hong Kong. But the import tax was 12.83 *yuan*, so white sugar imported to Guangzhou was priced at 22.85 *yuan* per picul at a minimum. Imported white sugar could not compete with the provincial sugar, which was priced at 19 *yuan* per picul in Guangzhou. During the sugar cane crushing season between January and May 1935, the average cost of manufacturing in the Xinzao and Shitou sugar factories reached as much as 18.7 *yuan* per picul. This means that without the tariff protection the provincial sugar would not have been competitive with the imported sugar in terms of price. However, the manufacturing cost of the provincial sugar factories fluctuated. For example, the cost of white sugar was 15.64 *yuan* from the Shitou Sugar Factory and 17.64 *yuan* from the Xinzao Sugar Factory during the 1934–35 sugar cane season. These government-run factories had a great advantage: even if the manufacturing costs were to change, the GDP could secure profits from the sugar factories by adjusting the sales price through the monopoly.[23]

Of course, this only occurred in Guangdong, not the other markets in China. At that time, Shanghai's imported white sugar was sold at prices

21 C. P. Wong→B&S Hong Kong, 23 August 1934, JSS 5-1-9.

22 Hong Kong→London, 31 May 1935, JSS 5-1-10; Hong Kong→London, 16 April 1937, JSS 5-1-11.

23 Xi Zisi, "Ban tangye jingguo jiqi zhenxiang" [History of the building of the sugar industry and its true story], in *Nantian suiyue: Chen Jitang zhu Yue shiqi jianwen shilu* [Days of the southern sky: Records of personal experiences about Guangdong under the rule of Chen Jitang], ed. Guangdongsheng zhengxie wenshi ziliao yanjiu weiyuanhui (Guangzhou: Guangdong renmin chubanshe, 1987), 255–256.

as high at 24 *yuan* per picul because of the high tariffs in 1933. Feng Rui thought if they could produce white sugar at 12 *yuan* per picul, even with the shipping and other fees, provincial sugar from Guangdong would be competitive in the Shanghai market. However, the initial cost from actual operations soared to 19.4 *yuan* per picul due to supply difficulties and poor operations in the plants. Meanwhile, by 1936 the price of imported sugar in Shanghai fell to 21.5 *yuan* per picul. Therefore, with shipping and other fees, the Guangdong provincial sugar could not expect high returns from sales in the Shanghai market.[24]

In comparison with the native sugar made by private mills, provincial sugar produced by the new government-run sugar factories had an upper hand in terms of profit per unit. In crushing 100 piculs of sugar cane, the private sugar mill could produce 10.5 piculs of native sugar, at a manufacturing cost of 52.2 *yuan*, while the mechanized sugar factories could produce 9.5 piculs of white sugar with a manufacturing cost of 28.5 *yuan*. Since the price of white sugar at 256.5 was far higher than the price of native sugar at 168 *yuan*, the profits for white sugar (228 *yuan*) was almost double that of native sugar (115.8 *yuan*). Of course, such high profits within Guangdong province were due to the high price set by the sugar monopoly.[25]

Production at the sugar factories consistently increased during the Three-Year Plan period. The first year (the second half of 1934 and the first half of 1935) recorded 143,322 piculs, the second year (the second half of 1935 and the first half of 1936) recorded 330,000 piculs. Because all six factories were in operation from January 1936 and operations improved with training and experience, production in the second year more than doubled that in the first year.[26]

Nevertheless, it is difficult to calculate the financial contribution of the sugar business to provincial revenue. The average amount of provincial revenue during the period 1932–1935, excluding during the anti-Jiang movement of 1931 and 1936, was 56 million *yuan*. Combined with the national tax revenue, which was actually withheld in Guangdong for provincial use, the total revenue per year was about 80 million *yuan*.[27] In the first year (June 1934–May 1935), the National Products Sales Department of Guangdong province (*Guangdongsheng guohua tuixiaochu*, which in April 1935 was renamed the Provincial Products Management Office, *shengying wuchan*

24 Xi Zisi, "Ban tangye jingguo jiqi zhenxiang," 250, 255; Nihon tōgyō rengōkai, *Shina no tōgyō*, 26, 58–59.

25 Shiyebu Zhongguo jingji nianjian bianzuan weiyuanhui, *Zhongguo jingji nianjian*, 37.

26 Nihon tōgyō rengōkai, *Shina no tōgyō*, 25.

27 Qin Qingjun, "Minguo shiqi Guangdongsheng caizheng shiliao," 87, 103–104, Table 8.

jingjichu) raised as much as 25.1 million *yuan* in revenue. Among this, revenue from the sugar monopoly must have contributed the major portion. Table 5.4 shows the total value of sugar sold by the National Products Sales Department in Guangdong from June 1934 to April 1935.

Table 5.4 Value of sugar sold by the National Products Sales Department, June 1934–April 1935 (unit: 1,000 *haoyang yuan*)

Month	Sales	Month	Sales	Month	Sales
June 1934	737	October	1,214	February	515
July	1,093	November	958	March	611
August	1,529	December	1,040	April	504
September	1,770	January 1935	969	Total	10,944

Source: "Kuangtung Government Sugar-Factory," 165–66.

The sales figure for the sugar monopoly from June 1934 to April 1935 was 10.944 million *yuan*. Although the cost needs to be deducted to arrive at the net profit, the figure is still enormous, amounting to about 16 percent of Guangdong's fiscal revenue (July 1934–June 1935). Furthermore, considering the transactions were also settled for the First Force military account of Chen Jitang, the actual financial contribution of the sugar factories and the sugar monopoly must have been significant.

According to a May 1935 Hong Kong report of B&S, the National Products Sales Department of the GPG purchased 21,300 tons (355,000 piculs) of Java White, 2,500 tons (41,666 piculs) of Java Brown, and 3,150 tons (52,500 piculs) of Taikoo refined sugar by 1 June 1934, less than one year after the start of the sugar monopoly. A large amount of Brown Candy was also imported from Chinese sugar merchants in Hong Kong. The Huiyang Sugar Factory under direct military control separately imported 10,000 tons (166,666 piculs) of Java White. In sum, the GPG and Guangdong Army purchased 615,832 piculs of imported sugar in total.[28] Considering that the sales margin per picul was over 10 *yuan*, the GPG could make a net profit of more than 6 million *yuan* just from the repackaged sales of imported sugar, not including profits from the sales of provincial factory sugar and sugar candy. Therefore, actual revenue from construction of the sugar industry business must have been substantial. As people at the time used to say, the "Guangdong army is fed on sugar."[29]

28 Hong Kong→Shanghai, 23 May 1935, JSS 5-1-10.

29 Xie Yingming, "Shengying gongye gaikuang yishu" [Recollections about the condition of government industries], in *Nantian suiyue*, 230.

6 The Sugar Monopoly: From Local to National

Abstract
The project of the Guangdong provincial government to revive the sugar industry consisted of the building of state-run sugar factories for production and strict official control over distribution. Guangdong's sugar monopoly was the first such attempt in Republican China. Chapter 6 examines the abortive state monopoly trial of the Nationalist Government in Nanjing in 1935. The success of Guangdong's sugar monopoly has led to an unexpected collaboration between the two rivals in Nanjing and Guangzhou. The central government would run a national sugar monopoly, while Guangdong's refineries would act as sugar suppliers. It was an ambitious plan to expand the state-owned sugar monopoly in Guangdong nationwide. However, this trial ended in suspension due to the strong opposition from Shanghai sugar merchants and foreign sugar capitals.

Keywords: sugar, monopoly, Guangdong, Nanjing Nationalist Government, Shanghai, Butterfield & Swire

Merchants and the sugar monopoly

The project of the Guangdong provincial government to revive the sugar industry consisted of the building of state-run mechanized sugar factories for production and strict official control over distribution. Guangdong's sugar monopoly, characteristic of the industrialization led by the Guangdong provincial government (hereafter, the GPG), was the first such attempt in Republican China, and the policy had a significant impact on the provincial economy.

The GPG abolished the existing native sugar tax (*tutangjuan*) and instead imposed the Special Tax on Imported Sugar in May 1934. It was claimed this

Kang, Jin-A, *The Guangdong Model and Taxation in China*. Taylor & Francis Group, 2022
DOI: 10.5117/9789463725248_CH06

measure would protect both native sugar and refined sugar produced by the future state-run sugar factories. The following month (June 1934), the Sugar Office of the National Products Sales Department was established to administer the sugar monopoly in Guangdong.[1]

The sugar monopoly in Guangdong province was modeled after the 2,000-year-old Chinese salt monopoly. The peasants grew the sugar cane, the government produced the sugar in state-run refineries, and the merchants delivered and sold the sugar. The Sugar Office of the National Products Sales Department divided the provincial territory into ten districts for sugar sales and selected ten licensed merchants (*quansheng tangye yingyunshang*), who contracted the wholesale sugar released by the Sugar Office in each district. These merchants were part of the Merchants Union (sugar syndicate) and had the right to select sub-agents in their respective districts. The Sugar Office selected thirteen public sugar storehouses across the province. The ten licensed merchants managed the distribution and sales by subcontracting 240 sub-agents.

According to the Guangdong provisional regulation on transportation of sugar, all sugar was required to have a shipment license issued by the Sugar Office prior to shipment. For all imported sugar and other province-produced sugar, an application had to be made to the Sugar Office for an entry license before the sugar could enter Guangdong. Furthermore, regardless of whether it was provincial sugar or non-provincial sugar, an exit license had to be applied for in order for any sugar to be exported out of Guangdong. Shipments without a license were heavily penalized. Additionally, from when the Sugar Office was first established, in order to receive a license all sugar dealers were first required to report their sugar stock, and any retail trade of sugar weighing over five *jin*.[2]

With official support to crackdown on private sugar, all sugar entering Guangdong province was required to be distributed exclusively by ten

1 Nihon tōgyō rengōkai, *Shina no tōgyō: Kotoni nanshi saikin no tōgyō jijō ni tsuite* [China's sugar industry: Especially on the recent situation of the sugar industry in South China] (Tokyo: Nihon tōgyō rengōkai, 1939), 24; Xi Zisi, "Ban tangye jingguo jiqi zhenxiang" [History of the building of the sugar industry and its true story], in *Nantian suiyue: Chen Jitang zhu Yue shiqi jianwen shilu* [Days of the southern sky: Records of personal experiences about Guangdong under the rule of Chen Jitang], ed. Guangdongsheng zhengxie wenshi ziliao yanjiu weiyuanhui (Guangzhou: Guangdong renmin chubanshe, 1987), 256.

2 Chen Shaoyu, *Guangdong tangye yu Feng Rui* [The Guangdong sugar industry and Feng Rui] (Hong Kong: n.p., 1937), 57–58; Shiyebu Zhongguo jingji nianjian bianzuan weiyuanhui [China Economic Yearbook Compilation Committee of the Ministry of Industry and Commerce], *Zhongguo jingji nianjian* [China Economic Yearbook], Vol. 2 (Shanghai: Shangwuyin shuguan, 1934), 37; *Shenbao*, 22 October 1935.

licensed merchants.[3] According to Wong, however, among these ten only two merchants had prior experience in the sugar trade. One of the two was Y. K. Mok, a former Taikoo sugar comprador. The licensed merchants paid a security deposit of 40,000 *yuan* but they received 6 percent annual interest on their deposits. At least 70 percent of the selling price had to be paid with every purchase. Credit was allowed only up to 12,000 *yuan*. The monthly sales quota of the licensed merchants was 5,000 piculs, and their commission was 3 percent of the sales price, while the monthly sales quota of the sub-agents was 100 piculs.[4] Furthermore, the licensed merchants could demand a deposit of less than 2,000 *yuan* from the sub-agents in their respective districts.

Despite the strict penalties and the crackdown, the sugar monopoly was not successful. One year later, Japanese General Consul in Guangzhou Kawai Tatsuo reported to the minister of Foreign Affairs in Tokyo about various problems with the sugar monopoly. These problems included that the ten licensed merchants, in collusion with the sub-agents, were selling sugar above the regulated price to increase their profits. On 1 May 1935, the GPG announced amended regulations (the Provisional Regulations on Sugar Licensed Merchants), which entered into effect on 1 June. The name of the licensed merchants was changed from "management and transportation merchant" (*yingyunshang*) to "transportation and sales merchant" (*yunxiaoshang*). The sub-agents were abolished. Instead, the licensed merchants had to make up for any losses with their deposits if they failed to meet their quotas. Out of the thirteen public sugar storehouses, the four main storehouses in Guangzhou, Shantou, Jiangmen, and Haikou remained, but the rest were abolished. The licensed merchants had to build and operate storehouses in their respective districts with their own money.

The amended regulations did not benefit the merchants, whereas the GPG could secure stable income regardless of sales. Of course, there was an incentive for above-quota sales to be profitable. However, as Table 6.1 below reveals, profitability was unlikely.

3 Wong's list of ten selected wholesalers is the following: company name (manager name). Lap Shing Kung Si (Y. K. Mok), Wang Tai (Mok Wing Sun and Mok Hing), Tai Shing (John Shing Chung), Yue Hing (Kwok Siang Ngau), Sum Mon (Kwok Chang Dick), Tung On Ngau Yue Kung), Siang On (Yuen Lai Chuen), Shing Fat (U Chik Fong), Man Sang (Fung Kam Ngo), Shun Lee (Chan Chung).

4 Chen Zhen, ed. *Zhongguo jindai gongyeshi ziliao* [Materials on the modern industrial history of China] Vol. 3 (Beijing: Sanlian shudian, 1961), 1174.

Table 6.1 New and old sales quotas for major sugar districts in Guangdong (unit: picul)

Sugar district	Old quota	New quota	Percentage change
Guangzhou city	20,000	21,000	+5%
Chaomei	25,000	14,000	-44%
Qiongya	15,000	700	-95.3%
Nanlu	10,000	1,300	-87%
Total	70,000	37,000	-47%

Source: Kawai Tatsuo, Consul General of Guangdong→Gaimushō Tōa kyokuchō (Director of the East Asia Bureau, Ministry of Foreign Affairs, Japan), 3 June 1935, S5100-3, Satō no bu [Sugar File], Nihon Gaimushō monjo kantonshō no bu [Diplomatic Archives of the Ministry of Foreign Affairs of Japan], Microfilm Collection, National Assembly Library of Korea.

Within a year, the quota was cut by 47 percent. Except for Guangzhou city, where administrative powers were strong, all other periphery areas remote from the provincial capital experienced rapid drops in the minimum sales quota. This means that the original quotas might have been set too high, or that the government crackdown had been unsuccessful in blocking the trafficking of private sugar. But even the adjusted quotas were not low enough for merchant profitability.

Table 6.2 Quota based on the minimum consumption estimates and the highest bid sales quota for a license in seven sugar districts

Sugar district	Minimum quota	Bidder	Highest bid quota
Guangzhou city	21,000	Tongxing Company	24,500
Chaomei	14,000	-	-
Dongjiang	2,000	Honghe Company	1,300
Qiyi	11,000	Dacheng Company	11,650
Nanshaolian	5,000	Chengfa Company	4,700
Nanlu	1,200	-	-
Qiongya	700	-	-

Source: Kawai Tatsuo→Gaimushō Tōa kyokuchō, S5100-3, 367.

Table 6.2 shows the results from the bidding for annual license rights in seven sugar districts. Among the seven districts, there was no bid for Chaomei district because the licensed merchant had just been changed in the spring. Meanwhile, the bids for Nanlu and Qiongya districts were aborted because there were no bidders. Even with a large drop in the quota it was impossible to find bidders. Only two districts, Guangzhou and Qiyi, had bids higher than the minimum quota, and the others ended with decreased quotas after the bidding.

The monopoly system gave the Guangdong government exclusive benefits, but the merchants clearly suffered the damage. A petition by merchants in Shantou to abolish the sugar monopoly after centralization of Guangdong was characteristic of the problematic management of the sugar monopoly under rule by Chen Jitang. According to the petition, the GPG brought sugar from Hong Kong (at a cost of 4 *yuan* per 1 picul) to Shantou where the price was listed at 23 *yuan* per picul. This system forced people to consume costly sugar because the contract sellers and the crackdown teams were allowed to ransack private shops.[5] Sugar subject to the monopoly system included not only sugar produced in the state-run sugar factories but also imported finished sugar from Hong Kong. The government actually stripped the sales profits of the sugar merchants. The sugar monopoly was neither a part of the policy to build the national economy nor a local friendly policy supporting the provincial economy for the merchants. On the contrary, it was merely cover for the reality that "the government is contending with the people for profits (*yumin zhengli*)."

However, elevation of the price of imported sugar was not just an exploitive policy. Rather, if we consider the fundamental concerns of the GDP to secure time and money for future economic building, it was a completely complementary step. In the end, the GPG achieved some success in imposing strict control over sugar imports to Guangdong province. In 1933, 800,000 piculs of sugar were shipped from Hong Kong to Macau, and about 300,000 piculs were shipped to Guangzhou Bay. With Macau's annual sugar consumption of up to 10,000 piculs, the remaining 790,000 piculs were smuggled into Guangdong province through the web-like river line in Zhongshan county. However, in 1936 the amount of contraband sugar from Hong Kong to Macau and Guangzhou was reduced to 412,474 piculs.[6] It is ironic that part of this decline was due to the increase in the volume of direct shipment by the GPG from Hong Kong to Huangpu, Guangzhou.

5 *Shenbao*, 22 October 1935; Chen Shaoyu, *Guangdong tangye yu Feng Rui*, 71.

6 Yokotake Heitarō, Commerce Counselor of the Foreign Ministry of Japan in Shanghai, "Saikin Kantonshō keizai jij" [Recent economic affairs in Guangdong province], *Kaigai keizai jijō* 13 (1935): 255, S5100-3.

Trends in native sugar mills constituted another part of the multifaced construction of the sugar industry in Guangdong. The following table indicates the changes in the output of native sugar before and after the Three-Year Plan for Rejuvenation of the Sugar Industry.

Table 6.3 Trends in native sugar production in Guangdong

	Production output (1933–1934)		Production output (1936–1937)		Increase index
	Unit: 1,000 piculs	Share (%)	Unit: 1,000 piculs	Share (%)	
Shantou	958	48.0	1,600	55.7	167
Guangzhou	530	26.5	590	20.6	111
Leizhou	289	14.5	240	8.1	83
Hainan Island	219	11.0	250	6.9	114
Sugar at state-run factories	-	-	198	8.7	*
Total	1,995	100.0	2,878	100.0	144

Source: Nihon tōgyō engōkai, *Shina no tōgyō: Kotoni nanshi saikin no tōgyō jijō ni tsuit* [China's sugar industry: Especially on the recent situation of the sugar industry in South China] (Tokyo: Nihon tōgyō rengōkai, 1939), 15.

During the 1934–35 and 1935–36 periods (where there are missing data) there was fierce competition between native sugar and the refined sugar of the state-run factories. However, the impact of the Three-Year Plan on native sugar production is clearly apparent. According to the table, native sugar production increased by 34 percent, from 1,995,000 to 2,878,000 piculs, within three years. The GPG's policy package of reviving Guangdong sugar reversed the previous ever-decreasing trend in native sugar in Guangdong. The GPG and Feng Rui tried to prevent native sugar manufacturing from hampering the state-run sugar factories. Nevertheless, it was inevitable that the private sugar sector and the government sugar factories became competitors in the supply and sales of sugar cane.[7] However, within three years, both sectors rapidly increased production to replace the shrinking volume of sugar imports.

7 Kang Jin-A, "1930 nendai kanton Chinsaitō seiken no seitōgyō kensetsu," 88–89.

Spread of the Guangdong model: An aborted attempt by the national sugar monopoly in 1935

The advance of Guangdong sugar into the Shanghai market

Feng Rui's ultimate dream was to achieve sugar self-sufficiency in China by promoting sugar cane cultivation and modernizing the sugar industry in Guangdong. Once China restored tariff sovereignty, private capital and government-run factories envisioned a similar plan.[8] But only the GPG and Feng Rui could realize it, and within a very short period. Above all, the Guangdong model to combine state-run industry and the sugar monopoly attracted not only locals but also the Nanjing Nationalist Government (hereafter NNG). With this combination of the GPG taking on the role of sugar supplier and the NNG administering the national sugar monopoly, both sides could share in the enormous profits. Furthermore, this contributed to the great cause of "self-sufficiency" to replace "foreign sugar" with "national sugar." The potential confrontation between the GPG and the NNG, however, worked against such cooperation. Under-the-table negotiations and a tug-of-war between the two sides took place in relative secrecy. One year after the beginning of the sugar monopoly in Guangdong, the NNG announced a national sugar monopoly, starting from 1 June 1935. Several months later, after the start of the sugar monopoly in Guangdong (1 June 1934), Feng Rui sought to sell the sugar refined in the government sugar factories in the Shanghai market.

According to a report in the Swire Archives sent from Butterfield & Swire in Hong Kong (hereafter B&S) to London, Feng Rui visited Nanjing and Shanghai in November 1934 to explore a way to sell Guangdong sugar in Shanghai, the center of the domestic sugar trade. His visit to Nanjing was reportedly related to the abrupt intervention by Guangzhou Customs in the shipment of sugar by the military between Hong Kong and Guangzhou. From May to October, Customs had overlooked and tolerated these unreported shipments. Feng Rui must have considered Guangdong and Nanjing's cooperation to resolve this issue, but it is unclear whether the sugar monopoly was discussed at this stage.[9]

8 "A proposal for the development of the sugar industry on Hainan Island," H. C. Lin→Messrs. Dodwell & Co., Ltd, 24 May 1934 JSS 5-1-9. John Swire & Sons Ltd Archive, London University SOAS Library Special Collections.

9 Messrs. Butterfield & Swires. Hong Kong (hereafter Hong Kong)→Messrs. John Swire & Sons, Ltd. London (hereafter London), 16 November 1934, JSS 5-1-9.

In fact, when Guangdong enacted its sugar monopoly in June, Song Ziwen frequently made inquiries about the effect of high tariffs on the sugar trade and, moreover, asked the Shanghai branch of B&S to estimate the amount of sugar smuggling in 1933 through the services of Gustav Amann, foreign adviser to the NNG. B&S in Shanghai submitted the data on 21 June. Therefore, B&S must have been anticipating that the NNG was considering a type of government monopoly, "envying the success of the Canton sugar monopoly," but the most plausible scenario might have been not a government monopoly but an import quota system.[10] Another important sign was the establishment of Xinghua Company, a sales agency for Guangdong sugar in Shanghai. The official opening of the company took place in December, but the Shanghai B&S reported it in November with detailed information about the partners.[11] In sum, the move to sell Guangdong sugar in Shanghai, the NNG's intervention, and the beginning of talks between the GPG and the NNG through Feng Rui were all interwoven in the events of November 1934.

On 27 November, three Hong Kong sugar merchant guilds that were sugar exporters to Shanghai and northern China wired a telegram to the NNG to debunk the myth of "smokeless sugar," stating that "most white Sugar has been bought from Java and is being packed as native sugar." Therefore, collaboration between Xinghua Company and the GPG could threaten their business. However, several days later, on 4 December, these three guilds wired another telegram to the NNG, with a completely different message. It stated, "we ... now regret to inform you that a mistake has been made regarding the truth about this. As a matter of fact, several of our members have recently inspected the Government Sugar Mills, and we know that the Kwangtung Government [sic] has built three large Sugar Mills and booked large quantities of Sugar Cane from farmers for crushing at the beginning of December. Since this is to revive the Sugar industry, we are very pleased to learn of it, and the truth now being fully understood, we regret having dispatched the last telegram and tender our apologies to the Kwangtung Officials." The B&S Shanghai explained the details of the event to London headquarters. Upon hearing of this report, Feng Rui stopped by in Hong Kong on his way home from Shanghai and threatened that all members of the Hong Kong sugar merchants' guild would be arrested as soon as they

10 Messrs. Butterfield & Swires. Shanghai Branch (hereafter Shanghai)→Hong Kong, 12 October 1934, JSS 5-1-9; Hong Kong→London, 22 June 1934, 5-1-9.

11 Shanghai→Hong Kong, 12 November 1934, JSS 5-1-9.

set foot in Guangzhou, and that in the future Hong Kong sugar merchants supplying candy and sugar powder to the GPG would not be paid.[12]

On 27 December 1934, the first shipment of Guangdong sugar, 800 bags, arrived in Shanghai, and another 2,000 bags of sugar was shipped from Guangzhou headed toward Shanghai.[13] Officially, with acknowledgment by the NNG, Guangdong sugar could enter the Shanghai market beginning from January 1935. Many questioned the source of this sugar. Was this Guangdong sugar actually fake domestic sugar (repackaged as foreign sugar) or genuine domestic sugar? However, B&S flatly rejected any doubts, saying all repackaged foreign sugar had been sold in Guangdong and Guangxi territory to raise revenue. The GPG and Feng Rui prepared refined sugar in new government factories for export to Shanghai.

The GPG and the NNG reached an agreement to import 6,000 tons of real Guangdong sugar into Shanghai. The first shipment of 96 tons (16,000 piculs) of white sugar and 540 tons (9,000 piculs) of acceptable quality was produced by Huiyiang Sugar Factory under the jurisdiction of the First Force of the Guangdong military (*Guangdong diyijun junkenchu*). B&S reported that the factory had initially crushed and refined the local sugar cane but ended operations due to a lack of local sugar cane, a result of the rivalry with the native sugar manufacturers.[14] This B&S document refutes the accusations of Japanese and Hong Kong merchants that all Guangdong sugar exported to Shanghai was "smokeless sugar." Meanwhile, Japanese scholar Hirai Kensuke calculates that the total amount of Guangdong sugar amounted to 9,600 tons (160,000 piculs), which consisted of 100,000 piculs of government factory sugar and 60,000 piculs of "smokeless sugar" (repackaged Java white), citing a contemporary Japanese report.[15] We will have to wait for in-depth discussion and new historical materials to be determined before the differences of opinion on this point can be resolved.

Guangdong sugar, Jianyuan, and Shanghai sugar merchants

Xinghua Company was established by three stores—Yuantaiheng, Yuaxing, and Changxing—for commissioned sales of Guangdong sugar in Shanghai. Yuanxing and Changxing were shops affiliated with Jianyuan

12 Shanghai→London, 7 December 1934, JSS 5-1-9.

13 Hong Kong→London, 4 January 1935, JSS 5-1-10.

14 Hong Kong→Shanghai, 23 May 1935, JSS 5-1-10.

15 Hirai Kensuke, *Satō no teikoku nihon shokuminchi to ajia shijō* [Empire of sugar: External forces of change in the economies of the Japanese colonies] (Tokyo: Tōkyō daigaku shuppankai, 2017), 119.

(Kian Guan, Kian Gwan), the largest Chinese sugar capital in Java. Y. C. Sze of Yuantaiheng, as a representative of Xinghua Company, signed a contract with Feng Rui. Instead of obtaining exclusive sales rights, Xinghua Company lent 1 million *yuan* to the GPG, with an annual interest rate of 6 percent to fund the development of government sugar factories.[16] At about this time, the Ministry of Finance opened a temporary institution, called the Sugar Distribution Commission (*shitang yunxiao guanli weiyuanhui*) to conduct research on the monopoly. There were two standing members on this commission: Liang Jingchun, a former senior treasury official, and Huang Jiangchuan, a representative of Jianyuan in Shanghai.[17]

Jianyuan was involved with the sales agency for Guangdong sugar as well as with the NNG's preliminary sugar-monopoly institution. The involvement of capital of Java sugar in the sugar monopoly aroused wide speculation. In terms of manufacturing and trading, the Jianyuan company represented the largest Chinese sugar capital in Java. When China imposed high tariffs on sugar imports, this company sent its representative Huang Jiangchuan to Shanghai in 1932 to build a refinery in Shanghai by direct investment. He was said to hold a post in the Ministry of Communications.[18] On the one hand, he tried to buy up the Minghua Sugar Refinery, a branch factory of Japanese Meiji Sugar in Shanghai. On the other hand, he lobbied the NNG to grant preferential tariffs for raw sugar imports to a Chinese sugar refinery in Shanghai. After failed attempts to buy Minghua, Jianyuan built a new sugar mill called Kwang Hua Refinery (sic), which entered into operation in May 1933. In that sense, with the emergence of Guangdong sugar in late 1934, a new combination among Jianyuan, the NNG, and the GPG was envisioned.

16 Hong Kong→London, 26 November 1934, JSS 5-1-9. The exchange rate between "Big Money" and "Small Money" in 1934 was approximately 100 silver dollars in Shanghai (Big Money), equal to 130 silver dollars in Guangdong ("Small Money"), and equal to 91 Hong Kong dollars. For reference, the exchange rate in 1933 when the NNG abolished the *liang* (teal) standard (*biliang gaiyuan*) to adopt the *yuan* (dollar) standard, one silver teal in Shanghai was equal to 1.29 silver dollars in Shanghai and 1.23 Hong Kong dollars. For detailed information about currencies and exchange rates, see Jin-A Kang, *1930 nyŏndae Chungguk ŭi chungang, chibang, sangin: Kwangdongsŏng ŭi chaejŏng kwa kukka kŏnsŏl* [Center, provinces, and merchants in China in the 1930s: Finance and nation-building in Guangdong province] (Seoul: Sŏul taehakkyo ch'ulp'anbu, 2005), Part 4.

17 Mitsubishi Corporation, Shanghai Branch→Chief of Agricultural Department, Tokyo, 2 May 1935, S5100-3, Satō no bu [Sugar File], Nihon Gaimushō monjo kantonshō no bu [Diplomatic Archives of the Ministry of Foreign Affairs of Japan], Microfilm Collection, National Assembly Library of Korea.

18 Hong Kong→London, 6 January, 19 May, 1 December 1933, JSS 5-1-8.

From January to April 1935, 3,600 tons (6,000 piculs) of Guangdong sugar were shipped to Shanghai. Upon its arrival, the NNG's plan to sell sugar nationwide by organizing a general sales agency was discussed among Shanghai's sugar merchants. In January, members of the Shanghai Sugar Business Association held a general meeting to decide on the organization of the Shanghai Sugar Business-Cooperative Company (*Shanghai tangye hezuo gongsi*). The goal of the organization was to develop domestic sugar ("national sugar"). However, because domestic sugar production was insufficient to meet domestic demand, this new company was to deal with imported sugar as well. The Shanghai sugar merchants who joined this cooperative company were responsible for distributing both domestic and imported sugar nationwide. In their discussion, the domestic sugar refers to Guangdong sugar, and the imported sugar was exclusively Java sugar. Xinghua Company, the sales agency for Guangdong sugar, also participated in this cooperative venture to recommission the franchise. Native sugar produced in traditional Chinese sugar mills and other foreign imported sugar, such as Japanese sugar, could be freely traded. But only Guangdong sugar and Java sugar were to be traded nationwide through this cooperative company.[19]

The national sugar monopoly

On the establishment of the Shanghai Sugar Business-Cooperative Company, foreign companies and consulates held successive meetings with high-ranking NNG officials, such as President Wang Jingwei, chairman of the Executive Yuan, and Chen Gongbo. Their inquiries focused on two issues: whether this new company would be set up for the future sugar monopoly and whether the NNG would support a monopoly of Java sugar in the Chinese market. Despite an initial denial by NNG officials, a national sugar monopoly plan was suddenly announced on 1 May 1935, along with the establishment of a new monopoly institution. On the same day, the Sugar Distribution Commission was officially reopened as a regular institution, which expanded to one chairman and four members. Liang Jingchun, a Guangdong native and a former customs official, took the position of chairman. Huang Jiangquan, a Fujian native and a representative of Jianyuan, retained his post as a member. Liang and Huang had prepared the establishment of this institute from the preliminary stage. The additional members were Zhou Shaowen (Zhou Dian, a North China native, vice president of the National Taxation

19 Yokotake Heitarō, Commerce Counselor of the Foreign Ministry of Japan in Shanghai→Hirota Kōki, Minister of Foreign Affairs of Japan, 27 April 1935, S5100-3.

Commission), Wu Zengyu (a Fujian native, director of the Shanghai Postal Savings Office), and Feng Rui.[20]

There were rumors that Huang Jiangchuan was plotting a sugar monopoly led by Java sugar in cooperation with Chen Gongbo, Minister of Industry. These two, who were both overseas Chinese, had a close relationship. However, it turned out that Huang's plan was met with repeated rejections by Chen and this rejection was confirmed after he contacted Kong Xiangxi, Minister of Finance, through mediation by former Minister of Finance Song Ziwen.[21]

The list of announced members of the Sugar Distribution Commission convinced Japanese merchants that this sugar monopoly plan was a conspiracy by the GPG and Jianyuan to monopolize the Chinese market, with Guangdong and Java sugar pitted against other foreign sugars. Japanese sugar merchants in Shanghai and Japanese diplomats launched the official protest and campaign against the sugar monopoly in conjunction with European organizations such as NIVAS, a Dutch government-run Java sugar organization, and B&S Hong Kong, representing Taikoo Sugar.[22] In the beginning, B&S did not actively oppose the national sugar monopoly, as it had exclusively supplied refined sugar to the GPG and saw the potential to extend sales of Taikoo Sugar to northern China, where it was being outsold by Japanese sugar. However, the Maclaine Watson, a long-standing business partner supplying Java raw sugar to the Taikoo refinery, wanted a check on the dominance of its rival, Jianyuan. Eventually, B&S could not drop its name from the list of protestors led by the Japanese merchants.[23] In spite of strong protests by Japanese merchants and diplomats, the real support for blocking the national sugar monopoly plan came from among the Chinese sugar merchants themselves, who had been expected to execute the monopoly.

Their withdrawal of previous support for the monopoly became apparent when China Sugar Co., Ltd (*Zhonghua tangye gufen youxian gongsi*) was set up. This new, semi-official company was a joint venture of the government and private merchants to execute the sugar monopoly. On 25 May China Sugar Co. posted a public announcement in the Shanghai daily, *Shenbao*, about public offerings in stocks. On the very same day, the Shanghai Sugar

20 Yokotake Heitarō→Hirota Kōki, 2 May 1935, S5100-3.

21 Horiuchi, Secretary of the Consul General of Japan in Shanghai→Hirota Kōki, 14 May 1935, S5100-3.

22 Sakayori Hatsugorō, Shanghai branch of Masuyuki company→Yokotake Heitarō, Commerce Counselor of the Foreign Ministry of Japan in Shanghai, "Personal opinion on control of sugar sales," 8 May 1935, S5100-3.

23 Hong Kong→London, 30 March 1935, JSS 5-1-10; London→Hong Kong, 14 May 1935, JSS 5-1-10.

Business Association, which had been involved in organizing the Shanghai Sugar Business-Cooperative Company, held its twenty-eighth committee meeting to vote on whether they supported China Sugar Co. and the national sugar monopoly. The result of the vote was nine votes in favor and thirty-eight votes opposed.

On 30 May, twelve foreign sugar merchants, including Mitsui, Mitsubishi, Masuko Corporation, B&S, and Jardine, Matheson & Co., submitted a joint protest letter to the Ministry of Finance. On the same day, the Shanghai Sugar Business Association held its twenty-ninth committee meeting to hold another vote to decide its attitude to the monopoly. The result was even a bigger gap than in the previous vote, with forty-two votes opposed to participating in the government sugar monopoly with China Sugar Co. and only six votes in favor.

Based on the original schedule, 1 June would have been the starting date of the national sugar monopoly. Nevertheless, the plan was delayed by the Chinese sugar merchants' persistent opposition. To express their opposition, thirty-eight Shanghai sugar merchants posted a joint announcement in *Shenbao* on 25 June stating that they had no intention of participating in China Sugar Co. and that they were firmly against the sugar monopoly. In the evening of 25 June, a meeting of the relevant authorities was called by the Ministry of Finance to decide on an indefinite suspension of the sugar monopoly.[24]

The sugar industry after centralization of Guangdong

Despite suspension of the national sugar monopoly, the collaboration between the NNG and the GPG that Feng Rui had envisioned was able to survive. In July 1935, the NNG raised the upper limit of Guangdong sugar's exports to Shanghai from the previous 3,600 tons per year to 1,200 tons per month.[25] At the same time, Feng Rui suggested to B&S that it use the brown sugar from the government sugar factories as raw sugar instead of the Java raw sugar. He stressed that B&S sugar refined from Guangdong brown sugar

24 The studies by Kang, "1930nyŏn chungkukŭi kyŏngchekaepalesŏ nat'ananŭn sŏngkwa chungang" and Hirai, *Satō no teikoku nihon shokuminchi to ajiashijō*, have slight differences in terms of dates and numbers. The former mainly cites documents from the Ministry of Foreign Affairs of Japan, and the latter mainly cites materials from the Japan Sugar Industry Association.
25 For details, see Kang "1930 nyŏn chungkukŭi kyŏngchekaepalesŏ nat'ananŭn sŏngkwa chungang."

could be sold across the country as domestic sugar without import tariffs.[26] Nevertheless, B&S was hesitant about fully cooperating with Feng Rui. First, B&S worried about the inferior quality of Guangdong sugar. Second, it needed a promise from the NNG that the refined, processed Guangdong sugar would be treated as domestic sugar.[27]

In addition, Feng Rui was granted a preferential tax exemption by the NNG for raw sugar imports to the government sugar factories. The government sugar factories were allowed to pay only half the import tariffs on raw sugar imports, with the remainder suspended for three years.[28] It was in May 1936, however, that the collaborative mood changed. On 13 May, Hu Hanmin, a senior leader of the NNG, died. Chen Jitang and the Guangxi clique staged a coup d'état against Jiang Jieshi in the name of fighting against Japan (the Liangguang Incident, 1 June–18 July). The coup failed, Chen Jitang defected to Hong Kong, and Guangdong, in both name and substance, fell into the hands of the NNG.

In July, the NNG formed the National Sugar Distribution Association (*quanguo guotang chanxiao xiehui*), advocating the boosting of domestic sugar and control over Guangdong sugar. In August, the occupation officials from Nanjing as relatively peacefully reorganized the provincial government. Surprisingly, Feng Rui, chief of the Bureau of Agriculture and Forestry, was arrested on 10 August in his office and executed by a firing squad on 9 September (or 11 September).[29]

According to a B&S report, Liu Wei Chirk (sic) replaced Feng Rui as head of the Provincial Products Management Office. In addition, Yu Hanmou, a new Guangdong military leader who had replaced Chen Jitang, transferred management of two military sugar factories, Dongguan and Huiyang, to Xinghua Company (the Java Jianyuan capital mentioned above). Profits were divided at 80 percent for the military and 20 percent for Jianyuan.[30]

26 Hong Kong→London, 26 July 1935, JSS 5-1-10; Hong Kong→London, 24 April 1936, JSS 5-1-10-6.

27 Hong Kong→London, 24 April 1936, JSS 5-1-10-6. "For some reason, of which we are not aware, the Kwangtung Government are not at present prepared to approach Nanking in the matter unless they are reasonably assured of the latter agreeing to their request that Kwangtung Sugar refined by *the T.S.R. should not lose its native status* [emphasis added]." "On all the above general grounds, therefore, we reach the conclusion that everything possible should be done to encourage the Kwangtung Mills to send us their Browns for refining."

28 Hong Kong→London, 9 August 1935, JSS 5-1-10.

29 Zhu Chuxin, "Zhongguo de tangye wenti yu guotang chanxiao xiehui" [The problems of the Chinese sugar industry and the National Sugar Distribution Association], *Zhongguo jingji lunwenji* 3 (1936): 130; Chen Shaoyu, *Guangdong tangye yu Feng Rui*, 86.

30 Hong Kong→London, 16 April 1937, JSS 5-1-11.

In October 1936, the new GPG contacted B&S, Hong Kong, offering the same suggestion as that of Feng Rui about cooperation using Guangdong sugar as a raw material. The name of the institution on Guangdong's side was the "Commissioner of Reconstruction in Canton." B&S required "native status" for the refined product. In principle, the NNG granted unofficial approval, reportedly stating that "the tariff obstacle could be overcome."[31] In fact, there was no difference between the old GPG and the new GPG (that is, the NNG) in terms of their sugar policies.

The new GPG maintained the sugar monopoly in Guangdong. Facing fierce petitions from merchants both inside and outside of Guangdong to abolish the monopoly, the new GPG announced the abolishment of the monopoly and instead implemented the New Sugar Control Regulation (*xin tangye tongzhi banfa*) in November. Nonetheless, B&S commented that the new regulation was identical with the old sugar monopoly in terms of blocking free access by private merchants to sugar imports.[32] B&S continued to sell its refined sugar not to private merchants but to the Provincial Products Management Office of the new GPG.[33] It was in March 1937 that the monopoly was completely abolished in terms of canceling exclusive government sales of imported sugar and allowing private merchants to buy it freely. In return, the new GPG levied a 1 *yuan* "Reconstruction Fund Tax" and a 0.6 *yuan* "Agricultural Protective Tax" per 1 picul of sugar.[34] This represented a compromise between the sugar merchants and the government, trading the monopoly for tax revenue. Part of the reason for the new GPG's concessions was the government's deteriorating management of the government sugar factories. A report from B&S Hong Kong on 2 July 1937 details the situation in the government sugar factories, describing how the government sugar factories had been abandoned and the experienced original workers had left after the death of Feng Rui. Due to corruption, poor care of the production facilities, and ineffectiveness in the takeover, the factories had virtually closed down. B&S, however, alerted its London office, stating that "we must take account of the fact that the mills are in existence now, and in proper hands are capable of a large production of sugar."[35]

Paradoxically, the final winners in this contestation were native sugar makers, who gained a great leap in production. During the Three-Year Plan

31 Hong Kong→London, 16 October 1936, JSS 5-1-10.

32 Hong Kong→London, 20 November 1936, JSS 5-1-10.

33 Hong Kong→London, 11 December 1936, 7 March 1937, JSS 5-1-10.

34 Hong Kong→London, 16 April 1937, JSS 5-1-11.

35 Hong Kong→London, 2 July 1937, JSS 5-1-11.

period, the high sugar price under the monopoly and the special protective tax against imported sugar brought huge benefits and profits to manufacturers of native sugar in Guangdong. In addition, because of the incentive scheme in the former GPG to encourage sugar-cane farming, sugar-cane cultivation increased significantly, thereby easing the bottlenecks caused by shortages of raw materials. But along with the abolition of the monopoly, the compulsory state procurement was discontinued. Farmers were able to hand over their products to the private sugar mills for a better price. This market liberalization exacerbated the supply problems in the government sugar factories.[36]

The export of Guangdong native sugar totaled only 26,495 tons (441,592 piculs) in 1932, doubling to 49,545 tons (825,763 piculs) in 1933, and increasing to 73,092 tons (1,218,212 piculs) in 1934.[37] There are no exact post-1935 statistics, but B&S Hong Kong reported in 1938 that thriving production and sales of native sugar had significantly cut Taikoo sugar sales in Guangdong, indicating the continued prosperity of native sugar after the Three-Year Plan.[38] In contrast, after being taken over by the NNG, the government sugar factories suffered from poor management. They would have to wait a long while before reconstruction.

The legacy of the Guangdong model in the sugar monopoly

The financial and industrial success of the Guangdong sugar monopoly must have impressed the NNG. In June 1937, one month before the outbreak of the Second Sino-Japanese War, the Executive Yuan of the NNG passed the National Sugar Control Committee Act (*quanguo tangye guanli weiyuanhui an*), and Song Ziwen drafted the Hainan Island Development Plan, which focused on the development of Hainan Island as the center of sugar production in Guangdong.[39] Hainan Island was the hometown of Song Ziwen, and Panyu county, where the Sinzao and the Shitou sugar factories were built, was the home county of Feng Rui. The drafting of the Hainan plan can be interpreted as part of an attempt by the NNG to expand the

36 Kang Jin-A, "1930 nendai kanton Chinsaitō seiken no seitōgyō kensetsu," 88.

37 Hong Kong→London, 31 May 1935, JSS 5-1-10.

38 Hong Kong→London, 22 April 1938, JSS 5-1-12.

39 Xi Zisi, "Song Ziwen longduan Guangdong tangye de jihua he wo canjia chouban Guangdong tangchang de jingguo" [Song Ziwen's plan to monopolize the Guangdong sugar industry and my experience in organizing Guangdong sugar factories], *Guangdong wenshi ziliao* 62 (1990): 205–208.

Guangdong model nationwide. This effort was cut short due to the Marco Polo Bridge Incident, on 7 July 1937, which triggered the launch of a full-scale war between China and Japan.

To secure wartime resources, the GDP returned to the legacy of the old Guangdong sugar monopoly in February 1938. In this system, one merchant was exclusively responsible for the sale of sugar across the province, unlike in the previous system in which ten licensed merchants undertook collective management. The security deposit was set as 150,000 *yuan*, and the monthly sales quota was set at 25,500 piculs. As before, the commission was 3 percent of the sales price. The newly appointed licensed merchant was Iu Chak Fong (sic), who had been one of the ten licensed merchants during the earlier period. However, two months later, Guangzhou was heavily bombed by the Japanese Air Force. In early April, three sugar refineries were hit and severely damaged.[40] The Xinzao and Shitou factories in the Guangzhou district could not recover from the destruction caused by the Japanese bombing. Jieyang Sugar Factory in Chaozhou district was rented out to a private merchant in 1937 because of financial difficulties, and the Dongguan and Shunde factories, following suit, were rented out in 1941 for a contract period of three years.[41]

During the Chinese Civil War, Song Ziwen, appointed as governor of Guangdong province in 1947, once again dreamed of the large-scale reconstruction of the Guangdong sugar industry. The legacy of the earlier Guangdong sugar monopoly had survived for over ten years, and in consultation with Weng Wenhao, Minister of Economic Affairs and chairman of the National Resources Commission, Song Ziwen launched the "Guangdong Sugar

40 Hong Kong→London, 8 April 1938, JSS 5-1-12. "The Japanese have recently concentrated on bombing Kwangtung Government factories and it is reported that three of the sugar factories have been more or less badly damaged and put out of action."

41 Immediately after the outbreak of the Sino-Japanese War, Škoda Co. signed a contract with Kong Xiangxi, Minister of Finance, in August 1937 to sell £10 million worth of weapons and sugar-refining machinery. Further, Škoda was in negotiation to build a sugar refinery with the Sichuan provincial government. However, as the war progressed, Škoda ended up giving up its business in China. Although Škoda had already completed the contracted installation of the machinery to expand the Shitou Sugar Factory, during the war, the company did not receive payment. Furthermore, the factory was destroyed by bombing by the Japanese Air Force. It is said that the Japanese air raids did not stop until the factory raised the Czech flag. The Czech government demanded payments and indemnity from China and Japan through diplomatic channels, but with no significant results. Its £300,000 claim for compensation continued after the Sino-Japanese War until the establishment of the People's Republic of China. However, the Communist governments of Czechoslovakia and China resolved the issue politically, ending in 1957 with an agreement to cancel all claims regarding events prior to 9 May 1945. Aleš Skřivan, "Škodovy závody a výstavba cukrovarů v Číně před druhou světovou válkou," 323–324.

Business Development Plan (*Guangdong tangye kaifa jihua*)." The goal of this plan was to set up forty mechanized sugar factories, producing raw sugar, and three sugar refineries, which together would produce 1 million tons of sugar annually, enough not only to achieve self-sufficiency but also to send exports abroad. By the time the plan was revealed, Song Ziwen had already reclaimed, through diplomatic negotiations, the machinery and equipment of Dongguan Sugar Factory that had been dismantled and taken to Japan. In addition, he relocated machinery and equipment from sugar factories in Taiwan as enemy assets. The attempt to restart the government sugar factories left significant assets to the Chinese Communist Party (CCP) to rebuild its sugar industry, producing 200,000 tons of sugar annually and 500,000 *mu* of sugar cane farmland. The dream of self-sufficiency was finally realized under socialist CCP control.[42]

42 The above process is detailed in the following studies. Jin-A Kang, "1930nyŏn Chungkukŭi kyŏngchekaepalesŏ nat'ananŭn sŏngkwa chungang"; Jin-A Kang, "Naejŏn'gi kwangdongsŏngŭi sŏngyŏnggongŏp chaegŏnjŏngch'aekkwa songjamun" [Song Ziwen and the reconstruction of provincial industries in Guangdong during the Chinese Civil War], *Chungguk kŭnhyŏndaesa yŏngu* 24 (2004); Emily M. Hill, *Smokeless Sugar: The Death of Provincial Bureaucrat and the Construction of China's National Economy* (Vancouver: University of British Columbia Press, 2001).

Part 3

Reform of Tax Collection

7 The Building of Public Administration and Taxation

Abstract
Chapter 7 discusses the process of the Guangdong provincial government's efforts to reform its administration of tax collection. The tax collection in Guangdong province relied heavily on a tax-farming system where contractors varied from traditional merchant guilds to professional tax-farmers. The co-existence of various currencies and their daily fluctuating exchange rates added to the difficulty of tax collection. The provincial governments tried to set up tax bureaus locally and create a unified and top-down tax collection system in Guangdong. However, the complete abolition of the contract system was never declared due to the financial vulnerability of the provincial government. The Chen Jitang regime in Guangdong heavily depended on fund-raising through loans from merchants.

Keywords: tax-farming, Guangdong, China, tax collection

Various evaluations of the tax-farming system

The tax-farming system is a taxation method that allows the government to delegate administrative affairs to private organizations. It is based on a mutual agreement between the government and a private organization. However, tax-farming in Chinese history always had negative implications. Delegating administration to middlemen, particularly in taxation, was linked to exploitation of the people and the malfunctioning of state administration.

Prasenjit Duara's study of rural areas in North China in the 1920s analyzes the penetration of state power to the grassroots level by shifting from a tax system through traditional gentlemen and local communities to the rise of tax "brokerism" during Republican China. According to Duara, the tax-farming system was part of a violent process in which state power infiltrated the private sector to obtain financial resources, and the tax farmers were

Kang, Jin-A, *The Guangdong Model and Taxation in China*. Taylor & Francis Group, 2022
DOI: 10.5117/9789463725248_CH07

profit-seeking because they did not belong to local communities.[1] Meanwhile, Susan Mann describes the transition between the two systems as "liturgical." In the 1930s, the bidding system introduced professional tax contractors, which Mann depicts as the demise of the liturgical tax strategies.[2] In Mann's research, the tax-farming system was introduced by the state's aspirations to expand financial resources, and tax-farming and traditional taxation through guilds were established incompatible binarities.

Mann's study focuses mainly on the emergence and characteristics of the *likin* tax in the late Qing and it lacks a detailed analysis of the professional tax-farming merchants during Republican China. The question of why the tax-farming system thrived in China in the 1930s is not answered. In that regard, Duara's research describes the change in the tax system as strategic penetration of state power, but it does not overcome the simplified dichotomy between traditional guild taxation and brokerism.

As the above studies show, the meaning of tax-farming in Chinese financial history has differing connotations, but there is also a common thread. First, tax-farming is equated with penetration by state power. The reason why tax-farming was so popular in the 1930s is always explained as a combination of state efforts to infiltrate the private sector. Second, the guild tax system is equated with a self-protective system and the tax-farming system is equated with an anti-community system.

This dichotomy generally fits the Chinese situation of the 1920s, but it does not fit the reality of China in the 1930s. The Nanjing Nationalist Government (hereafter NNG) of the 1930s strongly criticized the tax-farming system and tried to disable it. One of the main goals of the NNG's "nation-building" was to abolish tax-farming and to introduce direct taxation by the state. Because tax-farming practices had prospered in Guangdong and Guangdong was where the Kuomintang (hereafter KMT) had established its home base, it was here that there was an attempt to replace the tax-farming system with direct taxation. Even though Guangdong maintained its de facto independence from the NNG from 1932 to 1936, its financial and fiscal policy basically inherited the legacy of the KMT in the 1920s. Consequently, the thriving tax-farming system in Guangdong in the 1930s provides a clue to the riddle of why tax-farming flourished in the 1930s when nation-building was so eagerly pursued. This chapter will take a comprehensive look at attempts

1 Prasenjit Duara, *Culture, Power and the State: Rural North China, 1900–1942* (Stanford, CA: Stanford University Press, 1988).

2 Susan Mann, *Local Merchants and the Chinese Bureaucracy, 1750–1950* (Stanford, CA: Stanford University Press, 1987), 186–199.

to build a modern taxation administration by overcoming "brokerism" and the complex reactions by Chinese society in Guangdong.

Song Ziwen's reform of the tax-farming tradition in Guangdong province

The problems with the widespread contract system of taxation in Guangdong were pointed out early on. The preface to the *Guangdong Financial Statement*, published in 1911, stresses the disturbances caused by the contract system of taxation, stating:

> The most severe strain on Guangdong's finances is the contract merchants' collection of a gambling tax. In addition, under the contract system there is also a slaughter tax, an opium tax, a wine tax, an entertainment tax, and a prostitution tax. The cases may vary. In one case, many merchants may jointly contract a single tax, and in other cases, a merchant may contract a single tax within one or several prefectures or a single county. In some cases, one merchant receives the contract rights for a single tax item, then he subcontracts it with sub-agencies according to district, and then the sub-agencies divide it again according to guild, forming a staircase-like structure.[3]

This passage shows that tax-farming was widespread in Guangdong province at the end of the Qing dynasty. The political unrest in the early Republican era in fact rapidly expanded the tax-farming system, called *baoshang-zhi* or *chengshang-zhi*, to an unprecedented level. Even the regular taxes, such as the land tax, were generally collected by the contractors in the 1920s. Because the tax collection system for a single tax in Guangdong frequently oscillated between a contract system and direct collection by the state, it is difficult to determine the ratio of tax revenue collected by the contract system among the total tax revenue. Nonetheless, collection of the gambling tax, opium tax, and *likin*, the three largest tax resources in Guangdong province, was always based on a contract system. Furthermore, commercial taxes in Guangdong were primarily collected by tax-farming merchants; the proportion of commercial taxes relative to total tax revenue could be as

3 Guangdongsheng caizheng kexue yanjiusuo [Fiscal Science Research Center, Department of Finance, Guangdong], ed., *Guangdong caizheng shuomingshu* [Guangdong financial statement] (Guangzhou: Guangdong jingji chubanshe, 1997), 8.

much as 80 percent. Therefore, it is no exaggeration to say that the contract system was the major way of collecting taxes in Guangdong during the Republican period.

The right to select the contractors belonged not only to the governments at all levels (province, city, prefecture, and county) but also to the military or a senior contractor, called a "general company" (*zonggongsi*) or a "general merchant" (*zongshang*). In some cases, contract rights were even sold abroad. For example, during the period of occupation by the Guangxi military clique in the 1920s, Military Governor Lu Rongting and Provincial Governor Mo Rongxin financed military expenses with foreign loans provided by the Bank of Taiwan in exchange for tax revenue put up as security. At that time, the tobacco and wine taxes, *likin*, the cowhide tax, the cow butchery tax, and the entertainment tax were all collected by contractors chosen by the comprador of the Bank of Taiwan.[4]

All governments in Guangdong during the Republican era attempted to unify their tax collection systema under their direct control so as to be able to monopolize funds. However, since it was nearly impossible to immediately eliminate the system of middlemen based on contracts, the governments sought to simplify and systemize the widely divided tax-farming practices. An example is the introduction of the general merchant at the provincial level. To prevent local garrisons from withholding revenue, the Guangdong provincial government under Chen Jiongming applied the idea of a general merchant to supervise collection of the tobacco and wine taxes throughout the province. But this attempt was thwarted by local military intervention. It was Song Ziwen's reform that, to some extent, restored some order to the confused taxation administration after The Guangdong Nationalist Government was established in 1925.[5]

In short, Song's reform sought to unify financial sources. Appointed director of Finance in September 1925, Song Ziwen had rushed to reform Guangdong finance to help relieve the Guangdong Nationalist Government of its financial predicament. The reform focused first on reclaiming the tax revenue controlled by the local garrisons, and second on reforming tax-farming practices and drawing up a government budget. In reality, because reclaiming the tax revenue was identical to removing the military's right to appoint contractors, these two reforms were inter-connected in the

4 Yu Yanguang and Chen Fulin, *Nanyue geju: Cong Long Jiguang dao Chen Jitang* [The separatist regime of southern Guangdong: From Long Jiguang to Chen Jitang] (Guangzhou: Guangdong renmin chubanshe, 1989), 102–103.

5 Yu and Chen, *Nanyue geju*, 114.

reform of the tax-farming system. To accomplish his goal, he had to not only subdue complaints from the military but also to allow access to taxation information. The latter was a more complicated issue.

The core of Song's strategy to increase revenue was placed on expanding indirect tax revenue by raising the rates of the freight tax, the tobacco and wine taxes, and the stamp tax, and so on. For this purpose, the government had to have accurate information about the market and to secure accurate statistics for taxation. Song Ziwen ordered that the *likin* tax contractors report periodic statistics on the value and volume of cargo in and out of the checkpoints. Meanwhile, Song separately sent finance officials to the tax offices and required them to issue monthly reports. Furthermore, the tax-farming merchants were required to produce periodic reports on the number, capital, and sales of stores in their respective contracted districts. At the higher administrative levels, a Tax Improvement Committee, installed in the Department of Finance, recruited educated finance officials by examination. These officials were dispatched to the local tax offices to study the local situations, and their promotions by the Department of Finance were based in part on these reports.

To some extent, Song Ziwen's reform was successful and it eventually succeeded in recovering the *likin* taxation rights in southern Guangdong and the Xi River area from the First Force and the Fourth Force. Because the central government had no information about the local situation due to the long-standing contract system, rather than abolishing all contract practices, Song Ziwen introduced an open and competitive bidding system to select the contractors.[6] The bidding system could supply more revenue to the government. However, Song also promoted a monopoly system as an essential means of financial unification. Song Ziwen successfully raised government tax revenue by implementing a monopoly on the stamp tax, the tobacco and wine taxes, and the opium tax.[7]

In spite of success in increasing revenue, Song Ziwen's reforms could not fundamentally change the contract tax-collecting tradition in Guangdong. This was also the case of the newly introduced monopoly. Originally, the opium tax had been collected by a unit of the divided districts where the

6 Gaimushō tsūshōkyoku [Trade Bureau, Ministry of Foreign Affairs, Japan], *Saikin no kanton keizai jijō* [The recent economic situation in Guangdong] (Tokyo: Gaimushōtsūshōkyoku, 1927), 25–30.

7 Song Ziwen, "Yinian yilai guoku shengku shouru ji zhengdun caizheng zhuangkuang wenti" [An analysis of the adjustment of revenue between the national treasury and the provincial treasury during the past year], 5 November 1925, *Guangdongsheng caizheng jishi*, Vol. 1, Part 1, 51.

troops or the contractors controlled tax collection. Song decided to implement a monopoly on opium tax collection for the next four years, beginning in September 1925. However, this so-called monopoly did not mean that the government directly controlled the sales and taxation of opium; rather it meant that the Ministry of Finance would hold exclusive rights to appoint the district tax-collection contractors. In other words, the contract system was maintained while supervision by the government was strengthened. In practice, this monopoly was no different from the previous attempt to introduce general merchants during the period of rule by Chen Jiongming.

In December 1925, Song Ziwen placed the opium tax office of the Anti-Opium Supervision Office (*duyan dubanshu*) under the direct control of the Ministry of Finance. However, a sharp decrease in the amount of tax revenue in May 1926 forced Song Ziwen to restore the old system of entrusting tax collection to contractors. Moreover, as private opium flooded the market, the monopoly system remained nominal.[8] Later, during the period of Chen Jitang's rule, the gambling tax and the opium tax were exclusively commissioned by the Dalai Company operated by a Chen Jitang insider, Huo Zhitang. The revenue from the two taxes was appropriated for military spending rather than for the provincial budget.[9]

Song Ziwen's efforts to reform finance in Guangdong were decisively interrupted by the revival of warlordism and the political unrest after the Nationalist government left Guangdong following the Northern Expedition. In November 1927 Chen Jitang, who garrisoned in Chaozhou and Mei county, announced the withholding of tax revenue in the name of autonomy.[10] Guangdong's financial situation returned to what it had been in the days before Song Ziwen's reform. Nonetheless, Song Ziwen's 1925 reform eventually became a model for the financial restructuring of the successive Guangdong provincial governments.

The banquet tax issue

To understand the tax contract system in Guangdong, it is necessary to consider why Song Ziwen could not but compromise to maintain the contract

8 Guangdongsheng Caizhengting [Department of Finance, Guangdong], *Guangdongsheng caizheng jishi* [Record of finance in Guangdong province] (Guangzhou: Guangdongshengcaizhengting, 1933), Vol. 1, Part 1, 51–52.

9 Yu and Chen, *Nanyue geju*, 134.

10 *Shenbao*, 28 November 1927.

system. If the tax contract system or the tax-farming system were simply evil exploitation of the taxpayers, the reform would have easily won the support of the merchant groups that represented the tax base of the commercial taxes. The fundamental reason for the persistence of the contract system was not only because the existing tax contractors resisted the reform but also because the merchants as taxpayers preferred the contract system to direct taxation.[11]

To increase revenue to fund the Northern Expedition, the Nationalist government in Guangdong mobilized all kinds of financial strategies. In this picture, the traditional tax contracting system was resisted by the merchants to avoid excessive taxation. The Banquet Tax issue in 1930 revealed the complicated characteristics of the tax contract system in Guangdong.

Guangdong could take a breath when the Nationalist government moved northward after the victory of the Northern Expedition in 1927. The military leader Li Jishen, who ruled thereafter, sought to establish a separatist regime. But, when the NNG detained Li Jishen in March 1929, Guangdong again fell into the hands of the Nationalist Party. This would last until the anti-Jiang movement by Chen Jitang in 1931. During this takeover period, reform of the tax collection contract system was attempted, as seen in the case of the banquet tax in Guangzhou.

This tax was literally a tax on banquets, a kind of entertainment tax or business tax paid by restaurants and bars in the city. Before 1930, the banquet tax was customarily collected by a contractor. This contactor, called a "tax merchant" (*juanshang*), was usually a member of the restaurant and tea house guild. Once the total amount of contracted tax was fixed, the contractor would allocate the tax burdens according to district based on negotiations with the guild members. The contractor would subcontract collection according to district. In principle, the amount of tax paid by individual shops was determined by the basis of the size of the business. Meanwhile, the grading of shops, tax amounts, and subcontracts were determined conventionally by the guild's bylaws. In reality, the banquet tax was collected by the guild.

However, the Guangdong provincial government (hereafter, the GPG) announced a new rule for the banquet tax beginning in 1930. This action followed "abolition of the *likin* and implementation of a new tax" in 1929. The GPG delegated all taxation authority to a newly appointed contracting

11 John Fitzgerald's book on the Nationalist regime's exploitation of Guangdong society during the 1920s can help understand this point. John Fitzgerald, *Awakening China: Politics, Culture and Class in the Nationalist Revolution* (Stanford, CA: Stanford University Press, 1996).

agency and canceled the districts' conventional subcontracting. Instead, the GPG adopted a fixed tax-rate system that collected 16.5 percent of sales. The Dean Company was selected as the new contractor under the condition of a yearly tax quota of 30,000 *yuan*. The owner of this company, Wu Zhefu, confidently declared that 1 million *yuan* of tax revenue per year was expected on a fixed-rate basis. This attracted investments from all walks of life. Contemporaries called the Dean Company the Banquet Tax Company.

The success of the new policy depended on access to concrete sales information. Therefore, the Banquet Tax Company forced all stores to submit a "tax report form" on every banquet. However, even though tax collectors monitored the business of each restaurant, the restaurants would fabricate the tax report form to manipulate the sales amount and to evade the taxes. As a countermeasure, the company introduced a new regulation regarding the tax report form called the three connected forms (*liandan banfa*), for the restaurant, the customer, and the tax collector. The company was thus confident about determining the exact sales amount for taxation.

The restaurant guild and the merchants began negotiations with the company, suggesting a restoration of the traditional district contract at the cost of raising the tax amount. The company declined this offer. The Liquor Industry Association and the Guangzhou Chamber of Commerce petitioned the Department of Finance to abolish the Banquet Tax Company, stating that the new method was very cumbersome and difficult to implement. When the Department of Finance rejected this petition, as an action of last resort they decided to engage in a strike. Beginning on 6 September 1930, all restaurants in Guangzhou went on strike. When the strike began, the price of food in the city plummeted, with duck, chicken, and meat prices plunging by about 30 percent compared to before the strike. The GPG took a hardline policy, including the arrest of three leading merchants, but the strike did not end. Eventually, on 30 September, the Department of Finance decided to abolish the Banquet Tax Company and promised to maintain the prior "self-operation" (*ziban*) of tax collection (i.e., a conventional guild-contract system). The restaurants resumed business on 1 October, but the Department of Finance exacted a tax increase from the restaurant guild as a condition for concessions. Merchants could restore the contracting practice partly because of their persistent resistance and partly because of the government's priority to increase revenue.[12]

12 *Shenbao*, 8, 12, 18, and 30 September, and 3 and 4 October 1930; Chen Boren, "Caizheng he shuijuan" [Finance and taxes and levies], in *Nantian suiyue: Chen Jitang zhu Yue shiqi jianwen shilu* [Days of the southern sky: Records of personal experiences about Guangdong under the rule

The confrontation between the merchants and the Department of Finance over the banquet tax probably strengthened the government's commitment to reform the contract system. As soon as the merchants withdrew from the strike, on 6 October, the director of Finance, Fan Qiwu, announced that he would completely abolish the tax-farming system as soon as military tensions due to the anti-Jiang movement in Guangdong could be eased. Fan proposed a reform plan to the Southwest Political Council of the Nationalist Party to replace the local contracting taxation with direct tax collection by the government. For this purpose, Fan suggested the creation of the General Tax Bureau (*shuiwu zongju*) under the Tax Office of the Department of Finance to be in charge of taxation. In addition, each prefecture and each county were to set up a tax office, varying in rank from 1 to 4, to be in charge of regional taxation affairs. The Southwest Political Council recommended implementing this system in a few counties on a trial basis and then expanding it to all provinces. In the following year, 1931, the reform of the tax-farming system in Guangdong province was also discussed within the NNG. On 31 August 1931, the Nanjing Government Finance Commission (*Nanjing zhengfu caizheng weiyuanhui*) submitted a proposal to abolish the tax contract system in Guangdong by adopting the government agency system (*weiban*). The NNG approved this proposal.[13] However, because Chen Jitang's regime separately administered Guangdong, the actual reform was left in the hands of the GPG under Chen Jitang.

The tax contract system had a dual nature that swung between the merchants as taxpayers and state power as tax collectors. Song Ziwen's reform was an attempt to pull the contract system away from the taxpayers' side and to attract it to the state's side through open bidding for the contract and unified administration for selecting a general contractor at the

of Chen Jitang], ed. Guangdongsheng zhengxie wenshi ziliao yanjiu weiyuanhui (Guangzhou: Guangdong renmin chubanshe, 1987), 300–301; Suma Yakichirō, Acting Consul General of Guangdong→Shidehara Kijūrō, Minister of Foreign Affairs of Japan, "Tōshi ryōri ten dōmei higyō ni kansuru ken" [Our city restaurant allied strike], 9 September 1930, E.1.3.2.1-003 Chūgoku ni okeru sozei oyobi futankin kankei zakken [Miscellaneous matters related to taxes and contributions in China, Vol. 3], Gaimushō, Gaikō Shiryōkan (Diplomatic Archives of the Ministry of Foreign Affairs of Japan), Tokyo.

13 Suma Yakichirō→Shidehara Kijūrō, "Zaiseichō no kakushu zeien ukeoi seido haishi kata keikaku ni kansuru ken" [The plan of the Department of Finance to abolish various tax contract systems], 9 October 1930, E.1.3.2.1-003; Suma Yakichirō→Shidehara Kijūrō, 3 September 1931, E.1.3.2.1-003. According to Uchida's research on Shanxi province, most tax collection was executed by a contract system, depending on the merchant guild. Uchida Tomoyuki, "1930 nendai ni okeru En Sekizan seiken no zaisei seisaku" [Fiscal policy of the Yan Xishan regime in the 1930s], *Ajia Keizai* 25(7) (1984): 16.

provincial level. In other words, as a way to collect taxes, the contracting system itself was the neutral concept. It could not be said to be simply a tool for state power to penetrate the private sector or, on the contrary, a means to ensure guild protection. The roles and implications of the tax contract system had already been changing and being reinterpreted in the context of the contemporary reformers. The banquet tax issue in 1930 demonstrated that the tax contractors were about to change from being members of the business communities to being members of a government organization. The reorganized contract system in Republican China was an unfamiliar tax system that was not ruled by traditional social norms. It became a weapon to destroy the self-defensive walls of traditional society and to allow infiltration by state power. This conversion, plotted by Song Ziwen's reform, was inherited by the Guangdong provincial government in the 1930s.

The tax contract system under Chen Jitang

Readjustment of financial institutions

Chen Jitang took over military leadership of Guangdong province after Li Jishen, who was detained by the NNG in 1929. Despite the initial cooperation between Chen and the NNG in the course of replacing Li Jishen, in May 1931 Chen decided to join the anti-Jiang movement and support the establishment of an alternative Nationalist government in Guangzhou led by Hu Hanmin. After dissolution of the Guangdong Nationalist Government in January 1932 and a May coup, Chen strengthened separatist control of Guangdong, and the Southwest Political Council of the Nationalist Party, stationed in Guangzhou, maintained the legitimacy of Chen's separatist regime until the death of Hu Hanmin in 1936.

Under the slogan "Reconstructing Guangdong with Guangdong people's own hands," the GPG under Chen's rule attempted modern state-building at the provincial level by promoting economic, social, and administrative modernization. The person leading the financial reforms during practically the whole of Chen Jitang's time in power was Qu Fangpu, director of Finance in Guangdong from 6 May 1932 to 21 August 1936. In principle, Qu's financial management project followed Song Ziwen's financial strategy faithfully.

The GPG was asked to finance the growing military spending to maintain the Guangdong separatist regime. The decentralization of financial authorities was one of the obstacles thwarting the GPG's efforts to raise revenue.

The GPG actively sought to rebuild the tax administration, and its ultimate goal was to replace the tax contract system with direct tax collection by finance officials and to build tax offices throughout the province. The GPG thus sought to reorganize fiscal administration at the county level.

At the time, county finance, as well as lower administrative localities, faced the task of "balancing the budget by itself" (*ziwei shouzhi*). Each district had its own budget (*qushou*), and each village had its own budget (*xiangshou*) as well. Each county in Guangdong had a Finance Bureau (*caizhengju*) set up under direct control by the Department of Finance in Guangzhou. However, the chief of the Finance Bureau was appointed by the county magistrate. Many county magistrates in Guangdong maintained their positions regardless of the change of power in Guangzhou. Accordingly, the chiefs and the county magistrates were highly interconnected local people. The magistrates did not blindly follow orders of the GPG, and the chiefs often violated the chain of command issued by the Department of Finance. In addition, the operating expenses of the Finance Bureau came not from the Department of Finance but from the county government. Therefore, it was said that "the county magistrate largely manages county finance." District and village finance was seized by the local gentry, and the so-called "chief of the Finance Bureau was nothing more than the private accountant of the county magistrate."[14] Seeking to understand the local economies and local finance and to reform the above situation, Qu Fangpu attempted to enhance the status of the Finance Bureau and to incorporate it into the chain of command under the Department of Finance.[15]

As a first step, in March 1933 the GPG announced the Provisional Regulations of the County Finance Bureaus (*gexian caizhengju zanxing zhangcheng*). Article 1 of the General Rules of the regulation articulated that the Finance Bureau was responsible for the collection, remittance, storage, and arrangement of all local taxes. According to Article 2, the chief of the Finance Bureau was to be appointed by the GPG based on a recommendation from the Department of Finance.[16]

14 In July 1927, Guangdong province abolished the prefectural collegial system and restored a prefectural magistrate system. *Shenbao*, 13 July 1927.

15 *Guangdongsheng caizheng jishi*, Vol. 1, Part 1, 99; Qin Qingjun, "Duiyu Guangdongsheng sannian caizheng jihua zhi shangquan" [Discussion on the Three-Year Financial Plan of Guangdong province], *Xin Guangdong* 1(1933): 4; Gu Yu, "Guangdongsheng sannian shizheng jihua xia zh[illegible] Guangdong caizhenglun" [On finance in Guangdong under the Three-Year Administrative Pl[illegible] of Guangdong province], *Xin Guangdong* 5 (1933): 4.

16 Gu Yu, "Guangdongsheng sannian shizheng jihua xia zhi Guangdong caizhenglu," 3.

On 14 February, the GPG therefore implemented the screening and examination process to select the county magistrate and the chief of the Finance Bureau. On 14 February, 1933, the GPG implemented a screening regulation regarding the chief of the Finance Bureau at the county level. Then, in April, the Provisional Regulations for the Examination of General Public Officials in Guangdong Province (*Guangdongsheng putong gongwuyuan kaoshi zanxing zhangcheng*) was implemented, which stipulated the selection of the chief of the Finance Bureau through regular examinations to be held every May.[17]

Prior to this, the examination for selecting the county magistrate took place on 1 April 1933, with fifty-one successful applicants. But the number of qualified candidates was not enough to fill the ninety-four slots for county magistrate in Guangdong province. Subsequently, the GPG conducted an additional examination to determine the current county magistrates' qualifications based on academic background, experiences, and work performance.[18] In the wake of the screening of the current county magistrates, in July 1934 the GPG established a "Public Officials Qualification Committee" (*gongwuyuan zhenbie weiyuanhui*) in July 1934. The committee sought to expand the screening process of the GPG to public servants and public officials in counties, cities, and government-affiliated organizations.

Second, the GPG attempted to raise the education level of the required public officials. Entering 1935, along with the examination and screening, the GPG recruited graduates and students from the School of Military Politics and the Advanced Course on Politics for county magistrates and public officials in the county governments.[19] The above endeavors by the GPG, which were a precondition for fiscal reform, aimed to establish a modern state administrative system based on a disciplined civil service system.

"Dingqi kaoxuan gexian caizheng juzhang" [Regular examination for selecting the County
f the Finance Bureau], *Xin Guangdong* 4 (1933): 118.
ng xianzhang kaoshi yu shixing sannian jihua" [Examination for selecting County
nd implementing the Three-Year Plan], *Xin Guangdong* 1 (1933): 70; "Zhenbie xianren
g juzhang kezhang" [Screening for the current head chiefs and section chief of
u in all counties], *Xin Guangdong* 8 (1933): 112. For detailed information about
e Kang Jin-A, "1930 nendai chūgoku niokeru chōzei ukeo seido no kaikaku
d reform of the tax-farming system in China in the 1930s], *Rekishigaku*

nian shengzheng sheshi zhi huigu" [Review of the performance of
e twenty-third year of the Republic of China (1934)], *Xin Guangdong*
iyu Guangdongsheng sannian caizheng jihua zhi shangquan"
cial plan of Guangdong province], *Xin Guangdong* 1 (1933):

Third, a periodic provincial finance conference was called to compile reports from each county and to discuss the reform plan. This idea was reminiscent of the National Finance Conference held by the NNG, when each province was to dispatch a representative to discuss the national financial reform agenda. Finally, the GPG declared that the balances of local finance at the provincial and county levels should be publicized monthly. Thereafter, the Provincial Assembly and the councils in about eighty counties would vote on their own local budgets. As to the lower localities, the Representative Congress of the District, the Villagers' Congress, and the Town Congress would decide on their own budgets.

However, the effectiveness of these administrative reforms is questionable. There had already been a plan to establish a county budget during Chen Jitang's rule, but it was never implemented. It was during the Second Sino-Japanese War that the wartime provincial government had several counties draw up their own budgets on a trial basis.

Besides, the tax contract system, which was to be abolished with the reform of financial administration, was still prevalent until the centralization of Guangdong province in 1936. Chen Songguang writes in his book *Local Finance in the Counties of Guangdong Province* that each county government financed its own expenditures because the Chen Jitang regime had adopted a policy of noninterference.[20] He suggests that the delegation of the chief of the Finance Bureau to each county in 1933 did not have much of an effect and that the county continued to manage itself.[21]

In the long run, GPG administrative reforms were necessary to establish a modern tax administration, but in the short run they were not expected to be very effective.

Full implementation of open bidding in 1932

When he took office as director of Finance in May 1932, Qu Fangpu announced an "Outline on the Rearrangement of Taxes" (*zhengli shuijuan dagang*). The Outline mandated that all taxes for which the contract had expired were to be chosen through open public bidding (*dangzhong mingtou*). As to the contracts already ratified by Qu's predecessor, if the contract began before the end of September, the contract would be recognized, but the contracted amount would be raised by 20 to 30 percent. Those

20 Chen Songguang, *Guangdong zhi xian difang caizheng* [Local finance in the counties of Guangdong province] (Qujiang: Mandihong banyue kanshe, 1941), 17.
21 Chen Songguang, *Guangdong zhi xian difang caizheng*, 12–13.

contracts that were to start after September, however, would be canceled, and open bidding would be held for contract rights.[22] Under this policy, Qu Fangpu secured an increase of about 150,000 *yuan* for three months (8 May–5 August) after his inauguration. Beginning in July 1932, the tax contractors, regardless of whether they were national taxes or local taxes, were selected by open public bidding. The amount of the tax contracts raised provincial incomes but this also led to a rise in prices, which hurt the livelihoods of ordinary people.[23]

Bidding under Qu was different from the earlier bidding system in that it introduced full open bidding. This means that the GPG was attempting to increase tax revenue by introducing the principles of openness, fairness, and competition in the contract system instead of replacing the tax contract system with direct tax collection. After implementing the "Outline on the Rearrangement of Taxes," government income increased daily and the harmful effects of the contract system reportedly decreased. In fact, the idea of open bidding had already been proposed by Song Ziwen. However, unlike Song, Qu suspended the instant change to direct tax collection and to some extent introduced a public contractor selection process. Qu apparently had his own reasons for acting in this way. Since January 1932, the GPG had been under extreme financial pressure to fund the expenditures for the anti-Jiang movement and the alternative Nationalist government in Guangzhou. Qu's predecessors, like Qu himself, had no choice but to borrow money from the tax contract merchants. Most of these debts consisted of "advanced taxation," whereby the tax contractors prepaid the amount of the future tax contract to the GPG in advance. When Qu took office, the government had so far already spent 1.5 million *yuan* from the future revenue of the pawn tax, 1 million *yuan* from the tax contractors' security, and about 2.7 million *yuan* from the future revenue of other miscellaneous taxes. To repay the above debts, after taking office Qu had to deduct an average of 440,000 *yuan* from the monthly tax revenue for eight months (May 1932–December 1932).

Meanwhile, Qu searched for every way possible to raise money and repay the 3.3 million *yuan* of debt during the same period. However, up until the point of Qu's resignation, when funds were required to finance military tensions it was necessary to repeatedly borrow cash from the contractors. The abolition of the tax contract system could not have been possible in

22 *Guangdongsheng caizheng jishi*, Vol. 1, Part 1, 90.

23 Guangdong dang'anguan, *Chen Jitang yanjiu shiliao, 1928–1936* [Historical materials for research on Chen Jitang] (Guangzhou: Guangdongsheng dang'anguan, 1985), 289.

the absence of a capacity to repay the debt. Therefore, the GPG chose open bidding to increase tax revenue while maintaining the contract system.[24]

The introduction of open bidding was also intended to prevent military interference in finance. The local military garrison would often borrow cash from the local tax contractor and give him a military receipt. The local tax contractor would submit the receipt to the Department of Finance as part of his tax collection quota. Therefore, the tensions between the Department of Finance and the military continued. According to the recollections of Chen Boren, who had worked as a high-ranking official in the Department of Finance during the tenures of both Feng Zhuwan and Qu Fangfu, in many cases the tax contractors would use assumed names. The military and political leaders often exerted influence on the Department of Finance by selecting the tax contractors. Thus, in fact, Qu's "open bidding" was intended to block the military's influence in appointing the contractors.[25]

Furthermore, the full implementation of the open bidding can be interpreted in the context of the financial unification promoted by the GPG. The Three-Year Plan beginning in 1933 sought to prevent double and triple taxation. The GPG therefore took various measures to merge the miscellaneous taxes on the same item into a single tax. During Chen Jitang's rule, the consolidation and unification of taxes mostly ended up in the adoption of the contract system for collection. Paradoxically, the government still made progress in unifying taxes by merging various taxes into a single contracted tax.[26]

The last attempt at full-scale reform of the tax contract system in 1934 was a unique experiment. In 1933, in the midst of the world depression and the subsequent economic recession in China, Guangdong's economy, especially Shantou, was hard hit by financial crises, including the bankruptcy of native banks, bank runs, and silver drains. As a countermeasure, the GPG pushed ahead with its efforts to strengthen its grip on the economy and finance. In April 1934, the Department of Finance thus announced a plan to collect all taxes by direct official collection. The entire territory of Guangdong was divided into eight tax districts and a General Office of Provincial Levies (*quansheng shuijuan zongchu*) was to be established.[27] The Department of Finance imposed an active measure against the Special Taxes, which

24 *Guangdongsheng caizheng jishi*, Vol. 1, Part 1, 96.

25 Chen Boren, "Chen Jitang tongzhi jituan de hengzheng baolian" [Tyrannical rule and excessive exploitation by the ruling group in the Chen Jitang regime], *Guangzhou wenshi ziliao* 16 (1965): 108–109.

26 Qin Qingjun, "Duiyu Guangdongsheng sannian caizheng jihua zhi shangquan," 5–6.

27 *Shenbao*, 27 and 29 April 1934.

constituted about 30 percent of the total tax revenue. Seven kinds of Special Taxes that had been collected by the contractors were integrated into the direct collection by the Bureau of Provincial Special Taxes on Agricultural Imports. As a result, all Special Taxes, except for those on wax and dried goods, were collected by the government tax office. The Special Tax had been advertised as a "modern tax" that took the system one step farther away from the *likin*. A reformist agenda was thus applied to the Special Tax earlier than to the other taxes.[28]

However, except in the case of the Special Tax, complete abolition of the contract system was never declared. This was because of the financial vulnerability of the GPG. As explained above, the GPG depended heavily on fundraising through loans from merchants. In April 1934, the GPG borrowed 5 million *yuan* from merchants in Guangzhou to deal with the financial crisis caused by the plunge in the market value of Guangdong Provincial Notes.[29] Meanwhile, the GPG forced the tax contractors to purchase provincial government bonds and to raise money through advance tax payments. These additional burdens on the tax contractors mainly occurred in 1935 as military tensions with the NNG were escalating. In the end, the GPG could not escape from the existing tax collection practice until it found a new way to raise funds.

The tax contract system after centralization of Guangdong

The NNG harshly criticized the harmful effects of the tax contract system that was prevalent in Guangdong prior to 1936. However, once the NNG took over Guangdong province, the NNG took a cautious attitude toward reform, stating, "In principle, taxes should be collected by government agencies, but because there are special circumstances for some taxes, for the time being

28 Harada Chūichirō, Consul of Shantou→Arita Hachirō, Minister of Foreign Affairs of Japan, 17 April 1936, E.1.3.2.1-2-1 Santō mondai kome senzei [The Shantou issue: the Special Tax on Rice]. In addition, in 1934 the GPG adopted the commissioner system for collection of the banquet tax referred to above. "Yanxi fujia juan wei zhun chexiao" [Additional charge of the banquet tax is not allowed to be cancelled], *Shishanghui zhoukan* 19 (1934). It is not clear how close the 1934 commissioner system was to direct collection by the government because in most cases the status of the commissioner was contracted. After the Japanese occupation of Guangzhou, an open bidding system for tax contracts was reintroduced in 1942. Zai kanton nihon taishikan jimusho [Office of the Embassy of Japan in Guangdong], ed., *Kantonshō chihōzei zeisoku* [Local tax regulations in Guangdong province] (Guangzhou: Printed in November 1943), (collection of Sun Yat-sen Library, Guangzhou), 79–84. Policy continued to vacillate between direct tax collection and tax contracting.
29 *Shenbao*, 13 April 1934, 19 January 1935.

we will continue to allow tax contracts for merchants, but we will adopt an open bidding method."[30] Full reform was thus suspended.

Finally, in 1937 the NNG and the new GPG adopted a full fiscal reform in Guangdong province. The first obstacle that the new GPG faced was strong opposition from the merchants against the introduction of a business tax. A business tax had been partially implemented in Guangdong on 1 May 1931, but it had failed to be executed properly. The NNG rushed to introduce a business tax in Guangdong based on the same regulation as that in other provinces of China. In early January 1937, the Department of Finance announced the "New Regulations on the Business Tax" (*yingyeshui xinzhang*), in which the tax rate was set at 0.5 percent of the amount of sales. All merchants in Guangzhou, under the lead of the Guangzhou Chamber of Commerce, immediately launched a campaign against this business tax. The reason for the opposition was not much different from the rationale during the anti-taxation movement against the banquet tax in 1930. Merchants were reluctant to disclose their sales conditions to the government and they demanded changes to the tax base and lower tax rates. After a month-long demonstration, in February 1937 the Ministry of Finance in Nanjing eased the regulation stipulating that the tax base could be adjusted from the sales amount to the merchants' assets according to the circumstances. Again, the NNG reduced the tax rate from 0.5 percent to 0.2 percent. However, merchants in Guangzhou did not end their resistance and they continued to stage a strike. As a result, in March the NNG promised an overall re-examination of the tax base of the business tax and the regulations.[31]

At the same time, the NNG and the new GPG declared that the six tax contracts that had expired would not be renewed, while tax-farming on three taxes under the direct official collection would be restored.[32] The general contract merchant system was also reformed. The GPG decided to withdraw the general merchants' subcontracting rights and to hold open bidding in each district to select subcontractors. Finally, the Department of Finance delegated collection of the banquet tax to the county governments, except in the case of the banquet tax in Guangzhou, where collection was managed by the Business Tax Bureau. According to a 1937 report on these reforms, in 1936 the amount of the tax contracts that were to be abolished

30 Guangdong caizhengting mishushi [Secretary's Office, Department of Finance, Guangdong], *Guangdong caizheng jiyao* [Financial summary of Guangdong] Guangzhou: Guangdong caizhengting, 1937), 57.

31 *Shenbao*, 13, 23 January, 6, 18 February, 24, 26, 27 March, and 1 April 1937.

32 Chen Boren, "Caizheng he shuijuan," 299.

amounted to 24.8 million *yuan* in provincial tax and 0.87 million *yuan* in county and city taxes. This means that more than 80 percent of local tax revenue from Guangdong taxes (31.19 million *yuan*) was collected through tax contract merchants.[33] This amount does not include the revenue from the contracted opium tax and the gambling tax revenue that had been abolished after the NNG took over Guangdong. The revenue of these two taxes in 1935 was as much as 19.32 million *yuan*. Despite the fact that Guangdong's local tax revenue was nearly halved in 1936 due to the centralization, it can be said that at least 70–80 percent of total tax revenue in Guangdong was collected through the tax contract system in the 1930s.[34]

The reform plan went into effect on 1 July 1937. At the same time, Zeng Yangfu, the new director of Finance in Guangdong, made an effort to reform fiscal administration throughout the province. The focus of the reform was the drawing up of county budgets and the separation of provincial finance from county finance. Zeng's idea was partially realized during wartime.[35]

The outbreak of the Second Sino-Japanese War interrupted the course of the reform. Ironically, it was the war itself that outdated the prevalent tax contracting practices. Emergency fiscal requirements strengthened the government's control of financial and fiscal operations. Nevertheless, the agenda for long-term modernization of fiscal administration was frustrated by the war.

In the 1930s, the GPG under the rule of Chen Jitang and the NNG envisioned replacing the irregular taxation under the tax contract system with a modernized taxation, by which the government could access information regarding the tax base so as to levy taxes such as the business tax and the income tax at legal rates. But the introduction and expansion of these new taxes had to be delayed until the end of the war. The role of the tax contracting system in funding provincial finance declined. Meanwhile, the sources that supported the wartime finances were the land tax in-kind, the miscellaneous taxes, and irregular allotments similar to those in the late Qing.

33 *Guangdong caizheng jiyao*, 57–58.

34 Guangdong's provincial revenue was halved from 61.81 million *yuan* in 1935 to 31.19 million *yuan* in 1936. Guangdongsheng difang shizhi bianzuan weiyuanhui [Compilation Committee for The Gazetteer of Guangdong Province], *Guangdongsheng zhi: Caizheng zhi* [Gazetteer of Guangdong Province: Finance] (Guangzhou: Guangdong renmin chubanshe, 1999), 51.

35 Chen Songguang, *Guangdong zhi xian difang caizheng*, 17–27. For experimentation of county reforms in Sichuan province, see Yamamoto Shin, "Nicchūsensō kaishi zengo shisenshō Shinto ken ni okeru kensei kaikaku no jikken to sono zasetsu: hōi jiken ni taisuru ichikōsatsu" [Aborted experiment of the county administration reforms in Xindu county, Sichuan province around the time of the outbreak of the Sino-Japanese War: In light of the Siege Incident], *Hitotsubashi ronsō* 120(2) (1998).

8 Regularization of the Tax-farming System

Abstract
The tax contract system reform in Guangdong province under the separatist rule in the 1930s faithfully adopted Song Ziwen's original reform program in the 1920s. But Guangdong provincial government in the 1930s attempted to systematize it more skillfully by introducing a full-scale open-bid contract. This chapter demonstrates the specific process of the tax-farming contract using five files related to the tax contractors, found among the documents of the Department of Finance, Guangdong Provincial Archives. Chapter 8 shows the vitality and merits of the tax contract system to appeal to the government and the taxpayers. For a government with weak administrative capacity, soliciting tax contractors was an attractive option to minimize tax costs and secure a fixed amount of tax revenue.

Keywords: tax-farming. Guangdong, tax contractors, Republican China

The process of tax-farming

This chapter demonstrates the specific process of the tax-farming contract using five files related to the tax contractors, found among the documents of the Department of Finance, Guangdong Provincial Archives. Table 8.1 below provides an overview of each cited file.

File No. 3 focuses on a provincial level contractor completing a one-year contract term without a problem. The other files are all related to sub-provincial contract issues. No. 5 is a compilation of documents about the process of changing from a contract to a government agency for tax collection. File Nos. 1, 2, and 4, related to debt collection, provide many clues to understanding the operations of the contract company. These contractors were all in default on their monthly rent. The Department of Finance confiscated their securities and assets, and sometimes ordered

Kang, Jin-A, *The Guangdong Model and Taxation in China*. Taylor & Francis Group, 2022
DOI: 10.5117/9789463725248_CH08

Table 8.1 List of files on tax contractors found among the documents of the Department of Finance, Guangdong Provincial Archives

No.	Tax	Tax contractor	Representative merchant	Contract locality	Archive No.
1	Miscellaneous gambling levies	Dayuan Company	Mai Ruiqi	Jiangmen city	4(5)10
2	Defense fee	Hongli Company Wanli Company	He Dingfang	Jiangpu and Zhubo	4(5)103
3	Slaughter tax	Wanquan Company	Xie Kaoling	Guangdong province	4(5)155
4	Pig export tax on Hainan Island	Yongchang Company		Qiangya (Hainan Island)	4(5)11
5	Stamp, Tobacco, and Wine tax				4(2)175

Source: 4(5)10 Jiangmenshi dayuan gongsi qianxiang chafeng shanghao zubaodian shou qianlei deng laiwang wenjian [Communications on the involved guarantee shops and the seized shops through an investigation of the debt of Dayuan Company, Jiangwen city, 1932–1935]; 4(5)103 Jiangpu zhubo liangsi fangwu Hongli gongsi ji jiujiang fangwu Wanli gongsi chengjiao qian xiang baozheng wuye qiju (shuiqi) [Deed of guarantee for payment of debts submitted by Hongli Company, the gambling tax contractor of the two districts of Jiangpu and Zhupbo (present-day Shunde county), and Wanli Company, the gambling tax contractor of Jiujiang, 1933–1934]; 4(5)155 Quansheng tujuan, Wanquan gongsi jiexiang ji shangren Xie Kaoling yu caiting hanjian [Remittance of the tax quotas of Wanquan Company, the provincial slaughter tax contractor, and letters between the representative merchant Xie Kaoling and the Department of Finance]; 4(5)11 Qiongya shengzhu chukou juan bugao zhangcheng hanjian [Letters on the regulation on the pig export tax in Qiongya county].1933–1938); 4(2)175 Caizhengbu Guangdong yinhua yanjiushuiju youguan yingye shuishou wenti de xunling bugao ji yu Luodingxian de (gong?)han [Instructions and notices from the Bureau of the Stamp Tax and the Tobacco and Wine Taxes under the Ministry of Finance about business tax issues, and official letters from Luoding county], Guangdong Provincial Archives, Guangzhou.

that the company's shareholders be arrested in order to collect the debt. In the course of events, the merchants began to bargain with the authorities and requested that the government reduce rent arrears or release what had been confiscated.

The bid opening and the process of awarding a contract

Beginning in 1932, the Guangdong provincial government (hereafter, the GPG) introduced public bidding competition for all tax-farming in Guangdong. Yongchang Company of in File No. 4 won the contract for the 1933 taxation on pig exports from Hainan Island. The pig export tax from Hainan Island, the first of its kind in Guangdong, was levied on pig exports by steamer from Haikou port on Hainan Island to Hong Kong. In May 1921, collection of this tax was changed from direct official tax collection to tax contract collection.[1] The bidding regulations, announced on 19 May 1933, are cited below.

> Article 1. The term of the contract shall be one year; the company awarded the contract cannot be changed or replaced during the period of the contract.
> Article 4. A participant in a bid shall register his/her name and pay 800 *yuan* as a registration deposit.
> Article 9. A contractor may establish a tax office in Haikou city to collect taxes and may set up outposts according to local circumstances. However, the establishment of a general tax office or outposts requires permission from the Department of Finance.
> Article 4. A contract merchant shall not use the collected tax for a mortgage and shall not form a partnership or offer stock with foreign nationals or foreign merchants.
> Article 15. The supervisor dispatched by the Department of Finance to the general tax office shall be to oversee the process. A monthly salary of 60 *yuan* (*haobi*) shall be remitted by the Department of Finance in the middle of every month.

The purpose of Article 2 was to ensure transparency by specifying fair bidding. The ban on involvement of foreigners in the tax contract, in Article 4, seems to have been derived from the anti-imperialist sentiment of the 1920s when a substantial amount of tax revenue was transferred to foreign banks or foreign companies as collateral.

Based on the above regulations, the bidding took place at 2 p.m. on 1 July 1933, at the office of the Guangzhou Chamber of Commerce. However, no one participated in the bidding on that day. Thereafter, the Ministry of Finance lowered the minimum bid price by 1,000 *yuan*, from the original 18,500 *yuan*, to 17,500 *yuan*, and again to 16,000 *yuan*. But, again, there was no bidder for the second and third bids. In the fourth bid (9 August), when the minimum bid was set at 15,000 *yuan*, two merchants, one in Sanhe and one in Weiyi, registered for the first time. But the bid was again delayed due to failure to satisfy a legal quorum. There was also no bidder in the fifth round.

1 Guangdongsheng Caizhengting [Department of Finance, Guangdong], *Guangdongsheng caizheng jishi* [Record of finance in Guangdong province] (Guangzhou: Guangdongshengcaizhengting, 1933), Vol. 2, Part 3, 863–865.

Finally, on 6 August the Department of Finance lowered the amount of the minimum bid to 14,000 *yuan*, producing bidders (30 August). By bidding three times, Yongchang Company, led by Zhang Jiheng, won the contract, with a yearly rent amount of 14,500 *yuan* (*nianxiang*). All ten bidders had the title of "company" (*gongsi*), but only one representative merchant from each appeared in the negotiations or the official documents filed with the Department of Finance.[2]

The next step after the bidding was for the winning merchant to submit to the Department of Finance the payment of the monthly rent as a deposit (*anxiang*), an advance payment of the monthly rent (*yuxiang*), and a security deposit. Although all three items were required to be submitted for any tax contract, the amount of the monthly rent as a deposit and the amount to be submitted as an advance payment varied from contract to contract. The value of the security deposit depended on the amount of the yearly rent. Interestingly, most of the security deposits in the contract regulations prior to 1929, found in the *Handbook on Guangdong Finance* (*Guangdong caizheng yaolan*), were in a fixed-rate currency, while those from the 1930s consisted of real property, primarily stores. The fact that in the 1930s Guangdong province was frequently hit by financial panic or bank runs, whereby currency was an easily discounted asset, might be the reason for the change to real estate.[3]

In the case of Yongchang Company, it submitted two months' deposit, one month's advance rent, and title deeds for the security deposit. The collateral real estate was Rongan Inn store in the city of Guangzhou. The Department of Finance sent two people to investigate the value of the inn on 6 September. The survey considered the value of the inn, whether it had a business license, and whether its business would be able to cover as much as 50 percent of the monthly rent (604.15 *yuan*), which was the standard for

2 Weiyuan Jia Chongji (Commissioner Jia Chongji)→Caizhengting [Department of Finance, Guangdong Province, (hereafter DFG)], 1, 14, 27 July 1933, 4(5)11; Weiyuan Wu Yongji (Commissioner Wu Yongji)→Caizhengting, 9, 19, 30 August 1933, 4(5)11.

3 For financial panic and the monetary policy of the GPG, see Kang Jin-A, "20 shiji 30 niandai Guangdongsheng de huobi tongyi zhengce de bengkui guocheng: Waihui weiji yu xiaoyangquan" [Collapse of currency control in Guangdong province in the 1930s: Financial crisis and the "small money" system], in *Shijie jingji tizhi xia de Minguo shiqi jingji* [The Chinese economy during the Republican era under the world system], ed. Zhang Donggang (Beijing: Zhongguo caizheng jingji chubanshe, 2005), 44–56. For the tug-of-war between Nanjing and Guangzhou over the exchange rate, see Jin-A Kang, "Monetary war between Nanjing and Guangzhou during the great depression: Financial unification and national versus local politics in China in the 1930s," in *Strenuous Decades: Global Challenges and Transformation of Chinese Societies in Modern Asia*, ed. Chi-cheung Choi, Tomoko Shiroyama and Venus Viana (Berlin, Boston: De Gruyter Mouton, 2022).

collateral. After receiving a positive report on 21 September, the Department of Finance issued an official letter to each county magistrate instructing them to fully cooperate with the tax collectors of Yongchang Company. The company thus became a formal tax contractor.[4]

The process of open bidding seems to have been a tug-of-war between the government and the merchants. Bidding up to six times can be considered a type of negotiation process over the minimum bid by exploring the parties' intentions. The attitude of the Department of Finance was quite compromising, in contrast with how it appeared in the stipulated regulation. It is no wonder that the Department of Finance did not issue any comment about Yongchang's one-day-late payment of the deposit, in spite of the strict regulation that if the due date passed, the merchant would be stripped of contract rights. Such flexibility also applied to the Department of Finance's response to complaints about the fairness of the bidding.[5]

The public open bidding originally was part of Qu Fangpu's reform policy to prevent bribery and bid-rigging. But interestingly, two days after the open bidding was completed, a person by the name of Huo Bing, who was a representative of Hecheng Company, filed a complaint with the Department of Finance claiming that bid-rigging had occurred and demanding a rerun of the bid. He said, "Their nine-vote coalition was so intimidating. Furthermore, they threatened me they would use force if I didn't cooperate, so I had no choice but to follow them." According to Huo Bing's petition, these ten bidders had a separate meeting after the official bidding had been completed, where they opened real competitive bidding. Huo Bing's testimony proved that the purpose of the bid-rigging was to lower the amount of the winning quotation. However, it is not clear how the winner of the private bidding could cooperate with Yongchang Company, the official winner. The petitioner certainly disclosed the bid-rigging because he had lost the private bidding. In reacting to the petition, Qu Fangpu ordered that the petition remain secret and that the petitioners

4 Caizhengting (DFG)→Yongchang gongsi (Yongchang Company), 31 August 1933, 4(5)11; Yongchang gongsi Zhang Jiheng (Zhang Jiheng, representative of Yongchang Company) Jiheng→Caizhengting, 4 September 1933, 4(5)11; Caizhengting→Weiyuan Wu Yongji, 6 September 1933, 4(5)11; Weiyuan Wu Yongji→Caizhengting, 11 September 1933, 4(5)11; Guangdongsheng zhengfu (Guangdong Provincial Government)→Caizhengting, 21 September 1933, 4(5)1.

5 The value of the annual contract for the pig export tax in Hainan Island increased sharply from 11,400 *yuan* in 1930, to 12,000 *yuan* in 1931, and again to 19,750 *yuan* in 1932. It is likely that there was a boycott to reduce the quota of the first 18,000 *yuan* in 1933.Therefore, the final bid amount was set at 14,500 *yuan*, but this was still higher than the annual contracted amount in 1930 and 1931. *Guangdongsheng caizheng jishi*, Vol. 2, Part 3, 867.

be investigated, rather than checking into whether there had indeed been bid-rigging.[6]

The Department of Finance advertised the introduction of open bidding as a measure to increase fairness and transparency. But in reality, securing the revenue always took precedence over any principles. The petition demonstrated that the tax contractors had their own network through which to collect information and respond collectively to the Department of Finance to voice in their own interest. Behind the five failed bids, there must be a collective action to lower the minimum bid.

Taxation, remittances, and disputes during the term of the contract

Once they had received the tax contract, the contractor would begin to collect the tax according to the legal tax rate and the taxation method stipulated in the tax contract regulations. There was a deadline for the monthly remittances to the provincial treasury, and interest was added daily if the deadline passed before the remittance. Wanquan Company, which had contracted the slaughter tax, left the referable documents due to collection of unpaid interest.

The Guangdong slaughter tax was established in 1902 and every corner of Guangdong province except Guangzhou was subject to taxation. In 1910, the previous separate county tax-farming system was integrated into a provincial six-year contract. During the Republican era, taxation frequently changed between separate local contracts and provincial unified contracts. The provincial unified tax contract resumed beginning in July 1929,[7] and Wanquan Company became a contract merchant in September 1935. Although Wanquan Company was a general contractor for the entire province, it did not directly collect local taxes. It divided Guangdong into districts so as to subcontract local taxation to sub-agencies. Table 8.2 below lists the amount of rent that Wanquan Company paid during the contract period, based on the remaining receipts.

Wanquan Company was required to pay an initial six-month deposit. Considering that a two-month-deposit was quite common in the 1930s and a three-month deposit became more frequent in 1935, paying half a year's rent at once was definitely a burden. In 1935, when financial difficulties were

6 Toucheng Qiongya shengzhu chukou juanshang gongsi Hecheng (Hecheng Company, a bidder for the pig export tax contract in Hainan Island)→Caizhengting, 1 September 1933, 4(5)11.

7 *Guangdongsheng caizhengjishi*, Vol. 2, Part 3, 744–745.

Table 8.2 Monthly payments of Wanquan Company, September 1935–November 1935 (uniti: *yuan, haoyang*)

Date	Item	Amount
September	Deposit	The amount of six months' rent paid in advance at once
25 September	Supervisory fee for September	400 *yuan*
	Regular rent	155,246 *yuan**-6,555.96 *yuan***= 148,690.04 *yuan*
	20 percent special additional tax for financial stabilization	29,738.008 *yuan*
18 October	Supervisory fee for October	400 *yuan*
28 October	Regular rent	155,246 *yuan* - 9,833.94 *yuan* *** - 2,000 *yuan***** = 143,412.06 yuan
20 November	Supervisory fee for November	400 *yuan*
28 November	Regular rent	155,246 *yuan* - 9,833.94 *yuan* -2,000 *yuan* = 143,412.06 *yuan*
28 November	20 percent additional special tax	29,082.052 *yuan*
The above payments repeated unchanged until April 1936.		

Note:
*The figure for the regular rent by "Small Money" *haoyang* units (155,246 *yuan*) is derived from the following formula: 99,516.667 *yuan* (original contracted monthly rent, "Big Money" *dayang*) + 20 percent special additional tax (previous additional charge) + 30 percent exchange rate premium on *dayang* in the conversion to *haoyang*.
** the amount to be paid to the Meilu sub-treasury by the sub-agent of Gaolei county for 20 days
*** the above for 30 days
**** subsidy payment to Zhongshan county government

serious for the GPG, perhaps it required a large payment from a provincial-level contractor such as Wanquan.[8]

The regular payment was divided into three types: the regular rent (*zhengxiang*), the special additional tax (*zhuankuan*), and the supervisory fee (*jianbanfei*). The regular rent was the original contract tax revenue, a fixed monthly rent derived by dividing the annual contract rent by twelve months. A contractor was required to pay this monthly rent to the government regardless of whether the monthly tax revenue it had collected was greater than or less than this amount. The contract amount was nominally determined on a Big

8 Wanquan gongsi (Wanquan Company)→Caizhengting, 25 September 1935, 4(5)155. For instance, the deposit for the provincial contracts amounted to one month's rent in 1932. Guangdong yinhua yanjiushui ju (Guangdong Stamp Tax, Tobacco, and Wine Tax Bureau)→Xingning xian xianzhang (Xingning county magistrate), 17 June 1932, 4(2)175; Guangdong yinhua yanjiushui ju→Xingning xian xianzhang, 28 November 1932, 4(2)175.

Table 8.3 Wanquan Company's delayed payments and amount of added interest (unit: *yuan, haoyang*)

Item	Quota payment	Delayed days	Penalty amount	Date of the order for a penalty payment
Supervisory fee for September	400	5 days	3	28 September
Regular rent for early October	48,470.87	18 days	1,308.78	12 November
Regular rent for mid-October	48,470.87	8 days	581.68	12 November
20 percent special additional tax for early October	9,694.17	18 days	261.72	12 November
20 percent special additional tax for mid-October	9,694.17	8 days	116.32	12 November
Penalty for the delayed payment for October			2,268.5	6 December

Source: Quansheng tujuan, Wanquan gongsi jiexiang ji shangren xie kaoling yu caiting hanjian [Remittance of the tax quotas of Wanquan Company, the provincial slaughter tax contractor, and letters between the representative merchant Xie Kaoling and the Department of Finance]. 4(5)155. Guangzhou: Guangdong Provincial Archives.

Money silver dollar basis, while the taxpayer paid daily on a Small Money silver dollar basis in Guangdong. The GPG's accounting unit was actually *haoyang* (Small Money) *yuan* in the 1930s. Therefore, the contractor remitted the monthly rent after converting to *haoyang yuan* according to the exchange rate between the two units.[9] Big Money received a 25 percent premium over Small Money prior to 1 July 1932. However, Qu Fangpu raised the exchange rate premium from 25 to 30 percent when he took office.

As seen in Table 8.2, there were two special additional taxes: a 20 percent special tax was imposed on 21 July 1918, and thereafter it became part of the regular tax. The other special additional tax was categorized separately because it was a temporary tax imposed in response to the urgent need

9 For Guangdong's Small Money system and the separatist effort to unify currency against the *fabi* reform of the NNG, see Kang Jin-A, "20 shiji 30niandai Guangdongsheng de huobi tongyi zhengce de bengkui guocheng: Waihui weiji yu xiaoyangquan." The currency unit of taxation in Guangdong was generally Small Money (*haoyang*) until the 1920s. Entering the 1930s, the GPG changed the unit of tax to Big Money (*dayang*). Thereafter, the adjustment of the official exchange rate at between Small Money and Big Money on actual payments became a means of raising taxes.

to pool the reserves of the Guangdong Provincial Bank. This tax began in April 1934 when a discount rush on Guangdong Provincial Banknotes caused a financial crisis in Guangzhou.[10] This kind of unpredictable additional taxation could hurt not only the taxpayer but also the contractor. The third fee, the supervisory fee, was the supervisor's salary sent by the Department of Finance to the general tax office of the contractor. His job was to supervise management of the tax process. In the case of county-level contracts, this fee ranged around 60 *yuan* per month. Meanwhile, the supervisor of Wanquan Company was paid as much as 400 *yuan* per month.

The contractor delivered a monthly report about his remittances to the Department of Finance. However, actual remittance of the regular rent and the special additional tax occurred three times a month. The supervisory fee was deposited once a month. In cases where the contractor delayed delivery, he was charged a penalty of 3 percent. The Department of Finance issued an official letter to Wanquan Company on 25 October, stating it had been overdue for twenty-five days, warning that it would cancel the contract as soon as the due date exceeded a month.[11] However, this was often just a threat. In the 1930s, when the recession gripped the country, it was more likely that the government would not allow a company to step down from its position as contractor. In fact, the Department of Finance preferred debt collection, rather than replacing the contractor.

It is noteworthy that during the remittance process the company did not remit the entire allotment to the provincial treasury but rather deposited some fixed monthly amount directly in the county sub-treasury. Wanquan Company allowed Heyi Company, the subcontractor in Gaolei county, to deposit 9,833.94 *yuan* per month in the Meilu sub-treasury.[12] This means that the general contractor and the subcontractor worked directly in the financial management between the province and the county. In this system, the higher-ranking institution would reassign the financial allocation to the lower-ranking institution spontaneously in response to temporary financial needs. This method of operation is different from the so-called "unified revenues and expenditures" that were in effect later during the Communist period. Such management can be understood as an extension of the late Qing system, with no clear division between the national treasury, the provincial treasury, and the county treasury.

10 *Guangdongsheng caizheng jishi*, Vol. 1, Part 1, 744–745.

11 Caizhengting→Chengban (quansheng tujuan Wanquan) gongsi shangren (Wanquan Company), 25 October 1935, 4(5)155.

12 Yongchang gongsi→Caizhengting, 22 November 1933, 4(5)11.

Wanquan Company successfully continued the tax process until April of the following year (1936), when the file ends. It was rare that a contractor would continue throughout the entire term of a contract. Due to the economic recession, taxation became more difficult in the 1930s. Reduced tax revenues meant lower profit margins for the contractors. If the collected tax revenue could not cover their costs, the contractors had to supply the shortfall at their own expense. Sometimes, the outstanding payment of the monthly rent led to default. In such cases, disputes inevitably arose between the contactors and the Department of Finance.

The contractor of the gambling tax in Nanhai county, Hongli Company, applied to terminate the contract on two occasions—in August and October of 1933.[13] This gambling tax, called a defense fee (*fangwu jingfei*), imposed a tax on casinos that were popular sites for local gambling (*fantan*). Li Hongzhang legalized such gambling for the first time between 1899 and 1900 to raise funds for coastal defense, hence the reason for it being called a defense fee.[14] According to his explanation to the Department of Finance, the silk industry in the localities had declined, unemployed migrant workers had returned from Southeast Asia, and overseas remittances had decreased, all of which constituted a big blow to revenue from the gambling tax. The reason for termination of the contract was not approved by the government, therefore the company petitioned to lower the daily rent from 680 *yuan* to 200 *yuan*. However, the Department of Finance rejected both the petition and termination of the contract.[15]

Meanwhile, disputes over tax rates and tax collection methods were frequent. The experience of Yongchang Company, which had contracted the tax on pig exports from Hainan Island, was typical. The company had petitioned to terminate the contract or to decrease the amount of monthly rent, but the petition was rejected on both counts. Under these circumstances, in order to achieve its quota, the contractor had no choice but to resort to other means to the collect taxes from the taxpayers and, as a result, friction between the taxpayers and the contractor increased. The burden of securing tax revenue was passed on from the Department of Finance to the contractors and to the taxpayers.

On 17 February 1934, the chairman of the pig sales merchants' guild of Xincun port in Lingshui county petitioned the Department of Finance,

13 *Guangdongsheng caizheng jishi*, Vol. 2, Part 3, 973–974.

14 *Guangdongsheng caizheng jishi*, Vol. 2, Part 3, 973–974.

15 Hongli gongsi shangren He Dingbang (Hongli Company, merchant He Dingfang)→Caizhengting, 8 August 1933, 4(5)103.

claiming that Yongchang Company was collecting an illegal tax. He argued that the company's tax collector, Zhang Mei, had suddenly begun to tax pig transfers within the province, which, according to law, were not subject to the export tax. On this issue, the ordinary merchants (as taxpayers) and the contractor were clearly at odds.[16]

However, there were other cases where the merchants (as taxpayers) and the contractors united to oppose the Department of Finance. The new imposition of a 20 percent special additional tax in April 1934, seen in the above Wanquan Company case, resulted in the merchants and Yongchang Company forming a united front. On 3 June 1934, Wu Faying, chairman of the pig sales merchants' guild in Haikou city (*Haikoushi shengzhuye tongye gonghui*), and Zhang Chaoyuan and Wu Jiesan, two standing committee members, joined forces to petition for an exemption from the new additional tax. The three petitioners argued that the prefectural tax included an export tax on pigs (*shengzhu chukou shui*) which were already subject to the new additional tax. Therefore, to collect the additional tax on pig exports (*shengzhu chukou juan*) would have been double taxation.[17] Six days later, following the merchant association's petition, Yongchang Company issued a detailed report on the serious situation of double and multiple taxation on pigs and cows on Hainan Island.[18] Even though the Department of Finance publicly ordered an end to multiple taxation,[19] it did not withdraw the additional tax.[20] During the term of the contract, Yongchang Company was subject to the new surcharge. However, after the contract expired, the company's representative complained that he had been forced to apply it on orders.[21]

Why were the contractor and the taxpayers' guild in agreement against the new additional tax and the multiple taxation? Fundamentally, it was due to the human connection between the two. Wu Jiesan's name, one of the three petitioners, was found on the list of shareholders of Yongchang Company. Considering the overlap between the taxpayers and the contractor,

16 Lingshui xian Xincun gang shanghui zhuxi Lai Qingchao (President of the Chamber of Commerce, Xincun port, Lingshui county, Lai Qingchao)→Caizhengting, 17 February 1934, 4(5)11.

17 Haikoushi shengzhu ye tongye gonghui zhuxi Wu Faying, changwei Zhang Chaoyuan, Wu Jiesan (Wu Faying, chairman of the pig sales merchants' guild in Haikou city, two standing members Zhang Chaoyuan and Wu Jiesan)→Caizhengting, 3 June 1934, 4(5)11.

18 Yongchang gongsi→Caizhengting (9 June 1934) 4(5)11.

19 Caizhengting→Yongchang gongsi (19 June 1934) 4(5)11.

20 Qiongshan xian Haikoushi shengzhu tongye gonghui zhuxi Lin Kaidi, changwu weiyuan Wu Jiesan, Zhang Chaoyuan (Chairman of the Pig Sales Merchants' Guild in Qingshan county, Lin Kaidi, two standing members, Wu Jiesan, Zhang Chaoyuan)→Caizhengting, 19 August 1934, (5)11.

21 Yongchang gongsi→Caizhengting, 5 November 1934, 4(5)11.

the above bid-rigging can be reinterpreted as a strategy on the part of the merchants to prevent an increase in the tax burden due to the competitive bidding. In the case of Yongchang Company, contractor and the merchant guild were not necessarily incompatible.

In this regard, we can see the limitations of the reform by the GPG. The GPG tried to reorganize the tax contract system as a tool to effectively assert state power. It wanted to select a contract merchant who was devoted to the GPG, rather than a merchant through open competitive bidding. However, as in the case of Yongchang Company, the contractor selected from the competitive bidding still seemed to be closely connected with the merchants' guild. Compared to the checkpoint of the *likin* tax, it was difficult to obtain information, so the merchants' cooperation was needed. Therefore, it is highly likely that the contractor would be someone who was closely related to the business group. However, the relationship and the tensions between the merchants and the contractors differed from case to case and from place to place.

The tug-of-war between contractors and the Department of Finance over unpaid rent

Once the annual contract period was over, settlement would begin. If the contractor had failed to reach the quota, the unpaid monthly rent or other expenses were to be compensated for out of the contractor's own money. The cases of Hongli Company and Yongchang Company provide some examples.

On 20 December 1933, Hongli Company's contract expired, with 76,160 *yuan* still unpaid. The Department of Finance ordered the Nanhai county government to detain the staff of the company and to seize its property. In advance, the special forces of the Department of Finance had already arrested acting manager Qu Peiran.[22] It seems strange that the Department of Finance did not arrest the representative, He Dingfang, but he took the lead in negotiating with the government. Qu Peiran's father and He Dingfang jointly petitioned for Qu's release and leniency in reducing the debt. They appealed that Qu was not an original member of the company and was only entrusted with management when ex-manager Feng Jingshi had died. They argued that Qu's release would be indispensable to collect the unpaid rent from the subcontractors. Furthermore, according to their petition, the daily quota for Hongli Company in 1933 amounted to 680 *yuan*, which was

22 Nanhai xian xianzhang Li Haiyun (Nanhai county magistrate, Li Haiyun)→Caizhengting, 26 December 1933, 4(5)103.

much higher than the 365 *yuan* in 1932 and the 495 *yuan* charged in 1934. Therefore, they were petitioning to discount the daily quota to 150 *yuan* for the 112 days' worth of unpaid rent.[23]

The Department of Finance accepted the petition and reduced the amount of debt to 59,160 *yuan*. However, the company still did not pay it. When the Department of Finance dispatched an official to Nanhai, he found that all the key figures had fled, and that no stores had been offered in security. It was unusual to have no collateral, and this did not help the Department of Finance's efforts to collect the debt. But at the end of August 1934, the Department of Finance found a way to solve the problem.[24]

In August, the Department of Finance arrested the manager of Wanli Company, Cui Jingchang, in the course of collecting its debt. It confiscated the home of a shareholder of the company, Cui Fuquan. It turned out that Cui Fuquan was related to both Wanli Company and Hongli Company. He Dingfang, representative of Hongli, and Guo Taiqi, representative of Wanli, jointly petitioned for the release of Cui Fuquan's home that had been confiscated. He Dingfang promised to pay back the unpaid rent on an installment plan. Moreover, He Dingfang independently submitted a store as collateral and a house as joint security with Cui Fuquan to the Department of Finance on 27 September. In October, Guo Taiqi offered one more home as collateral. Looking at the above progress, He Dingfang initially had no intention of paying back the debt. The relationship between Hongli and Wanli was unclear. At the very least, the two were independent contractors, but the tax contracted was the same as the gambling tax. Therefore, Cui provided a clue about how to resolve the issue. Cui's assets were involved with another tax contractor, Yongli Company, which had been contracted for the collection of the gambling tax in Shaoshi and Quying counties. Cui might have been an influential investor in these gambling tax–contracting businesses. Consequently, by seizing his assets, the Department of Finance could effectively collect the unpaid rent and the debt from the contractor, who was presumably in default.[25]

The second case, that of Yongchang Company, is related to how far the contractor should be responsible for collecting the extra tax midway through the term of the contract. Initially, Yongchang Company had finished its

23 Ou Lu shi (Mr. Ou Lu)→Caizhengting, unknown date, 4(5)103; Xieban Jiangpu zhubo liangsi fangwu huiyi Hongli gongsi shangren He Dingbang (He Dingfang)→Caizhengting, 10 March 1934, 4(5)103; He Dingbang→Caizhengting, 23 August 1934, 4(5)103.

24 He Dingbang→Caizhengting, 23 August 1934, 4(5)103.

25 He Dingbang→Caizhengting, 27 September 1934, 4(5)103; Guo Taiqi→Caizhengting, 10 October 1934, 4(5)103.

contract period on 20 September 1934, with the regular rent fully paid. In November, however, the Department of Finance ordered that it pay the unpaid amount of the 20 percent additional tax quota from late July to mid-September. As noted above, this additional tax, starting in April 1934, was to fund financial stabilization. The company's representative merchant, Zhang Jiheng, paid the required amount of 483.36 *yuan* to the Haikou sub-treasury. The Department of Finance then asked it to pay another 1,208 *yuan,* which had already been added as the allotment for provincial bonds. Facing the possible arrest of the shareholders, Zhang was again forced to pay the 1,208 *yuan*. But this was not the end. On 21 February 1935, the Department of Finance required that Zhang pay another allotment for provincial bonds, amounting to 1,208 *yuan* and the unpaid supervisory fee, amounting to 720 *yuan*. Zhang protested that initially he had not been informed that he was to pay the supervisory fee. Nonetheless, the bidding regulation stipulated that the contractor should pay the supervisory monthly fee of 60 *yuan* (720 yuan per year). So his argument was no more than an excuse. Therefore, all three requests to the Department of Finance after the contract had expired were justified legally.[26]

But it is important to note why the Department of Finance did not liquidate the unpaid settlement when the contract expired but instead attempted to collect it at intervals. In fact, in 1934, a rural crisis was widespread in Hainan Island, just as it was in other parts of China. In addition to a series of disasters, the export of pigs from Hainan Island in 1934 reportedly had halved compared to 1933. Meanwhile, financial needs continued to grow due to the discount on banknotes and the increasing military expenses. Yongchang Company's winning bid quotation was 14,500 *yuan* for a one-year contract. Actual payment during the term of the contract amounted to 28,100 *yuan* due to the additional tax and the allotment for provincial bonds, which almost doubled the original amount.[27] In fact, such an amount of additional tax could only be possible in the tax-contracting system. Therefore, according to the regulations, the Department of Finance could not strictly collect the debt, and settlement of the accounts remained rather ambiguous. But whenever the government needed temporary income, the Department of Finance seemed to rummage through the account books and resume collection. Such invisible considerations and compromises were far from

26 Yongchang gongsi Zhang Jiheng→Caizhengting, 19 November 1934, 16 February 1935, 4(5)11; Caizhengting→Yongchang gongsi, 21 February 1935, 4(5)11.
27 Qiongshan xianzhang Liao Guoqi (Qingshan county magistrate, Liao Guoqi)→Caizhengting, February 1935, 4(5)11.

administrative enforcement based on laws and contracts; rather, they had their own rationale.

The internal structure of the contractors

In addition to the internal structure of the tax-contracting company, analysis of several cases of conversion from tax contracts to direct official tax collection in the 1930s helps explain why the tax contract system continued to survive in Guangdong.

It is challenging to identify the tax contracting company's shareholders or partners because only one representative acted publicly, from the bidding process to the correspondence with the government, and the contractors often employed puppet managers in preparation for possible debt collection. Fortunately, two files, relating to Dayuan Company and Yongchang Company, disclose the shareholders' names and identification in the course of debt collection. However, in the investigations, it should be noted that the reported shareholders usually gave fake and contradictory answers to protect their own interests. Despite these limitations, these two cases demonstrate the complexity of the tax contract organization and its link with the merchants' guild.

Dayuan Company contracted the gambling tax, called the "miscellaneous gambling tax" (*zadu*) in Jiangmen county.[28] When the contract expired in October 1933, the company had incurred a sizable amount of overdue rent—some 57,000 *yuan*. The Department of Finance confiscated two stores owned by Mai Ruiqi, a shareholder of Dayuan Company. Petitioning to have the two stores released, Mai insisted that the company debt should be collected from the shareholders differentially, depending on the value of their stock. For his own purposes, he reported the names and stakes of the shareholders'. According to Mai, the company had ten shareholders, with total share capital of 45,000 *yuan*, among which Manager Li Jianmin held 8,000 *yuan* of shares, Deputy Manager Tan Yongtang (Tan Furu) held 7,500 *yuan* (to which Guo Wan had contributed 1,300 *yuan*), Situ Zhongcheng, 5,000 *yuan*, Liang Guang, 5,000 *yuan,* Yu Shangzhi, 5,000 *yuan*, Feng Xianqi 5,000 *yuan* (Fang Xianqi and Feng Shuyun in fact are the same person), Ye Zhusan, 3,750 *yuan*, and Mai Ruiqi 3,750 *yuan* (he was a nominal shareholder; his own contribution was only 500 *yuan*), Feng Kunkang, 2,000 *yuan*, and

28 For military interference in tax farming and the function of the Finance Committee of the Three Forces, see Chen Boren, "Caizheng he shuijuan," 301–302.

so forth. Since his nominal share was 3,750, Mai argued that his obligation to pay the unpaid rent amounted to 4,750 *yuan*.

The Department of Finance arrested the manager of the store that had been put up as security and the four shareholders whom Mai had identified. However, statements by these people were inconsistent. Feng Shutang argued that he was not a shareholder and that Mai held shares in the value of 7,500 yuan. Furthermore, according to Feng, Mai was the most critical figure in the company after the military had arrested Manager Li, and Mai's relatives worked as staff in the company. The manager of the store put up as security claimed that the two key figures holding power were Mai and Deputy Manager Tan Yongtang and that Mai had allowed his relatives to manage the company. Guo Wan denied that he was a shareholder, and then he testified that Mai and Tang held shares valuing 7,500 *yuan*. Tan denied both that he was deputy manager and that he was a shareholder.[29]

Taken together, the testimonies suggest that after the arrest of Li Jianmin, who was in charge of the company, Mai and Tan cooperated as the two largest investors. Meanwhile, Mai then reported further detailed information about the assets of the ten shareholders in order to obtain release of the stores that had been seized.[30] At the same time, Mai lobbied, using his personal connections in the army. The Third Air Force Commander of Chen Jitang's First Force twice petitioned the Department of Finance on behalf of Mai, arguing that Mai was only a small shareholder and that he could not make a living after the seizure of his stores.[31] Finally, the Department of Finance began to seize the assets of the other shareholders and accepted Mai's plea to reduce his payment obligation to 4,750 *yuan* according to his shares of stock. However, the Department of Finance again raised the issue of the unpaid allotment of provincial bonds. It demanded that Mai pay another 2,374.95 *yuan,* derived from the total unpaid 28,500 *yuan* divided by his shareholding ratio. Mai held out without paying for half a year, arguing that the additional charge was unfair. Despite intervention by the military, the Department of Finance would not release the seized stores. Mai eventually paid the unpaid rent in the amount of 4,750 *yuan* and the

29 Caizhengting chengshengu guzhang Cai Xieyuan(Cai Xieyuan, chief, Tax Contract Section of the DFG)→Caizhengting tingzhang (Director, Department of Finance), 12 November 1934, 4(5)10.

30 Mai Ruiqi→Caizhengtingzhang (Director, Department of Finance), 8 November 1934, 4(5)10.

31 Guomin gemingjun diyi jituanjun kongjun silingbu feiji disan duibu Jiang Qiyan (Third Air Force Commander, First Force of the National Revolutionary Army, Jiang Qiyan)→Caizhengtingzhang, 19 October 1934, 4(5)10.

unpaid allotment of 949.996 *yuan* on 13 March 1935.[32] The allotment payment was discounted by 60 percent. Finally, on 22 March the two confiscated stores were returned.[33]

The above case shows that confiscation of the security assets was an effective strategy on the part of the Department of Finance to put pressure on the contractor to pay the debt. Stores in Guangzhou, in particular, suited the security demand because the Department of Finance could easily cancel their business licenses and suspend their operations.[34] However, it was difficult to seize real estate and stores in the sub-localities where the GPG's administrative intervention did not reach. For example, in the case of Mai, the Department of Finance tracked down the properties of the reported shareholders. Other than four homes in Guangzhou, it failed to identify all assets in the counties.[35] The Department of Finance could complete the negotiations with Mai and instead seize four houses located in Guangzhou and owned by Tan Yongtang.[36] Therefore, the security assets recorded in the archives of the tax contracts are mainly stores and homes in Guangzhou city, even in the cases of county-level contracts. Considering the requirements for security assets as collateral in Guangzhou and the fact that all bids were made in Guangzhou, the sub-provincial tax contractors formed a network of information and asset guarantees around Guangzhou.

The second case, involving Yongchang Company, provides a glimpse into the broad overlap between the shareholders of the tax contract company and the members of the merchants' guild. On 21 November 1934, the owner of a store that had been put up as security filed a petition to prevent his shop from being involved and instead, he reported the names of the shareholders. According to his account, Yongchang Company had four shareholders: Wu Jiesan, Wu Wenqi, Huang Dehua, and Zhang Chaoyuan. All four were part of the Fuxing pig farm.[37] In particular, Wu Sanjie and Zhang Zhaoyuan were two standing members of the pig sales merchants' guild in Haikou, which had petitioned on two occasions, 3 June and 19 August 1934, for an exemption from the new additional tax. Thus, the interests of the tax

32 Mai Ruiqi→Caizhengting, 13 March 1935, 4(5)10.

33 Weiyuan Xiao Songyou (Commissioner Xiao Songyou)→Caizhengting, 25 March 1935, 4(5)10.

34 Mai Ruiqi→Caizhengting, 16 April 1935, 4(5)10.

35 Kaiping xianzhang Yu Qimou (Kaiping county magistrate, Yu Qimou)→Caizhengting, 1 November 1934, 4(5)10; Chengshengu (Tax Contract Section of the DFG)→Caizhengting, 8 April 1935, 4(5)10.

36 Tan Yongfa. Tan Yongchang→Caizhengting, unknown date, 4(5)10.

37 Shen Jiaren (Mr. Shen Jiaren, owner of the guaranteed store)→Caizhengting, 21 November 1934, 4(5)11.

contractors and the merchants' guild seem to be virtually identical. This demonstrates that the merchants' guilds' traditional system of taxation based on self-reliance had survived despite the new policy of competitive open bidding.

Below is the official interrogation statement by Zhang Chaoyuan after he was arrested:

> Q: How many people joined as shareholders when Yongchang contracted taxation on pig exports from Hainan Island?
> A: Wu Sanjie and Huang Dehua managed this company's contract.
> Q: Mr. Shen [Shen Jiaren, the owner of the store that had been put up as security] said that you are a shareholder.
> A: I am not. My adopted younger brother is a shareholder.
> Q: How can Mr. Shen not know your brother when he knows you?
> A: I guess that when Wu Sanjie and I went to Guangzhou to manage the affairs of the cowhide tax, he saw that I was with Wu's party so he thought I was a shareholder.
> Q: When did the contract of Yongchang Company expire? How many sub-offices did you set up in the past?
> A: The contract had already expired. This company's tax office used to be located on the second floor of Fuxing Firm, Deshengsha Street, Haikou city.
> Q: Is Wu Wenqi the manager of the Fuxing Firm? What are Wu Wenqi and Huang Dehua doing now, and where?
> A: Wu Wenqi and Wu Wenqi are the same person, and he is the manager of Fuxing Firm. Huang Dehua is still in charge of tax services. His house is the northern 1st door of Yongle Street, Haikou city.
> Q: Where and what is your younger brother doing?
> A: He is currently a hired laborer at Jianchang pig farm in Hong Kong.[38]

Zhang Chaoyuan denied that he was a shareholder, but he identified as a shareholder his younger brother, Zhang Yinghui, who had remained in Hong Kong free from arrest. Considering that Zhang Chaoyuan was involved in two earlier petitions for tax cuts as a standing member of the merchants' guild, he must have been closely related to both Yongchang Company and the guild. It is thus likely that he was committing perjury.

Nonetheless, some facts can be inferred from his testimony. Wu Wenqi, one of the shareholders, was the manager of Fuxing Firm, which must have been the Fuxing pig farm referred to in the statement by the owner

38 Qiongshan xianzhang Liao Guoqi→Caizhengting, 18 December 1934, 4(5)11.

of the store that had been put up as security. This means that some of the contractors were also taxpayers. Furthermore, Wu Jiesan had earlier contracted the cowhide tax, and Huang Dehua was also engaged in another tax office. In other words, the fact that two people out of the four shareholders were involved in other tax contract businesses indicates that professional contractors were being drawn from among the tax-paying merchants. The difference between contract merchants (*baoshang*) and product merchants (*huoshang*) was apparent in Guangdong in the 1930s. The introduction of the full-scale open bidding system for tax contracting accelerated the formation of professional contractor groups or the professionalization of merchant contractors.

Even during the period of rule by Chen Jitang, there were several attempts to change the tax contract system to direct collection by the government, called "government agency collections" (*weiban*) or "government office collections" (*guanban*). Eventually, however, Chen's regime left to history the stigma of the "golden age of tax farming collection." The main reason for this was, along with the escalating conflict with the Nanjing Nationalist Government (hereafter NNG), securing military funds was a great challenge. At that time, the government could not afford to risk a reduction in tax revenue.

Of course, one of the reasons for changing to official tax collection was that the GPG hoped to raise more tax revenue by clearly identifying the sources of income. However, it was hard to predict whether the tax revenue would increase or decrease after the change in the method of tax collection. It often depended on the response of the tax-paying merchants and cooperation. News articles, books, and official documents urging fiscal reform for modern state-building appealed to how much the merchants had suffered from the harmful effects of the tax contracting practice. However, in reality, there were many cases where the merchants were more antagonistic toward the official direct taxation.

The vitality of the tax contract system had its merits, which appealed to both the government and the taxpayers. For a government with weak administrative capacity, soliciting tax contractors was an attractive option in terms of minimizing tax costs and securing a fixed amount of tax revenue. This was especially the case for commercial tax collection, where information about sales and incomes for taxation was hardly accessible without the voluntary cooperation of the taxpayers. For tax-paying merchants, the tax contracting system was less risky due to the fixing of the one-year tax burden within a somewhat predictable range, even if the government occasionally added the extra tax. It was safer than the official direct taxation in terms of the possibility that the tax rates could be raised at any time. In the 1930s the government actively tried to reorganize the features of the 1920s' Guangdong tax contract system. Progress was made through open bidding and active official supervision of the contractors. This weakened contractors' traditional connections with merchants and strengthened their roles as official agents.

The tax contract system cannot simply be called non-modern or feudal. Through elaborate public administration, the GPG and the NNG both attempted to build a "unified revenue and expenditure system" (*tongshou-tongzhi*). This term, which frequently appeared in the 1930s, refers to a system in which all tax revenue is collected in the national treasury of the central government and then distributed according to the budget. During the Sino-Japanese War, *tongshou-tongzhi* was implemented as a form of wartime finance and was maximized under the Communists after the Chinese Communist Party victory in 1949. In the 1930s and the 1940s, *tongshou-tongzhi* was considered antithetical to the corrupt and inefficient traditional finance. The evils of decentralization and tax contracting needed to be eradicated. Ironically, however, such unified, centralized finance under Communist China led to a rigidity of fiscal administration and became a new symbol of inefficiency. *Tongshou-tongzhi* gradually faded in the 1980s with the beginning of the reform and opening-up process. At the same time, central–provincial fiscal contracting systems were introduced to Guangdong and Fujian. All corners of Chinese society witnessed a revival of contracting practices.[39]

However, the legacy of negative aspects of the contract system remained. In the 1930s, idioms that satirized the reality of tax contracting were very popular: these included "colluding with bureaucrats to extract information" (*antong xiaoxi*), "formally an open bid, but determined by collusion (*anpan jueding*), "to threaten other bidders (*weixie picheng*), and "a state agency in public, but a contractor in fact (*mingwei anbao*). Such idioms are still applicable to contemporary China.

39 The topic of centralization and decentralization in public finance after the establishment of the People's Republic is systematically analyzed in Michel Oksenberg and James Tong, "The Evolution of Central-Provincial Fiscal Relations in China, 1971–1984: The Formal System," *The China Quarterly* 125 (1991). They explain that the introduction of the contracted fiscal system in Guangdong and Fujian provinces was an extension of the flow of fiscal decentralization during the Cultural Revolution era. My argument dates it earlier, from the evolution of the traditional tax-farming practices during the Republican era.

Part 4

The Transition of the Modern Chinese Tax Structure in a Global Context

9 Transition of the Modern Chinese Financial Structure

Abstract
Chapter 9 traces the long-term change in the Chinese fiscal structure compared to comparable counterparts and reference countries at each stage of development. Tax reform in contemporary China is examined as the interrupted but continuing efforts for fiscal modernization in China. It helps to identify the features of Chinse fiscal modernization and the impact of the Guangdong model. Tax structure in contemporary China is characterized by high dependence on the indirect tax and the significant fiscal weight of the corporate tax outplaying the individual income tax revenue. This reflects the legacy of Nationalist in socialist China. There is a continuing suspicious attitude toward profiteering private industries, and the goal is to support economic building driven by state-owned industries.

Keywords: China, Guangdong, direct tax, indirect tax, tax structure

The tax modernization pursued in modern and contemporary China did not proceed in a manner that was disconnected from the outside world. Rather, it was carried out with an awareness of and reference to trends in the tax systems in other countries. For example, the tax reforms of the late Qing empire and Republican China were profoundly influenced by the Japanese Meiji fiscal model. There is comparable example in the United States as the size of the country grew important during the Nationalist period. More recently, the People's Republic of China has been studying the United States as a reference model for future tax reforms.

A. K. Mehrotra, an American historian of legal history and tax law, suggests that historical research on taxation is an area that can shed new light on the

Kang, Jin-A, *The Guangdong Model and Taxation in China*. Taylor & Francis Group, 2022
DOI: 10.5117/9789463725248_CH09

history of capitalism.[1] Modern countries feature a legitimate monopoly over violence, such as the military and the police as well as legal and exclusive rights to collect taxes. They have also developed their own tax systems in line with their economic structures and stage of industrialization. The trajectory of tax policy varies in line with the various paths of capitalist development.

This chapter investigates long-term change in the Chinese fiscal structure in comparison with comparable counterparts and reference countries at each stage of development, with the aim of identifying the features of Chinese fiscal modernization and the impact of the Guangdong model.

Globalization and financial turbulence in the empire

Imperial finance and the World

Chinese imperial finance was not clearly divided into a central treasury and a local treasury. After retaining what was to be used for local expenses, the local governments submitted part of their tax revenue in cash or in kind to the capital in Beijing. This system was already established after the Anshi Rebellion in the late Tang dynasty, when tax revenue began to be divided into three levels: that which was to be sent to the capital (*gongjing, shanggong*), that which was to be retained and used for provincial (*dao*) finance by the regional military governors (*liushi, songshi*), and that which was to be preserved for prefectural finance (*liuzhou*).[2] This three-layered structure basically continued until the end of the Qing dynasty. R. Bin Wong points out that the morality and ideology of the imperial government took precedence over maintaining stability and balance in society and tapping economic and financial potential.[3]

1 Ajay K. Mehrotra, "A Bridge Between: Law and the New Intellectual Histories of Capitalism," *Buffalo Law Review* 64 (2016): 6.

2 Peng Yuxin, "Qingmo Zhongyang yu gesheng caizheng guanxi" [The financial relationship between the central government and the provinces in the late Qing dynasty], *Shehui kexue zazhi* 9(1) (1947): 83; Zhao Yunqi, *Zhongguo fenshuizhi caizheng tizhi yanjiu* [Research on the fiscal tax assignment system in China] (Beijing: Jingji kexue chubanshe, 2005), 154; Du Xuncheng, "Minguo shiqi de zhongyang yu difang caizheng huafen" [Financial division between the center and the provinces in Republican China], *Zhongguo shehui kexue* 3 (1998): 184. This system was called the "two tax-sharing system" (*liangshui fenshou zhi*). Okamoto Takashi, *Chūgoku keizaishi* [Chinese economic history] (Nagoya: Nagoya daigaku shuppankai, 2013), 114.

3 R. Bin Wong, *China Transformed: Historical Change and the Limits of European Experience* (Ithaca, NY: Cornell University Press, 1997), 113, 142, 147–148; R. Bin Wong, "Taxation and Good Governance in China, 1500–1914," in *The Rise of Fiscal States: A Global History, 1500–1914*, ed.

Thus, the Chinese empire had a significantly lower proportion of fiscal and tax revenue relative to its economic size in comparison with the countries of modern Europe. The basic unit of local governance was the province. The rich provinces were allocated an amount to pay to the central government or the amount that was to be paid in subsidies to neighboring poor provinces. The rest of the revenue was left to the provinces to meet provincial spending. Because the land-poll tax quota was quantitatively fixed for each region in Qing China, imperial finances were a repeat of the "status quo," except during periods of war and rebellion. Finance of the Qing imperial court mostly relied on land tax revenue sent from the provinces. Active economic intervention by the state was minimal. Income and expenditure items were executed almost regularly and conventionally, both by the central and local governments.[4]

Qing China during the Qianlong period was largely peaceful and stable. It is difficult to accurately estimate the fiscal size because the amount of tax varied greatly in the event of disaster or war. Local finance in a particular region also varied depending on the annual situation. However, 1766 might be considered one of the milder and more regular years during the mid-Qing period. Table 9.1 shows the revenue structure in this year.

Table 9.1 Tax revenue of the imperial Qing, 1766 (unit: tael)

Item	Tax revenue
Land tax	29,920,000
Reclaimed wasteland (*tuntian*) tax	780,000
Salt tax	5,750,000
Tariffs	5,420,000
Transport-loss surcharge	3,000,000
Regular contribution	3,000,000
Miscellaneous tax	1,000,000
Subtotal (tax revenue in silver tael)	49,320,000
Tax revenue in grain (converted to silver tael)	831 7,700 *shi* (12,980,000 taels)
Total	62,300,000

Source: Peng Zeyi, "Qingdai caizheng guanli tizhi yu shouzhi jiegou," 54; Kent G. Deng, "The continuation and efficiency of the Chinese fiscal state," 345, Table 14.4.

Bartolomé Yun-Casalilla and Patrick K. O'Brien (New York: Cambridge University Press, 2012), 353–355.

4 Iwai Shigeki, *Chūgoku kinsei zaiseishi no kenkyū* [A study of China's early modern financial history] (Kyoto: Kyoto daigaku shuppankai, 2004).

In terms of revenue, the land tax raises by far the most, more than 30 million taels. If the grain transported to Beijing as the imperial tax grain (*caoliang*) is added to this silver revenue, then more than 70 percent of the total tax revenue, amounting to about 60 million taels, came from the land tax. Meanwhile, the amount of miscellaneous taxes levied through the market on commerce and industry was insignificant, at 1 million taels. Historians estimate the proportion of tax revenue to GDP in the Qing period to be about 8 percent.[5]

Eighty years later, the Qing empire would be swept away by the tumult resulting from the confrontation with modern Europe after China's defeat in the Opium War against the British Empire. British structural features in the eighteenth century were vastly different from those during the Qing. In 1783, British fiscal revenue was about £12.677 million. The tax that brought in most revenue was the consumption tax (£5.479 million), accounting for 43 percent of fiscal revenue and about half of tax revenue. In second place was the customs duty (£2.949 million). Direct tax revenue from land and property came in third, at £2.595 million. From 1700 to 1810, indirect tax revenue, such as customs duties and consumption taxes, totaled nearly £10 million, constituting a share of more than 70 percent of total fiscal revenue. This was four times more the revenue from direct taxes, including the land tax. This structure basically continued to the nineteenth century.[6]

The British government could develop indirect tax–dependent finance thanks to earlier socioeconomic changes resulting from greater industrialization, whereby there was a higher proportion of secondary and tertiary industries than primary industries. In the eighteenth and nineteenth centuries, when war was frequent, Britain could raise its war budget by imposing indirect taxes and issuing bonds through the market, where there was weaker tax resistance than direct taxation on land.[7]

However, after the Napoleonic Wars ended in 1815, Britain had to face the latecomers' industrialization in continental Europe. The British government decided that a high dependency on indirect taxes was disadvantageous to British industry and trade and in 1816 it began to adjust the tax structure.

5 Kent G. Deng, "The continuation and efficiency of the Chinese fiscal State, 700 BC–AD 1911," in *The Rise of Fiscal States: A Global History, 1500–1914*, 342.

6 Teng Shuna, Xi Chuanying, and Han Daxue, "Jindai yilai Zhong Ying yanshui gongneng bianqian bijiao ji qishi" [Comparison and the implications of changes in the function of the salt tax: Comparing China and Britain in the modern period], *Yanyeshi yanjiu* 2 (2015): 27.

7 Patrick K. O'Brien, "The Political Economy of British Taxation, 1660–1815," *Economic History Review* 41(1) (1988): 9; Teng Shuna, Xi Chuanying, and Han Daxue, "Jindai yilai Zhong Ying yanshui," 27–28.

As a result, the fiscal share of customs duties and consumption taxes gradually decreased from 74.2 percent in 1841 to 65.3 percent in 1851, and then to 54.3 percent in 1881. British tax revenue had continued to grow with the expansion of economic and national power, which means that the imposition of direct taxes, such as land taxes, increased. Changes in the social atmosphere with regard to wealth and taxation contributed to a fiscal transformation. Since the 1820s, the issue of social inequality that had deepened with industrialization was actively discussed in British society. There was a social consensus on the pressing need to close the social gap and active use of taxation as a means of control gradually began to take shape in British society.[8]

A paradigm shift in taxation took place early in Britain as it experienced industrialization and capitalism. In 1799, for the first time in history, a personal income tax was imposed in Britain. At the end of the nineteenth century, the new tax policy package, including the introduction of progressive tax rates, an excess profits tax, and an inheritance tax, played a leading role in narrowing the absolute wealth gap. At the start of the early twentieth century, the proportion of direct taxes finally surpassed that of indirect taxes, and tax revenue was increasingly used for public expenditures such as welfare and education.[9]

The traditional Chinese empire seems to have been in line with the shift in British tax ideas in the late nineteenth century as the Qing state began to use financial logistics for social and regional balancing by communicating and distributing unequal resources rather than exploitative taxation as a means of fundraising. This might be the reason why R. Bin Wong captures a glimpse of the modern welfare state in Chinese imperial finance. However, important differences should not be overlooked. First of all, in Britain during the Middle Ages, the collection of taxes was legal only in cases of emergencies, such as war, and the king did not have authority to collect taxes on his own. The Magna Carta of 1215 and the Bill of Rights of 1689 did not allow arbitrary taxation without parliamentary permission. In modern times, parliament was the sole authority for taxation.[10] In China, where the emperor and the central government were given full legal taxation authority, there were no institutional and legal checks on excessive tax exploitation except for moral checks depending on precedent and practice.

8 Teng Shuna, Xi Chuanying, and Han Daxue, "Jindai yilai Zhong Ying yanshui," 28.

9 Kang Shumeng, "ZhongMei geren suodeshui zhidu duibi fenxi" [A comparative analysis of the Chinese and US personal income tax systems], *Caijing wenti yanjiu* 1(2016): 65.

10 Teng Shuna, Xi Chuanying, and Han Daxue, "Jindai yilai Zhong Ying yanshui," 30.

In fact, from the late Qing through Republican China, China did not adopt the new British fiscal model but rather adopted the older British model that prevailed in the eighteenth and early nineteenth centuries, which depended on highly exploitative indirect tax revenue. However, even in the late nineteenth and early twentieth centuries, China did not have a post-industrialization economic structure like that of the British economy in the eighteenth century. The economy of the late Qing and Republican periods was dominated by primary industry: 90 percent of the GDP came from agriculture. The difficulties that arose when the late Qing pursued an indirect tax–dependent model were due to the discrepancy between policymaking and economic reality. Under these circumstances, neighboring Japan became a new reference model.

Tax modernization efforts in the Qing dynasty and the Japanese model

Fiscal size during the Qianlong period, the peak age of the Qing dynasty, was about 60 million silver taels, which was a relatively low level compared to the size of the Chinese economy. But the situation changed significantly because of war. War can be a key driver in the development of tax history. It provides a reason for the mobilization of resources and fund-raising for the state. New taxes that emerge during wartime often survive after the war, thus changing both the tax structure and statecraft. It should be noted that China and America almost simultaneously witnessed very similar tax events due to war: the *likin* tax imposed during the Taiping Rebellion and the excise tax imposed during to the American Civil War.

During the British colonial era, there were local taxes in each US state, but the Continental Congress did not hold any taxation rights. The American Revolution took place against the British attempt to impose a stamp duty (1765) and a tax on tea (1773) in its colonies. The slogan of the American Revolution was "no taxation without representation" because the colonies did not have the right to vote for British lawmakers. Therefore, the perception that taxation was a form of government suppression took root, and a reluctance to impose federal taxation persisted even after victory in the American Revolution. With establishment of the federal government in 1789, tariffs and excise taxes began to be collected as a federal tax to pay off the debts of the American Revolution. But the excise tax was only temporary. A direct tax on property was introduced to help finance the war against France in the late 1790s, but it was revoked in 1802. The federal treasury has since relied on tariffs and intermittent excise taxes. It was with the outbreak of the American Civil War in 1861 that regularized excise taxes became a major tax resource for the federal government. To fund surging military spending, the federal government collected excise taxes across goods and services in 1861 and 1862, while also, for the first time, it collected personal income taxes. With the end of the war, some excise taxes were abolished in 1872, but excise taxes on key products such as alcohol and tobacco survived and became permanent sources of revenue.[11]

The Qing dynasty recognized the role of taxes in meeting the military expenses to suppress the Taiping Rebellion. But the *likin* commercial taxes in traditional imperial revenue came into conflict the imperial ideology that maintained that the state should not "contend with the people for profits (*yumin zhengli*)." After the second Opium War (1856–1860) and various regional rebellions, China's financial scale exceeded 100 million taels for the first time.[12] Crucially, defeat in the First Sino-Japanese War (1894–1895) and the Boxer Rebellion (1900–1901) resulted in a large amount of compensation, which led to a rapid expansion of finance. Entering the twentieth century, modern police, schools, and military reforms increased administrative costs. Central financial income during the Qing increased from 88 million taels in 1900 and 149.2 million taels in 1903 to 296.96 million taels in 1910.[13] Table 9.2 below summarizes the central government's budget for 1911.

In terms of ranking by financial weight, the land tax still ranked at the top. However, revenue from the land tax revenue, at about 48 million taels, was similar in value to the second-ranking income from state-run industry, the third-ranking tax on salt and tea, and the fourth-ranking income from the *likin*, all of which ranged between 43 million and 46 million taels. Overall, the top four income categories held a similar share of nearly 15 percent of total revenue. The drop in the share of revenue from the land tax is noticeable compared to the more than 70 percent revenue share of the land tax during the Qianlong era. In fact, the absolute value of revenue from the land tax did not decrease, while the expansion of total revenue more than quadrupled, making the relative weight of the land tax shrink. Because revenue from the land tax was almost fixed, taxation on commercial and

11 Fu Boying, "Meiguo lianbang gerensuodeshui de lishi bianqian yu qishi" [The historical transition and the implications of the individual income tax system in the Unnited States], *Caizhengshi yanjiu* 7 (2014): 321–322.

12 Kent G. Deng, "The continuation and efficiency of the Chinese fiscal State, 700 BC–AD 1911," 350.

13 Fu Zhiyu, "Jindai Zhongguo shuishou xiandaihua jincheng de sixiangshi kaocha" [An intellectual historical study on the modernization of taxation in modern China] (PhD diss., Hunan University, 2009), 31.

Table 9.2 Tax revenue budget of the central government, 1911 (unit: 10,000 taels)

Tax revenue budget					
Item	**Revenue amount**		**Item**	**Revenue amount**	
Land-poll tax	Regular	4,616	Miscellaneous taxes	Regular	2,616
	Temporary	193	*Likin*	Temporary	4,319
Salt and tea tax	Regular	4,631	Govern-ment enterprise revenue	Regular	4,660
Tariff		3,514	Miscellaneous income	Temporary	1,919
Domestic transit tax	Regular	699			
	Temporary	9		Regular	1,605
Temporary non-tax revenue					
Sale of official positions	565		Public bonds	356	
Total 296. 96 million taels					

Source: Fu Zhiyu, "Jindai Zhongguo shuishou xiandaihua jincheng de sixiangshi kaocha," 33–34.

industrial production and logistics filled the gap due to the inflated fiscal expenditures.

In terms of local budgets, according to a report on the total amount of revenue and expenditures of twenty-two provinces in 1908 (see Table 1.1 in Chapter 1), Jiangsu province was at the top with 46 million taels. Provincial revenue in Jiangsu province alone equaled the entire monetary tax revenue in 1766. Guangdong and Zhili recorded 27 million and 21.66 million taels in provincial revenue, respectively, ranking second and third. They were followed by Hubei (16.55 million taels), Fengtian (15.81 million taels), Sichuan (15.3 million taels), Zhejiang (11.7 million tael), and Shandong (11.3 million taels), while the revenue of the other provinces amounted to less than 10 million taels. The tax revenue of all twenty-two provinces totaled about 240 million taels.[14] Nonetheless, there is no clear way to determine the amount of revenue used within the provinces compared to the revenue that flowed out, including remittances to the capital, the neighboring poor provinces, or any other special allotments.

Another study calculates the average tax revenue of each province in the 1870s and 1880s: 2.5 million to 2.6 million taels in Shandong, 3 million taels

14 Han Xiang, "WanQing caizheng guimo gusuan wenti chutan" [Research on the problem of estimating the scale of public finance in the late Qing], Zhongguo jingjishi yanjiu 3 (2014): 26.

in Shanxi, 2.1 million taels in Henan, 5.7 million taels in Jiangsu, 3.7 million taels in Zhejiang, 2.8 million taels in Guangdong, 0.3 million taels in Guizhou, 1.5 million to 1.6 million taels in Shaanxi, 2.89 million taels in Fujian, and 5.2 million taels in Sichuan.[15] A comparison of these two groups of data reveals that the size of provincial revenue almost quadrupled within thirty years. The coast–inland gap was widened, and there was more rapid growth in the commercialized provinces than in the agricultural provinces. In particular, provincial revenue in Guangdong province increased nearly ten times.

In 1911, the Ministry of Finance compiled a revenue budget plan for 1912, for the first time applying the principle of dividing the national and local treasuries. This plan allocated most revenue, as much as 233.95 million taels, to the national budget, while it allocated only 25.96 million taels to the provincial budget.[16] Considering that the budget of the central government and the total provincial budgets were almost equal during the Republican era (in contemporary China as well), this budget plan was not a reflection of reality but an ideal target dreamed up by the imperial court. However, the outbreak of the Xinhai Revolution in 1911 thwarted this dream of fiscal centralization.

A proposal to compile a national budget was raised in earnest after the Sino-Japanese War. One way in which the victory of Meiji Japan was interpreted was that Japan had been able to finance the war through its efforts to transplant a Western fiscal and financial system in Japan, including its compilation of a national budget. Even earlier, however, in his pioneering writing, *Treatises on Japan* (*Riben guozhi*), Huang Zunxian, a Chinese diplomat and reformer, advocated the introduction of Japan's national budget system modeled after the Western countries. But Huang's work, which was completed in 1887 and printed in 1890, did not attract attention until after the Sino-Japanese War.[17]

With the New Policy reforms launched in 1901, fiscal modernization was an important item on the agenda. Chinese constitutional missions that toured abroad in 1905–1906 included inspections of the financial systems on their tours. In 1908, the Qing court dispatched Tang Shaoyi to inspect foreign financial systems. Simultaneously, introduction of a division between national and local taxes was actively discussed in court. For the

15 Ma Jinhua, "Waizhai yu wanQing zhengju" [Foreign loans and the political situation in the late Qing period] (PhD diss., Renmin University of China, 2004), 112, Table 4-4: Statistical table of the financial deficits in each province.

16 Fu Zhiyu, "Jindai Zhongguo shuishou xiandaihua jincheng de sixiangshi kaocha," 34.

17 Chen Feng, "WanQing caizheng yusuan de yunniang yu shishi" [Preparation and implementation of the financial budget in the late Qing dynasty], *Jianghan luntan* 1 (2009): 79–80.

first time, a "regulation on the division between national taxes and local taxes" was officially mentioned in the announcement about preparations for a preliminary constitution in the same year.[18]

The government of Meiji Japan had fought two wars, the First Sino-Japanese War and the Russo-Japanese War (1904–1905), which led to a decisive change in its tax revenue structure. The most significant change was the shift of the main tax revenue from a land tax to indirect taxes and an increase in the proportion of tax revenue from commercial and industrial entities. During the ten-year transition period from the nineteenth to the twentieth century, Japan established a revenue structure dependent on indirect taxes, similar to that which had been prevalent in Britain in the eighteenth and nineteenth centuries. Japan's revenue structure is examined in Table 9.3 below.

Table 9.3 Tax revenue structure, Meiji government (unit: 1 million Japanese *yen*)

Year	Total	Tariffs	Domestic taxes						
			Subtotal	Land tax	Income tax	Sales tax	Alcohol tax	Sugar consumption tax	Fabric consumption tax
1886	64	3	61	43			12		
1890	66	4	62	40	1		14		
1893	66	5	61	39	1		17		
1895	71	7	64	39	1		18		
1897	101	8	93	38	5	4	31		
1899	138	16	122	45	5	6	49		
1903	160	18	143	47	8	7	53	7	
1905	282	37	244	80	23	19	59	11	5
1909	354	37	317	86	33	25	91	13	19
1913	400	75	326	75	36	27	93	21	20

Source: Kamiyama Tsuneo, "Zaiseiseisakuto kinyūkōzō" [Fiscal policy and the financial structure], in *Nipponkeizaishi 2 sangyō kakumeiki* [An economic history of Japan 2: The industrial revolution period], ed. Ishi Kanji (Tokyo: Tokyo daigaku shuppankai, 2000), 91.

As Table 9.3 shows, in 1886 and 1890 Japan still maintained its traditional fiscal structure in which the land tax made up more than 60 percent of the total tax revenue. The fiscal weight of the land tax decreased to less than 40 percent in 1897, two years after Japan's victory in the First Sino-Japanese War,

18 Du Xuncheng, "Minguo shiqi de zhongyang yu difang caizheng huafen," 185; Fu Zhiyu, "Jindai Zhongguo shuishou xiandaihua jincheng de sixiangshi kaocha," 32.

and then it was surpassed by the alcohol tax in 1899. By 1910 and 1913, after the Russo-Japanese War, the share of the land tax decreased to below 20 percent. In fact, the absolute value of revenue from the land tax almost doubled during the same period, but Japan's total tax revenue expanded even more rapidly. The indirect tax on commerce and industry underpinned Japan's fiscal expansion. Revenue from indirect taxes, including tariffs, the sales tax, the alcohol tax, the sugar consumption tax, and the textiles and consumption tax, constituted 60 percent of total tax revenue. Remarkably, a personal income tax was introduced as early as 1890. Although its share of tax revenue remained at about 9 percent until 1913, its fiscal weight was not negligible.

The Meiji government could not afford to push ahead with a drastic land tax hike due to strong opposition from the Imperial Diet. Members of the House of Representatives who were elected in 1890 under the 1889 Meiji Constitution by eligible voters, mainly rural landlords and urban entrepreneurs, were reluctant to raise the land tax or any other direct taxation on property. When enacting a sales tax in 1897, the government faced strong opposition from urban entrepreneurs. Thus, the government and the Diet preferred indirect taxation, which was an easy way to pass the tax burden on to anonymous consumers who presented less tax resistance. The alcohol tax became the main tax resource because it ensured a moral legitimacy to protect public health and charges on luxury goods that were not necessities. The alcohol tax outplayed the land tax and the tariffs to become the primary source of tax revenue beginning in 1899.

The various excise taxes constituted another rising source of tax revenue. An indirect consumption tax started was levied on alcohol, soybean source, and sugar in 1901, and then on textiles in 1904. State monopolies was a new revenue source as well. The Japanese government implemented a state monopoly on tobacco leaves in 1898 and then expanded it to overall tobacco products such as cigarettes in 1904. Revenue from the alcohol tax reached 13.9 million *yen* in 1890 (approximately 13 percent of total tax revenue) and then jumped nearly seven times to 86.7 million *yen* (the same 13 percent of the total) in 1910. Whereas the total tax revenue in 1910 was 317.28 million *yen,* the combined revenue from the alcohol tax and the tobacco monopoly exceeded 100 million *yen*.[19]

Tax revenue in Meiji Japan remained at about 60 million *yen* before the Sino-Japanese War. But during the war it surpassed 100 million *yen*—200

19 Chang Segi, *Ilbon gyŏngje sa* [An economic history of Japan] (Seoul: Dunam Publisher, 2003), 272–273.

million *yen* with the outbreak of the Russo-Japanese War and 300 million *yen* during the latter part of the Russo-Japanese War. This amount was comparable to the total size of the tax budget in China. The Qing's total tax revenue budget in 1911 was slightly below 300 million taels (about 400 million Japanese *yen*). Even though the territory of Qing China was thirty times larger than that of Japan, their financial sizes were almost the same. The two countries had common features in their tax structures, such as the proportion of land taxes falling below 20 percent, and a dependence on indirect taxes such as tariffs and an increase in consumption taxes. Both countries were following the model of Britain's indirect tax–dependent financial system.

Nonetheless, there were also some differences between the tax structures in China and Japan. First, the income tax was introduced in Japan earlier in 1890 and it was rooted by 1913, when the income tax was still not on the agenda in China and it was legislated as a permanent tax for the first time in the United States. Second, there was a high level of regularization of tax administration in Japan. Due to its successful industrialization, factory manufactured products, such as alcohol, tobacco, and textiles, offered easy access to taxation for the Japanese government. The Meiji government levied various special consumption taxes at the factories before the products were shipped to the market. Taxation on the commercial and industrial sectors in China remained a form of non-regular taxes, such as *likins*, miscellaneous taxes, and extra charges. Unlike the state monopoly in Japan that targeted the modern sector, the traditional salt monopoly played a critical role in Chinese finance until the twentieth century. Third, related to the second point, China and Japan had similar tax structures at the start of the twentieth century but quite different economic structures. The transformation of the Japanese tax structure reflected the change in its economic structure. The size of the Japanese economy had increased rapidly, driven by growth in the modern sector, and the proportion of secondary and tertiary industries had already surpassed that of primary industries through successful industrialization. Thus, despite the explosive increase in tax revenue, the tax-to-GDP ratio remained stable. Japan's tax-to-GDP ratio was 5.2 percent during the First Sino-Japanese War and 7.5 percent during the Russo-Japanese War. From 1906 to 1909, the ratio increased more than 8 percent due to the burden of having to repay foreign debts. However, because of the subsequent rapid economic growth, the ratio fell below 7 percent from 1910 to 1913.[20] Compared with the 10 to 20 percent ratio in the European countries, Japan's taxation was

20 Kamiyama Tsuneo, "Zaiseiseisakuto kinyūkōzō," 91, 93.

not overly excessive. In contrast, at the beginning of the twentieth century, China remained an overwhelmingly agricultural country. Expansion of tax revenue was supported by excessive taxation on the commercial and industrial sectors. Although the tax structure appeared to be modern, this was not matched by the real tax base. This discrepancy continued to cause many problems in Republican China.

Republican China: A global taxation paradigm change and the catch-up of Chinese finance

Tax structure of the Beiyang government

The Republic of China followed the footsteps of the late Qing in its effort to learn from the Japanese fiscal model, with the shares of tariffs and indirect taxes in total revenue increasing. At the dawn of the Republican era, the effort to increase taxation on luxuries, such as alcohol and cigarettes, began in earnest. The possibility of a state monopoly over alcohol, cigarettes, and sugar was explored, and the Chinese state attempted to collect taxes in the form of a factory tax at the production stage, which targeted factories that produced modern consumer goods, including cotton fabrics. Restoration of tariff autonomy, with the dual goals of increasing tariff revenue and protecting domestic industries, was the primary item on the agenda of the Republican governments.[21] Discussions about an income tax and an inheritance tax began both inside and outside of government. These taxes were introduced to the Chinese public as "advanced" taxes, modeled after those in Britain, the United States, and Japan. The above attempts at fiscal reform looked to the earlier achievements in Japan.[22]

Unfortunately, the Republic of China, which opened its doors after the victory of the 1911 Revolution, failed to build a centralized and powerful

21 Kubo Tōru, *Senkanki chūgoku "jiritsueno mosaku" kanzei tsūka seisaku to keizai hatten* [Seeking for "self-reliance" in China during the interwar period: Tariff and monetary policy and economic development] (Tokyo: Tokyo daigaku shuppankai, 1999): 23–24.

22 For more detailed information about the attempt by the sugar monopoly in China, see Kang Jin-A, "1930nendai anton Chinsaitō seiken no seitōgyō kensetsu" [Building of the sugar industry under the Chen Ji-ang regime in Guangdong province in the 1930s], *Chikakini Arite* 30 (1996); Jin-A Kang, "1930 nyŏndae chunggugŭi sŏlt'ang chŏnmaewa hongk'ong t'aegodangbang: Taegonghwangesŏ saranamgi" [The politics of the Taikoo Sugar Refinery Co. in Hong Kong against the Chinese sugar monopoly during the 1930s: Survival during the Great Depression], *Chunggukkŭnhyŏndaesa yŏngu* 85 (2020).

Table 9.4 National tax revenue of the Beiyang government, 1911–1925 (Unit: 1,000 *yuan*)

Year	Land tax	Salt tax	Tariff	Domestic transit tax	Likin, freight tax	Stamp tax	Tobacco and wine taxes	Miscellaneous taxes	Miscellaneous fees	Total
1911	270		47,336					129,334	505	177,445
1913	82,404	77,566	68,224		32,711			37,863	3,944	302,712
1914	79,228	84,880	79,403		34,186			57,612	4,947	340,256
1916	97,554	84,771	72,346		40,290			108,649	18,564	422,174
1917		81,214	61,104			2,520	14,014	10,360		169,212
1918		89,831	58,153	6,359		2,780	12,531	5,755		175,409
1919	90,549	98,815	81,664	12,300	39,251	8,158	36,621	28,472	8,244	404,074
1920		89,248	79,712	7,017		2,990	14,950	4,245		198,162
1921		94,281	87,140	7,235		3,280	14,520	4,245		210,701
1922		99,238	93,815	6,908		3,382	15,070	6,289		224,702
1923		92,061	101,607	7,184		3,005		6,289		210,146
1924		81,433	111,352	6,682		3,048				202,515
1925	90,081	98,859	100,019	20,347	45,699	5,864	40,732	30,188	4,769	436,558

Source: Fu Zhiyu, "Jindai Zhongguo shuishou xiandaihua jincheng de sixiangshi kaocha," 48–49.

government like that in Japan. The Beiyang government, indicating the Yuan Shikai regime (1912–1916) and the subsequent central governments (1916–1928) in Beijing, only held administrative power within Beijing and Zhili province. Elsewhere warlordism divided the country into jigsaw puzzles. In spite of these circumstances, the Ministry of Finance of the government in Beijing divided national and local taxes in the drafts of related regulations (*guojia shuifa yu difang shuifa caoan, guojia feimu difang feimu biaozhun*). It is not clear whether the drafts follow a Japanese model or a French model. Either way, these regulations all proposed an unprecedented degree of financial centralization. But the issue of the allocation of the taxes has created widespread controversies. The tug-of-war over tax resources ended in a one-sided declaration in 1914 whereby the finalized amendment to the regulations allocated all major taxes to the national treasury, including land taxes, tariffs, salt taxes, *likin*, and consolidated levies (*tongjuan*). In contrast, the local treasuries were only allocated the additional charges on the land tax and the miscellaneous taxes. Ultimately, Yuan Shikai rejected this modest concession and eventually both local autonomy and the division of national–local taxes were canceled.

After the death of Yuan, the drafts were put back on the government agenda. In 1915, the Beiyang government implemented the so-called "special fund system" (*zhuankuan zhidu*), referring to the funds exclusively administered by the central government through the setting up of special tax offices across the country. The contract tax, stamp duty, tobacco and wine tax, sales license tax for tobacco and wine, and brokerage tax were included in this special tax. But the taxes assigned to the special tax continued to change. Under warlord autarky, local governments widely withheld the remittance of revenue that was part of the special tax.[23]

Table 9.4 presents the annual budget proposals, so these figures are likely different from the actual tax revenue collected each year. Moreover, the random but common withholding of tax revenue in the localities prevented the government in Beijing from realizing its budget plan estimates. However, since the budget was drawn up on the basis of earlier tax performance, the budget plan is still a valuable outline of the overall tax structure during this period.

The budget for national tax revenue for 1913 was 300 million *yuan*. Thereafter, the government's accounting unit was changed from the silver tael to the silver *yuan* (dollar). The Beiyang government issued the new silver one-dollar coins as legal tender. Although the market exchange rate fluctuated, the exchange rate between this one silver dollar (called *Guobi*) and the silver tael (*liang*) was generally one silver *yuan* = 0.75 silver tael. Therefore, the tax revenue in the 1913 budget plan amounting to 300 million *yuan* turned out to be a steep drop from about the 400 million *yuan* (300 million taels) in 1911. The total revenue in the 1916 budget plan increased significantly to 420 million *yuan* after Yuan Shikai promoted a centralization drive in 1915. However, it is unlikely that such sums would have actually been collected due to the death of Yuan Shikai and the subsequent political chaos in the Beiyang government. The estimated total tax revenue for 1917 halved to below 20 million *yuan* after six southwestern provinces declared independence from Beijing's central government. During the 1920s, total tax revenue remained at about 200 million *yuan* due to the ongoing civil war. Estimates in the 1925 budget bill doubled, making up for each missing item. Feng Yuxiang, who had seized power to establish a new central government in Beijing in 1924, may have set the budget at the same annual level.

The land tax was dropped during many years because few remittances were made to Beijing. The salt tax and tariffs were the primary tax source for the government in Beijing because these two taxes, as collateral for foreign loans, were administrated by special institutions under the control of foreigners, and the remainder of the tax revenue, subtracting for the redemption of loans, was transferred to the government in Beijing. Other

23 Du Xuncheng, "Minguo shiqi de zhongyang yu difang caizheng huafen," 185, 187.

indirect taxes on commerce and industry were primarily earned by Beijing and Zhili province. Many of these indirect taxes were managed under the "special fund system," but this revenue continued to decline. In 1917, the Beiyang government asked the provinces to remit 12.87 million *yuan*, but the total remittances only amounted to 10.36 million *yuan*. The government reduced the remittance quota to about 6 million won (1919–1923), but the provinces did not pay even this reduced amount. Actual remittances remained at about 4 million *yuan*.[24]

In the following table we examine the tax revenue of the local governments during the Beiyang government.

Table 9.5 Provincial tax revenue, 1915 and 1916 (unit: silver *yuan*)

Province	1915	1916	Comparable year's tax revenue
Zhili	19,948,843	-	9,670,894 (1924)
Fengtian	-	-	13,401,426 (1921)
Jilin	2,823,777	4,779,668	8,294,824 (1923)
Heilongjiang	2,806,098	5,184,843	6,788,128 (1923)
Shandong	13,525,430	11,552,369	10,495,054 (1923)
Shanxi	6,210,651	8,594,216	7,489,079 (1924)
Rehe	-	-	991,554 (1923)
Chahar	535,777	522,442	590,738 (1923)
Suiyuan	978,294	-	545,207 (1923)
Henan	6,760,683	8,473,051	10,215,346 (1923)
Shaanxi	4,705,094	5,695,720	5,673,806 (1923)
Hunan	9,571,599	4,800,879	6,072,996 (1919)
Hubei	10,801,096	12,421,520	8,347,444 (1923)
Zhejiang	16,582,506	16,343,981	12,177,868 (1921)
Jiangsu	15,370,185	18,585,897	17,551,031 (1923)
Jiangxi	8,835,943	8,254,952	8,202,810
Anhui	7,305,495	9,788,354	6,799,829 (1924)
Yunnan	3,139,507	2,805,772	2,219,988
Guizhou	2,423,918	4,485,266	1,573,946
Sichuan	-	-	12,747,834
Guangdong	16,626,092	-	12,711,737
Guangxi	4,379,076	-	4,109,501 (1921)
Fujian	6,284,519	5,576,249	6,023,318 (1924)
Xinjiang	3,823,739	3,782,565	2,306,308 (1923)
Gansu	3,265,050	3,348,646	2,958,505 (1924)

Source: Fu Zhiyu, "Jindai Zhongguo shuishou xiandaihua jincheng de sixiangshi kaocha," 49–50.

24 Du Xuncheng, "Minguo shiqi de zhongyang yu difang caizheng huafen," 185, 187.

In 1915, the year when Yuan Shikai attempted to centralize fiscal revenue, Zhili province collected 19.94 million *yuan* and was ranked first in terms of the amount of tax revenue brought in, followed by Guangdong (16.62 million), Zhejiang (16.58 million), Jiangsu (15.37 million), and Shandong (15.35 million). Meanwhile, in the 1920s Jiangsu (17.555 million) was at the top of the ranking, followed by Fengtian (13.4 million), Sichuan (12.74 million), Guangdong (12.71 million), Zhejiang (12.71 million), Henan (10.21 million), and Shandong (10.49 million). Tax revenue in Zhili was recorded at only 9.67 million *yuan*. Financial reports during the warlord period generally lacked credibility and were distorted by political factors. For example, in 1915 Zhili province had the highest tax revenue because Yuan Shikai's regime held strong administrative control. In contrast, the government changes and the interregnum in 1924 resulted in decreased tax collection in Zhili. During the warlord era, the needs of local warlords may have required some provinces to collect excessive taxes (for example, Henan or Fengtian). In contrast, tax revenue in Jiangsu, the richest province, appeared to be relatively low during certain years, probably due to poor reporting.

Therefore, distribution of local tax revenue during this period does not fit well with that of the late Qing. The primary source of provincial revenue was the land tax, which was generally withheld by the localities. However, tax structure varied from province to province. Hunan and Jiangsu retained the traditional structure where the land tax constituted the overwhelming share of tax revenue. The revenue from the gambling tax in Guangdong was three times more than the revenue from the land tax.

State-building efforts by the Nanjing Nationalist government and fiscal reform

The Nanjing Nationalist Government (hereafter NNG) inherited the previous reform efforts by both the late Qing court and the Beiyang government and it eventually succeeded in dividing national and local taxes and restoring tariff autonomy. Another major achievement was abolition of the *likin* and establishment of the consolidated tax (*tongshui*). Similar to the special consumption tax in Meiji Japan, the consolidated tax was a national tax levied on modern factory products, such as cigarettes, cotton cloth, matches, flour, and cement, during the product shipment phase. To compensate for the loss of the *likin* tax, the NNG allocated the land tax to local governments, which had an ongoing demand from the provinces since the Xinhai Revolution in 1911. Tax reform had been attempted several times, for example, the first individual income tax was introduced in 1936, and even during wartime (1937–1945) and the subsequent Civil War period (1946–1949). But with the outbreak of the Sino-Japanese War in 1937, collected revenue was transferred to wartime emergency finance. After the Civil war and the resultant hyperinflation, the economy faced anarchy in 1947. Therefore, here we will focus on the pre-war NNG period.

National tax revenue in 1928, when the NNG reunified China after completion of the Northern Expedition, amounted to 20 million *yuan*. This amount was below the average revenue during the Beiyang government. But thereafter national tax revenue began to increase rapidly, and by 1936 it reached 760 million *yuan*. The tax revenue in 1937 was affected by the Sino-Japanese War, so 1936 is the most appropriate year to evaluate the economy and tax reforms of the NNG. Despite the economic recession and financial crisis during the 1930s, by late 1935 the NNG was able to unify the national currency and successfully implement a managed currency system. The success of this *Fabi* currency reform placed the struggling Chinese economy back on the road to recovery. In 1936, the NNG retook control of Guangdong and Guangxi in the course of an aborted coup in these two provinces. As a reflection of these positive factors, China in 1936 witnessed a significant increase in tax revenue and the introduction of a new income tax. Table 9.6 summarizes the tax structure under NNG rule.

Table 9.6 National tax revenue of the Nanjing Nationalist Government, 1928–1937 (unit: *yuan, fabi*)

Year	Salt tax	tariff	Consoli-dated tax	Stamp tax	Wine and tobacco tax	Mining tax	Bourse tax	Bank tax	Income tax	Total
1928	29,542,421	179,141,917	27,691,337	3,034,342	3,549,380	90,182	-	-	-	243,049,579
1929	122,146,170	275,545,215	36,566,506	5,426,844	6,830,995	-	-	-	-	446,515,730
1930	150,484,086	312,986,653	53,330,705	6,111,114	8,617,127	-	-	-	-	531,529,685
1931	144,222,716	369,742,637	88,681,798	4,798,950	7,625,785	-	-	-	-	615,071,886
1932	158,073,565	325,534,850	79,596,999	5,118,580	9,506,988	-	-	-	-	577,830,982
1933	174,414,230	337,647,767	98,870,926	8,182,864	12,332,395	2,465,814	3,063	1,526,940	-	635,443,999
1934	175,466,172	337,973,541	139,658,310	10,162,184	18,363,404	3,958,644	326,674	1,613,539	-	687,522,468
1935	192,745,843	272,455,806	116,088,172	7,589,389	9,835,526	3,045,033	260,442	1,716,810	-	603,737,021
1936	170,144,384	408,141,422	146,469,713	8,740,023	14,266,450	5,120,130	307,373	37,875	7,316,986	760,544,356
1937	228,625,553	369,267,522	176,313,905	11,300,000	24,767,524	5,522,718	170,000	1,600,000	20,237,589	837,804,811

Source: Fu Zhiyu, "Jindai Zhongguo shuishou xiandaihua jincheng de sixiangshi kaocha," 66, Table 4.1.

Table 9.7 Tax structure and shares of national tax revenue, 1928–1937 (unit: %)

Year	Salt tax	Tariff	Consolidated tax	Stamp tax	Wine and tobacco tax	Mining tax	Bourse tax	Bank tax	Income tax	Total
1928	12.15%	73.71%	11.39%	1.25%	1.46%	0.04%	-	-	-	100%
1929	27.36%	61.71%	8.19%	1.22%	1.53%	-	-	-	-	100%
1930	28.31%	58.88%	10.03%	1.15%	1.62%	-	-	-	-	100%
1931	23.45%	60.11%	14.42%	0.78%	1.24%	-	-	-	-	100%
1932	27.36%	56.34%	13.78%	0.89%	1.65%	-	-	-	-	100%
1933	27.45%	53.14%	15.56%	1.29%	1.94%	0.39%	*0.00%	0.24%	-	100%
1934	25.52%	49.16%	20.31%	1.48%	2.67%	0.58%	0.05%	0.23%	-	100%
1935	31.93%	45.13%	19.23%	1.26%	1.63%	0.50%	0.04%	0.28%	-	100%
1936	22.37%	53.66%	19.26%	1.15%	1.88%	0.67%	0.04%	*0.00%	0.96%	100%
1937	27.29%	44.08%	21.04%	1.35%	2.96%	0.66%	0.02%	0.19%	2.42%	100%

Source: Table 9.6.
* The amount is extremely small and does not fall within the second decimal place.

As land taxes were classified as local taxes, they disappeared from the category of a national tax. Tariffs and the salt tax constituted the largest tax among the indirect taxes, accounting for 90 percent of national tax revenue. In 1936, the total tax revenue of 760 million *yuan* consisted of tariffs, at 400 million *yuan* (ranking first if we arrange the amounts in order of size), the salt tax, at 170 million *yuan* (ranking second), the consolidated tax, at 140 million *yuan* (ranking third), the tobacco and wine taxes, 14 million *yuan* (fourth), the stamp tax, at 8.74 million (fifth), and income tax, 7.81 million *yuan* (the sixth largest amount). The continuing trend of relying on indirect taxes reached its apex in 1936.

The above table, categorized by tax items, shows that income from the tobacco and wine taxes during the NNG period ranged from 10 million *yuan* to 20 million *yuan*, accounting for less than 2 percent of total revenue. However, income from taxation on tobacco and wine was actually far more than is indicated by these statistics because more than 60 percent of the revenue from the consolidated tax revenue came from taxation on cigarettes, ranging from 50 million *yuan* to 80 million *yuan*. Thus, a large amount of income, close to 100 million *yuan*, was derived from the total taxes on tobacco and wine.[25] Such a high dependence on a tax for luxury goods was also found in Meiji Japan and the United States in modern times. However, the increased dependence on the traditional salt tax was a unique fiscal feature of modern China.

25 See Chapter 3.

In 1698, the British taxed salt for the first time to fund the war against the Netherlands. Thereafter, the salt tax was an easy way to raise funds during wartime. When the British government steeply raised the rate of the salt tax to prepare for war with France in 1805, the selling price of salt was thirty times greater than the cost. In 1815, British salt tax revenue amounted to £1.6 million. However, because of growing public criticism that the salt tax would hurt the livelihood of ordinary people, in 1825 the government abolished it forever.[26] In comparison, the share of the salt tax to total revenue actually increased in China under the NNG. The salt tax rate increased from 3.11 *yuan* per picul in 1928 to 4.76 *yuan* in 1936 and 5.98 *yuan* in 1937. While Britain and Meiji Japan were able to diversify their tax bases through rapid industrialization and urbanization, China remained primarily an agricultural country, with agriculture generating over 60 percent of GDP. Therefore, although total tax revenue increased significantly during the NNG period, the tax-to-GDP ratio in China remained at about 5 percent, even in 1936, far lower than the federal tax-to-GDP ratio of 13–15 percent during peacetime in the United States in the 1920s and 20 percent during wartime in the United States, and even the 8 percent of the late Qing.[27]

Local finance of the NNG (except for that in Japanese-occupied Manchuria) is shown in Table 9.8 below.

What stands out most in the above table is how overwhelmingly Jiangsu's revenues outstrip those of every other province. Tax revenue in Jiangsu province jumped from 40 million taels (about 53 million *yuan*) in the late Qing to 417.56 million *yuan* in 1936. Hebei (Zhili) ranked second. But these top two provinces experienced a sharp decline in revenue in 1937 due to the war. According to the table, Hubei followed Hebei to rank third. In fact, Guangdong's real tax revenue might have been higher than that in Hubei. The low tax revenue of below 40 million *yuan* in Guangdong during the 1933–1935 period lacks credibility because Guangdong reported as little revenue to the NNG as possible in order to gloss over its military expenses and its withholding of taxes. The revenue of over 60 million *yuan* in 1936, when the NNG took over Guangdong, may be close to reality. Sichuan, which became a wartime capital, witnessed a steep increase in tax revenue, amounting to 93.51 million *yuan* in 1937. The combined total

26 Teng Shuna, Xi Chuanying, and Han Daxue, "Jindai yilai Zhong Ying yanshui," 25.

27 Fu Boying, "Meiguo lianbang geren suodeshui de lishi bianqian yu qishi," 324; Fu Zhiyu, "Jindai Zhongguo shuishou xiandaihua jincheng de sixiangshi kaocha," 120. Kubo assesses the ratio of Chinese finance relative to all national economic activities to be 6 percent. Kubo Tōru, *Chūgoku keizaishi nyūmon* [Introduction to Chinese economic history] (Tokyo: Tokyo daigaku shuppankai, 2012), 128.

Table 9.8 Provincial tax revenue under the Nationalist government, 1933–1936 (unit: silver *yuan*)

Province	1933	1934	1935	1936	1937
Hebei	75,906,638	80,504,393	67,561,126	85,172,864	37,214,891
Shandong	48,146,377	52,548,214	46,891,624	58,013,695	19,377,691
Henan	9,788,212	12,061,800	12,229,213	14,031,596	9,547,214
Shanxi	6,180,087	6,707,890	7,239,937	5,824,760	3,450,081
Shaanxi	1,715,388	2,221,329	2,230,807	2,366,276	2,717,308
Xinjiang	-	-	22,354	56,169	59,221
Chahar	1,184,129	1,284,690	1,483,708	287,138	279
Jiangsu	326,930,069	347,517,330	303,678,175	417,569,777	121,414,553
Zhejiang	20,841,115	22,274,058	18,598,362	27,091,373	19,953,236
Anhui	10,321,796	10,656,719	10,204,297	13,381,956	7,668,186
Jiangxi	13,090,953	15,093,976	13,016,318	18,352,406	13,975,347
Hubei	39,480,034	42,513,114	37,809,119	54,049,990	44,553,895
Hunan	18,281,482	20,285,100	22,104,490	25,106,515	30,615,856
Guangdong	36,569,256	32,789,852	34,895,829	65,385,212	78,826,747
Guangxi	1,894,671	1,572,104	1,619,780	2,685,508	8,043,229
Fujian	10,433,663	13,505,957	12,874,619	17,547,599	13,604,081
Yunnan	4,724,514	4,985,583	6,111,522	6,237,092	6,277,979
Guizhou	-	1,299	16,757	39,079	170,568
Sichuan	15,190,801	16,800,596	30,002,022	31,692,533	93,516,448
Gansu	-	550,828	518,024	1,924,071	1,849,025
Ningxia	-	44	292	-	106
Qinghai	-	3,027	3,484	-	6,459
Suiyuan	-	76,331	102,560	476	19

Source: Fu Zhiyu, "Jindai Zhongguo shuishou xiandaihua jincheng de sixiangshi kaocha," 67, Table 4.2.

provincial revenue in 1936 amounted to about 850 million *yuan*. However, other research estimates that the total tax revenue of 1.6 billion *yuan* (equal to about 1.2 billion silver taels) in 1936 consisted of 870 million *yuan* of national tax revenue, 534 million *yuan* of provincial tax revenue, and 190 million *yuan* of prefectural tax revenue. In sum, total tax revenue might have more than doubled in twenty-five years (1911–1936) compared to 540 million taels (300 million taels in the national treasury and 240 million taels in the local treasury).

The original plan drafted by the first minister of Finance, Gu Yingfen, in 1927 provides a useful criterion for understanding the fiscal policy orientation and the fiscal performance of the Nationalist Government (1927–1949) as a central government. Gu Yingfen formulated five tax-reform principles that included in his "Provisional Standards for Dividing National and Local

Income" (*huafen guojia shouru difang shouru zanxing biaozhun an*). The key points are summarized as follows: First, to facilitate collection, consumer goods such as salt, alcohol, cigarettes, and oils would be taxed before shipment from the factories. All the above taxes belonged to the national tax, while the *likin* taxes and other local charges were to be abolished. Instead, the land tax and taxes on real estate, contracts, slaughter, and pawnshops were to belong to the local taxes. Second, new national taxes were to be created, including an income tax, inheritance tax, banknote issuance tax, tax on the bourse, and a registration tax on companies and trademarks. A business tax and building tax, modeled after those overseas, were to be newly created for the local treasury. Third, the way to divide the tax revenue between the central government and the local government would be decided after wide reference to overseas cases. Globally, there were two ways to divide taxes: one to separately designate whether each tax source was to be national or local tax revenue. The other way was to divide the tax revenue in the form of shared taxes between the central and local governments at a certain rate. Traditionally, China had allocated the regular tax to the imperial government and the additional charges to the local governments, but this method was to be abandoned and it was recommended that the tax sources be clearly divided.

In 1928, Gu's proposal was discussed, partly amended, and passed at the National Finance Conference presided over by the new Minister of Finance, Song Ziwen. Gu's proposal formed the basis for the future tax reform of the Nationalist Government. It is useful to regard Gu's proposal as a cornerstone to estimate the achievements of the NNG before 1949. The consolidated tax represented the successful realization of Gu's plan. But allocation of the land tax to the local treasuries was reversed due to the war, and the land tax was returned to the national tax category to fund wartime expenses. After the end of the war in 1945, a petition by the provincial governments to reclaim the revenue from the land tax revenue was partially accepted and in 1946 the idea of a shared tax, at the ratio of 3 to 7, was applied to the land tax. The land tax revenue was divided between the central government and the provincial government. Out of a list of new national taxes, an inheritance tax could not be implemented due to strong opposition, whereas an income tax was introduced in 1936. However, unlike the Western income taxes that began as taxation on the rich, the income tax in China initially started as a mass tax that was levied on the urban middle class whose monthly salary was over 30 *yuan*. The lack of administrative ability hindered tax collection from high-income earners. Consequently, the income tax base was limited to the salaries of civil servants and teachers. The proportion of the income tax revenue relative to the total tax revenue never exceeded 3 percent.[28]

During the Beiyang government, the transportation clique (*jiaotong-xi*) who starting their careers as technocrat officials in the late Qing period played a leading role in fiscal policymaking. Meanwhile, many officials in the NNG who had studied in the United States were also active in policymaking, especially in departments related to finance and the economy. Therefore, these technocrats within the NNG paid a lot of attention to the US model, and this explains why the introduction of an income tax and an inheritance tax was consistently attempted in spite of sluggish progress.

The NNG period coincided with a historical change in US taxation. The era of indirect and proportional taxes that dominating the nineteenth century had ended, and the era of direct and progressive taxes opened with the twentieth century.[29] The federal government, whose revenue had depended on tariffs and the excise tax, eventually acquired permanent and primary tax sources to finance the increasing role of the federal government during the First and Second World Wars. The income tax had first been introduced during the American Civil War, on a temporary basis, and it was legalized as a permanent tax in 1913.[30] Initially, the income tax was applied to individuals with an annual income of more than $500,000, which was the highest income bracket of less than 1 percent of the US population. The tax rate was low, at 1–7 percent. With the outbreak of World War I in the following year, income taxes were firmly established. The US Congress expanded the scope of individual income taxes and increased the tax rate to 2–15 percent in 1916 and further to 6–77 percent in 1918, becoming the primary tax source for the federal government, and constituting one-third of total tax revenue. An inheritance tax and excess profits tax, following the British precedent, were introduced in the United States during wartime. At that time, only 5 percent of the US residents with an annual income of more than $40,000 paid income taxes, while 20 percent of wage-earners paid income taxes.

During the Great Depression and World War II income tax rates soared. When the Great Depression caused a sharp decrease in federal tax revenue, the US Congress in 1936 decided to raise the income tax rate

28 Du Xuncheng, "Minguo shiqi de zhongyang yu difang caizheng huafen," 189.

29 Ajay K. Mehrotra, "The Notion of Tax Reform in Historical Perspective," Last modified 13 July 2017, at http://www.processhistory.org/mehrotra-tax-reform/ (accessed 30 September 2018).

30 Wang Huayu, "Wenhua yanjin, zhidu bianqian yu shuishou fazhi: Fali yujing xia de ZhongMei shuizhi bijiao" [Cultural evolution, institutional change, and rule of law in taxation: A comparison government discourse in China and the US], *Dongfang faxue* 5 (2013): 89–90.

to 4–79 percent. World War II constituted a decisive turning point in the history of the US income tax by a shift from a class tax to a mass tax. Not only the tax rate but also the number of taxpayers increased significantly. Individuals with less than $2,000 annual income were subject to a 23 percent minimum tax rate, while those with incomes exceeding $200,000 were subject to the highest tax rate of over 94 percent. The income tax-to-GDP ratio increased from 0.8 percent to 9.4 percent in 1944 in order to fund the war.[31]

The table below illustrates the explosive growth of US income tax revenue.

Table 9.9 Tax revenue structure of the US federal government, 1880–1930

Year	1880	1890	1900	1910	1917	1920	1930
Tariffs	56%	57%	41%	49%	21%	5%	14%
Excise tax on wine and tobacco	34%	35%	43%	39%	35%	7%	11%
Income tax	-	-	-	-	33%	66%	59%
Other	10%	8%	16%	12%	11%	22%	16%
Total	100%	100%	100%	100%	100%	100%	100%

Source: Ajay K. Mehrotra, *Making the Modern American Fiscal State: Law, Politics, and the Rise of Progressive Taxation, 1877–1929* (New York: Cambridge University Press, 2013), 7, Table I.I: Federal Government Receipts by Source, 1880–1930, as Percentage of Total.

The tariffs and the excise tax on alcohol and tobacco generated more than 80 percent of federal tax revenue between 1880 and 1910. However, in the four years since its introduction the income tax had already become the primary tax in 1917. It accounted for about 60 percent of federal tax revenue in 1920 and 1930. The NNG's fiscal reform reflects its awareness of global fiscal trends. The NNG must have referred to the tax experience of the United States at that time. Due to the Sino-Japanese War and the subsequent Civil War, the NNG's fiscal-reform efforts were interrupted, not to be picked up again until after the reform and opening-up policy of 1978. By 1949, the world's advanced regions had moved away from a dependence on indirect taxes and to a tax system based on a progressive income tax. Meanwhile, the Nationalist government in Nanjing still relied on traditional tax revenues such as salt tax and deepened dependency on indirect tax.

31 Ajay K. Mehrotra, "The Notion of Tax Reform in Historical Perspective"; Fu Boying, "Meiguo lianbang geren suodeshui de lishi bianqian yu qishi," 323–325.

Tax reform in the post-opening era and the legacy of the Republic of China

The continuing wars and socialization of production after the Communist victory created a rupture in the process of fiscal modernization from the late Qing. Modern fiscal state-building attempts resumed after the reform and opening-up policy in 1978. The goals of the fiscal reforms at that time were to simultaneously carry out two tasks: to raise funds and to balance social inequalities. The Chinese Communist Party (hereafter CCP) tried to adjust the tax system according to various production modes. An individual income tax (in fact limited to foreigners) was introduced in 1980, and an income tax on foreign enterprises (corporate tax) was promulgated in 1981. Comprehensive domestic tax reform was implemented in 1983 and 1984, called a "tax-for-profit" reform (*li gai shui*). An enterprise income tax had replaced the previous profit remittances. At the same time, the industry and commercial tax that had been integrated during the Cultural Revolution period was again divided into four categories: a product tax (*chanpinshui*), a value-added tax (*zengzhishui*), a salt tax (*yanshui*), and a business tax. The 1984 resource tax was applied to the development of state-owned natural resources such as coal mines. For local treasuries, the CCP created several new taxes related to land and property.[32]

From 1980 to 1988 the central government had divided the country into four groups to administer local finance. The first group consisted of Beijing, Shanghai, and Tianjin, whose remittances to the national treasury were adjusted yearly according to the previous performance of the provincial tax revenue. Sixteen provinces belonged to the second group for which the remittance amount was decided at a fixed rate for five years. The remittance amount of the third group, consisting of the two provinces of Guangdong and Fujian where the special economic zones were located, was a fixed quota. The last group consisted of the poor provinces and autonomous regions, which had no remittances and instead received subsidies from the national treasury.[33] Even though there is a difference between a fixed amount and a fixed-rate, their management is quite similar to that in traditional China where there was a balance

32 Ho-lim Yoo, "Chungkukŭi hyŏntae sechesae kwanhan koch'al" [Research on the history of comtemporary China's tax system], *Semuwa hoegyejŏnŏl* 12(1) (2011): 133.

33 Ik-soo Kim, "8onyŏntae chungkukŭi chaechŏngkwanlicheto kaehyŏkkwa t'uchap'aengch'ang" [China's fiscal system reforms and the expansion of fixed investments in the 1980s], *Tongbuga gyŏngje yŏn'gu* 9(1) (1997): 220.

between rich and poor provinces through financial flows of "annual subsidies" (*xiexiang*).

In 1994 there was yet another comprehensive tax reform. This fiscal reform introduced a "tax-assignment system" (*fenshuizhi*) that organized taxes into three types: a national tax, a local tax, and a shared tax.[34] This system was quite similar to the NNG's division between national and local taxes in 1928 and 1941 and its introduction of a shared tax in 1946.[35]

Another important action was taken in terms of tax administration. The Law on the Administration of Tax Collection was enacted in 1992, whereby the State Administration of Taxation (SAT, *guojia shuiwu zongju*) was given legal authority to administer the substantive tax laws and to prevent the arbitrary application of laws on tax affairs by local governments.[36] In addition, the value-added tax, which had already been partially implemented, was expanded to all goods and services.

Notably, the 2,600-year-old salt tax disappeared from among the separate tax items to be merged into the resource tax. The reason for this move was that the financial weight of the salt tax had become insignificant. The share of revenue from the salt tax in total national tax revenue had fallen from 5.49 percent in 1950 to 0.04 percent in 2006.[37] In contrast, taxation on tobacco and wine, which had become a main source of tax revenue in Republican China, was further strengthened. A consumption tax was newly added for certain products, including tobacco, wine, automobiles, and crude oil. Tobacco had the highest tax rate at 45 percent. This consumption tax,

34 Even before the "tax-assignment system," a tax-sharing system was attempted in 1985. The Chinese government announced that "sharing tax income" (*gongxiang shouru*) would be introduced in 1987 after a two-year grace period. But due to strong opposition, even by 1987 it had not yet been implemented. The tax-sharing system was first and partly introduced in 1992 and was fully implemented in 1994. Young-jin Kim, "Kaehyŏkki chungkuke issŏsŏ chungangkwa chipangŭi chaechŏngkwankye: Chaechŏngkaehyŏkŭi kwachŏngkwa sŏngkwae taehan silchŭng" [The fiscal relationship between the center and the provinces during China's reform period: An empirical analysis of the process and result of fiscal relationship], *Sahoe gwahak* 34(1) (1995): 189.

35 [5] For a comparison of the tax reforms in the 1990s with the NNG tax reform, see Jin-A Kang, "Chungkukŭi ch'echekaehyŏkkwa taeoekaepang: kŭntaehwaŭi yŏksasŏng" [The reform and opening policy of China: The historicity of modernization], in *Chungguk kaehyŏk: Kaebangŭi chŏngch'i gyŏngje 1980–2000* [China reform: The politics and economy of opening-up, 1980–2000], ed. Jea-ho Jung (Seoul: Kkach'i kŭlpang, 2002).

36 Lorenzo Riccardi, *Introduction to the Chinese Fiscal System* (Singapore: Springer, 2018), 17–18; John Brondolo and Zhiyong Zhang, "Tax Administration Reform in China: Achievements, Challenges, and Reform Priorities," IMF Working Paper WP/16/68, 2016, 12–13.

37 Teng Shuna, Xi Chuanying, and Han Daxue, "Jindai yilai Zhong Ying yanshui," 26.

similar to the consolidated tax in the NNG era, was assigned to national taxes under the jurisdiction of the SAT.[38]

The 1994 tax reforms significantly improved the fiscal balance. The central government that had faced chronic fiscal deficits gained more than 100 billion *yuan* in annual revenue after 1994, and more than 200 billion *yuan* after 2000.[39] In line with the increasing central government budget, voices calling for fiscal policy to reduce the growing social inequalities began to grow. The idea, which was widely discussed in 1994, was to establish a property tax, inheritance tax, and gift tax to resolve the social imbalances. But in China these are not national taxes and they only exist in some local pilot programs or they are at a theoretical stage.[40] The work of the Republican era has still not been completed.

Meanwhile, like the fiscal features of imperial China, there are generous taxation exemptions and deductions for the poor. In 2006, the agricultural tax, which had been the largest tax source in the traditional imperial economy, collected from farmers, who constituted 70 percent of the population, was abolished. Like the salt tax, tax revenue from farmers in 2006 was only about 60 billion *yuan*, thus allowing the Chinese government to abolish it as a preferential measure for the low-income classes.[41] Instead, in the same year the consumption tax was drastically revised to expand the subjects of taxation, adding golf goods as a new luxury item.[42]

38 The total amount of taxes related to the tobacco industry was 735 billion *yuan* in 2011, accounting for 7.26 percent of China's fiscal revenue. If we add the tax revenue from liquor, the tax revenue from tobacco and alcohol is almost 1 trillion *yuan*, and the ratio of tax revenue is close to 15 percent; Yu Baohua, "Dangqian woguo yancao chanye shuizhi bianqian yanjiu" [Study of the tax system changes in the Chinese tobacco industry], *Guanli xuekan* 25(4) (2012): 60; Jiang Yuanjian and Huang Xiaoli, "Maotai jituan qiansanjidu wancheng shuishou shouru 100.8yiyuan, zengzhang41%" [The Maotai group received tax revenues of 10.08 billion and grew by 41 percent at the third quarter], *Niangjiu keji* 12 (2016): 121. The tax revenue ratio for the liquor and tobacco tax during the period of Republican China was 14 percent, or almost the same.

39 Ho-lim Yoo, "Chungkukŭi hyŏntae sechesae kwanhan koch'al," 140.

40 Gongshang shuizhi gaige pingxi ketizu [Research Group on the "Report on the Reform of the Industrial and Commercial Tax System], "1994 nian Zhongguo de gongshang shuizhi gaige pingxi" [An analysis of the Chinese industrial and commercial tax reform in 1994], *Caizheng jingji* 7 (1997): 19, 21, 25; Wang Linlin, "Jianguo yilai woguo shuishou zhidu de bianqian yu fazhan qushi" [The change and development trends in China's tax system since the founding of the people's Republic of China], *Gongshang luntan* 16(2) (2010): 58.

41 However, at the same time as the agricultural tax was abolished, the Chinese government created a new tax on tobacco leaf and collected tax at a ratio of 20 percent of the price from tobacco leaf farmers. Yu Baohua, "Dangqian woguo yancao chanye shuizhi bianqian yanjiu," 60.

42 Ho-lim Yoo, "Chungkukŭi hyŏntae sechesae kwanhan koch'al," 142–143.

Table 9.10 outlines the changes in the average tax burden per capita from 1999 to 2016. For eighteen years, a Chinese resident who earned an average annual income of 6,251 *yuan* paid an average of 1,075 *yuan* in taxes. The income tax payment averaged only 67 *yuan* annually, while the VAT payment was 520 *yuan*. This average income per capita is consistent with macroscopic trends, so it can be extended to the national level. The indices (1) and (2) are indicators that make macro trends easier to understand. On average, during the eighteen-year period analyzed in Table 9.10, 48.4 percent of tax revenue came from the VAT, whereas the individual income tax remained insignificant at 6.3 percent (average index [1]). This means that China's finances are still heavily dependent on indirect taxes. The income tax, which is the primary tax in advanced economies such as the United States, Japan, and South Korea, accounts for only 6–7 percent of tax revenue in China. In 2013, the indirect tax-to-GDP ratio was 4.47 percent in the United States, 5.14 percent in Japan, and 8.17 percent in South Korea, whereas in China it was still high, at 12.07 percent.[43] The fiscal role in narrowing the gap between rich and poor is still insufficient.

Table 9.10 Actual value per capita of production, expenditures, and taxes for seventy-two quarters, 1999–2016 (unit: RMB)

	GDP	Financial expenditures	Tax revenue			
			Total	Income tax	Corporate tax	VAT
Average	6,251.8	1,351.7	1,075.1	67.8	210.7	520.5
Median	5,860.6	1,071.8	976.4	63.5	197.7	486.7
Maximum	11,763.7	3,087.2	2,070.4	161.1	517.8	1,011.2
Minimum	2,077.9	274.2	232.2	8.4	19.7	123.0
Average Index (1)	581.5	122.4	100	6.3	19.6	48.4
Average Index (2)	100	21.6	17.2	1.1	3.4	8.3

Source: Based on Lee Jong-ha, Lee Jong-chan, and Hwang Jin-yeong, "Chungkukŭi chaechŏng mich' hangmokpyŏl choseŭi oesaengchŏk ch'ungkyŏkkwa saengsanlyang pyŏntong" [Output impacts of exogenous shocks on public finance and tax policy in China], *Chaejŏng jŏngch'aeng nonjip* 20(2) (2018): 140, Table 1.
Note: Average Indexes (1) and (2) are added here.

43 Guojia fagaiwei jingji yanjiusuo ketizu [Research Group of the Economic Research Institute of the National Development and Reform Commission], "Woguo hongguan shuifu yanjiu" [Research on the macro tax burden in China], *Jingji yanjiu cankao* 2 (2014): 18.

However, the Chinese tax-to-GDP ratio recorded an average of 17 percent between 1999–2016, a substantial increase from the 5–6 percent during the NNG period. This increase has grown faster in recent years. In 2010, the tax-to-GDP ratio in China surpassed 20 percent.[44] Although this ratio is still lower than that of other developed countries, it still represents sharp growth compared to the 13 percent in the mid-1990s.[45]

Another feature of the tax structure in contemporary China is the significant weight of the corporate tax (the Enterprise Income Tax), the second-largest tax after the VAT. In advanced countries, revenue from the individual income tax is basically the primary tax, outplaying the revenue from the corporate income tax. This unique feature of the Chinese tax structure reflects the immaturity of administration of the individual income tax as well as the legacy of Nationalist and socialist China, where suspicious attitudes toward profiteering private industries persist and the goal is to support economic building driven by state-owned industries.

44 Wang Linlin, "Jianguo yilai woguo shuishouzhidu de bianqian yu fazhanqushi," 58.

45 According to the 2017 revenue-to-GDP ratio ranking of 191 countries, the ratios in the Nordic welfare countries (Norway, Finland, Denmark, etc.) and France were more than 50 percent, with Japan (33 percent, 59th) and the United States (30 percent, 69th) in the middle. China continued its tax growth trend, rising sharply to 28 percent, but remained at the bottom. Moreover, mass taxation in China remained the primary source of taxation. Korea ranked 121st (23 percent), making it a low taxation country. Meanwhile, the upper 10 percent of taxpayers' payments made up 90 percent of the income tax revenue of Korea's primary tax. http://ecodb.net/ranking/imf_ggr_ngdp.html (accessed 10 October 2018).

10 Afterword: Between Chinese Exceptionalism and Modern Fiscal State-building

Abstract

Chapter 10 belongs to the concluding part of the book that contains an overview of fiscal state-building efforts in modern Guangdong and a general evaluation of the experience of Guangdong in the context of China's process of financial modernization. As reviewing the experience of Guangdong, the modern fiscal state-building efforts should not be judged a success or a failure based solely on the standpoint of the central government. Despite a few features underpinning China's exceptionalism, the Chinese experience in the fiscal state-building beginning in the mid-nineteenth century was a process of convergence with the modern model in the rest of the world. Modern nation-building was strategically promoted as part of its catch-up development.

Keywords: China, Guangdong model, fiscal state-building, tax structure, Chinese model

China recently joined the group of G2 countries, alongside the United States, but the Chinese model has been offered as an alternative to the Western model. The Beijing consensus includes not only other political and socioeconomic options but also cultural and philosophical replacements. Professor R. Bin Wong argues that the traditional China of the Ming and Qing dynasties has something in common with today's welfare state. By examining Chinese notions of good governance (*shanzheng*), based on light taxation and the provision of social goods – pursued between 1500 and the mid-nineteenth century – and the pre-1850 success of this ideological

Kang, Jin-A, *The Guangdong Model and Taxation in China*. Taylor & Francis Group, 2022
DOI: 10.5117/9789463725248_CH10

state-operation,[1] he finds that, ideologically, the traditional Chinese state was a transcendental arbitrator between contradictory interests among social groups and played the role of agency to flatten social inequality.[2]

Meanwhile, to win routine wars, Europe gradually created military-fiscal nations and developed a technique for fiscal operations of modern states by adopting indirect taxes, such as commercial and excise taxes, and raising finance from the private sector and overseas capital markets by issuing bonds. This model contrasts sharply with that of the Chinese moral economy where it is not permitted for the state to "contend with the people for interests." Superficially, this Chinese large-scale granary system to relieve famine and the fiscal subsidy system to move finances between the rich and poor provinces is similar to the current welfare state.[3]

But what about the reality? According to the governing philosophy of the Chinese empire, the widening of wealth inequalities often led to rebellion and turmoil. To manage risks, it was necessary, to some extent, to suppress the merchants (at least ideologically), even though the Chinese empire actively utilized the merchants and the commercial economy for governance. Although its financial scale was small, much needed to be done to realize a moral socio-economy, so administrative and financial matters were "allocated" by region and left to the local elites. These administrative and financial contracting systems were rational in China where there was a large land area and a large population.

When the Manchus conquered the Ming empire to mark the beginning of the Qing dynasty, the Manchus, with a population of 2 million, faced the task of governing the Han Chinese, with a population of 100 million. As such, administrative finance required the support of the local Han Chinese elite. Although the number of Qing bureaucrats was about the same as that of the Tang dynasty one thousand years earlier, the population during the Qing dynasty exceeded 450 million until the end of the eighteenth century, whereas the population during the Tang dynasty numbered only about 90 million. Therefore, during the Qing a county magistrate, the lowest-level local official dispatched from the central government, had to rule an average of 300,000 people.

Although their monthly salaries were meager, county magistrates assigned to govern counties with populations of hundreds of thousands had to hire,

1 R. Bin Wong, "Taxation and Good Governance in China, 1500–1914," 353.

2 R. Bin Wong, *China Transformed: Historical Change and the Limits of European Experience*, 142–151; R. Bin Wong, "Taxation and Good Governance in China, 1500–1914," 353–355.

3 R. Bin Wong, "Taxation and Good Governance in China, 1500–1914," 353–355.

with their own money, three to five private secretaries (*muliao*) as financial and legal experts. Furthermore, if the quota for tax collection was not met, the imperial court would cut their annual salary. If a disaster were to occur in a jurisdiction, the magistrate, calling on his personal sense of integrity, would volunteer to reduce his own salary. To match this spending, "non-regular accounting" and flagrant corruption were widespread. In the early Qing, a county magistrate's annual salary was 90 taels, and by the late Qing, through the Yongzheng emperor's action to support the bonus (*yanglianyan*) of realizing the official salary, it increased to 1,590 taels. However, this salary still could not cover the necessary spending. A magistrate would be praised for being a reasonably clean official if he received less than 100,000 taels a year.[4] Under the institutional weakness in which there was a mismatch with reality, "intermediate exploitation" was rampant. There was a huge gap between the fiscal scale that was reported to the central government and the taxpayers' real burden. Moreover, distribution of tax burdens within local communities was unfair due to the "proxy principle" of relying on local elites to oversee administrative and financial matters. Since tax collection was based on a regional quota system, tax burdens were easily passed on to the vulnerable.

Nevertheless, under such circumstances, the power of the central government was not weak. The basis for China's exceptionalism is that China maintained a political unit over such a vast demographic and territorial scale for thousands of years, a rare feat in human history, but its success was due to a combination of loose, indirect control over the localities and strong imperial power. Over a period of two thousand years, there were ups and down in imperial power but it was strengthened to an absolute level by Zhu Yuanzhang, the vagrant-turned-rebel leader who ushered in the beginning of the Ming dynasty. The Qing dynasty was foreign-dominated, so the emperor's reign was more tyrannical. The ability of the Qing dynasty to successfully control the population of more than 400 million, one-quarter of humankind, with only a handful of bureaucrats, rested on its seamless control over bureaucrats based on despotic power. From time to time, the imperial court would impose harsh punishments on corrupt bureaucrats and local elites to show that the emperor was not an exploiter but a guardian of the people.

4 Li Kaizhou, "WanQing shiqi de zhixian shouru jihe? Bu tanwu jiuyao beichao youyu" [What was the income of a county magistrate in the late Qing? If you didn't embezzle, you would be fired], *Yangcheng wanbao*, 23 July 2018.

Chinese fiscal-state building from a global perspective

Despite this feature underpinning China's exceptionalism, Chinese experience in fiscal state-building beginning the mid-nineteenth century was a process of convergence with the modern model in the rest of the world. Modern nation-building was strategically promoted as part of its catch-up development. The imperial court and ruling elites shared a belief in the necessity of adopting a Western model of state operations for defense against intrusion by foreign powers and survival in the competitive international order. The early model, for the late Qing court and the Beiyang government during the Republican era, was Japan. Although Japan had started as an agricultural nation similar to China, it had successfully transformed itself into a prosperous modernized power, training a modern army and reforming its fiscal system. In terms of fiscal reform, both China and Japan pursued an indirect-taxation model that supported an expansion of taxation, a model that had been pioneered by the British empire, the hegemon of the nineteenth-century.

However, by the end of the nineteenth century, the British government was already trying to transform its primary tax to direct taxes, such as an income tax and an inheritance tax. A prerequisite for shifting from a tax structure that depended on indirect tax was to break away from the agricultural society and reorganize the economic base into a commercial and industrial society. Japan, which succeeded in industrialization, had made a successful transition to indirect tax–centered public finance. But tax reforms such as those in Japan resulted in irregular deprivation of the commercial sector in China. These reform programs were not realistic in China, where the economy was still highly dependent on agriculture. Even in the mid-1930s, tax reforms without a fundamental change in the economic structure had limited fiscal success. The revenue to the Nanjing Nationalist Government (hereafter NNG) in the 1930s remained at about 5 to 6 percent of national income.[5]

Moreover, political instability fueled a struggle for financial resources between the central and local governments. As an example, Guangdong province consistently resisted the central government's fiscal concentration efforts in the late Qing, and the reforms to centralize public finance and build a modern fiscal state were never implemented as originally designed. The imperial court was flooded with telegrams as the supervisors who had been dispatched to each province announced their resignations. Such

5 Kubo Tōru, *Chūgoku keizaishi nyūmon*, 128.

conflicts between supervisors and provincial governors were widespread, especially in Guangdong. After tenacious appeals to Beijing, the Guangdong provincial government eventually postponed their implementation of the imperial instruction to eliminate the *likin* and to create unified levies (*tongjuan*). With respect to the stamp duty reform, merchants in Guangzhou went on strike in protest.[6] But on the eve of the Xinhai Revolution, the central government in Beijing sought to centralize public finances by canceling the rights of provinces to issue money and establish a public treasury system. The Qing government nationalized the Canton Mint, a cash cow for provincial revenue, and set up a Guangzhou branch of the Great Qing Bank to replace the provincial Official Silver Copper Money Bureau that served as a provincial treasury. Attempts by the central government to neutralize provincial finance were the primary reason why each province, in the course of the Xinhai Revolution, sought to declare independence.

Importantly, the modern fiscal state-building efforts should not be judged a success or a failure based solely on the standpoint of the central government. Efforts to build a modern fiscal state were continued through the work of local provinces, while the process of division and decentralization by warlords was deepened during the Republican era. Even today, when implementing national policies, China often implements them on a trial basis in limited localities and then expands them based on their success. In this way, the central and local governments effectively communicate and refer to each other in policy development in a complementary manner. Guangdong became a model for the construction of a modern fiscal state in China, taking the lead in absorbing central government policies and implementing them locally, and vice versa. The relationship between central and local governments should not be regarded as merely a conflict over financial resources during either the Republic of China or the People's Republic of China.

The Guangdong model

Beginning in the late Qing, finance of Guangdong province differed from those of other provinces in that there was a lower proportion of land tax revenue and a higher proportion of commercial tax revenue relative to total

6 Yang Huashan, "Lun WanQing "caili tongjuan" yu "caili renjuan" de changshi ji yaozhe" [On the aborted attempt to "abolish the *likin* and create unified levies" and to "abolish the *likin* and the tax-farming of levies" in the late Qing dynasty], *Shixue yuekan* 2 (2014): 59, 61.

revenue. As the imperial court in Beijing passed on the burden of military spending and foreign debt to local public finance, the scale of provincial finance expanded. The increasing revenue from taxation in Guangdong, second only to that in Jiangsu province, tapped the industrial and commercial sectors to support the expanding provincial budget. In particular, income from government-owned enterprises emerged as a new financial source. The most profitable government-run business was the Canton Mint. Furthermore, construction of industries run by the Guandong provincial government had begun during the late Qing. Guangdong province was the most favorable area for industrial building in terms of attracting overseas Chinese capital and it took the lead in tapping financial resources to build modernized government-owned industries. Such potential manifested during Republican China, especially in the 1930s when Guangdong witnessed large-scale development of government industries.

Beginning in the late 1910s, Guangdong province was intermittently the base of the KMT's Nationalist Revolution, led by Sun Wen. From the Nationalists' return to Guangdong in 1923 to the Northern Expedition and finally to the Nationalists' departure from Guangdong in 1927, Guangdong province endured the heavy financial burden of funding the revolution. Using the opportunity of the anti-Jiang movement in the 1930s, the military leader of Guangdong, Chen Jitang, announced a separatist regime. The GPG mobilized various administrative and financial tools of the Nationalist government in the 1920s and designed new fiscal programs to support the separatist regime. The KMT government, which succeeded in establishing a national government in Nanjing in 1927 and in uniting China again in 1928, had developed financial policies for modernized fiscal state-building. Many of these programs had been discussed, but ultimately had failed, in the late Qing. Under the NNG's rule, the *likin* was abolished instead of restoring customs autonomy. The NNG introduced new taxes, such as a consolidated tax, an income tax, and a business tax, as well as a division between national and local taxes. In this process of fiscal reform, Japan and the United States played critical roles as significant reference models.

The NNG promoted construction of a powerful nation-state through national integration. In contrast, the Chen Jitang regime in Guangdong, denounced as an autarky damaging national integration, emphasized regional autonomy. Nevertheless, apart from its ideological pursuits, the fiscal policy of the GPG was almost the same as that of the central government in Nanjing. As the NNG cultivated tax sources centered around tariffs, the GPG made up for the loss of the *likin* tax by creating the Special Tax, which was a local tariff. Meanwhile, as the NNG policy combined tariff increases with the development of import substitution industries, the GPG sought to protect local industries through the Special Tax and the effects of import substitution by provincial government industries. In the field of tax administration, the tax contract system reform in Guangdong province, under the rule of Chen Jitang, faithfully adopted Song Ziwen's original reform program. But Chen Jitang's administration attempted to systematize it more skillfully by introducing a full-scale open-bid contract.

The GPG's fiscal policy achieved considerable success both in budgetary and economic terms. But ironically these desired results were due to the NNG. For example, previous attempts by the GPG to collect a Tax on Imported Rice ended in failure. But in 1933 the GPG succeeded in levying a Special Tax on Imported Rice because the NNG had imposed tariffs on imported rice as national policy. In November 1935, the GPG's drive on monetary reforms based on the provincial banknotes was really an adjusted version of the currency reform of the NNG. Overall, the state-building efforts seen from the GPG's fiscal policy were also part of the state-building efforts of the Nanjing government.

Globality in the 1930s

The GPG, in much the same way as the NNG, endeavored to unify provincial finance, rebuild a modernized industry, and improve administration. The results were realized by easing the budget deficit, reducing the miscellaneous taxes, and developing government-run modern sectors. However, the openness of the provincial economic structure qualified this success. Imports and remittances from the overseas Chinese in Southeast Asia supported the Guangdong provincial economy. But the Special Tax on Imports did not benefit the overseas Chinese, the import traders, and domestic consumers who were familiar with cheap imported goods. But tax collection on food, such as imported rice, struck a chord with the government-led sugar industry project and the sugar monopoly. Despite this mismatch between the economic structure and fiscal policy, the GPG adhered to a firm control policy. This promotion of substantial control is a characteristic of the GPG's fiscal policy in the 1930s.

The Three-Year Administration Plan for Guangdong was the definitive strategy. The GPG rushed to strengthen control over the private economy to secure finances. But this policy decision took place against the background of the effects of the Great Depression. The wave of the Great Depression, which subsumed China in 1932, pushed the Chinese economy into a full-scale recession beginning in 1933. As a countermeasure, there was active government intervention, but there were no signs that the private-sector industries would survive the recession on their own. Similar to the 1933 US New Deal policy, the NNG in the 1930s embarked on the construction of infrastructure, such as roads, railways, and large-scale public works projects. National investment increased. The NNG's *fabi* reform can be understood in this global context in which each country was strengthening financial controls by adopting a managed currency system and by tightening regulations on the foreign exchange market. The same can be said for policies in Guangdong. In other words, in the 1930s China experienced the rise of a modern fiscal state in that the state's financial and industrial policy exerted a significant influence on the private economy.

In this sense, Chinese fiscal-state building was deeply linked to global trends. Noriyuki Ishijima stresses the importance of the globally popular controlled economy in understanding the policies of the NNG. According to Ishijima, the Nanjing government, led by Jiang Jieshi after the mid-1930s, intended to awaken Sun Wen's idea of national economic adjustment in the wake of the Great Depression and the successful experience of the Soviet Union in economic-building under the national plan.[7]

The meaningful success of Guangdong's experiment with its Three-Year Plan should have provided food for thought for the Nanjing government. Many of the policies tried out in Guangdong were later adopted by the NNG. In practice, the Nationalist government and the KMT were strongly motivated to develop state-led fiscal and economic policies based on Sun Wen's Three Principles. Tōru Kubo refers to this intrinsic tendency as " proxyism," which is consensus that the state should take a proxy role in developing the national economy, rejecting the private sector's autonomous development. Chinese traditional ideology on statecraft and Nationalist ideas were thus a far cry from laissez-faire. The 1928 state-owned factory construction plan of Kong Xiangxi and the 1931 Four-Year Plan for Industry drafted by Chen Gongbo for the NNG supported radical state-led import

7 The Great Depression spread disillusionment with liberalism among intellectuals, and the success of the Soviet Five-Year Program strengthened voices calling for state control of the economy. Even if the favored models among Chinese intellectuals varied between German-style totalitarianism, the American New Deal, and the Soviet planned economy, "state control over the economy is a global devotion today." Ishijima Noriyuki, "Nankinseiken no Keizai kensetsu ni tsuiteno ichi shiron" [An essay on the economic construction of the Nanjing administration], *Ibaraki daigaku jinbun gakubu kiyō bungakka ronsō* 11 (1978): 8.

substitution industrialization.[8] These early plans in Nanjing must have inspired the policy decisions of the provincial governments, including Guangdong. However, the Nanjing government failed to mobilize funds and it therefore canceled its plans in the face of fierce opposition from the private sector, such as the Shanghai merchants.

In contrast, the GPG put its plan into practice. It achieved significant results during the Great Depression as a successful example of fiscal mobilization through economic construction and control. These results were also reflected in the wartime fiscal and economic policies of the NNG. In this way, the NNG and the GPG both made interrelated efforts toward state-building.[9]

In the 1930s, considerable traditional or feudal elements remained in Chinese finances. However, the state-building efforts of the 1930s created a new atmosphere. These efforts were also a part of global trends. During the Great Depression, many countries, not just in the West, raised tariff barriers to protect their own industries and they curtailed imports. The recession in Southeast Asia bottomed out in 1936, and trade began to expand again in 1937. Despite this revival, the raw material export industry, particularly in rice and sugar, continued to suffer from sluggish growth because the previous import countries, including China, had raised the entry barriers.[10] Without the full-scale war between China and Japan in 1937, the proportion of foreign rice in the Guangdong market would have declined further. Burgeoning nationalism clarified the division between states drawn by borders and tariffs. National finance and the private economy grew closer. The period of private currencies had come to an end and a managed currency system

8 Kubo Tōru, "Kingendai chūgoku ni okeru kokka to keizai: Chūka minkoku ki Keizai seisaku shiron" [The state and the economy in modern China: The history of economic policy in the Republic of China], in *Rekishi no nakano gendai chūgoku* [Modern China in history], ed. Yamada Tatsuo (Tokyo: Keisoshoho, 1996).

9 For example, during the Second Sino-Japanese War, the Nationalist government in Guangdong appointed Qu Fangfu, who was working as director of the Department of Finance in Chen Jiang's administration, to be chief senior advisor of the Ministry of Agriculture. This appointment was related to the fact that the Nationalist government had once again adopted self-sufficiency and control of food as a wartime policy. Guangdongsheng Zhongshan tushuguan, *Guangdong jinxiandai renwu cidian* [Biographical dictionary of modern people in Guangdong] (Guangzhou: Guangdong kexue chubanshe, 1992), 25.

10 Kano Hiroyoshi, "Kokusai bōeki kara mita 20 seiki no tōnan ajia shokuminchi keizai: Ajia taiheiyō shijō eno hōsetsu" [The twentieth-century Southeast Asian colonial economy from the perspective of international trade: Inclusion in Asia-Pacific markets], *Rekishi hyōron* 539 (1995): 49.

was established. It was at this point that a modern financial state clearly emerged in China.

A Chinese model still in progress?

After the beginning of the reform and opening-up period, China put tax reform, which had never been completed during the Republican era, back on the agenda. The division between national and local taxes, the introduction of various direct taxes, and the abolition of agricultural and salt taxes all took place by about 2000. The success of the fiscal reforms was ensured by the accompanying rapid economic growth, combined with expansion of the commercial and industrial sectors. However, the tax structure in contemporary China is still characterized by low porportion of income taxes and high dependency on indirect taxes. It seems that China has not yet entirely escaped from the indirect tax–dependent model of the nineteenth century.

The current situation in contemporary China can also be explained in another way. At the time of the reform and opening-up period in the 1980s, the model pursued in the United States in the early twentieth century, which centered on direct and progressive tax, suddenly declined in the wake of Reagan's fiscal reforms. The neo-liberalist regime instead preferred a pro-corporate and wealthy-friendly tax model to boost the economic engine. Global fiscal trends had thus changed by the time China reconsidered its tax reforms at the end of the twentieth century. Many countries were shifting the focus of their tax policies to strengthen national competitiveness and stimulate the economy, rather than to redistribute wealth and narrow the social gap. As in the United States, the Chinese government has had a limited social redistribution role in the tax sector during the reform period, as a result of which social imbalances have been exacerbated.

In his keynote speech to the 2018 World Economic History Convention in Boston, French economic historian Thomas Piketty, in seeking to explain the growing phenomenon of economic inequality in the twentieth century, based his argument on an interesting sociological analysis of the relationship between voting trends and legislation. Piketty observed that inequalities in global wealth had declined sharply during the Great Depression and World War II and then they remained stable in the postwar period. But beginning in the 1980s and thereafter the concentration of wealth among the top 10 percent increased sharply. He suggested that state policies to prevent a concentration of wealth and to redistribute social wealth began to malfunction due to changing voting trends. In the case of France, by the 1960s the majority of highly educated people were voting for the right-wing parties. But since the 1970s, more than half of highly educated voters have supported the left-wing parties. As a result, the composition of the left-wing parties has become more complicated, leading to growing internal conflicts and a weakening of reform-minded activism. Overall, the left-wing parties failed to be effective policymakers.[11]

The world today is again facing the challenge of capitalist economic expansion, questioning the role of the state in developing the economy. The fourth Industrial Revolution will call for a reconsideration of employment and distribution in a capitalist society. Resource depletion will require resource conservation for sustainable economic growth. Global pandemics, such as Covid-19, have already exposed the weaknesses of the global supply chain. Under these challenging new circumstances, the roles of both the state and finances are again attracting attention as complementary entities to maintain production in the twenty-first century.

As a result, there has been a focus on China's fiscal and governance models. Traditional Chinese finance, which focuses on the sustainability of a social balance, has been transformed, and it has become necessary to learn from Western Europe and Japan so as to "mobilize" preparations to confront the threat of the Western powers. The process of learning modern fiscal state-building and adapting it to China's social environment is an essential case study in any discussion about public finance in global history.

It is important to note that the Chinese model is being discussed not only by intellectuals but also by the Chinese government in the context of the rivalry between the global hegemons. The Chinese government is taking the lead in creating its own model of governance. From the late Qing to Republican China, and then to the period of reform and opening-up the logics of "mobilization" and modern state-building have overwhelmingly been on the political agenda and there no longer is a focus on the "premodernity" of the moral economy of traditional China. But in the twenty-first century, as regional and class disparities have emerged as social problems in China, the "distribution" logic is being emphasized and "premodernity," or "Chineseness," have grown stronger.

The Chinese government envisions its economic and financial goals as *wenbao* for all people—that is, a stage in which people have basically no problems in obtaining food and clothing. The government has assumed the

11 Thomas Piketty, "Brahmin Left vs Merchant Right: Rising Inequality and the Changing Structure of Political Conflict," at http://piketty.pse.ens.fr/fr.

role of agent, or proxy, in order to realize such social goals and to obtain the legitimacy to rule the people. Such proxyism, whereby the state should adopt a proxy role in developing the national economy to the exclusion of the role of the people in state-building, is essential to promote the legitimacy of Communist Party rule.[12]

The mechanism to overcome the malfunctioning of capitalism, or the agenda of postmodernism, in China has been exclusively and cleverly linked to reinstating the tradition of the moral economy as well as to the ideological governance in traditional China. Unlike elsewhere in the world, the attempt in China to produce an alternative governance, culture, and civilization to overcome modern capitalism has uniquely been aligned with the revival of Chinese tradition. There are indeed parallels between current-day China and traditional China. Socialist morality has replaced Confucian ethics, and the high-income, urban, middle-class, and educated intellectuals now constitute the ranks of the former gentry literati.

The art of governing in China today is very similar to how it was in traditional China, whereby the Chinese empire achieved ultra-stable rule by making full use of ideology to tame the elites. By sorting out the defective from the elite group, such as the capitalists, the bureaucrats, and the intellectuals, through campaigns accusing those who are corrupt or reactionary, the state may achieve two goals. Firstly, to the general public, the government can present itself not as a guardian of the upper classes but as a supreme and neutral executor, protecting social morality. But secondly, the elites remain docile while being reminded of the source of their power. Such performances are part of the politics of both traditional China and present-day China. In traditional society, moral condemnation gained traction by uncompromisingly separating orthodoxy from heresy. Even in China today, the final decision as to whether or not something is in line with the "people's interests" is decided by state power. Condemnation of the "people's enemies" is extrajudicial and threatening. The shadow of Confucian society is beginning to overcome capitalist modernity.

Lastly, a return to Chinese exceptionalism. Initially, comparative history and academic endeavors enjoyed popularity by overcoming orientalism. Today, however, orientalism is often mobilized to rationalize the revival of tradition and the logic of rebutting external criticism. The term *guoqing* (national conditions) means that China, with its large population and vast

12 Jin-A Kang, "G2 shidaeŭi chungguk sahoejuŭi: yŏksajŏk kwanjŏm esŏ pon chunggug ŭi kaehyŏkkaebang" [On Chinese socialism in the age of the G2: China's reform and opening-up from a historical perspective], *Yŏksabip'yŏng* 106 (2014): 287–322.

territory, has a unique historical background and its own style of governance. However, now is the time to transcend the division between "premodern" and "modern," or "the West" and "the East." Instead, the priority should be creating global alternatives for future governance and society. It is time to discuss from a long-term perspective how governance and the state fiscal policy have changed in human history and what kind of system we should adopt for the future. There is no country whose history and national conditions are not unique. No country is exceptional, and no country is not universal. This is the case for finance as well.

Bibliography

Primary Materials and Newspapers

Beijing tushuguan chubanshe yingyinshi, ed. *Qingmo Minguo caizheng shiliao jikan diyice* 清末民国财政史料辑刊 [Historical financial materials on the late Qing dynasty and the Republic of China, Vol. 1]. Beijing: Beijing tushuguan chubanshe, 2007.

Bogong 博公 (pen name). "Yangmi mianshui jinkou wenti" 洋米免税进口问题 [Duty- free imports of foreign rice]. *Banyue pinglun* 半月评论 1(5) (1937): 6–9.

"Caizhengbu liangshi yunxiaoju chengli" 财政部粮食运销局成立 [Establishment of the Food Transportation Bureau of the Ministry of Finance]. *Yinhang zhoubao* 银行周报 21(1) (1937): 6.

Chaomei shanghui lianhehui 潮梅商会联合会 [Chaozhou and Mei county district Chamber of Commerce Federation]. "Shantou fenjinku yiyuefen shouru zhi diaocha" 汕头分金库1月份收入之调查 [Survey of the revenue in the Shantou sub-treasury in January]. *Chaomei shanghui lianhehui banyuekan* 潮梅商会联合会半月刊 1(3/4) (1929).

Chaomei shanghui lianhehui 潮梅商会联合会 [Chaozhou and Mei county district Chamber of Commerce Federation]. "Shantou lai chunmi ji doubing shijia zhi yuce" 汕头来春米及豆餅市価之予测 [Prediction of the market price of spring rice and soybean cake entering Shantou]. *Chaomei shanghui lianhehui banyuekan* 潮梅商会联合会半月刊 1(2) (1929): 19–20.

Chaomei shanghui lianhehui 潮梅商会联合会 [Chaozhou and Mei county district Chamber of Commerce Federation]. "Shantou mishi zhi diaocha" 汕头米市之调查 [Survey of the market price of rice in Shantou]. *Chaomei shanghui lianhehui banyuekan* 潮梅商会联合会半月刊 1(1) (1929): 12–15.

Chen, Baozhi 陈宝芝. "Ershisannian shengzheng sheshi zhi huigu 二十三年省政设施之回顾 [Performance of the provincial administration in the twenty-third year of the Republic of China (1934)]. *Xin Guangdong* 新广东 26 (1935): 1–28.

Chen, Baozhi 陈宝芝. "Minguo ershisinian shengzheng sheshi gaikuang" 民国二十四年省政设施概况 [The performance of the provincial administration in the twenty-fourth year of the Republic of China (1935)]. *Xin Guangdong* 新广东 36 (1935): 1–18.

Chen, Shaoyu 陈昭宇. *Guangdong tangye yu Feng Rui* 广东糖业与冯鋭 [The Guangdong sugar industry and Feng Rui]. Hong Kong, 1937 (Harvard Yenching Library Collection).

Chen, Songguang 陈松光. *Guangdong zhi xian difang caizheng* 广东之県地方财政 [Local finance of counties in Guangdong province]. Qujiang: Mandihong banyue kanshe, 1941.

Chen, Xingyuan 陈星源. Zenyang fazhan huanan zhi shangye 怎様发展华南之商业 [How to develop commerce in South China]. *Xianggang huashang zonghui yuekan* 香港华商总会月刊 1(5) (1935): 5.

Chen, Zhen 陈真, ed. *Zhongguo jindai gongyeshi ziliao* 中国近代工业史资料 [Materials on the modern industrial history of China]. Vol. 3. Beijing: Sanlian shudian, 1961.

"Dingqi kaoxuan gexian caizheng juzhang" 定期考选各県财政局长 [Regular examination for selecting the chief of the county Financial Bureau]. *Xin Guangdong* 新广东 4 (1933): 118.

Gaimushō tsūshōkyoku 外務省通商局 [Trade Bureau, Ministry of Foreign Affairs, Japan]. *Saikin no kanton keizai jijō* 最近ノ広东経済事情 [The recent economic situation in Guangdong]. Tokyo: Gaimushō tsūshōkyoku, 1927.

Gu, Yu 古煜. "Guangdongsheng sannian shizheng jihua xia zhi Guangdong caizhenglun" 广东省三年施政计划下之广东财政论 [On finance in Guangdong under the Three-year Administrative Plan of Guangdong province], *Xin Guangdong* 新广东 5 (1933): 1–18.

Gu, Yu 古煜. "Guangdongsheng sannian shizheng jihua zhong bizhi gaige fang'an zhi niyi" 广东省三年施政计划中币制改革方案之拟议 [The draft currency reform during the Three-year Administrative Plan of Guangdong province]. *Xin Guangdong* 新广东 3 (1933): 12–20.

Guangdong caizhengting 广东财政厅 [Department of Finance, Guangdong], ed. *Guangdong caizheng* 广东财政 [Finance of Guangdong]. Qujiang: Guangdongsheng caizhengting, 1941.

Guangdong caizhengting mishushi 广东财政厅秘书室 [Secretary's Office, Department of Finance, Guangdong], ed. *Guangdong caizheng jiyao* 广东财政纪要 [Financial summary of Guangdong]. Guangzhou: Guangdong caizhengting, 1937.

Guangdong nonglinju 广东农林局 [Bureau of Agriculture and Forestry of Guangdong province]. "Yuesheng migu zengchan wunian jihua" 粤省米谷增産五年计划 [The five-year plan for increasing rice and grain production in Guangdong province]. *Yinhang zhoubao* 银行周报 22(15) (1938): 7–9.

"Guangdong yuchou minshi wenti" 广东予筹民食问题 [Guangdong plans to solve the people's food problem]. *Yinhang zhoubao* 银行周报 21(30) (1937): 4–6.

Guangdongsheng caizheng kexue yanjiusuo 广东省财政科学研究所 [Fiscal Science Research Center, Department of Finance], ed. *Guangdong caizheng shuomingshu* 广东财政说明书 [Guangdong financial statement]. Guangzhou: Guangdong jingji chubanshe, 1997.

Guangdongsheng caizhengting 广东省财政庁 [Department of Finance, Guangdong], ed. *Guangdongsheng bolai wuchan zhuanshui zhanshi shuize* 广东省舶来物産専税戦时税则 [Wartime temporary tax regulations with respect to the Guangdong special tax on imported products]. 1 January 1940 (Sun Yat-sen Library Collection, Guangzhou).

Guangdongsheng caizhengting 广东省财政厅 [Department of Finance, Guangdong], ed. *Guangdongsheng caizheng jishi* 广东省财政纪实 [Record of finance in Guangdong province]. Guangzhou: Guangdongsheng caizhengting, 1933.

Guangdongsheng caizhengting 广东省财政庁 [Department of Finance, Guangdong], ed. *Guangdongsheng geji zhengshou jiguan zuzhi guiding* 广东省各级征収机関组织规定. Qujiang: 19 December 1939 (Sun Yat-sen Library Collection, Guangzhou).

Guangdongsheng dang'anguan 广东省档案馆 [Guangdong Provincial Archives]. *Shenbao Guangdong ziliao xuanji* 《申报》广东资料选辑 [Selected materials on Guangdong in *Shenbao Daily*]. 17 Vols. Guangzhou: Guangdongsheng dang'anguan, 1996.

Guangdongsheng difang shizhi bianzuan weiyuanhui 广东省地方史志编纂委员会 财政志 [Gazetteer of Guangdong Province Compilation Committee], ed. *Guangdongsheng zhi: Caizheng zhi* 广东省志.财政志 [Gazetteer of Guangdong province: Finance]. Guangzhou: Guangdong renmin chubanshe, 1999.

Guangdongsheng jianshe taolunhui 广东省建设讨论会 [Conference on Guangdong Provincial Construction], ed. *Guangdong caizheng yaolan* 广东财政要覧 [Handbook on finance in Guangdong]. Guangzhou: Guangdongsheng jianshe taolunhui, 1929.

Guangdongsheng shengying chanwu jinglichu 广东省営産物経理処 [Guangdong Provincial Products Management Bureau], ed. *Guangdong shengying chanwu jinglichu yi zhounian yingye tongji* (1934.5–1935.4) 广东省営産物経理処一周年営业统计 [Sales statistics of the Guangdong Provincial Products Management Bureau in the first year, May 1934–April 1935]. Guangzhou, 1935 (Sun Yat-sen Library Collection, Guangzhou).

Guangdongsheng yinhang 广东省银行 [Guangdong Provincial Bank]. "Appendix: Provincial revenue of Guangdong" *Guangdongsheng yinhang yuekan* 广东省银行月刊 [Monthly journal of the Guangdong Provincial Bank]. Inaugural issue (1937)

Guangdongsheng yinhang 广东省银行 [Guangdong Provincial Bank]. "Ben shengshi ge xianshi caizheng jinxun" 本省市各県市财政近讯 [Recent news on finance at all levels in cities in our province]. *Guangdongsheng yinhang yuekan* 广东省银行月刊 1(1) (1937): 131–132.

Guangzhoushi shanghui 広州市商会 [Guangzhou Chamber of Commerce]. Untitled article, *Shishanghui zhoukan* 市商会周刊 1 (1934): 4.

Guangzhoushi shanghui 広州市商会 [Guangzhou Chamber of Commerce]. Untitled article. 广东省银行月刊18 (1934): 1–5.

Guangzhoushi shanghui 広州市商会 [Guangzhou Chamber of Commerce]. "Yanxi fujia juan wei zhun chexiao" 筵席付加捐未准撤销 [Additional charges on the banquet tax are not allowed to be cancelled]. *Shishanghui zhoukan* 市商会周刊 19 (1934): 4.

Guangzhoushi shanghui 広州市商会 [Guangzhou Chamber of Commerce]. "Zhaoji ge hangshang taolun zhengshou waihuo teshui qingxing" 召集各行商讨论徵収外货特税情形 [Calling on all merchants to discuss the situation of the special tax on foreign goods]. *Shishanghui zhoukan* 市商会周刊 9 (1934): 2–5.

Hirano, Ken 平野健. *Kanton no genjō* 広東之現状 [The current situation in Guangdong]. Guangzhou: Kanton nihon shōgyō kaigisho, 1943.

"Jiang weizhang hezhun yangmi mianshui ru Yue" 蒋委长核准洋米免税入粤 [Chairman Jiang approves duty-free entry of foreign rice into Guangdong]. *Yinhang zhoubao* 银行周报 22(10) (1938): 4–5.

"Juxing xian zhang kaoshi yu shixing san nian jihua" 举行県长考试与施行三年计划 [Examination for selecting county magistrates and implementation of the Three-year Plan]. *Xin Guangdong* 新广东 1 (1933): 70.

"Kuangtung government sugar-factory." *Chinese Economic Journal and Bulletin* 18(2) (1936): 160–168.

Ma, Yinchu 马寅初. "Cong weichi mijia wenti shuodao qianbi geming" 従维持米価问题説到銭币革命 [Speaking about issues about maintaining the price of rice to the currency revolution]. *Yinhang zhoubao* 银行周报 17(7) (1933): 5–15.

Min, Shu 敏树. "Guangdong shiliang wenti zhi jiantao" 广东食粮问题之検讨 [Examination of the food problem in Guangdong]. *Xin Guangdong* 新广东 38 (1936): 23–24.

Minguo 24 niandu xian difang suiru suichu yusuan diaocha biao 民国24年度県地方岁入岁出予算调查表(1935年7月–1936年6月) [Survey of county revenue and expenditure budgets in the twenty-fourth year of the Republic of China, July 1935–June 1936] (Sun Yat-sen Library Collection, Guangzhou).

"Miye qingjin yangmi maifen jinkou" 米业请禁洋米麦粉进口 [Rice business circles request a ban on the import of foreign rice and wheat flour]. *Yinhang zhoubao* 银行周报 15(14) (1931): 6–7.

"Nankin seifu no kantonshō kinyu zaisei seiri no genkyō" 南京政府の広東省金融.財政整理の現況 [The current financial and fiscal consolidation situation in Guangdong led by the Nanjing Government]. *Tōa* 東亜 9(11) (1936): 79–94.

Nihon tōgyō rengōkai 日本糖業連合会, *Manshūkoku chūkaminkoku no satō bōeki narabini juyōryō ni kansuru tōkeiteki ichikōsatsu* 満州国・中華民国の砂糖貿易並に需要量に関する統計的一考察 [A statistical consideration of sugar demand as well as sugar trade in Manchuria and the Republic of China]. Tokyo: Nihon tōgyō rengōkai, 1938.

Nihon tōgyō rengōkai 日本糖業連合会, *Shina no tōgyō: Kotoni nanshi saikin no tōgyō jijō ni tsuite*支那の糖業：殊に南支最近の糖業事情に就 [China's sugar industry: Especially on the recent sugar industry situation in South China]. Tokyo: Nihon tōgyō rengōkai, 1939.

Qin, Qingjun 秦庆钧. "Duiyu Guangdongsheng sannian caizheng jihua zhi shangquan" 对于广东省三年财政计划之商権 [Discussion of the three-year financial plan of Guangdong province]. *Xin Guangdong* 新广东 1 (1933): 1–7.

Qin, Qingjun 秦庆钧. "Guangdong sannian shizheng jihua xia yi nianlai caizheng zhi huigu" 广东三年施政计画下一年来财政之回顾 [Review of finance during the past one year under the Three-year Administrative Plan of Guangdong province]. *Xin Guangdong* 新广东 15 (1934): 1–38.

Quanshi 権时 (penname). "Yuesheng qingqiu yangmi mianshui wenti" 粤省请求洋米免税问题 [Guangdong province's request for a tax exemption on foreign rice]. *Yinhang zhoubao* 银行周报 21(3) (1937): 1–2.

"Rikin teppai mondai" 釐金撤廃問題 [Abolition of the *likin* tax]. *Tōa* 東亜 4(4) (1931): 100–107.

Shenbao [Shen Bao Daily]

13 July 1927; 28 November 1927; 18 November 1928; 13 March 1929; 1 September 1929; 8, 12, 18, 30 September 1930; 3, 4 October 1930; 27 February 1931; 2 April 1931; 1 December 1932; 31 March 1933; 19, 20, 30 September 1933; 1, 3, 7, 9, 18 October 1933; 10 November 1933; 21 December 1933; 26 February 1934; 16 March 1934; 13, 27, 29 April 1934; 16 May 1934; 19 January 1935; 31 March 1935; 20 May 1935; 31 August 1935; 1, 3, 6, 10, 12, 15, 17, 19, 20 September 1935; 1, 3, 4, 6 October 1935; 6 February 1936, 29 March 1936; 5, 11, 16 April 1936; 9, 11, June 1936; 24, 31 July 1936; 3, 10, 25 August 1936; 1 December 1936; 9, 13, 17, 20, 23 January 1937; 6, 18 February 1937; 15, 24, 26, 27, 28 March 1937; 1 April 1937; 26 December 1938.

Sheng, Huanming 盛焕明. "Yuesheng yang gumi mianshui wenti" 粤省洋谷米免税问题 [The controversy over tax exemptions on foreign rice and grain in Guangdong province]. *Yinhang zhoubao* 银行周报 21 (16) (1937): 13–19.

Shiyebu Zhongguo jingji nianjian bianzuan weiyuanhui实业部中国经济年鉴编纂委员会 [China Economic Yearbook Compilation Committee of the Ministry of Industry and Commerce]. *Zhongguo jingji nianjian* 中国経済年鑑 (中卷 [China Economic Yearbook, Vol. 2]. Shanghai: Shangwuyin shuguan, 1935.

"Song Ziwen deng chouzu liangshi yunxiao gongsi" 宋子文等筹组粮食运销公司 [T. V. Soong and others are preparing to set up a food transportation company]. *Yinhang zhoubao* 银行周报 21(8) (1937): 1–2.

Tang, Qijun 唐啓均. "Xiangmi xiao Yue wenti" 湘米销粤问题 [On the issue of selling Hunan rice to Guangdong]. *Yinhang zhoubao* 银行周报 20(36) (1936): 27–28.

Tōa dōbunkai 東亜同文会, ed. *Shina shōbetsu zenshi daiikken kantonshō fuhonkon makao* 支那省別全誌第一巻広東省附香港澳門 [Complete gazetteer of each Chinese province of, Vol. 1 Guangdong province, Appendix: Hong Kong and Macau]. Tokyo: Tōa dōbunkai, 1917.

"Xiangmi xiao Yue cheng wenti" 湘米销粤成问题 [The problem of selling Hunan rice to Guangdong]. *Yinhang zhoubao* 银行周报 20(49) (1936): 5–6.

"Xiangmi xiao Yue yu Xiang Yue jingji hezuo" 湘米销粤与湘粤経済合作 [Sales of Hunan rice to Guangdong and economic cooperation between Hunan and Guangdong]. *Yinhang zhoubao* 银行周报 20(38) (1936): 1–2.

Xiong, Li 熊理. "Yuebi shiyao" 粤币史要 [A brief history of currency in Guangdong]. *Guangdongsheng yinhang yuekan* 广东省银行月刊 1(1) (1937): 53–74.

"Yang gumi yun Yue an gao yi duanluo" 洋谷米运粤案告一段落 [The case of transporting foreign rice to Guangdong has come to an end]. *Yinhang zhoubao* 银行周报 21(17) (1937): 5.

"Yangmi jinkoushui jiang shixing zhengshou." 洋米进口税将实行施行徵収 [Import duty on foreign rice import duty to be issued]. *Yinhang zhoubao* 银行周报 17(37) (1933): 8.

"Yangmi zhengshui wenti" 洋米徵税问题 [On the issue of levying an import duty on foreign rice]. *Yinhang zhoubao* 银行周报 17(38) (1933): 1–2.

Yu, Qizhong 余啓中. *Guangdong yanjiushui yange* 广东烟酒税沿革 [The evolution of the tobacco and wine taxes in Guangdong]. Guangzhou: Guoli Zhongshan daxue chubanbu, 1933.

"Yuesheng kuoda zengjia nongye shengchan" 粤省拡大增加农业生産 [Guangdong province to increase agricultural production]. *Yinhang zhoubao* 银行周报 22(14) (1938): 2.

"Yuesheng tongzhi churukou maoyi" 粤省统制出入口贸易 [Guangdong controls import and export trade]. *Yinhang zhoubao* 银行周报 22(20) (1938): 4–5.

"YueHan lu yanxian wuchan diaocha" 粤汉路沿线物產调查 [Investigation into the products in the region along the Guangzhou–Hankou railway]. *Yinhang zhoubao* 银行周报 20(38) (1936): 5–8.

"Yueshe minshi tiaojiehui" 粤设民食调节会 [Guangdong province's establishment of the Food Regulation Association]. *Yinhang zhoubao* 银行周报 21(1) (1937): 6–8.

"Yuesheng juban bolai nongchanshui" 粤省挙办舶来农産税 [Tax on imported agricultural products in Guangdong province]. *Yinhang zhoubao* 银行周报 17(39) (1933): 6–7.

"Yuesheng nongchanshui yijiu cunzai" 粤省农産税依旧存在 [The Guangdong agricultural tax still exists]. *Yinhang zhoubao* 银行周报 21(21) (1937): 7–8.

"Yuesheng she liangshi teweihui" 粤省设粮食特委会 [Guangdong province sets up special food committee]. *Yinhang zhoubao* 银行周报 22(5) (1938): 1.

"Yuesheng yangmi mianshui wenti" 粤省洋米免税问题 [On the issue of a foreign rice tax exemption in Guangdong province]. *Yinhang zhoubao* 银行周报 21(13) (1937): 3–6.

Yuesheng yangmi mianshui wenti huiji 粤省洋米免税问题汇辑 [A collection of discussions on foreign rice tax exemptions in Guangdong province]. Guangzhou, 1937 (Sun Yat-sen Library Collection, Guangzhou).

"Yuesheng zushe liangshi zong gongsi" 粤省组设粮食总公司 [Guangdong province sets up a food company]. *Yinhang zhoubao* 银行周报 20(48) (1936): 2–3.

Zai kanton nihon taishikan jimusho 在広東日本大使館事務所 [Office of the Embassy of Japan in Guangdong], ed. *Kantonshō chihōzei zeisoku* 広東省地方税税則 [Local tax regulations in Guangdong province]. Guangzhou, November 1943 (Sun Yat-sen Library Collection, Guangzhou).

Zhang, Gonglue 张公畧. "Xin shangren" 新商人 [New merchant]. *Chaomei shanghui lianhehui banyuekan* 潮梅商会联合会半月刊 1(1) (1929): 13.

Zhang, Ouru 张藕如. "Shantou neidi shuiju houlun lingdan fengchao zhi jingguo jiqi ganxiang" 汕头内地税局候轮领单风潮之経过及其感想 [The experience and thoughts about the unrest over ticket regulations prior to the shipment of the Shantou Inland Tax Bureau]. *Chaomei shanghui lianhehui banyuekan* 潮梅商会联合会半月刊 1(1)(1929): 16–18.

“Zhenbie xianren gexian caizheng juzhang kezhang” 甄别现任各県财政局长科长 [Screening for the current head and section chiefs of the Financial Bureau in all counties]. *Xin Guangdong* 新广东 8 (1933): 112.

“Zhengshou yangmi jinkoushui wenti” 徵収洋米进口税问题 [On the issue of import duties on foreign rice]. *Yinhang zhoubao* 银行周报 17(35) (1933): 1–3.

Zhongguo dier lishi dang’anguan 中国第二歷史档案馆 [Second Historical Archives of China], ed. *Zhonghua Minguo shi dang’an ziliao huibian diwuji diyibian caizheng jingji* 中华民国史档案资料滙编 第五辑第一编财政経済 [Archival compilation on the history of the Republic of China, Collection 5, Part 1: Finance and economy, Vols. 1–9]. Nanjing: Jiangsu guji chubanshe, 1994.

Zhongguo renmin yinhang zonghang canshishi 中国人民银行総行参事室 [Counselor’s Office of the People’s Bank of China], ed. *Zhonghua Minguo huobishi ziliao dierji* 中华民国货币史资料第二辑 [Monetary history of the Republic of China, Part 2]. Shanghai: Shanghai renmin chubanshe, 1991.

Zhu, Chuxin 朱楚辛. “Zhongguo de tangye wenti yu guotang chanxiao xiehui” 中国的糖业问题与国糖产销协会 [Problems in the Chinese sugar industry and the National Sugar Distribution Association], *Zhongguo jingji lunwenji* 中国经济论文集 3 (1936)

Archives

Guangdongsheng dang’anguan 广东省档案馆 [Guangdong Provincial Archives]. Guangzhou.

[GPA 4(2)108]

Gexian baosong shuijuan yusuan xinhui taishan zengcheng xinyi deng xian guanyu shuijuan wenti de qingshi baogao yu pifu 各県报送税捐予算新会台山增城信宜等県関于税捐问题的请示报告与批復 [Provincial counties’ reports on tax budgets: Requests for instructions and reports from Xinhui, Taishan, Zengcheng, Xinyi, and other counties on tax issues, and replies from the Department of Finance]. 4(2)108. Guangzhou: Guangdong Provincial Archives.

Sanshuixian xianzhang Chen Zhuolin 三水県県长陈卓霖→ Caizhengting 财政厅, 5 March 1938, 4(2)108.

[GPA 4(2)130(1)]

Haifeng lufeng Xiangyangxian Shantoushi chengqing huanan miye gongsi fanggou liangshi ji junmin wenti de wenjian 海豊陆豊湘阳県汕头市呈请华南米业公司放购粮食济军民问题的文件 [Document on the petitions from Haifeng, Lufeng, and Xiangyang counties and the city of Shantou to the South China Rice Company to release the purchased grains for the army and the people]. 1937–1938. 4(2)130(1). Guangzhou: Guangdong Provincial Archives.

Shantoushi Chaoyang gonghui changwu dongshi Ma Zonghan, Deng Jieqing, Wu Huisheng, Hong Zijian, Lin Weimin 汕头市潮阳公会常务董事马宗汉.邓介卿.呉晖生.洪子建.林伟民→Caizhengting财政厅. 6 October 1937, 4(2)130(1).

Lufengxian xianzhang Ou Rujun 陆豊県県长欧汝钧→Caizhengting tingzhang Zeng Yangfu 财政厅厅长曾养甫, 27 October 1937, 4(2)130(1).

Shantoushi Chaoyang gonghui changwu dongshi Ma Zonghan deng 汕头市潮阳公会常务董事马宗汉等→Caizhengting 财政厅, 3 November 1937, 4(2)130(1).

[GPA 4(2)175]

Caizhengbu Guangdong yinhua yanjiushuiju youguan yingye shuishou wenti de xunling bugao ji yu Luodingxian de (gong?)han, 财政部广东印花烟酒税局有関营业税収问题的训令布告及与罗定県的(公?)函 [Instructions and notices from the Bureau of the Stamp Tax and the Tobacco and Wine Taxes under the Ministry of Finance about business tax issues, and official letters from Luoding county]. 4(2)175. Guangzhou: Guangdong Provincial Archives.

Guangdong yinhua yanjiushuiju xunling (juzhang Su Chenliang) 广东印花烟酒税局训令第, no. 3577号(局长苏陈亮)→Xingningxian xianzhang 兴宁県県长, 17 June 1932, 4(2)175.

Caizhengbu Guangdong yinhua yanjiushuiju xunling, no. 7286 (juzhang Su Chenliang) 财政部广东印花烟酒税局训令第7286号(局长苏陈亮)→Xingning xian xianzhang 兴宁県长, 28 November 1932, 4(2)175.

[GPA 4(5)10]

Jiangmenshi dayuan gongsi qianxiang chafeng shanghao zubaodian shou qianlei deng laiwang wenjian 江门市大源公司欠饷查封商号租保店受牵累等来

往文件 [Communications on the involved guarantee shops and the seized shops through an investigation of the debt of Dayuan Company, Jiangwen city] 1932–1935 4(5)10. Guangzhou: Guangdong Provincial Archives.
Guomin gemingjun diyi jituanjun kongjun silingbu feiji disan duibu Jiang Qiyan 国民革命军第一集团军空军司令部飞机第三队部蒋其炎→Caizhengtingzhang 财政厅, 19 October 1934, 4(5)10.
Kaiping xianzhang Yu Qimou 开平县长余棨谋→Caizhengting 财政厅, 1 November 1934, 4(5)10.
Mai Ruiqi 麦瑞岐→Caizhengtingzhang 财政厅长, 8 November 1934, 4(5)10.
Caizhengting chengshengu guzhang Cai Xieyuan 财政厅承审股股长蔡夑垣→Caizhengting tingzhang 财政厅厅长, 12 November 1934, 4(5)10.
Mai Ruiqi 麦瑞岐→Caizhengting 财政厅, 13 March 1935, 4(5)10.
Weiyuan Xiao Songyou 委员萧颂猷→Caizhengting 财政厅, 25 March 1935, 4(5)10.
Mai Ruiqi 麦瑞岐→Caizhengting 财政厅, 16 April 1935, 4(5)10.
Chengshengu 承审股→Caizhengting 财政厅, 8 April 1935, 4(5)10.
Tan Yongfa．Tan Yongchang 谭永発.谭永昌→Caizhengting 财政厅, unknown date, 4(5)10.

[GPA 4(5)11]
Qiongya shengzhu chukou juan bugao zhangcheng hanjian 琼崖生猪出口捐布告章程函件 [Letters on the regulation on the pig export tax in Qiongya county]. 1933–1938. 4(5)11. Guangzhou: Guangdong Provincial Archives.
Weiyuan Jia Chongji 委员贾崇纪→Caizhengting 财政厅, 1, 14, 27 July 1933, 4(5)11.
Weiyuan Wu Yongji 委员呉镛斉→Caizhengting 财政厅, 9, 19, 30 August 1933, 4(5)11.
Caizhengting 财政厅→Yongchang gongsi 永昌公司, 31 August 1933, 4(5)11.
Toucheng Qiongya shengzhu chukou juanshang gongsi hecheng 投承琼崖生猪出口捐商公司合成→Caizhengting 财政厅, 1 September 1933, 4(5)11.
Yongchang gongsi Zhang Jiheng 永昌公司张济亨→Caizhengting 财政厅, 4 September 1933, 4(5)11.
Caizhengting 财政厅→Weiyuan Wu Yongji 委员呉镛斉, 6 September 1933, 4(5)11.
Weiyuan Wu Yongji 委员呉镛斉→Caizhengting 财政厅, 11 September 1933, 4(5)11.
Guangdongsheng zhengfu 广东省政府→Caizhengting 财政厅, 21 September 1933, 4(5)11.
Yongchang gongsi 永昌公司→Caizhengting 财政厅, 22 November 1933, 4(5)11.
Lingshu xian xincungang shanghui zhuxi Lai Qingchao 陵水県新村港商会主席頼庆朝→ Caizhengting 财政厅, 17 February 1934, 4(5)11.
Haikoushi shengzhuye tongye gonghui zhuxi Wu Faying, Changwei Zhang Chao yuan, Wu Jiesan 海口市生猪业同业公会主席呉発英、常委张超元.呉杰三→Caizhengting 财政厅, 3 June 1934, 4(5)11.
Yongchang gongsi 永昌公司→ Caizhengting 财政厅, 9 June 1934, 4(5)11.

Caizhengting 财政厅→Yongchang gongsi 永昌公司, 19 June 1934, 4(5)11.
Qiongshanxian Haikoushi shengzhu tongye gonghui zhuxi Lin Kaidi, changwu weiyuan Wu Jiesan, Zhang Chaoyuan 琼山県海口市生猪同业公会主席林开第常务委员呉杰三张超元→Caizhengting 财政厅, 19 August 1934, 4(5)11.
Yongchang gongsi 永昌公司→Caizhengting 财政厅, 5 November 1934, 4(5)11.
Shen Jiaren (Guangdong Nanhai ren baozheng shangdian zhuren) 沈家仁(广东南海人, 保証商店主人)→Caizhengting 财政厅, 21 November 1934, 4(5)11.
Yongchang gongsi Zhang Jiheng 永昌公司张济亨→Caizhengting, 财政厅 19 November 1934, 4(5)11.
Qiongshan xianzhang Liao Guoqi 琼山県长廖国器→Caizhengting 财政厅, 18 December 1934, 4(5)11.
Qiongshan xianzhang Liao Guoqi 琼山県长寥国器→Caizhengting 财政厅, February 1935, 4(5)11.
Yongchang gongsi Zhang Jiheng 永昌公司张济亨→Caizhengting财政厅, 16 February 1935, 4(5)11.
Caizhengting财政厅→Yongchang gongsi永昌公司, 21 February 1935, 4(5)11.

[GPA 4(5)16]
Shuiwu wenti laiwang wenjian 税务问题来往文件 [Correspondence on tax issues]. 1930–1939. 4(5)16. Guangzhou: Guangdong Provincial Archives.
Caizhengting 财政厅→Longchuanxian xianzhang 龙川県県长, 21 April 1938, 4(5)16.

[GPA 4(5)103]
Jiangpu zhubo liangsi fangwu Hongli gongsi ji jiujiang fangwu Wanli gongsi chengjiao qian xiang baozheng wuye qiju (shuiqi), 江浦主薄两司防务宏利公司及九江防务万利公司呈缴欠饷保証物业契据(税契) [Deed of guarantee for payment of debts submitted by Hongli Company, the gambling tax contractor of the two districts of Jiangpu and Zhupbo (present-day Shunde county), and Wanli Company, the gambling tax contractor of Jiujiang]. 1933–1934. 4(5)103. Guangzhou: Guangdong Provincial Archives.
Hongli gongsi shangren He Dingbang 承办江浦主薄(防务会议)宏利公司商人何定邦→ Caizhengting 财政厅, 8 August 1933, 4(5)103.
Nanhaixian xianzhang Li Haiyun 南海県県长李海云→Caizhengting 财政厅, 26 December 1933, 4(5)103.
Ou Lu shi (Guangdong Nanhai ren)区卢氏(广东南海人)→ Caizhengting 财政厅, unknown date, 4(5)103.
Xieban Jiangpu zhubo liangsi fangwu huiyi Hongli gongsi shangren He Dingbang 卸办江浦主薄两司防务会议宏利公司商人何定邦→Caizhengting 财政厅, 10 March 1934, 4(5)103.
He Dingbang 何定邦→Caizhengting 财政厅, 23 August 1934, 4(5)103.

He Dingbang 何定邦→Caizhengting 财政厅, 27 September 1934, 4(5)103.

[GPA 4(5)155]
Quansheng tujuan, Wanquan gongsi jiexiang ji shangren Xie Kaoling yu caiting hanjian 全省屠捐, 万全公司解饷及商人谢考凌与财厅函件 [Remittance of the tax quotas of Wanquan Company, the provincial slaughter tax contractor, and letters between the representative merchant Xie Kaoling and the Department of Finance]. 4(5)155. Guangzhou: Guangdong Provincial Archives.
Wanquan gongsi 万全公司→Caizhengting 财政厅, 25 September 1935, 4(5)155.
Caizheng ting xunling 财政厅训令→Chengban quansheng tujuan Wanquan gongsi shangren→承办全省屠捐万全公司商人, 25 October 1935, 4(5)155.

Diplomatic Archives of the Ministry of Foreign Affairs of Japan (2 sources)

Lists of Source 1: Gaimushō, Gaikō Shiryōkan. Tokyo. 外務省外交史料館 Diplomatic Archives of the Ministry of Foreign Affairs of Japan. Tokyo.

E1.3.2.1-001 Chūgoku ni okeru sozei oyobi futankin kankei zakken 中国ニ於ケル租税及負担金関係雑件 [Miscellaneous matters related to taxes and contributions in China, Vol. 1].
E1.3.2.1-002 Chūgoku ni okeru sozei oyobi futankin kankei zakken 中国ニ於ケル租税及負担金関係雑件 [Miscellaneous matters related to taxes and contributions in China, Vol. 2].
E1.3.2.1-003 Chūgoku ni okeru sozei oyobi futankin kankei zakken 中国ニ於ケル租税及負担金関係雑件 [Miscellaneous matters related to taxes and contributions in China, Vol. 3].
E1.3.2.1-004 Chūgoku ni okeru sozei oyobi futankin kankei zakken 中国ニ於ケル租税及負担金関係雑件 [Miscellaneous matters related to taxes and contributions in China, Vol. 4].
E1.3.2.1-005 Chūgoku ni okeru sozei oyobi futankin kankei zakken 中国ニ於ケル租税及負担金関係雑件 [Miscellaneous matters related to taxes and contributions in China, Vol. 5].
E.1.3.2.1-2-1 Santō mondai kome senzei 汕頭問題(米専税) [Shantou issue: the Special Tax on rice]
E.3.4.0.3-4-2 Chūgoku zeikan kankei zakken-Kaikan kanshō mondai/Kanton Kaikan 中国税関関係雑件一海関干渉問題/広東海関 [China customs-related

miscellaneous matters. Issue of interference in Maritime Customs/Maritime Customs Office in Guangdong].

Lists of Source 2: NihonGaimushō monjo 日本外務省文書 [Diplomatic Archives of the Ministry of Foreign Affairs of Japan]. Microfilm Collection, National Assembly Library of Korea.

S5100-3 Satō no bu 砂糖の部 [Sugar File]
S5160-25 Kantonshō no bu 廣東省の部 [Guangdong Province File]

Reports (in alphabetical order by sender)

Beppu Kumakichi→Yoshizawa Kenkichi 芳沢謙吉 Minister Extraordinary and Plenipotentiary of Japan to China, "Kanton zengo kinyū iji oyobi shinsai fukazei ni kansuru ken" 広東善後金融維持及賑災付加税ニ関スル件 [Additional tax charges for financial maintenance and disaster relief in Guangdong], 13 March 1928, E.1.3.2.1-001.

Beppu Kumakichi 別府熊吉→Tanaka Giichi 田中義一, "Kaku shōgyō kōkai no naichi zeikyoku saitetsu undō ni kansuru ken" 各商業公会ノ内地税局裁撤運動ニ関スル件 [Commercial Associations' Movement for the abolition of the Inland tax Bureau], 18 April 1928, E.1.3.2.1-002.

Beppu Kumakichi→Yoshizawa Kenkichi, "Shinsai fukazei wo naichi zeigyoku ni chōshū seshimuru no ken" 賑災付加税ヲ内地税局ニ徴収セシムルノ件 [Collection of a disaster relief tax surcharge by the Inland Tax Bureau], 27 April, 8 June 1928, E.1.3.2.1-001.

Beppu Kumakichi→Tanaka Giichi, Yunyū mugiko ni taishi unshōzei kafu kata ni kansuru ken 輸入麦粉ニ対シ運銷税課賦方ニ関スル件 [How to levy the transit and sales tax on imported wheat flour], 18 August 1928, E.1.3.2.1-001.

Beppu Kumakichi 別府熊吉, Consul of Shantou→Tanaka Giichi 田中義一, Minister of Foreign Affairs of Japan, "Shūsei naichisanka shukkō hōzei Benhō hantai undō ni kansuru ken" 修正内地産貨出口報税辯法反対運動ニ関スル件 [Report on the movement against revised regulations on exports of local products], 14 September 1928, E.1.3.2.1-004.

Beppu Kumakichi→Shidehara Kijūrō 幣原喜重郎, Minister of Foreign Affairs of Japan, Kokuzei ni taishi niwari huka ni kansuru ken 国税ニ対シ二割付加ニ関スル件 [20 percent additional charge on the national tax], 2 August 1930, E.1.3.2.1-002.

Commander of the Five Water Wars→Vice Chief of the Army General Staff, Chief of Staff of the Three Fleets, 3, 4 October 1935, E.1.3.2.1-2-1.

Harada Chūichirō→Hirota Kōki, "Dōgyōkumiai ni kansuru kō sanji mōshide hōkoku no ken" 同業組合ニ関スル黄參事申出報告ノ件 [Report on Huang's proposal about the industry union], 13 September 1935, E.1.3.2.1-2-1.

Harada Chūichirō→Hirota Kōki, 15 September 1935, E.1.3.2.1-2-1.

Harada Chūichirō 原田忠一郎, Consul of Shantou→Hirota Kōki 広田弘毅, Minister of Foreign Affairs of Japan, 広東省米専税ニ関スル件」, 20 September 1935, E.1.3.2.1-2-1.

Harada Chūichirō→Hirota Kōki, "Kantonshō kome zenzei ni kansuru ken" 広東省米専税ニ関スル件 [The special tax on rice in Guangdong province], 8 October 1935, E.1.3.2.1-004.

Harada Chūichirō→Hirota Kōki, 8 October 1935, E.1.3.2.1-2-1.

Harada Chūichirō→Arita Hachirō 有田八郎, Minister of Foreign Affairs of Japan, 17 April 1936, E.1.3.2.1-2-1.

Harada Chūichirō→Arita Hachirō, 17 April 1936, E.1.3.2.1-2-1.

Hattori Tsuneo 服部恒雄, Acting Consul General of Guangdong→Hirota Kōki, "Kantonshō no zatsuzei seiri jijō ni kansuru ken, Kantonshō zaisei tōkyoku no haishi zatsuzei ichibetsu hyō 広東省ノ雑税整理事情ニ関スル件, 広東省財政当局の廃止雑税一瞥表 [A glance at Guangdong province's consolidation situation for the miscellaneous taxes. Table of the miscellaneous taxes abolished by the finance authorities of Guangdong province], 18 August 1934, E.1.3.2.1-004.

Hirota Kōki 広田弘毅, Minister of Foreign Affairs of Japan→Kawai Tatsuo, 3 October 1935, E.1.3.2.1-2-1.

Horiuchi 堀内, Secretary of the Consul General of Japan in Shanghai→Hirota Kōki, 14 May 1935, S5100-3.

Hu Shi 胡適, Xinnian de mengxiang 新年ノ夢想, Dagongbao 大公報 [Dagongbao Daily], 20 December 1934, newspaper clippings, E.1.3.2.1-004.

Katō Hiyoshi 加藤日吉, Acting Deputy Consul of Shanghai→Taiwan seitō kabushiki kaisha kōbe seitōjo 台湾製糖株式会社神戸製糖所 [Taiwan Sugar Co., Ltd Kobe Sugar Refinery], 19 June 1928, E.1.3.2.1-004.

Kawagoe Shigeru 川越茂, Consul General of Guangdong→Hirota Kōki,第159號, 19 June 1934, S5160-25.

Kawai Tatsuo→Gaimushō Tōa kyokuchō 外務省東亜局長, Director of the East Asia Bureau, Ministry of Foreign Affairs, Japan, 3 June 1935, S5100-3.

Kawai Tatsuo→Hirota Kōki, "Gaikoku hikaku zei no zeiritsu hikiage ni kansuru ken" [On the increase in the tax rate on foreign leather], 6 July 1935, E.1.3.2.1-004.

Kawai Tatsuo 河相達夫, Consul General of Guangdong and Harada Chūichirō→Hirota Kōki, "Nihonjin mitsuyusha shikei no ken" 日本人密輸者死刑ノ件 [Japanese smugglers executed], 6 September 1935, E.1.3.2.1-2-1.

Kawai Tatsuo→Hirota Kōki, “Goma abura ni gaikoku nōsanpin senzei tekiyō kata ni kansuru ken 胡麻油ニ外国農産品専税適用方ニ関スル件 [Application of the special tax of on sesame oil agricultural products], 10 September 1935, E.1.3.2.1-004.

Kawai Tatsuo 河相達夫→Hirota Kōki, 11 September 1935, E.1.3.2.1-2-1

Mitsubishi Corporation, Shanghai Branch 三菱商社(上海)→Chief of the Agricultural Department, Tokyo, 2 May 1935, S5100-3.

Mizuzawa Kōsaku 水沢孝策, Consul General of Hong Kong→Hirota Kōki, 16 September 1935, E.1.3.2.1-2-1.

Morita Kanzō 森田寛蔵, Consul General of Guangdong→Tanaka Giichi 田中義一, Shinsai fukazei chōshū ni kansuru ken 賑災付加税徴収ニ関スル件 [Collection of the disaster relief tax surcharge], 29 May 1928, E.1.3.2.1-001.

Nakahara Saburō 中原三郎, Japanese Naval Officer and Military Attaché in Guangdong→Vice Chief of the Army General Staff, Chief of Staff of the Three Fleets, Commander of the Five Water Wars, Satō Okota 佐藤脩 Military Attaché with the Chinese Legation, 6 September 1935, E.1.3.2.1-2-1.

Nakahara Saburō 中原三郎 Japanese Naval Officer and Military Attaché in Guangdong→Vice Chief of the Army General Staff, Chief of Staff of the Three Fleets, Commander of the Five Water Wars, Satō Okota 佐藤脩 Military Attaché with the Chinese Legation, 24, 27 September 1935, E.1.3.2.1-2-1.

Nakamura Toyoichi 中村豊一, Consul General of Guangdong→Hirota Kōki, 1 September 1936, E.1.3.2.1-005.

Sakayori Hatsugorō 酒寄発五郎, Shanghai Branch of Masuyuki Company→Yokotake Heitarō 横竹平太郎, Commerce Counselor of the Foreign Ministry of Japan in Shanghai, “Personal opinion on controls over sugar sales,” 8 May 1935, S5100-3.

Suma Yakichirō 須磨弥吉郎, Acting Consul General of Guangdong→Shidehara Kijūrō, Sekitan fuka zei chūshi ni kansuru ken 石炭付加税中止ニ関スル件 [Cancellation of the coal surcharge tax], 7 September 1931, E.1.3.2.1-003.

Suma Yakichirō→Shidehara Kijūrō, Tōshi ryōri ten dōmei higyō ni kansuru ken 当市料理店同盟罷業二関スル件 [Strike by our city’s allied restaurants], 9 September 1930, E.1.3.2.1-003.

Suma Yakichirō→Shidehara Kijūrō, “Zaiseichō no kakushu zeien ukeoi seido haishi kata keikaku ni kansuru ken” 財政庁ノ各種税捐請負制度廃止方計画二関スル件 [Department of Finance’s plan to abolish various tax contract systems], 9 October 1930, E.1.3.2.1-003.

Suma Yakichirō→Shidehara Kijūrō, 6 July, 22 July 1931, E.1.3.2.1-003.

Suma Yakichirō→Shidehara Kijūrō, “Kōshū shi ni okeru zari hōdai hi fukki kata ni kansuru ken” 広州市ニ於ケル坐厘砲台費復帰方ニ関スル件 [How

to restore the fortress and cannon fee in Guangzhou city], 16 July 1931, E.1.3.2.1-003.
Suma Yakichirō→Shidehara Kijūrō, "Sekitan fuka zei chōshū kata ni kansuru ken" 石炭付加税徴収方ニ関スル件 [How to collect the coal surcharge tax], 27 July, 14 August 1931, E.1.3.2.1-00.3
Suma Yakichirō→Shidehara Kijūrō, "Sekitan fuka zei chūshi setsu ni kansuru ken" 石炭付加税中止説ニ関スル件 [Rumor on cancellation of the coal tax], 20 August 1931, E.1.3.2.1-003.
Suma Yakichirō→Shidehara Kijūrō, 3 September 1931, E.1.3.2.1-003
Suma Yakichirō→Inukai Tsuyoshi 犬養毅, Minister of Foreign Affairs of Japan, Zari hōdai hi teppai ni kansuru ken "坐厘台砲費撤廃ニ関スル件 [Cancellation of the fortress and cannon fee], 26 December 1931, E.1.3.2.1-003.
Tsukamoto Tsuyoshi 塚本毅, Consul of Amoy→Hirota Kōki, 18 December 1933, E.1.3.2.1-004.
Usuda Hirozo 臼田寛三, Japanese Army Officer, Lieutenant Colonel, Military Attaché in Guangdong→Vice Chief of the Army General Staff, 3 October 1935, E.1.3.2.1-2-1
Yano Makoto 矢野真, Consul General of Guangdong→Tanaka Giichi, 30 January 1929, 1929, E.1.3.2.1-002.
Yokotake Heitarō 横竹平太郎, Commercial Counselor of the Foreign Ministry of Japan in Shanghai, "Saikin Kantonshō keizai jijō" 最近広東省経済事情 [Recent economic affairs in Guangdong province], Kaigai keizai jijō 海外経済事情 13 (1935): 255, S5100-3.
Yokotake Heitarō→Hirota Kōki, 2 May 1935, S5100-3.
Yoshida Tanichirō→Uchida Kōsai, "Zaiseichō no zatsuen haishi kata ni kansuru ken" 財政庁ノ雑捐廃止方ニ関スル件 [How to abolish the miscellaneous levies of the Department of Finance], 4 January 1933, E.1.3.2.1-004.
Yoshida Tanichirō→Uchida Kōsai, "Kanton koku shō zeien tōitsu kensa iinkai no seiritsu ni kansuru ken" 広東国省税捐統一検査委員会ノ成立ニ関スル件 [Establishment of the United Guangdong Inspection Committee on National and Provincial Taxes and Levies], 18 March 1933, E.1.3.2.1-004.
Yoshida Tanichirō→Uchida Kōsai, "Kōshū santō sansui kōmon kaku kensajo shokuin ninmei no ken" 広州.汕頭.三水.江門各検査所職員任命ノ件 [Staff appointments for the Guangzhou, Shantou, Sansui, and Jiangmen Inspection Offices], 28 March 1933, E.1.3.2.1-004.
Yoshida Tanichirō→Uchida Kōsai, "Kanton zaiseichō no kenshi zeien oyobi Tesūryō nado chōsadan soshiki ni kansuru ken" 広東財政庁ノ県市税捐及手数料等調査団組織ニ関スル件 [Guangdong's organization of a special investigation team on taxes, levies, and charges in counties and towns, Department of Finance], 20 July 1933. E.1.3.2.1-004.

Yoshida Tanichirō→Uchida Kōsai, "Kanton zaiseichō shusai no kenshi zeien chōsadan so no go" 広東財政庁主催ノ県市税捐調査団其ノ後 [The situation after the Department of Finance, Guangdong, organized a special investigation team on taxes, levies, and charges in counties and towns], 15 August 1933, E.1.3.2.1-004.
Yoshida Tanichirō 吉田丹一郎, Acting Consul General of Guangdong→Uchida Kōsai 内田康哉,Minister of Foreign Affairs of Japan, "Kanton zaiseichō shūshi sōsho ni kansuru ken" 広東財政庁緝私総処ニ関スル件 [Anti-smuggling General Office, Department of Finance, Guangdong], 29 September 1933, E.1.3.2.1-004.
Yoshitake Sadaharu 吉竹貞治, Acting Consul General of Guangdong→Arita Hachirō 有田八郎, 2 September 1936, E.1.3.2.1-005.

John Swire & Sons Ltd Archive, London University, SOAS Library Special Collections

[JSS 5-1-8] Sugar Refinery letters
Messrs. Butterfield & Swires. Hong Kong (hereafter, Hong Kong)→Messrs. John Swire & Sons, Ltd London (hereafter, London), 6 January 1933, JSS 5-1-8.
Hong Kong→London, 19 May 1933, JSS 5-1-8.
Hong Kong→London, 26 September 1933, JSS 5-1-8.
Hong Kong→London, 29 September 1933, JSS 5-1-8.
London→Hong Kong, 27 September 1933, JSS 5-1-8.
Hong Kong→London, 1 December 1933. JSS 5-1-8.

[JSS 5-1-9] Sugar Refinery letters
Hong Kong→London, 27 April 1934. JSS 5-1-9.
Hong Kong→London, 18 May 1934, JSS 5-1-9.
H. C. Lin→Messrs. Dodwell & Co., Ltd, 24 May 1934, JSS 5-1-9.
* Hong Kong→London, 3 August 1934, JSS 5-1-9. Attachment (3)
Hong Kong→London, 22 June 1934, JSS 5-1-9.
Hong Kong→London, 21 June 1934, JSS 5-1-9.
C. P. Wong→Hong Kong, 23 August 1934, JSS 5-1-9.
* Hong Kong→London, 31 August 1934, Attachment
Hong Kong→London, 24 August 1934, JSS 5-1-9
Messrs. Butterfield & Swires. Shanghai (hereafter, Shanghai)→Hong Kong, 12 October 1934, JSS 5-1-9
Shanghai→Hong Kong, 12 November 1934, JSS 5-1-9.
Hong Kong→London, 16 November 1934, JSS 5-1-9.
Hong Kong→London, 26 November 1934, JSS 5-1-9.
Shanghai→London, 7 December 1934, JSS 5-1-9.

[JSS 5-1-10] Sugar Refinery letters
Hong Kong→London, 4 January 1935, JSS 5-1-10.
Hong Kong→London, 30 March 1935, JSS 5-1-10.
Hong Kong→London, 24 April 1936, JSS 5-1-10
London→Hong Kong, 14 May 1935, JSS 5-1-10.
Hong Kong→Shanghai, 23 May 1935, JSS 5-1-10.
Hong Kong→London, 31 May 1935, JSS 5-1-10.
Hong Kong→London, 26 July 1935, JSS 5-1-10.
Hong Kong→London, 16 October 1936, JSS 5-1-10.
Hong Kong→London, 20 November 1936, JSS 5-1-10.
Hong Kong→London, 11 December 1936, JSS 5-1-10.
Hong Kong→London, 7 March 1937, JSS 5-1-10.

[JSS 5-1-11] Sugar Refinery letters
Hong Kong→London, 16 April 1937, JSS 5-1-11.
Hong Kong→London, 2 July 1937, JSS 5-1-11.

[JSS 5-1-11] Sugar Refinery letters
Hong Kong→London, 8 April 1938, JSS 5-1-12.
Hong Kong→London, 22 April 1938, JSS 5-1-12.

Secondary Sources

Boecking, Felix. *No Great Wall: Trade, Tariffs and Nationalism in Republican China, 1927–1945*. Cambridge, MA: Harvard University Asia Center, 2017.

Brondolo, John and Zhang Zhiyong. "Tax Administration Reform in China: Achievements, Challenges, and Reform Priorities." IMF Working Paper WP/16/68, 2016.

Cai, Renlong 蔡仁龙. "Huang Zhonghan jiazu yu Jianyuan gongsi" 黄仲涵家族与建源公司 [Oei Tiong Ham's family and Kian Gwan Company]. *Nanyang wenti* 南洋问题 1 (1983): 15–26.

Caizhengbu Guokusi 财政部国库司 [Treasury Department of the Ministry of Finance]. "2016 nian caizheng shouzhi qingkuang" 2016年财政收支情况 [The budget balance of 2016]. *Zhongguo caizhen*g 中国财政 3 (2017): 70–71.

Chang, Segi. *Ilbon gyŏngje sa* [Economic history of Japan]. Seoul: Dunam Publisher, 2003.

Chen, Boren 陈伯任. “Caizheng he shuijuan” 财政和税捐 [Finance and taxes and levies]. In *Nantian suiyue: Chenjitang zhu Yue shiqi jianwen shilu* 南天歲月: 陈济棠主粤时期见闻实录 [Days of the southern sky: Records of personal experiences in Guangdong under the rule of Chen Jitang], ed. Guangzhoushi zhengxie wenshi ziliao yanjiu weiyuanhui 广东省政协文史资料研究委员会 [Committee on the Study of Historical Materials of the Guangzhou Municipal Branch of the Chinese People’s Political Consultative Conference], 294–305. Guangzhou: Guangdong renmin chubanshe, 1987.

Chen, Boren 陈伯任. “Chen Jitang tongzhi jituan de hengzheng baolian” 陈济棠统治集团的横政暴敛 [Tyrannical rule and excessive exploitation by the ruling group of the Chen Jitang regime]. *Guangzhou wenshi ziliao* 广州文史资料 16 (1965)

Chen, Feng 陈锋. “20 shiji di wanQing caizhen shi yanjiu” 20世纪的晚清财政史研究 [Research on the financial history of the late Qing dynasty in the 20th century]. *Jindaishi yanjiu* 近代史研究 1 (2004): 245–281.

Chen, Feng 陈锋. *Qingdai caizheng zhengce yu huobi zhengce yanjiu* 清代财政政策与货币政策研究 [Research on fiscal and monetary policy in the Qing dynasty]. Wuhan: Wuhan daxue chubanshe, 2008.

Chen, Feng 陈锋. “WanQing caizheng yusuan de yunniang yu shishi” 晚清财政预算的酝酿与实施 [Preparation and implementation of the financial budget in the late Qing dynasty]. *Jianghan luntan* 江汉论坛 1 (2009): 78–90.

Chŏng, Chi-ho. “Ch’ŏngmal yanggyech’oŭi chaejŏnggaehyŏgan’gwa kungmin’gukka” [Liang Qichao’s financial reform plan and the idea of a nation-state in the late Qing dynasty]. *Myŏngch’ŏngsa yŏn’gu* 39 (2013): 145–180.

Chŏng, Yŏng-gu. “1902–1930 Chungguk paeksŏlt’angshijangŭi sŏnggyŏk” [Features of the Chinese white sugar market, 1902–1930]. *Chungguksa yŏn’gu* 121 (2019): 165–208.

Coble, Parks Jr. *The Shanghai Capitalists and the Nationalist Government, 1927–1937*. Cambridge, MA: Harvard University Press, 1986.

Deng, G. Kent. “The Continuation and Efficiency of the Chinese Fiscal State, 700 BC–AD 191.” In *The Rise of Fiscal States: A Global History, 1500–1914*, ed. Bartolomé Yun-Casalilla and Patrick K. O’Brien, 335–352. New York: Cambridge University Press, 2012.

Deng, Shaohui 邓绍辉. *WanQing caizheng yu Zhongguo jindaihua* 晚清财政与中国近代化 [Late Qing finance and China's modernization]. Chengdu: Sichuan renmin chubanshe, 1998.

Deng, Yanbin 邓衍彬. "Chen Jitang kaizheng meiyan fanmai yingye shui" 陈济棠开征煤烟贩売营业税 [Chen Jitang's launch of a sales tax on petroleum]. *Guangzhou wenshi ziliao* 广州文史资料 16 (1965): 43–48.

Du, Xuncheng 杜恂诚. "Minguo shiqi de zhongyang yu defang caizheng huafen" 民国时期的中央与地方财政划分 [Financial division between the center and the provinces during the Republic of China]. *Zhongguo shehui kexue* 中国社会科学 3 (1998): 184–195.

Duara, Prasenjit. *Culture, Power and the State: Rural North China, 1900–1942*. Stanford, CA: Stanford University Press, 1988.

Eng, Robert Y. "Chinese Entrepreneurs, the Government, and the Foreign Sector: The Canton and Shanghai Silk-Reeling Enterprises, 1861–1932." *Modern Asian Studies* 18(3) (1984): 353–370.

Fang, Jianchang 房建昌. "Neimenggu yancao xiaoshi: Jianlun Minguo qianqi Neimeng de yanshui ji youguan jigou" 内蒙古烟草小史-兼论民国前期内蒙古的烟税及有关机构 [History of tobacco in Inner Mongolia: The cigarette tax in Inner Mongolia and related organizations in the early Republic of China]. *Yinshan xuekan* 阴山学刊 1 (1998): 62–68.

Faure, David. "The Plight of the Farmers: A Study of the Rural Economy of Jiangnan and the Pearl River Delta, 1870–1937." *Modern China* 11(1) (1985): 3–37.

John Fitzgerald, *Awakening China: Politics, Culture and Class in the Nationalist Revolution* (Stanford, CA: Stanford University Press, 1996).

Fitzgerald, John. "Increased Disunity: The Politics and Finance of Guangdong Separatism, 1926–1936." *Modern Asian Studies* 24(4) (1990): 745–775.

Fitzgerald, John. "The Misconceived Revolution: State and Society in China's Nationalist Revolution, 1923–26." *Journal of Asian Studies* 49(2) (1990): 323–343.

Fitzgerald, John. "Warlords, Bullies, and State Building in Nationalist China: The Guangdong Cooperative Movement, 1932–1936." *Modern China* 23(4) (1997): 420–458.

Fu, Boying 付伯颖. "Meiguo lianbang geren suodeshui de lishi bianqian yu qishi" 美国联邦个人所得税的历史变迁与启示 [The historical transition and implications of the individual income tax system in the United States]. *Caizhengshi yanjiu* 财政史研究 7 (2014): 318–338.

Fu, Zhiyu 付志宇. "Jindai Zhongguo shuishou xiandaihua jincheng de sixiangshi kaocha" 近代中国税收现代化进程的思想史考察 [Intellectual historical study on the modernization of taxation in modern China]. PhD diss., Hunan University, 2009.

"Global tax-to-GPD ratio ranking in 2017." Last modified 14 October 2020. http://ecodb.net/ranking/imf_ggr_ngdp.html (accessed 10 October 2018).

Gongshang shuizhi gaige pingxi ketizu 《工商税制改革评析》课题组 [Research Group for the "Report on the Reform of the Industrial and Commercial Tax System"]. "1994 nian Zhongguo de gongshang shuizhi gaige pingxi" 1994年中国的工商税制改革评析 [An analysis of China's industrial and commercial tax reform in 1994]. *Caizheng jingji* 财政经济7 (1997): 2–28.

Guangdong dang'anguan 广东省档案馆 [Guangdong Provincial Archives]. *Chen Jitang yanjiu shiliao, 1928–1936* 陈济棠研究史料 [Historical materials for research on Chen Jitang]. Guangzhou: Guangdongsheng dang'anguan, 1985.

Guangdongsheng zhengxie wenshi ziliao yanjiu weiyuanhui 广东省政协文史资料研究委员会 [Committee for the Study of Historical Materials of the Guangzhou Municipal Branch of the Chinese People's Political Consultative Conference]. *Nantian suiyue: Chen Jitang zhu Yue shiqi jianwen shilu* 南天歲月: 陈济棠主粤时期见闻实录 [Days of the southern sky: Records of personal experiences in Guangdong under the rule of Chen Jitang]. Guangzhou: Guangdong renmin chubanshe, 1987.

Guangdongsheng Zhongshan tushuguan 广东省中山图书馆 [Sun Yat-sen Library of Guangdong]. *Guangdong jinxiandai renwu cidian* 广东近现代人物词典 [Biographical dictionary of modern and contemporary people in Guangdong]. Guangzhou: Guangdong kexue chubanshe, 1992.

Guo, Xu 郭旭. "Qingmo minchu jiushuizhidu yingelun" 清末民初酒税制度因革论 [History of the liquor tax system in the late Qing and the early Republic]. *Guizhou wenshi congkan* 贵州文史丛刊 4 (2011): 25–32.

Guojia fagaiwei jingji yanjiusuo ketizu 国家发改委经济研究所课题组 [Research group of the Economic Research Institute of the National Development and Reform Commission]. "Woguo hongguan shuifu yanjiu" 我国宏观税负研究 [Research on the macro tax burden in China]. *Jingji yanjiu cankao* 经济研究参考 2 (2014): 3–42.

Hamashita, Takeshi 浜下武志. "Imin to shōgyō nettowāku chōshū gurūpu no tai imin to hongoku sōkin" 移民と商業ネットワーク一潮州グループのタイ移民と本国送金 [Immigration and commercial network: Chaozhou immigrants in Thailand and their remittances to China]. *Tōbunken kiyō* 東洋文化研究所紀要 116 (1992): 61–106.

Han, Xiang 韩祥. "WanQing caizheng guimo gusuan wenti chutan" 晚清财政规模估算问题初探 [Research on the problem of estimating the scale of public finance in the late Qing]. *Zhongguo jingjishi yanjiu* 中国经济史研究 3 (2014): 25–41.

He, Hanwei 何汉威. "Qingmo fushui jizhun de kuoda jiqi juxian: Yi zashui zhong de yanjiushui he qishui weili" 清末赋税基准的扩大及其局限: 以杂税中的烟酒税和契税为例 [Expansion and the limitations of the tax basisin the late Qing: The case of the tobacco and wine taxes and the deed tax in the miscellaneous taxes]. *Taiwan zhongyang yanjiuyuan jindaishi yanjiusuo jikan* 台湾中央研究院近代史研究所集刊 17(2) (1988): 69–98.

He, Lie 何烈. *Qing Xiantong shiqi de caizheng* 清咸同时期的财政 [Finance in the Qing under the reign of the Xianfeng and Tongzhi emperors]. Taipei: Guoli bianyi guan Zhonghua congshu bianshen weiyuanhui. 1981.

Hill, Emily M. "The Life and Death of Feng Rui (1899–1936): Sugar Mills, Warlord Rule in Guangdong, and China's Agrarian Economy." PhD diss., Cornell University, 1996.

Hill, Emily M. *Smokeless Sugar: The Death of a Provincial Bureaucrat and the Construction of China's National Economy*. Vancouver: University of British Columbia Press. 2001.

Hirai, Kensuke 平井健介. *Satō no teikoku nihon shokuminchi to ajia shijō* 砂糖の帝国: 日本植民地とアジア市場 [Empire of sugar: External forces of change in the economies of the Japanese colonies]. Tokyo: Tōkyō daigaku shuppankai, 2017.

Ishijima, Noriyuki 石島紀之. "Nankinseiken no Keizai kensetsu ni tsuiteno ichi shiron" 南京政権の経済建設についての一試論 [An essay on the economic construction of the Nanjing administration]. *Ibaraki daigaku jinbun gakubu kiyō bungakka ronsō* 茨城大学人文学部紀要文学科論集 11 (1978): 41–77.

Iwai, Shigeki 岩井茂樹. *Chūgoku kinsei zaiseishi no kenkyū* 中国近世財政史の研究 [Study on China's early modern financial history]. Kyoto: Kyoto daigaku shuppankai, 2004.

Iwai, Shigeki 岩井茂樹. "Chūka teikoku zaisei no kindaika" 中華帝国財政の近代化 [Modernization of finance in the Chinese empire]. In *Shirīzu 20 seiki Chūgokushi 1: chūka sekai to kindai* ツリーズ20世紀中国史 1: 中華世界と近代 [Series on twentieth century Chinese history 1: The Chinese world and modernity], ed. Ijima Wataru 飯島渉, Tokyo: Tokyo daigaku shuppankai, 2009.

Iwai, Shigeki 岩井茂樹. "Yōeki to zaisei no aida: Chūgoku zei·eki seido no rikai teki ri kai ni mukete (1–4)" 徭役と財政のあいだ一中国税·役制度の歴史的理解にむけて (1–4) [Between corvée and finance: Toward a historical understanding of the Chinese tax and corvée System (1–4)]. *Keizai keiei ronsō* 経済経営論叢 28(4), 29(1), 29(2), 29(3) (1994): 153–210, 105–154, 62–130, 188–276.

Ji, Haopeng 纪浩鹏. "Ningshu haishi sushu: Xinren zhiji Jiangsu shenghui zhizheng" 宁属还是苏属：辛壬之际江苏省会之争 [Belonging to Ningshu or to Suzhou: Debate during the Jiangsu Provincial Conference in 1911–12]. *Jiangsu shehui kexue* 江苏社会科学 2 (2017): 239–246.

Jiang, Yuanjian 江源荐 and Huang Xiaoli 黄筱鹂. "Maotai jituan qiansanjidu wancheng shuishou shouru 100.8 yiyuan, zengzhang41%" 茅台集团前三季度完成税收收入100.8亿元, 增长41% [The Maotai Group achieved tax revenue of 10.08 billion and grew by 41 percent in the third quarter]. *Niangjiu keji* 12 (2016): 121.

Jung, Myeong-jin. "Namkyŏng kukminchŏngpuŭi chosekaehyŏkkwa kŭ sŏngkyŏk, 1929–1937" [The Nanjing Nationalist Government's fiscal policy and its characteristics]. *Sŏultae tongyangsahakkwa nonjip* 25 (2001): 161–205.

Kamiyama, Tsuneo 神山恒雄. "Zaiseiseisakuto kinyūkōzō" 財政政策と金融构造 [The fiscal policy and financial structure]. In *Nipponkeizaishi 2 sangyō kakumeiki* 日本経済史2産业革命期 [Economic history of Japan 2: The industrial revolution period], ed. Ishi Kanji 石井寛治. Tokyo: Tokyo daigaku shuppankai, 2000.

Kaneko, Hajime 金子肇. "Chūgoku no tōitsuka to zaisei mondai: 'Kokuchi zaisei kakubun' mondai o chūshin ni" 中国の統一化と財政問題: 「国地財政劃分」問題を中心に [China's unification and financial problems: Focusing on the "division between national and local taxes"]. *Shigaku kenkyū* 史学研究 179 (1988): 19–39.

Kaneko, Hajime 金子肇. "Sanhai shihonka kaikyū to kokumintō tōchi" 上海資本家階級と国民党統治(一九二七一二九) [The Shanghai capitalist class and Guomindang governance (1927–29)]. *Shigakukenkyū* 史学研究 176 (1987): 27–47.

Kano, Hiroyoshi 加納忠良. "Kokusai bōeki kara mita 20 seiki no tōnan ajia shokuminchi keizai: Ajia taiheiyō shijō eno hōsetsu" 国際貿易から見た20世紀の東南アジア植民地経済: アジア太平洋市場への包摂 [The Southeast Asian colonial economy in the twentieth century from the perspective of international trade: Inclusion in Asia-Pacific markets]. *Rekishi hyōron* 歴史評論 539 (1995): 39–55.

Kang, Jin-A 姜抮亚. "1930 nendai chūgoku niokeru chōzei ukeoi seido no kaikaku to kokka" 1930年代中国における徵税請負制度の改革と国家 [State and reform of China's tax-farming system in the 1930s.]. *Rekishigaku kenkyū* 歴史学研究 771 (2003): 32–44.

Kang, Jin-A 姜抮亚. "1930 nendai kanton Chinsaitō seiken no seitōgyō kensetsu" 1930年代广东陈济棠政权の製糖业建设 [Building of the sugar industry in Guangdong under the Chen Jitang regime in the 1930s]. *Chikakini Arite* 近きに在りて 30 (1996): 78–97.

Kang, Jin-A. "1930 nyŏn Chungkukŭi kyŏngchekaepalesŏ nat'ananŭn sŏngkwa chungang—'kwangtongtang'ŭi sanghaechinch'ulkwa namkyŏngchŏngpu" [Center and local in Chinese economic development in the 1930s: The launch of the Guangdong sugar industry in Shanghai and the Nanjing government]. In *Chungkuk kŭnhyŏntaesaŭi chaechomyŏng* [Reconsideration of the history of modern China], ed. Sŏultaehakkyo tongyangsahakkwa yŏn'gushil, 283–319. Seoul: Jisiksanupsa, 1999.

Kang, Jin-A. *1930 nyŏndae Chunggukŭi chungang, chibang, sangin: Kwangdongsŏng ŭi chaejŏng kwa kukka kŏnsŏl* [Center, provinces, and merchants in China in the 1930s: Finance and nation-building in Guangdong province]. Seoul: Sŏul taehakkyo ch'ulp'anbu, 2005.

Kang, Jin-A, "1930 nyŏndae Chunggukŭi kŭmyung t'ongil kwajŏng esŏ pon chungang kwa chibang: Kwangdongsŏng ŭi chibang hwap'ye chŏngni kwajŏng ŭl chungsim ŭro" [Financial unification and central versus local politics in China in the 1930s: Reforms of the local currency in Guangdong province, 1936–1938]. *Chungkuk hakpo* 46 (2002): 315–336.

Kang, Jin-A. "1930 nyŏndae kŭmyunggaehyŏk esŏ nat'anan kukkagwŏllyŏk kwa min'gan kŭmyung: Kwangdongsŏng Sandu ŭi sarye" [State power and private finance in the financial reforms of China in the 1930s: The case of Shantou in Guangdong]. *Chungguk kŭnhyŏndaesa yŏn'gu* 16 (2002): 119–139.

Kang, Jin-A. "1930 nyŏndae Kwangdongsŏng ŭi suimmi kwasenonjaeng kwa Namgyŏng chŏngbu" [Debates over taxation on imported rice in Guangdong province and the Nanjing Nationalist Government in the 1930s]. *Tongyang sahak yŏn'gu* 75 (2001): 159–196.

Kang, Jin-A 姜抮亚. "1935 nian de Shantou shijian: 1930 niandai Guangdong difang guanshui yu Riben" 1935年的汕头事件：1930年代广东地方关税与日本 [The Shantou Incident in 1935: The Guangdong provincial tariff and Japan in the 1930s]. In *1930 niandai de Zhongguo* 1930 年代的中国 [China in the 1930s], ed. Sichuan shifan daxue lishi wenhua xueyuan 四川师范大学历史文化学院, and Zhongguo shehui kexueyuan jindaishi yanjiusuo Minguoshi yanjiushi 中国社会科学院近代史研究所民国史研究室. 323–337. Beijing: Shehui kexue wenxian chubanshe, 2006.

Kang, Jin-A 姜抮亚. "20 shiji chu de dongya shichang yu Zhongguo zhi tangye" 20世纪初的东亚市场和中国制糖业 [East Asian markets and the Chinese sugar industry in the early twentieth century]. In *Jindai Zhongguo: Jingji yu shehui yanjiu* 近代中国-经济与社会研究 [Modern China: Research on the economy and society], 447–473. Shanghai: Fudan daxue chubanshe, 2006.

Kang, Jin-A 姜抮亚. "20 shiji 30 niandai Guangdongsheng de huobi tongyi zhengce de bengkui guocheng: Waihui weiji yu xiaoyangquan" 20世纪30年代广东省的货币统一政策的崩溃过程: 外汇危机与小洋券 [Collapse of currency control in Guangdong province in the 1930s: Financial crisis and the "small money" system]. In *Shijie jingji tizhi xia de Minguo shiqi jingji* 世界经济体制下的民国时期经济 [The Chinese economy during the Republican era under the world system], ed. Zhang Donggang 张东刚, 44–56. Beijing: Zhongguo caizheng jingji chubanshe, 2005.

Kang, Jin-A. "Cheguk chaejŏngŭi kŭndaejŏk pyŏnyong: ch'ŏngmal kwangdongŭi chibangjaejŏngŭl chungshimŭro" [Modern transformation of imperial finance:

The case of Guangdong provincial finance in the late Qing period]. *Chungguk kŭnhyŏndaesa yŏngu* 69 (2016): 39–70.

Kang, Jin-A. "Chunghwamin'guk shigi kwangdongsŏngŭi sul tambae kwase kaehyŏkkwa chaejŏng kŭndaehwa" [The taxes on wine and tobacco in Guangdong province and the modernization of finance during the Republic of China]. *Tongyang sahak yŏngu* 138 (2018): 237–286.

Kang, Jin-A. "Chungkukŭi ch'echekaehyŏkkwa taeoekaepang: kŭntaehwaŭi yŏksasŏng" [The reform and opening-up policy of China: The historicity of modernization]. In *Chungguk kaehyŏk: kaebangŭi chŏngch'I gyŏngje 1980–2000* [China reform: The politics and economy of opening-up, 1980–2000], ed. Jung Jea-ho. Seoul: Kkach'i kŭlpang, 2002.

Kang, Jin-A 姜抮亚. *Dongyahuaqiao ziben he jindai chaoxian: Guangbang jushang tongshuntai hao yanjiu* 东亚华侨资本和近代朝鲜: 广帮巨商同顺泰号研究 [The Chinese merchant network in East Asia and modern Korea: Cantonese big business Tongshuntai]. Guangzhou: Guangdong renmin chubanshe, 2018.

Kang, Jin-A. "G2 shidaeŭi chungguk sahoejuŭi: yŏksajŏk kwanjŏm esŏ pon chunggug ŭi kaehyŏkkaebang" [On Chinese socialism in the age of the G2: China's reform and opening-up from a historical perspective]. *Yŏksabip'yŏng* 106 (2014): 287–322.

Kang, Jin-A. "Kŭndae chunggugŭi chaejŏnggaehyŏge issŏsŏ chŏnt'ongsŏnggwa kŭndaesŏng chaego: 1930nyŏndae kwangdongsŏngŭi chingsech'ŏngbujedoŭi unyŏnggwa shilt'ae" [Rethinking tradition and modernity in the financial reform of modern China: Management and the reality of the tax-farming system in Guangdong province in the 1930s]. *Inmun nonch'ong* 50 (2003): 3–89.

Kang, Jin-A. "Kŭntae tongasia sŏlt'ang sichangkwa hongk'ong chetangŏp: sangin tiasŭp'olanŭn chisok kanŭnghanka?" [The sugar market in modern East Asia and the Hong Kong sugar industry: Is the merchant diaspora sustainable?]. *Yŏksa pip'yŏng* 130 (2020): 381–428.

Kang, Jin-A. "Monetary war between Nanjing and Guangzhou during the great depression: Financial unification and national versus local politics in China in the 1930s." In *Strenuous Decades: Global Challenges and Transformation of Chinese Societies in Modern Asia*, ed. Chi-cheung Choi, Tomoko Shiroyama, and Venus Viana, 253–276. Berlin, Boston: De Gruyter Mouton, 2022.

Kang, Jin-A. "Naejŏn'gi kwangdongsŏngŭi sŏngyŏnggongŏp chaegŏnjŏngch'aekkwa songjamun" [T. V. Soong and the reconstruction of provincial industries in Guangdong during the Chinese Civil War]. *Chungguk kŭnhyŏndaesa yŏngu* 24 (2004): 69–90.

Kang, Jin-A. "Segyesaŭi shigagesŏ pon kŭnhyŏndae chungguk chose kujoŭi chŏnhwan" [The transition of the modern Chinese tax structure from the perspective of global history]. *Ihwa saha kyŏn'gu* 57 (2018): 181–241.

Kang, Myŏng-hŭi. "Mobŏmsŏng ŭi hŏ wa shil: Min'guk shigi sansŏsŏng chŏngbu ŭi chŏngch'I gaehyŏk kwa kyŏngje kŏnsŏl" [The rhetoric and reality of the model province: Political reform and economic construction of the Shanxi provincial government during the Republic of China]. PhD diss., Seoul National University, 1995.

Kang, Shumeng 康姝萌. "Zhong Mei geren suodeshui zhidu duibi fenxi" 中美个人所得税制度对比分析 [A comparative analysis of the individual income tax system in China and America]. *Caizheng wenti yanjiu* 财政问题研究 12 (2016): 61–65.

Ke, Weiming 柯伟明. "Minguo shiqi shuishou zhidu de shanbian" 民国时期税收制度的嬗变 [The evolution of tax system during the Republican China]. *Zhongguo shehui kexue* 中国社会科学 11 (2019): 149–170.

Kikuchi, Kazutaka 菊池一隆. Kōnichi sensō jiki no kakyō to chūgoku kōgyō gassaku undo" 抗日戦争時期の華僑と中国工業合作運動 [Overseas Chinese and the Chinese Industrial Collaboration Movement during the Anti-Japanese War]. *Rekishi hyōron* 歴史評論 549 (1996): 28–43.

Kim, Du-hyeong. "Chungkuke issŏsŏ secheŭi palchŏnkwa hyŏnhwang" [The development of tax policy in China]. *Sahoe iron* 26 (2004): 73–123.

Kim, Ik-soo. "80 nyŏntae chungkukŭi chaechŏngkwanlicheto kaehyŏkkwa t'uchap'aengch'ang" [China's fiscal system reforms and the expansion of fixed investments in the 1980s]. *Tongbuga gyŏngje yŏn'gu* 9(1) (1997): 213–239.

Kim, Jee-hwan. "Namgyŏnggungminjŏngbu shigi t'ongse kaejŏngŭi sŏnggyŏk yŏn'gu: 1934nyŏndo myŏnsa t'ongse kaejŏngŭi paegyŏnggwa yusanŭl chungshimŭro" [Research on the nature of the consolidated tax reform of the Nanjing Nationalist Government: The case of the background of the cotton yarn consolidated tax reform and its abolition in 1934]. *Chungguk hakpo* 48(2003): 349–372.

Kim, Young-jin. "Kaehyŏkki chungkuke issŏsŏ chungangkwa chipangŭi chaechŏngkwankye: chaechŏngkaehyŏkŭi kwachŏngkwa sŏngkwae taehan silchŭng" [The fiscal relationship between the center and the provinces in China during the reform period: An empirical analysis of the process and result of the fiscal relationship]. *Sahoe gwahak* 34(1) (1995): 108–208.

Knight, G. Roger. "Exogenous Colonialism: Java Sugar between Nippon and Taikoo before and during the Interwar Depression, c. 1920–1940." *Modern Asian Studies* 44(3) (2010): 477–515.

Kubo, Tōru 久保亨. "1930 nendai chūgoku no kanzei seisaku to shihonka kaikyū" 一九三〇年代中国の関税政策と資本家階級 [China's tariff policy and the capitalist class in the 1930s]. *Shakai Keizai shigaku* 47(1) (1981): 42–64.

Kubo, Tōru 久保亨. *Chūgoku keizaishi nyūmon* 中国経済史入門 [Introduction to Chinese economic history]. Tokyo: Tōkyō daigaku shuppankai, 2012.

Kubo, Tōru 久保亨. "Chūgoku kokumin seifu ni yoru kanzei seisaku kettei katei no bunseki: 1932. 1934 nen" 中国国民政府による関税政策決定過程の分析: 一九三二一一九三四年 [Analysis of the process of tariff policy-making by the Nationalist government of China: 1932–1934]. *Tōyō bunka kenkyūjo* 92 (1983): 141–217.

Kubo, Tōru 久保亨. *Gendai chūgoku no genkei no shutsugen: Kokumintō tōchi kano minshū tōgō to zaiseikeizai* 現代中国の原型の出現: 国民党統治下の民衆統合と財政経済 [The emergence of the prototype of modern China: People's integration and the financial economy under Chinese Nationalist Party rule]. Tokyo: Kyūko shoten, 2020.

Kubo, Tōru 久保亨. "Kingendai chūgoku ni okeru kokka tokeizai: Chūka minkoku ki Keizai seisaku shiron" 近現代中国における国家と経済: 中華民国期経済政策史論 [The state and the economy in modern China: History of economic policy in the Republic of China]. In *Rekishi no nakano gendai chūgoku* 歴史のなかの現代中国 [Modern China in history], ed. Yamada Tatsuo 山田辰雄. 82(116). Tokyo: Keisoshoho, 1996.

Kubo, Tōru 久保亨. "Kokumin seifu no yushutsu sokushin seisaku to chūka kōgyō kokugai bōeki kyōkai: 1930 nendai chūgoku ni okeru yushutsu shikō kōgyōka no mosaku" 国民政府の輸出促進政策と中華工業国外貿易協会: 一九三〇年代中国における輸出志向工業化の模索 [The export promotion policy of the Nationalist government and the Chinese Industrial Foreign Trade Association:

The search for export-oriented industrialization in China in the 1930s]. *Tōyō bunka kenkyūjo* 100 (1987): 81–113.

Kubo, Tōru 久保亨. "Kokumin seifu no zaisei to kanzei shūnyū, 1928–1937 nen" 国民政府の財政と関税収入、一九二八一一九三七年 [Finance in the Nationalist government and Customs revenue, 1928–1937]. In *Chūgokushi ni okeru shakai to minshū* 中国史における社会と民衆 [Society and people in Chinese history], ed. Masubuchi tatsuo sensei taikan kinen ronshū kankōkai 增淵龍夫先生退官記念論集刊行会 [Publication Committee for Tatsuo Masubuchi's Retirement Memorial Collection], 213–232. Tokyo: Kyūko shoin, 1983.

Kubo, Tōru 久保亨. "Nankin seifu no zaisei kinyū seisaku" 南京政府の财政金融政策 [The financial and banking policy of the Nanjing government]. In *Chūgoku kokumin seifushi no kenkyū* 中国国民政府史の研究 [Research on the history of the Nationalist government of China], ed. Chūgoku gendaishi kenkyūkai 中国现代史研究会, 215–249. Tokyo: Kyūko shoin, 1986.

Kubo, Tōru 久保亨. *Senkanki chūgoku "jiritsueno mosaku" kanzei tsūka seisaku to keizai hatten* 戦间期中国<自立への模索—一関税通货政策と経済発展 [Seeking "self-reliance" in China during the interwar period: Tariff and monetary policy and economic development]. Tokyo: Tokyo daigaku shuppankai, 1999.

Kubo, Tōru 久保亨, Kajima Jun 加島潤, and Kigoshi Yoshinori 木越義則, eds. *Tōkeidemiru chūgokukingendai keizaishi* 統計でみる中国近現代経済史 [China's modern economic history as seen from statistics]. Tokyo: Tokyo daigaku shuppankai, 2016.

Lee, Jong-ha, Lee Jong-chan, and Hwang Jin-yeong. "Chungkukŭi chaechŏng mich' hangmokpyŏl choseŭi oesaengchŏk ch'ungkyŏkkwa saengsanlyang pyŏntong" [Output impact of exogenous shocks on public finance and the tax policy in China]. *Chaejŏng jŏngch'aeng nonjip* 20(2) (2018): 133–158.

Lee, Seong-gi and Won Seok-jo. "Kaehyŏkkaepang ihu chungkukŭi sahoepuchokaehyŏkkwa chungang-chipangchŏngpu kan kwankye" [Social assistance reforms and inter-governmental relations since the open policy in China]. *Sahoe bokchi jŏngch'aek* 41(1) (2014): 267–288.

Li, Guorong 李国荣. "Tangshaoyi chushi Ri Ou baguo kaocha caizheng shiliao" 唐绍仪出使日欧八国考察财政史料 [Historical sources on Tang Shaoyi's economic mission to Japan and the West]. *Lishi dang'an* 历史档案 2 (1990): 64–72.

Li, Qingyu 李庆宇. "Minguo Beijing zhengfu yanjiu gongmai shulun" 民国北京政府烟酒公卖述论 [Research on the tobacco and liquor monopoly of the Beiyang government]. *Lishi jiaoxue* 历史教学 10 (2017): 49–56.

Li, Zongling 黎宗玲. "Wanshan woguo geren suode shuizhi de sikao: Jiyu Zhong Mei bijiao shijiao" 完善我国个人所得税制的思考: 基于中美比较视角 [On improvements in China's personal income tax system: Based on a comparative perspective between China and the United States]. *Zhongguo waizi* 中国外资 265 (2012): 96.

Lian, Bingyi 练秉彝. "Chen Jitang Yu Hanmou shiqi Chaoshan ji zong duirishijian" 陈济棠余汉谋时期潮汕几宗对日事件 [Several anti-Japan incidents in Chaozhou-Shantou district during the period of rule by Chen Jitang and Yu Hanmou]. *Guangzhou wenshi ziliao* 广州文史资料 4 (1961): 171–179.

Lian, Haowu 连浩鋈 (Alfred H. Y. Lin). "Ershi shiji sanshi niandai Guangdong mihuang wenti de yanjiu" 二十世紀三十年代广东米荒問題的研究 [Research on the rice famine in Guangdong in the 1930s]. *Zhongguo jingjishi yanjiu* 中国经济史研究 4 (1996): 10–20.

Lian, Haowu 连浩鋈. "Sanshi niandai Guangdong nanlu de tudi liyong yu nongye gaikuang yanjiu" 三十年代广东南路的土地利用与农业概况研究 [A study on land use and agriculture in Nanlu district of Guangdong in the 1930s]. In *Shisi shiji yilai Guangdong shehui jingji de fazhan* 十四世纪以来广东社会経济的发展 [Development of society and the economy in Guangdong since the fourteenth century], ed. MingQing Guangdongsheng shehui jingji yanjiuhui 明清广东省社会経济研究会, 74–94. Guangzhou: Guangdong gaodeng jiaoyu chubanshe, 1992.

Lian, Haowu 连浩鋈 "WanQing shiqi Guangdongsheng de duiwai maoyi jiqi dui nongcun shehui jingji de yingxiang" 晚清时期广东省的对外贸易及其对农村社会経济的影响 [Foreign trade in Guangdong and its impact on the rural social economy in the late Qing period]. In *Qingdai quyu shehui jingji yanjiu (xia)* 清代区域社会経济研究(下册) [Research on the regional social economy during the Qing dynasty. Vol. 2], ed. Ye Xianen 叶顕恩, 1165–1192. Beijing: Zhonghua shuju, 1992.

Liang, Yong 梁永. "Chen Jitang tongzhi jituan de hengzheng baolian" 陈济棠统治集团的横政暴敛 [Tyrannical rule and excessive exploitation by the ruling group during the Chen Jitang regime]. *Guangzhou wenshi ziliao* 广州文史资料

16 (1965): 123–125. (Note: this article has the same title as an article written by Chen Boren, in the same publication.)

Lin, Alfred H. Y. "Building and Funding a Warlord Regime: The Experience of Chen Jitang in Guangdong, 1929–1936." *Modern China* 28(2) (2002): 177–212.

Liu, Decheng 刘德成. "Qingmo 'Caizheng Shuomingshu' jiqi shiliao jiazhi" 清末《财政说明书》及其史料价值 ["Instructions on Guangdong finance" in the late Qing period and its historical value]. *Dang'an yu jianshe* 档案与建设 4 (2016): 53–54.

Liu, Han 刘菡 广东财政厅财政科学研究所 Fiscal Science Research Center, Department of Finance, Guangdong). "Bolai wuchan zhuanshui, kai ting zheng ji: Xiezai 'Guangdongsheng zhi: Caizhengzhi' chuban zhi qian" 舶来物産専税开停征记: 写在《广东省志.财政志》出版之前 [The beginning and end of collecting the special tax on imported products: Written before the publication of the *Gazetteer of Guangdong Province: Finance*]. Unpublished draft. Presented by the author on a visit to the Fiscal Science Research Center, July 1999.

Liu, Qi 刘琦 and Huang Tianhua 黄天华. "Minguo shiqi zhuanmai zhidu yanjiu" 民国时期专卖制度研究 [Research on the monopoly system in the Republican period]. *Caizhengshi yanjiu* 财政史研究 4 (2012).

Liu, Zenghe 刘增合. "Qingji zhongyang dui waisheng de caizheng qingcha" 清季中央对外省的财政清查 [The central government's investigation of provincial finance in the late Qing period]. *Jindaishi yanjiu* 近代史研究 6 (2011): 102–123.

Ma, Jinhua 马金华. "Waizhai yu wanQing zhengju" 外债与晚清政局 [Foreign loans and the political situation in the late Qing period]. PhD diss., Renmin University of China, 2004.

Mann, Susan. *Local Merchants and the Chinese Bureaucracy, 1750–1950*. Stanford, CA: Stanford University Press, 1987.

Mehrotra, Ajay K. "A Bridge Between: Law and the New Intellectual Histories of Capitalism." *Buffalo Law Review* 64 (2016): 1–22.

Mehrotra, Ajay K. *Making the Modern American Fiscal State: Law, Politics, and the Rise of Progressive Taxation, 1877–1929*. New York: Cambridge University Press, 2013.

Mehrotra, Ajay K. "The Notion of Tax Reform in Historical Perspective," Last modified 13 July 2017. http://www.processhistory.org/mehrotra-tax-reform/ (accessed 30 September 2018).

Miyashita, Tadao 宮下忠雄. *Chūgoku heisei no tokushu kenkyū: kindai chūgoku ginryō seido no kenkyū* 中国幣制の特殊研究: 近代中国銀両制度の研究 [Special study on the Chinese monetary system: A study of modern China's silver system]. Tokyo: Maruzen kabushiki kaisha, 1952.

Miyata, Michiaki 宮田道昭. "Shinmatsu chōshū chihō ni okeru satō bōeki no tenkai to chiiki shakai: Santō kō no ryūtsū jōkyō o chūshin toshite" 清末、潮州地方における砂糖貿易の展開と地域社会: 汕頭港の流通状況を中心として [Development of the sugar trade and local communities in the Chaozhou region in the late Qing: A focus on the status of distribution at Shantou port]. In *Kanda nobuo sensei koki kinenronshū: Shinchō to higashi ajia* 神田信夫先生古希記念論集: 清朝と東アジア [Memorial Collection Celebrating the 70th Birthday of Prof. Nobuo Kanda: The Qing Dynasty and East Asia], ed. Kanda Nobuo Sensei koki kinen ronshū henshū iinkai 神田信夫先生古稀記念論集編纂委員会 [Compilation Committee of the Memorial Collection Celebrating the 70th Birthday of Prof. Nobuo Kanda], 489–512. Tokyo: Yamagawa shuppansha, 1992.

Mo, Yinggui (Mok Ying Kui) 莫应溎. "Yingshang Taigu yanghang jinbainian zai Huanan de yewu huodong yu moshi jiazu de guanxi" 英商太古洋行近百年在华南的业务活动与莫氏家族的关系 [The business activities of the British company, Butterfield & Swire Co. in the last 100 years and its relationship with the Mok family].]. *Guangdong wenshi ziliao* 广东文史资料 44 (1985): 77–131.

Mun, Myeong-ki. "Taeman·chosŏnch'ongtokpuŭi chŏnmaechŏngch'aek pikyoyŏnku: sahoekyŏngchechŏk yusankwa' kukka'nŭnglyŏkŭi ch'ai" [A comparative study on the monopoly policy of Taiwan and the general Chosen government]. *Sarim* 52 (2015): 377–424.

Na, Hyŏn-su. "Pukpŏl ch'ogi kungminjŏngbu ŭi taeoe gwan'gye ŭi chŏn'gae: Chamjŏng bugagwanse ŭi chingsu rŭl chungshim ŭro" [The Nationalist government's foreign relations during the early Northern Expedition period: A focus on collection of the 2.5% provisional tariffs]. *Yŏksa hakpo* (99/100) (1983): 261–312.

Nozawa, Yutaka 野沢豊. ed. *Chūgoku no heisei kaikaku to kokusai kankei* 中国の币制改革と国际関係 [Chinese currency reform and international relations]. Tokyo: Tokyo daigaku shuppankai, 1981.

O'Brien, Patrick K. "The Political Economy of British Taxation, 1660–1815," *Economic History Review* 41(1) (1988): 1–32.

Okamoto, Takashi 岡本隆司. *Chūgoku keizaishi* 中国経済史 [Chinese economic history]. Nagoya: Nagoya daigaku shuppankai, 2013.

Okamoto, Takashi 岡本隆司. *Kindai chūgoku to kaikan* 近代中国と海関 [Modern China and the maritime customs]. Nagoya: Nagoya daigaku shuppankai, 1999.

Oksenberg, Michel and James Tong. "The Evolution of Central-Provincial Fiscal Relations in China, 1971–1984: The Formal System." *The China Quarterly* 125 (1991): 1–32.

Park, Kyung-seok. "Namkyŏngkukminchŏngpuŭi sesuchŏngch'aekkwa chaechŏngkipanŭi sulip: ikŭm·t'ongsechŏngch'aekŭl chungsimŭlo" [Fiscal policy and revenue stablization of the Nanjing Nationalist Government: The case of the *lijin* and the consolidated tax policy]. *Tongyang sahak yŏn'gu* 61 (1998): 103–134.

Paulès, Xavier. "Unacceptable but Indispensable: Opium Law and Regulations in Guangdong, 1912–1936." *Cross-Currents: East Asian History and Culture Review* 1(7) (2013): 366–392.

Peng, Yuxin 彭雨新. "Qingmo Zhongyang yu gesheng caizheng guanxi" 清末中央与各省财政关係 [Financial relations between the central government and the provinces in the late Qing dynasty]. *Shehui kexue zazhi* 社会科学杂志 9(1) (1947): 83–110.

Peng, Zeyi 彭泽益. "Qingdai caizheng guanli tizhi yu shouzhi jiegou" 清代财政管理体制与收支结构 [The financial management system and the structure of the fiscal balance in the Qing dynasty]. *Zhongguo shehui kexueyuan yanjiushengyuan xuebao* 中国社会科学院研究生院学报 2 (1990): 48–59.

Qin, Qingjun 秦庆钧. "Minguo shiqi Guangdong caizheng shiliao 1911–1949" 民国時期广东财政史料 1911–1949 [Historical materials on finance in Guangdong province during the Republic of China, 1911–1949]. *Guangdong wenshi ziliao xuanji* 广东文史资料选辑 29 (1983): 33–153.

Riccardi, Lorenzo. *Introduction to Chinese Fiscal System*. Singapore: Springer, 2018.

Satō, Junpei 佐藤淳平. *Kindai chūgoku zaiseishi: 'gaishō' kara 'chihō' e* 近代中国財政史: 「外省」から「地方」へ [A fiscal history of modern China: Changing central-provincial relations in the late Qing and the early Republic]. Tokyo: Tōkyō daigaku shuppankai, 2020.

Shen, Xuefeng 申学锋, and Zhang Xiaoli 张小莉. "Jin shinian wanQing caizheng shi yanjiu zongshu" 近十年晚清财政史研究综述 [A summary of research on the financial history of the late Qing dynasty in the recent ten years]. *Shixue yuekan* 9 (2004): 102–108.

Shi, Zhihong 史志宏. and Xu Yi 徐毅. *WanQing caizheng 1851–1894* 晚清财政 [Finance in late Qing China]. Shanghai: Shanghai caijing chubanshe, 2008.

Skřivan, Aleš. "Czechoslovak Exports of Arms to China during the Interwar Period." *ÖT KONTINENS* 1 (2010): 233–243.

Skřivan, Aleš. "Škodovy závody a výstavba cukrovarů v Číně před druhou světovou válkou" [Skoda Works and construction of the sugar refineries in China before World War II], *LCaŘ* 127(11) (2011): 361–365.

Sugiyama, Shinya 杉山伸也. *Nichiei keizai kankeishi kenkyū* 日英経済関係史研究 1860–1940 [Historical study of Anglo-Japanese economic relations]. Tokyo: Keiō gijuku daigaku shuppankai, 2017.

Sung, See-il. "Cubic B-Spline Regression Modelŭl iyonghan chungkuk punseche punsŏk" [An analysis of the tax-distribution system in China using a Cubic B-Spline Regression Model]. *Hanjungsahoegwahakyŏn'gu* 8(1) (2010): 165–185.

Teng, Shuna 滕淑娜, Xi Chuanying 席传英, and Han Daxue 韩大学. "Jindai yilai Zhong Ying yanshui gongneng bianqian bijiao ji qishi" 近代以来中英盐税功能变迁比较及启示 [Comparison and implications of the changes in the function of the salt tax in China and Britain in the modern period]. *Yanyeshi yanjiu* 盐业史研究 2 (2015): 21–31.

Uchida, Tomoyuki 内田知行. "1930 nendai ni okeru En Sekizan seiken no zaisei seisaku" 1930年代における閻錫山政権の財政政策 [Fiscal policy of the Yan Xishan regime in the 1930s]. *Ajia Keizai* アジア経済 25(7) (1984): 11–39.

Uchida, Tomoyuki 内田知行. "En Sekizan seiken no zaisei seiri jigyō: 1930 nendai chūgoku ni okeru gunbatsu chihō kakkyo ni tsuite no ichikōsatsu" 閻錫山政

権の財政整理事業:一九三〇年代中国における軍閥地方割拠についての一考察 [The fiscal consolidation project of the Yan Xishan regime: A study of the warlords' regional separatism in China in the 1930s]. *Hitotsubashi ronsō* 一橋論叢 91(6) (1984): 827–846.

Wan, Bin 万斌. "Xin Zhongguo yancao zhuanmai zhidu gaige: Chengben yu shouyi fenxi" 新中国烟草专卖制度改革:成本与收益分析 [Reform of the tobacco monopoly system in new China]. PhD diss., Jiangxi University of Finance and Economics, 2010.

Wang, Hongxiao 王红晓 and Bai Taolin 白涛林. "Meiguo geren suodeshui shuilu de lishi bianqian ji qishi" 美国个人所得税税率的历史变迁及启示 [Historical changes in the personal income tax rate in the United States and its enlightenment]. *Shuiwu yanjiu* 税务研究 7 (2017): 73–76.

Wang, Huayu 王桦宇. "Wenhua yanjin zhidu bianqian yu shuishou fazhi: Fali yujing xia de ZhongMei shuizhi bijiao" 文化演进、制度变迁与税收法治—法理语境下的中美税制比较 [Cultural evolution, institutional change, and the rule of law in taxation: A comparison of government discourse in China and the US]. *Dongfang faxue* 东方法学 5 (2013): 87–103.

Wang, Huiying 王慧英. "Zhuanmai zhidu xia woguo yancao chanye de gaige yu fazhan" 专卖制度下我国烟草产业的改革与发展 [Reform and development of the tobacco industry by the monopoly system in China]. *Shanghai jingji yanjiu* 上海经济研究 4 (2009): 22–28.

Wang, Jingyu 汪敬虞. *Zhongguo jindai jingjishi, 1898–1927* 中国近代经济史, 1898–1927 [Modern Chinese economic history, 1898–1927]. Beijing: Renmin chubanshe, 2000.

Wang, Linlin 王琳琳. "Jianguo yilai woguo shuishou zhidu de bianqian yu fazhan qushi" 建国以来我国税收制度的变迁与发展趋势 [Change and development trends in China's tax system since the founding of the People's Republic of China]. *Gongshang luntan* 工商论坛 16(2) (2010): 57–58.

Wang, Song 王松, Jiang Shimin 蒋仕民, and Rao Fanghu 饶方虎. *Song Ziwen zhuan* 宋子文传 [Biography of T. V. Soong]. Wuhan: Wuhan Chubanshe, 1996.

Wang, Tingkui 汪廷奎. "Minguo yiqian weiyi de Guangdong caizheng jupian: Xijian Qingmo 'Guangdong caizheng shuomingshu' zhengliben wenshi" 民国以

前唯一的广东财政鉅篇: 喜见清末《广东财政说明书》整理本问世 [The sole comprehensive financial record of Guangdong provincial finance prior to the Republic of China: Gladly thinking about the publication of "Instructions on Guangdong finance" in the late Qing]. *Guangdong shizhi* 广东史志 2 (1998): 70–74.

Wang, Zhijun 王志军. "Lun Ying Mei yan gongsi yu jiu Zhongguo de 'xieding yanshui'" 论英美烟公司与旧中国的'协定烟税' [Research on the British American Tobacco Company and the 'Agreement on the Cigarette Tax' in old China]. *Xuchang xueyuan xuebao* 许昌学院学报 3 (2006): 99–101.

Wong, R. Bin. *China Transformed: Historical Change and the Limits of European Experience*. Ithaca, NY: Cornell University Press, 1997.

Wong, R. Bin. "Taxation and Good Governance in China, 1500–1914." In *The Rise of Fiscal States: A Global History, 1500–1914*, ed. Bartolomé Yun-Casalilla and Patrick K. O'Brien, 353–377. New York: Cambridge University Press, 2012.

Xi, Zisi 冼子思. "Ban tangye jingguo jiqi zhenxiang" 办糖业经过及其真相 [The history of sugar-industry building and its true story]. In *Nantian suiyue: Chen Jitang zhu Yue shiqi jianwen shilu*, 245–261. Guangzhou: Guangdong renmin chubanshe. 1987.

Xi, Zisi 冼子思. "Song Ziwen longduan Guangdong tangye de jihua he wo canjia chouban Guangdong tangchang de jingguo" 宋子文垄断广东糖业的计划和我参加筹办广东糖厂的经过 [T. V. Soong's plan to monopolize the Guangdong sugar industry and my experience in organizing Guangdong sugar factories]. *Guangdong wenshi ziliao* 广东文史资料 62 (1990): 205–208.

Xiang, Jun 向军. "WanQing huaqiao yu Zhongguo jingji xiandaihua yanjiu" 晚清华侨与中国经济现代化研究 [Overseas Chinese in the late Qing and China's economic modernization]. PhD diss., University of Ji'nan, 2007.

Xiao, Junsheng 肖俊生. "WanQing jiushui zhengce de yanbian lunxi" 晚清酒税政策的演变论析 [Analysis of change in the liquor tax policy during the late Qing]. *Shehui kexue jikan* 社会科学季刊 3 (2008): 150–155.

Xie, Hongmei 谢红梅. "Yinggai zeng dui jiudian hangye de shouyi yingxiang ji shuiwu chouhua" '营改增'对酒店行业的收益影响及税务筹划 [The effects on profits and the taxation plan of the hotel business of the 'Change from the Business Tax to the Value-Added Tax']. *Zhongguo jingmao* 20 (2016): 200–201.

Xie, Yingming 谢英明. "Shengying gongye gaikuang yishu" 省营工业概况忆述 [Recollection of the conditions of government industries]. In *Nantian suiyue: Chenjitang zhuyue shiqi jianwen shilu*, 219–240. Guangzhou: Guangdong renmin chubanshe, 1987.

Xu, Sidao 徐思道. "Guangdong tongyuan de zhuzao he liutong" 广东铜元的铸造和流通 [Casting and circulation of Guangdong copper ten cash]. In *Jindai Guangdong jinrong Guangdong wenshi ziliao diliushijiuji: Yinhai zong heng* 近代广东金融广东文史资料第六十九辑: 银海纵横 [Literature and history materials on modern Guangdong finance. Vol. 69: The wide sea of silver], ed. Zhongguo renmin zhengzhi xieshang huiyi Guangdongsheng weiyuanhui wenshi ziliao yanjiu weiyuanhui 中国人民政治协商会议广东省委员会文史资料研究委员会 [Committee for the Study of Historical Materials of the Guangzhou Municipal Branch of the Chinese People's Political Consultative Conference] and Zhongguo renmin yinhang Guangdongsheng fenhang jinrong yanjiusuo 中国人民银行广东省分行金融研究所 [Financial Research Institute of the Guangdong Branch of the People's Bank of China], 4–15. Guangzhou: Guangdong renmin chubanshe, 1992.

Xue, Gang 薛钢 and Li Shurui 李淑瑞. "Meiguo shuigai dui woguo shuizhi gaige de qishi" 美国税改对我国税制改革的启示 [Enlightenment of American tax reform on China's reforms of the tax system]. *Difang caizheng yanjiu* 7 (2018): 13–17.

Yamamoto, Shin 山本真. "Nicchūsensō kaishi zengo shisenshō shinto ken ni okeru kensei kaikaku no jikken to sono zasetsu: hōi jiken ni taisuru ichikōsatsu" 日中戦争開始前後,四川省新都県における県政改革の実験とその挫折: 包囲事件に対する一考察 [Aborted experiment on county administration reform in Xindu county, Sichuan province around the time of the outbreak of the Sino-Japanese War: A consideration of the Siege Incident]. *Hitotsubashi ronsō* 一橋論叢 120(2) (1998): 304–320.

Yang, Huashan 杨华山. "Lun wanQing 'caili tongjuan' yu 'caili renjuan' de changshi ji yaozhe" 论晚清 "裁厘统捐" 与 "裁厘认捐" 的尝试及夭折 [On the aborted attempt to "abolish the *likin* and create unified levies" and "abolish the *likin* and the tax-farming of levies" in the late Qing dynasty], *Shixue yuekan* 史学月刊 2 (2014): 57–63.

Yang, Zhiyong 杨志勇. "Xiandai shuishou zhidu jianshe: Sishinian geren suodeshui fazhan de sikao" 现代税收制度建设: 四十年个人所得税发展的思考 [Construction of a modern tax system: Reflection on the development of the personal income tax during the past forty years]. *Jingji zongheng* 经济纵横 6 (2018): 51–59.

Yoo, Ho-lim. “Chungkukŭi hyŏntae sechesae kwanhan koch'al” [Research on the history of China's contemporary tax system]. *Semuwa hoegyejŏnŏl* 12(1) (2011): 119–152.

Yoo, Ho-lim. “Chungkukŭi kuchochŏk kamsechŏngch'aeke kwanhan p'yŏngkawa sisachŏm” [Evaluation of China's structural tax reduction policy and its implications]. *Chose yŏngu* 14(2) (2014): 137–166.

Yoshihara, Kunio 吉原久仁夫 ed. and Zhou, Nanjing 周南京 trans. *Huang Zhonghan caituan: Dongnanya diyi qiye diguo* 黄仲涵财团: 东南亚第一企业帝国 [The Oei Tiong Ham concern: The first business empire of Southeast Asia]. Beijing: Zhongguo huaqiao chubanshe, 1993.

Young, Arthur N. *China's National-Building Effort, 1927–1937: The Financial and Economic Record*. Stanford, CA: Hoover Institution Press, 1971.

Yu, Baohua 喻保华. “Dangqian woguo yancao chanye shuizhi bianqian yanjiu” 当前我国烟草产业税制变迁研究 [Study of changes in the tax system for the tobacco industry in China]. *Guanli xuekan* 管理学刊 25(4) (2012): 59–64.

Yu, Chunsheng 喻春生. “Kong Xiangxi zai Guomindang wujie wuzhong quanhuishang de caizheng baogao” 孔祥熙在国民党五届五中全会上的财政报告 [Financial report of Kong Xiangxi at the fifth plenary session of the Fifth Central Committee of the Chinese Nationalist Party]. *Minguo dang'an* 民国档案 1(2006). 3–12.

Yu, Yanguang 余炎光 and Chen Fulin 陈福霖. *NanYue geju: Cong Long Jiguang dao Chen Jitang* 南粤割据: 従竜済光到陈済棠 [The separatist regime in southern Guangdong: From Long Jiguang to Chen Jitang]. Guangzhou: Guangdong renmin chubanshe, 1989.

Yun-Casalilla, Bartolomé and Patrick K. O'Brien, eds. *The Rise of Fiscal States: A Global History, 1500–1914*. New York: Cambridge University Press, 2012.

Zhang, Chuanming 张传明 and Ma Jie 马杰. “1949–1995: Zhongguo gongshang shuizhi bianqian de lishi kaocha (shang) 1949–1995” 中国工商税制变迁的历史考察(上) [A historical review of changes in the commercial taxes in China (I) 1949–1995]. *Shewai shuiwu* 涉外税务 6 (2000): 21–24.

Zhang, Chuanming 张传明 and Ma Jie 马杰. “1949–1995: Zhongguo gongshang shuizhi bianqian de lishi kaocha (xia)” 1949–1995” 中国工商税制变迁的历史

考察(下) [A Historical review of changes in the commercial taxes in China (II): 1949–1995]. *Shewai shuiwu* 涉外税务 7 (2000): 26–28.

Zhang, Jiuzhou 张九洲. "Lun Qingmo caizheng zhidu de gaige jiqi zuoyong" 论清末财政制度的改革及其作用 [On the reform and function of the financial system in the late Qing dynasty]. *Henan daxue xuebao* (*Shehui kexue ban*) 河南大学学报(社会科学版) 4 (2002): 51–57.

Zhang, Shouwen 张守文. "Shuizhi bianqian yu shuishou fazhi xiandaihua 税制变迁与税收法治现代化 [Changes in the tax system and modernization of the rule of law in tax collection]. *Zhongguo shehui kexue* 中国社会科学 2 (2015): 80–102.

Zhang, Xiaohui 张晓辉. *Minguo shiqi Guangdong shehui jingjishi* 民国时期广东社会经济史 [Socio-economic history of Guangdong during the Republic of China]. Guangzhou: Guangdong renmin chubanshe, 2005.

Zhang, Zhongli 张仲礼, Chen, Zengnian 陈曾年, and Yao, Xinrong 姚欣荣. *Taigu jituan zai jiu Zhongguo* 太古集团在旧中国 [Butterfield & Swire Co. in old China], Shanghai: Shanghai renmin chubanshe. 1991.

Zhao, Yunqi 赵云旗. *Zhongguo fenshuizhi caizheng tizhi yanjiu* 中国分税制财政体制研究 [Research on the tax assignment system in the fiscal system of China]. Beijing: Jingji kexue chubanshe, 2005.

Zhou, Bodi 周伯棣. *Zhongguo caizheng shi* 中国财政史 [Chinese financial history]. Shanghai: Shanghai renmin chubanshe, 1981.

Zhou, Yumin 周育民. *WanQing caizheng yu shehui bianqian* 晚清财政与社会变迁 [Late Qing finance and social change]. Shanghai: Shanghai renmin chubanshe, 2000.

Zhou, Zhichu 周志初. *WanQing caizheng jingji yanjiu* 晚清财政经济研究 [Research on finance and the economy in late Qing China]. Ji'nan: Qilu shushe, 2002.

Zuo, Zhisheng 左治生. *Zhongguo jindai caizheng shi conggao* 中国近代财政史丛稿 [A collection of manuscripts about modern Chinese financial history]. Chengdu: Xi'nan caijing daxue chubanshe, 1987.

Glossary

anpan jueding	"formally an open bid, but determined by collusion"
antong xiaoxi	colluding with bureaucrats to extract information
anxiang	deposit
baihuo lijin	*likin* on all kind of goods
baoshang	contract merchant
baoshangzhi or *chengshangzhi*	expanded tax-farming system
bianfa pingyi	"Discussion on the Reform"
bolai nongchanpin zaxiang zhuanshui	Special Tax on Agricultural Products
bolai tangleijuan	Special Tax on Imported Sugar
bubokuan	Board of Revenue (in Beijing)
buzhengshi	administrative commissioner
caili jiashui	"abolishing the *likin* and creating a new tax"
caizheng shuomingshu	Financial Statement
caizheng zonghuichu	Central Office of Finance
caizhengchu	Finance Office
caizhengju	Finance Bureau
caoliang	imperial tax grain
Changsha shangpin jianyanju	Changsha Bureau of Commodity Inspection
chanpinshui	product tax
chouxiang	Military Pay Fund
chuchuangshu	factory tax
dangshi tongyuan	copper ten cash
dangzhong mingtou	open public bidding
danhao	1 silver dollar (10 cents)
dantou fujiashui	additional tax on rice piculs
dao	tax revenue retained
Daqing yinhang	Great Qing Bank (Ta-Ching Bank
dayang, dayuan	"Big Money"
dianlifei	ceremonial expense
didingyin	land and poll tax

diyici xiuzheng jinkou xin shuizi	revised tariff rate
duyan dubanshu	Anti-Opium Supervision Office
duzhibu	Ministry of Finance
erwu sanding fujia guanshui	provisional 2.5 percent tariff
fabi	legal tender
fangwu jingfei	defense fee
fenshuizhi	"tax-assignment system"
gesheng liangshi huiyi	National Food Conference
gexian caizhengju	Provisional Regulations of the County Finance
zanxing zhangcheng	Bureaus
gexian xiaoshui	Miscellaneous Taxes of Each Prefecture
gongjing, shanggong	tax revenue sent to the capital
gongsi	company
gongwuyuan zhenbie weiyuanhui	Public Officials Qualification Committee
guan yinqianju	Official Silver Copper
guanban	"government office collection"
guandu shangban	"government supervised, privately-run company"
Guangdong caizheng gongsuo	Public Office of Finance in Guangdong
Guangdong caizheng shuomingshu	*Guangdong Financial Statement*
Guangdong caizheng yaolan	*Handbook on Guangdong Finance*
Guangdong diyijun junkenchu	First Force of the Guangdong military
Guangdong guosheng shuijuan tongyi jiancha weiyuanhui	committee to monitor unified taxation at local levels
Guangdong liangshi jingji weiyuanhui	Guangdong Food Economic Committee
Guangdong minshi tiaojie weiyuanhui	Guangdong Food Regulation Committee
Guangdong shizheng sannian jihua	Three-Year Administrative Plan of Guangdong
Guangdong tangye kaifa jihua	Guangdong Sugar Business Development Plan
Guangdong yanjiushui yange	*The Evolution of the Tobacco and Wine Taxes in Guangdong*

Guangdongsheng bolai wuchan zhuanshui zhanshi shuize	Wartime Tax Regulations for the Guangdong Special Tax on Imported Products
Guangdongsheng bolai wupinshui	Guangdong Province's Tax on Imported Products
Guangdongsheng difang shuize	Regulations on Guangdong Local Taxes
Guangdongsheng guohua tuixiaochu	National Products Sales Department of Guangdong Province
Guangdongsheng putong gongwuyuan kaoshi zanxing zhangcheng	Provisional Regulations for the Examination of General Public Officials in Guangdong Province
Guangdongsheng shanglianhui	Commercial Federation of Guangdong Province
guangshang heban	merchant joint venture
guanqianju	Official Copper Coin Bureau
guanye shouru	enterprise income
guanyinpiao	official silver banknote
guochan chukou weichi weiyuanhui	Committee Supporting Domestic Exports
guodi huafen	division of national and local taxes
guojia shuifa yu difang shuifa caoan, guojia feimu defang feimu biaozhun	divided national and local taxes in the drafts of related regulations
guojia shuiwu zongju	State Administration of Taxation
guoqing	national conditions
Haikoushi shengzhuye tongye gonghui	pig sales merchants' guild in Haikou city
heban xiangmi yunxiao	agreement for a joint venture for Hunan rice,
Yuesheng tiaoyue	transportation, and marketing in Guangdong province
heji mishi	Rice Market of Harmony
hōshō	national merchants (Japanese)
huafen guojia shouru difang	"Provisional Standards for Dividing
shouru zanxing biaozhun an	National and Local Income"
Huanan miye gufen youxian gongsi	Southern China Rice Business Limited Company
hubu	Board of Revenue
huoshang	product merchant
jianbanfei	supervisory fee

jiekuan, jingxiang	remittance to Beijing
jingji hezuo yuanze	principles for economic cooperation
jisi, yixian, weishi, kechang, xianggan, yizhan, chashan, caiban, gonglian shangxu, xiushan, zhizao	twelve major categories of official expenditures
jisi zongchu	inspection bureau to crack down on smuggling
jiuzeng paifei	"steaming bucket fee"
juanshang	tax merchant
juanshui	revenue from the sale of official positions
liandan banfa	three connected forms
liang juan	grain donation (tax)
liangguang tuyao tongshui	Guangxi Consolidated Opium Tax
liangshang guochang gongsi	joint company between the government and the merchants (in Shantou)
liangshi tongzhi weiyuanhui	Food and Grain Control Commission
liangshi yunxiao gongsi	Food Transport and Sales Company
liangshi yunxiaoju	Food Transport and Sales Bureau
liushi, songshi	regional military governors
liuzhou	tax revenue preserved for prefectural finance
liwu zongju	Central Bureau of *Likin*
meiyou teshui	new extra tax on gasoline
mihang	rice shop
mihang jie	"rice shop street"
mingwei anbao	"a state agency in public, but a contractor in fact "
minmi	mass rice (tax)
minshi huiyi	conference on food for the people
minshi wenti	"people's food problems"
muliao	private secretary
nanbeigang huowu yunshu gongshui, (*nanbeihang* for short)	South and North Guild
Nanjing zhengfu caizheng weiyuanhui	Nanjing Government Finance Commission
neidi erwu shui	inland 2.5 percent tax
neidi pilei lijin	domestic *likin* tax on cotton cloth

Ningshu	district of Jiangsu
paizhao fei	license fee
paizhao shui	license tax
Qichang yanghang	Russell & Co.
Qingchao xu wenxian tongkao	*Supplementary Documents in the Qing Dynasty*
qingli caizheng	financial reform
qingli caizhengju	Bureau of Financial Reform
quanguo caizheng huiyi	National Finance Conference
quanguo guotang chanxiao xiehui	National Sugar Distribution Association
Quanguo jingji weiyuanhui	National Economic Commission
quanguo tangye guanli weiyu-anhui an	National Sugar Control Committee Act
quansheng shuijuan zongchu	General Office of Provincial Levies
quansheng tangye yingyunshang	provincial territory divided into ten districts for sugar sales and ten selected licensed merchants
qushou	a district's own budget
Riben guozhi	*Treatises on Japan*
Sekimin	Japanese nationals (Japanese)
Shanghai tangye hezuo gongsi	Shanghai Sugar Business-Cooperative Company
Shanghaishi zaliang youbingye tongye gonghui	Shanghai association
shanhouju	Bureau of Military Revenue
shanzheng	good governance
shengwai geshu shou jiujuan baoxiao gekuan	"county tax on wine for levies and donations"
shengying wuchan jingjichu	Provincial Products Management Office
shengzhu chukou juan	additional tax on pig exports
shengzhu chukou shui	export tax on pigs
shidi huowu rukoushui	entry tax on cargo from lost territory
shitang yunxiao guanli weiyuanhui	Sugar Distribution Commission
shiye shouru	enterprise income
shuanghao	0.2 silver dollar (20 cents)
shuiwu xuetang	Tax School

shuiwu zongju	General Tax Bureau
shuiwuchu	Tax Office
Sushu	district of Jiangsu
taipao jingfei	"fortress and cannon fee"
tangye sannian fuxing jihua	Three-Year Plan for Rejuvenation of the Sugar Industry
tanpai	forced payment of the Boxer Indemnity
tanpai	tax apportionment to local governments
teshui	extra tax
tezhong xiaofeishui	special consumption tax
tianfu	land tax
tongjuan	unified levy
tongshou tongzhi	unified revenue and expenditure system
tongshui	consolidated tax
tongyuan	copper ten cash
tuixiao xiangmi banfa	regulation on the sale of Hunan rice
tuyangjuan	native sugar tax
tuyaoshui	tax on domestic opium
waixiao	unreported local spending
weiban	government agency system
weixie picheng	to threaten other bidders
wuben ban gongye	building industry without capital
wuyantang	smokeless sugar
Xiangmi xiaoYue	sell Hunan rice to Guangdong
xiangshou	a village's own budget
xiangYue yunmi gongsi	joint company between the government and the merchants ((in Guangzhou)
xiaoyang, haoyang, xiaoyuan, haozi, xiaoyinyuan, jiaoyang, haoyin	"Small Money"
xiaoyang yuan, haoyang yuan	five 20-cent silver coins, or one "Small Money *yuan*"
xiekuan, xiexiang	overlapping calculations of remittances to other provinces
xiekuan, xiexiang	subsidy to neighboring financially-poor provinces
xiexiang	annual subsidy

xin tangye tongzhi banfa	New Sugar Control Regulation
Xinzheng shiqi	Basic Principles of the New Policy
yangbu pitou zhuanshui	Special Tax on Machine-made Cotton Cloth
yanggu	imported grain
yanghetang	Hall of Nurturing
yanglianyan	onus
yangmi	imported rice
yanshui	salt tax
yingye shui	business tax
yingyeshui xinzhang	New Regulations on the Business Tax
yingyunshang	management and transportation merchant
Yinhang zhoubao	*Bank Weekly*
yinzhuang	native bank
youdou	special tax on beans
Yuehai guanzhi	*Gazetteer of Guangdong Maritime Customs*
YueHan tielu	Guangzhou-Hankou railway
Yuesheng migu zengchan	Five-Year Plan to increase rice and grain production
wunian jihua	in Guangdong
yuxian	advance payment of the monthly rent
za shouru	miscellaneous income
zaliang gonghui	Food Grain Trade Guild
zanshi Yuesheng mihuang banfa santiao, banshui jizhang jinkou banfa	temporary action for Guangdong
zaobi Yuechuang	Canton Mint
zengzhishui	value-added tax
zhengli shuijuan dagang	"Outline on the Rearrangement of Taxes"
zhengshou chuchan yunxiao wupin neidi shuiju	Inland Tax on Goods in Transit
zhengxiang	regular rent
zhengza gejuan	regular and miscellaneous levy
zhiqian	legal copper cash
Zhonghua tangye gufen youxian gongsi	China Sugar Co., Ltd
zhuankuan	special additional tax

zhuankuan zhidu	special fund system
zhuanshui	special tax
ziban	"self-operation"
ziwei shouzhi	"balancing the budget by itself"
ziyiju	provincial representative
zongban	chief manager
zonggongsi	general company
zongshang	general merchant
zouxiao	reported local spending

Index

Administrative Yuan 114
Advanced Course on Politics 186
Advance tax payment 188, 190
Agriculture and Forestry Bureau 107-108, 136, 146, 168
American Civil War 220, 237
American Revolution 220
Anti-British Movement of 1925 97, 141

Banquet tax 180-84
Beiyang Government 41, 50, 52, 55, 56, 58, 60-65, 90, 227-232, 237, 248
Bid-rigging 197-198, 204
Big Money (silver coin) 36-39, 61, 116-117, 164, 199-200
British American Tobacco (BAT) 62-63
Brockerism 15
Business tax 47, 50, 72, 74-75, 181, 191-192, 194, 236, 239, 250
Butterfield & Swire Co. 149-150, 152, 152, 1611-63, 166-170

C. P. Wong 150-152
California School 13
Canton Mint 34-39, 249-250
Chaozhou 89-91, 93-94, 96, 103, 108-109, 124, 131, 148, 171, 180
Chen Gongbo 128, 165-166, 252
Chen Guofu 113
Chen Jitang 40-45, 57-62, 68, 72, 77, 82, 98, 100, 102-103, 111, 117, 121, 123, 136, 144-146, 152, 154, 168, 180, 184, 250-251
Chen Shouming 131
China Sugar Co., Ltd 166-167
Chinese Civil War 41, 46, 136, 171-172, 232
Chinese Communist Party (CCP) 14, 46, 172, 239
Chinese General Chamber of Commerce in Hong Kong 86
Chinese General Chamber of Commerce in Thailand 131
Cigarettes 49-50, 60, 62-65, 225, 227, 231, 233, 236
Consolidated tax 14, 16-17, 43, 49-50, 60, 62-63, 65, 68, 74, 76, 114, 231-233, 236-241, 250
Copper ten cash 35, 38
County Finance Bureau 185-187
County magistrate 185-186, 197, 246-247
Currency reform of 1935 16, 36, 122, 200, 232, 251, 252

Dalai Company 180
Department of Finance, Guangdong province (DFG) 41, 68, 76-77, 80, 83-84, 90, 92, 103-105, 111-112, 115, 123, 125, 127, 128, 179-183, 185, 189, 191, 193-198, 200-209, 208-209
Division between national and local taxes 42, 52, 56, 73
Duara, Prasenjit 15-19, 175-176

Enterprise income (Qing China) 34, 45-46
Enterprise income Tax 243
Exchange market in Guangzhou 122
Excise tax 44, 220-221, 225, 237-238, 246

Fabi 42, 122, 200, 232, 252
Fan Qiwu 74, 183
Federation of Sugar Industry (Japan) 143
Feng Rui 83, 146-153, 160-164, 166-170
Feng Yuxiang 229
Feng Zhuman 82
Five Rams Brand 149, 151
Five-Year Plan to increase rice and grain production of 1938 136
food crisis in 1936 84, 107, 121-124, 131, 134-135

Gambling tax 32-34, 44, 71, 75, 79-80, 104, 177, 180, 194, 202, 205, 207, 231
General merchant 178
Gu Yingfen 57, 235
Guangdong Defense Fortress Debt 145
Guangdong Financial Statement 25-26, 29-31, 53-54, 177
Guangdong National Government 42, 77, 81, 253
Guangdong Provincial Bank 41-42, 82, 103, 146, 201
Guangdong Provincial Banknotes 201
Guangdong Sugar Business Development Plan 171-172
Guangzhou Chamber of Commerce 79, 86, 115, 125, 128, 182, 191, 195
Guangzhou–Hong Kong strike 96

Hong Kong 39, 86, 91, 96, 102, 110, 115, 140-141, 144, 149, 150, 152, 154, 159, 161-163, 168-170, 195, 210
Honolulu Ironworks Co. 146-148, 151
Hu Hanmin 57, 168, 184
Huang Yongyu 115
Huang Zunxian 223
Hunan province 27, 44, 230, 231, 235
  Hunan Rice 112, 117-118, 123-129, 132-133

Import substitution 83, 86, 139, 251
Income tax 192, 215, 219, 225-227, 232-233, 236-239, 242-243, 248, 250
Indirect taxes 18, 23, 50, 53-54, 85, 89, 179, 218, 220, 224-226, 230, 233, 238, 242, 246, 248, 254
Industrial and commercial taxes 18, 47, 50, 85
Inheritance tax 50, 219, 227, 236-237, 241, 248

Inland tax 81, 90-92, 97-98, 100
Iwai, Shigeki 16

Japan 13, 15, 18, 134, 142, 157, 168, 172, 231, 233, 234, 242, 255
Japanese taxation on wine 54, 64
Japan as a fiscal model 64-65, 215, 220, 223-228, 248, 250
Japanese smuggling 95-97, 105
Japanese opposition against the likin tax 97-103
Japanese sugar 140-141, 145, 163-165
Japanese policy on sugar 143
Jardine Matheson & Co. 110, 141, 167
Jianyuan(Kian Gwan) Company 150, 163-166, 168
Jiang Jieshi 44, 55, 98, 133, 135, 168, 252
John Swire & Sons Ltd. 149

Kaneko, Hajime 15-16
Kong Xiangxi 71-72, 102-103, 133, 166, 171, 252
Kubo, Tōru 11, 15-16, 128, 252
Kuomintang(KMT) 14, 18, 40-42, 51, 55, 57, 63, 82, 176, 250, 252
Kwang Hua Refinery 164

Land and poll tax 31, 33
Land tax 18, 23, 26, 33, 43-44, 49, 64, 67, 70-72, 75, 81, 84-85, 90, 177, 192, 217-219, 221, 224-226, 228-229, 231, 233, 236, 249
Li Jishen 181
Li Quanshi 132
Liangguang Incident 57, 68, 168
license tax 52, 59, 61-62, 77, 229
licensed merchants 139-140, 156-158, 171
likin tax 14, 25-26, 30, 51-52, 77, 81, 97, 101, 109, 113, 116, 176-179, 190, 204, 220-222, 226, 228, 249
Fiscal weight of *Likin* in Guangdong 32-34, 47, 49
Abolition of the *likin* 44, 67-70, 72-75, 79-80, 181, 231, 236, 250
Likin and the Tobacco and Wine taxes 50-51, 53, 61, 64
Lin Yungai 77, 84
liturgic tax systems 15-16, 176

Ma Yinchu 113
Maclaine Watson 166
Manchuria 94-96, 101-102, 141-142, 144
Mann, Susan 15-16, 176
May Thirtieth Movement of 1925 96, 141
Military Pay Fund 71
Ministry of Finance, Beijing (Qing China) 24-26, 35, 39, 223
Ministry of Finance, Beijing (Republican China) 61, 228
Ministry of Finance, Guangzhou (Republican China) 180
Ministry of Finance, Nanjing (Republican China) 56, 60, 62, 71, 91, 113-134, 127-128, 130, 134, 164, 167, 191
Modern fiscal state-building 11, 13-14, 16, 47, 83, 211, 231, 239, 245, 248-251, 253, 255-256
Mok YingKwai (Y. K. Mok) 149-150, 157

National Finance Conference 77
National Food Conference 118
National Products Sales Department of Guangdong 149-150, 157
National Resources Commission 171
National Rice Group 123, 130, 132-133
National Sugar Control Committee Act 170
Native sugar 140, 145, 147, 156, 162-163, 165
Prices of native sugar 153
Tax on native sugar 155
Production of native sugar 160, 169-170
New Policy reform 23-24, 31, 51, 54, 75, 182, 210, 223

Official Silver Copper Money Bureau 34, 249
Open bidding system 183, 187-191, 197-198, 210-212
Opium tax 30, 32-33, 40, 42-44, 79, 104, 177, 179-180, 192
Overseas Chinese 40, 109, 131-134, 166, 251

Pentreath & Co. 150
Preferential tariff 84, 105, 130, 164, 168
Provincial Products Management Office 153, 168

Qu Fangpu 80, 184-185, 187-188, 197, 200

R. Bin Wong 216, 219, 245
Reform and opening-up policy 16, 50, 65, 212, 238, 254, 255
Rice 16, 31, 50, 51, 65, 212, 238, 254-255
Import in Guangdong 108-111,119
Consumption of Guangdong 107, 108
Production of Guangdong 107, 108
Prices 112-113, 120-121
Southeast Asian rice 87, 93, 109
Taxation on rice import 101-114
Sales of Hunan rice to Guangdong 122-129
Controversy over tariff exemption 129-136
Rice Wholesalers' Association in Guangzhou 115

Sales Tax on Petroleum 46, 69-71, 77, 104-105
salt monopoly 139-140, 156, 226
Salt tax 30, 32-33, 39, 43, 74, 82, 217, 228-229, 232-234, 238-241, 254
School of Military Politics 186
Shanghai 36, 45, 84, 110, 118, 120, 141-142, 148, 164, 239, 253
Money 36-38
Shanghai and Guangzhou 86-89, 106, 121, 132

Shanghai merchants against taxation on rice in Guangdong 94-95, 102-105, 112, 123, 130, 132-133
Shanghai merchants against sugar monopoly 166-167
Shanghai Chamber of Commerce 86, 105, 132, 133
Shanghai Sugar Business Association 167
Shanghai Sugar Business-Cooperative Company 165, 167
Shantou 80, 89, 94, 108, 110, 117-118, 122, 125, 127, 132, 135
Strikes against taxation 90-92, 95
Economy and trade 92-94, 96-97, 189
Sugar 140, 151, 157, 159-160
Shantou Incident 98-103
Shantou Chamber of Commerce 90
Shared tax 236, 240
Sichuan province 27, 192, 222-223, 230-231, 234
Tax on tobacco and wine 52, 54-55, 58
Sugar 140, 142, 172
Sino-Japanese War of 1894 31, 51-53, 221, 223, 224-226
Sino-Japanese War of 1937 14, 23, 41, 46, 58, 64, 106, 129, 131, 135, 170-171, 187, 192, 212, 232, 238, 253
Škoda Works 146-148, 151, 171
Small Money (silver coin) 36-39, 61, 75, 116, 164, 199-200
Smuggling 40, 95-98, 100, 102, 120, 145, 162
Official smuggling 46, 149
Crack down on smuggling 76, 91, 98-99, 151
Song Ziliang 103, 127-128
Song Ziwen (T. V. Soong) 57, 103, 113, 128, 135, 147, 166, 170, 236-51
Reform in Guangdong (1920s) 42, 81, 177-180, 183-184, 188, 193
Activities in Guangdong during the Civil War 136, 171-172
South and North Guilds 93
South and North Trade Union 100
Southwest Government Committee of the KMT 57
Southwest Political Council of the Nationalist Party 113-114, 121, 146, 183-184
Soybean cakes 94-96
Special fund system 230
Special Tax Bureau of Agricultural Products 69-70
Special Tax on Artificial Fiber 68-69, 78
Special Tax on Imported Fertilizers 93-94
Special Tax on Imported Rice 101-103, 107, 111-112, 114-117, 119, 121-123, 251
Special Tax on the Agricultural Products 70, 71-72, 77, 93, 104-105
State-run enterprise (government-run industry) 34, 45-46, 64, 83-84, 89, 152, 153, 161, 221, 250-251
Sugar refineries 79, 93-94, 143-144, 147-152, 155-156, 159-161
Sugar Distribution Commission 164-166
sugar monopoly (Guangdong) 139-140, 145-147, 150, 153-54
Sugar monopoly (National) 155-157, 159-162, 164-167, 169-170
Sugar Office of the National Products Sales Department 156
Sun Wen 40, 55, 63, 81, 131, 250, 252

Taikoo Sugar 83, 141, 149-150, 152, 157, 166, 170, 227
Taiping rebellion 52, 220-221
Taiwan 96, 100-101, 103
Taiwanese smuggling 100-101, 103
Taiwanese sugar 140, 143, 172
Bank of Taiwan 178
Tanpai 31, 51
Tariff sovereignty (autonomy) 18, 67, 73, 90, 97, 101-102, 141-143, 145, 161, 227, 231, 250
Tax Improvement Committee 179
Tax-assignment system of 1994 240
Tax-farming system 15-16, 94-95, 175-179, 181, 183, 191, 193-194, 198, 212
Tax-for-profit reform of 1983 239
Thai Chinese 109, 131
Thailand 109-110, 118-119, 131, 133
Three-Year Administrative Plan of Guangdong 45, 70, 139
Three-Year Plan for Rejuvenation of the Sugar Industry 147, 160
Tobacco and wine public sale system 61
Tobacco and wine taxes 49-55, 58-61, 64-65, 178-179, 194, 233
Tongshou-tongzhi 212

Value-added tax 239-240

Warlord autarky 46, 229, 250
Weng Wenhao 171

Xicun Cement Plant 34, 39, 45
Xinghua Company 162-165, 168
Xinhai Revolution 14, 223, 231, 249

Yu Hanmou 126, 168
Yuehan railway 110, 124-125

Zeng Yangfu 104-105, 127, 135
Zengyuan Paper Company 39
Zhili province 24, 27, 56, 222, 228, 230, 231, 234
Tobacco and wine taxes 51-52, 54-55, 61

For Product Safety Concerns and Information please contact our EU
representative GPSR@taylorandfrancis.com
Taylor & Francis Verlag GmbH, Kaufingerstraße 24, 80331 München, Germany

www.ingramcontent.com/pod-product-compliance
Ingram Content Group UK Ltd.
Pitfield, Milton Keynes, MK11 3LW, UK
UKHW020017200926
475702UK00014B/1928

* 9 7 8 1 0 4 1 1 8 8 1 0 0 *